INNOCENT UNTIL PROVEN MUSLIM

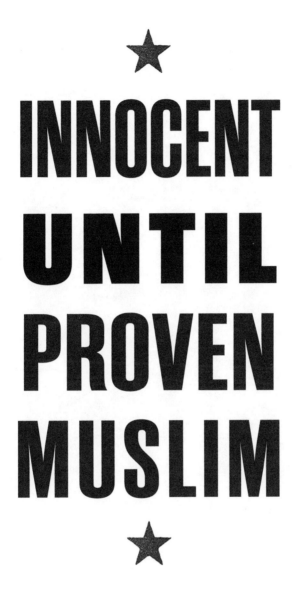

INNOCENT UNTIL PROVEN MUSLIM

ISLAMOPHOBIA, THE WAR ON TERROR, AND
THE MUSLIM EXPERIENCE SINCE 9/11

MAHA HILAL

BROADLEAF BOOKS
MINNEAPOLIS

INNOCENT UNTIL PROVEN MUSLIM
Islamophobia, the War on Terror, and the Muslim Experience since 9/11

Cover Design: Faceout Studios

Print ISBN: 978-1-5064-7046-7
eBook ISBN: 978-1-5064-7047-4

To all the victims of the War on Terror:
May you find justice or may justice find you, wherever you are.

This book is dedicated to the following people:

My father (1945–92), whose love and care shaped my road to success and who taught me the value of persistence and perseverance. Although he is no longer with us, I feel his presence every day. I wish he could be here to witness the completion of this book, but I am confident that he would be proud of me.

My beautiful mother, who has been my rock all my life and in particular while I was writing this book. In the early days of writing my manuscript, I would frequently tell her that I had writer's block. She would always repeat an Arabic proverb to me that translates to "Rain begins with one drop and then it pours down." So it was with this book. I love her more than words can describe.

My sister and brother-in-law, who encouraged me to write and finish this book and who have shown me the importance of getting new ideas out in the world. They are as brilliant as they are accomplished, and anyone would be lucky to have them as professors.

My niece and nephew, who won't understand the contents of this book just yet (and I hope it's a long time before they do), but for whom I have infinite love. They are the beautiful beings I remember when I think about why this world has to change and what my role is in creating a better world for them.

Because night is here but the barbarians have not come
Some people arrived from the frontiers
And they said that there are no longer any barbarians
And now what shall become of us without any barbarians?
Those people were a kind of solution.
—C. P. CAVAFY, "WAITING FOR THE BARBARIANS"[1]

CONTENTS

     Muslim American Narratives Post 9/11   225

     Conclusion   257

     Acknowledgments   265
     Notes   267

INTRODUCTION

How Did We Get to Where We Are?

This book has been a long time in the making, yet nothing could have prepared me for the task of writing it. While I knew writing this book would involve serious time and commitment, nothing could have mentally prepared me for the trauma of spending hours, days, and weeks researching, examining, and writing about the level of violence that Muslims have experienced post-9/11 and long before.

I was eighteen years old when the attacks of September 11, 2001, happened. Even though I did not then know how to articulate the concept of collective responsibility, after seeing the images of the twin towers of the World Trade Center collapsing, I somehow knew immediately that if the perpetrators were Muslim, I would have to contend with what this meant for me as a Muslim—not as an American. This realization was a reflection of my implicit understanding of how the United States treated marginalized communities.

I think back on my eighteen-year-old self now and wonder how and why this attack on the United States cued me to think about collective responsibility for Muslims. My parents, both immigrants, had endured vicious religious and ethnic discrimination, though my dad died when I was ten and therefore too young to understand the extent of what he had gone through. After that, my mom put all of her considerable energy into making sure my sister and I felt taken care of and safe. So, while I was certainly aware of anti-Muslim sentiment, I was insulated from its worst effects—at least initially. And I didn't connect it to the state—whether due to my age or to ignorance—but attributed it to vague, ill-defined social forces.

The moment the towers fell, however, I knew instinctively that anti-Muslim sentiment was more than that. I knew that the state would leverage its power in support of the anti-Muslim sentiment that had been in the background my whole life. Twenty years later, I think a lot about what it means to exist in a country where one's very humanity is contingent on whiteness, a country where my niece and nephew, ages seven and two, will learn what it means to be antagonized and otherized probably before they learn simple division.

To say that this topic is personal to me would be an understatement. For the last fourteen years, I have focused my research, writing, advocacy, and organizing on the War on Terror. Conducting this work has been difficult, to say the least—especially because the War on Terror is rooted in marginalizing an identity I hold dear. Moreover, I know that doing this work as a Muslim American comes with great risks, whether surveillance or worse. But I have always been driven by the courage of other Muslims and Muslim Americans who shoulder this burden because they believe in justice for Muslims and in collective liberation.

When I started writing this book in 2020, a Black man named George Floyd had been recently murdered by the police. His murder came just three months after a Black woman named Breonna Taylor was murdered by the police while she slept in her apartment. As I came close to finishing this book, another Black man, Jacob Blake, was shot seven times by police officers in Kenosha, Wisconsin. As uprisings persisted across the country, Black communities powerfully resisted—and called on others to resist the violence of a country so rooted in anti-Blackness that police brutality is the norm, not the exception.

Injustice never takes a break in the United States. But 2020 brought the COVID-19 pandemic as well. As if to belie former president Donald Trump's slogan "Make America Great Again," the pandemic exposed exactly the opposite, laying bare the human consequences of the United States' misplaced priorities. In contrast to governments nearly everywhere else in the world, the Trump administration took no action to contain the spread of the virus, to bolster the capacity of the health-care system, which was soon overwhelmed, or to mitigate the economic effects of the pandemic on ordinary Americans. As a result, the pandemic raged to epic proportions in the United States, and as usual, Black and brown communities were hit the hardest.

Neither has Islamophobia missed a beat during the COVID-19 crisis. From articles on the virus accompanied by irrelevant pictures of Muslims—praying, for example—to hashtags such as #CoronaJihad, Muslims have been scapegoated for yet another global problem.[1] The Trump administration, meanwhile, despite its lack of decisive action to combat the virus, didn't hesitate to invoke the threat of COVID-19 in defending its racist and Islamophobic immigration policies, saying in a statement, "The President's authority to restrict travel into the United States has been central to the Administration's ongoing efforts to safeguard the American people against the spread of COVID-19."[2]

The aim of this book is to explore the impact of state violence on Muslims in the War on Terror. It should be noted, however, that the violence against Muslims in this country did not begin in the aftermath of 9/11. It began with the transatlantic slave trade, which brought many enslaved Black Muslims to the shores of the United States. Their perseverance, steadfastness, and resistance laid a powerful foundation for all the Muslims who came after them. We can only hope to absorb and apply some of their power to the violence we are experiencing now.

As has been the case in other critical eras of American history, how a person relates to this ongoing movement of resistance is indicative of their place in society and the privileges they hold. The relative privilege, or not, of any individual's position in the current moment is not an accident but a legacy of historical violence. Without understanding how this cumulative violence affects each and every moment of change in the United States, we might see the violence against Indigenous and Black people, and the rampant anti-Blackness that is being challenged and resisted, as separate from the War on Terror. But there is a continuity in the United States' official violence that begins with the genocide of Indigenous people and the enslavement of Africans. Centuries later, Black and brown communities have continued to be targets, whether of the War on Drugs or the War on Terror, in both cases based on constructions of their criminality.

However, the War on Terror is unique in that a confluence of circumstances allowed the executive branch of the federal government to garner unprecedented power, operating largely outside the normal political system and thus insulating those gains against the checks and balances American government was designed to ensure. Supported by a powerful public narrative rooted in virulent Islamophobia, three successive administrations—those of George Bush, Barack Obama, and Donald Trump—worked to consolidate this power and use it to build, maintain, and expand the vast official apparatus of the War on Terror. The increasingly invisible nature of these structures obscures the connection between them and the violence that underlies interactions between the state and marginalized communities, both domestic and foreign. As the priorities of the War on Terror have become more deeply embedded in law and policy and in our concept of business as usual—that is, the more invisible the structure has become—the greater the harm has been to marginalized communities.

Although the apparatus of the War on Terror is unprecedented in breadth and depth, what is not new is the way it has proven self-perpetuating in its violence. Too often we believe the myth that wars end when troops are withdrawn or treaties are signed. But wars only end when the violence ends—not just direct violence, but the violence of malnutrition, economic instability, birth defects, poverty, and/or death that happens both during the war and in its aftermath. When we broaden our view to consider this ongoing violence, we see that the wars of the United States have never ended; they have only morphed and transitioned into new wars that preserve the brutality of wars past.

The cost of the War on Terror so far has been estimated at $6.4 trillion.[3] This only includes militarism and warfare abroad, not any costs of the war on the domestic front, making the War on Terror the most expensive war in US history.[4] Moreover, the financial cost of the war does not and indeed cannot possibly capture the amount of destruction and the number of lives lost because of it. For this, of course, there is no price tag. But both the human and economic costs of the war have continued to increase—because the War on Terror was designed to be a never-ending conflict. Compounding the negative social impact, especially on vulnerable segments of the population, is the fact that funds spent on endless war have been redirected away from schools, affordable housing, and other social services.

After twenty years, it is time to dismantle the War on Terror.

This book is, in part, about explaining how we got to where we are today. It's a look at how, over the last twenty years, the War on Terror has become so normalized that a world without TSA body scanners, a no-fly list, or Guantánamo Bay prison seems unfathomable. It is a reflection on the fact that as with all US wars, there's no going back, only going further and deeper into the violence—violence that is as much about subduing marginalized communities as about sustaining and strengthening systems of oppression.

To understand the War on Terror as fully as possible, this book considers the role of narrative, how it was formed to advance the laws and policies of the War on Terror, and how it continues to justify the policies that have shaped the post-9/11 landscape. This book also seeks to undo the narrative of the state—not by engaging with the dominant narrative as a legitimate starting point for argument, but by challenging its underlying and fundamental assumptions.

Although the War on Terror was designed to almost exclusively target Muslims, in the larger narrative and among policy and advocacy organizations, Muslim identity is treated as a coincidence or neglected altogether. For this reason, this book also highlights this violence from Muslim perspectives and experiences that have consistently been sidelined or invisibilized, even in progressive and liberal circles. The War on Terror is addressed as a campaign of violence rooted in Islamophobia by examining the anti-democratic laws and policies put in place post-9/11. This necessarily takes into account policies that were implemented in the immediate aftermath of 9/11, which are often treated as distant history, even while they remain firmly lodged in the trajectory of the violence of the War on Terror today.

From here, this book looks at the impact of the War on Terror on Muslim Americans. This includes internalized Islamophobia as a particular response to the War on Terror in addition to Muslim Americans' lived experiences.

For Muslims, I hope this book offers insight into what it means to reject and dismantle oppressive systems instead of becoming part of them based on the false pretense that engagement can or will ever lead us down the path toward liberation. This cannot be the way forward. Too much is at stake.

What Is Islamophobia?

Many terms attempt to capture the phenomenon of the targeting of Muslims. Some people use the term *anti-Muslim racism*, acknowledging how the abuse and mistreatment of Muslims fits into the United States' violent racial hierarchy. Others refer to the abuse and mistreatment of Muslims as *anti-Muslim bigotry*. Though there are valid and brilliantly articulated ideas on the choice of these terms, I refer to the phenomenon of anti-Muslim targeting as Islamophobia. *Islamophobia* is the term that is more widely used in the mainstream and is generally understood to capture bias against Muslims and people perceived as Muslim. More than that, though, I believe it best captures the essence of a system of oppression rooted in anti-religious animus. Specifically, I believe that negative constructions of Islam are not only used as an initial mechanism to dehumanize Muslims, but are also used to justify violence against a people whose religion is constructed as irredeemable. At the same time, my definition of *Islamophobia* acknowledges that Muslims have different intersecting identities resulting in stark and different experiences of Islamophobia.

Together with the growing body of work on systemic violence against Muslims, I hope that this book makes a contribution to the field while providing ways that we can collectively end this violence. My focus here is primarily on institutionalized Islamophobia—the form of Islamophobia that is deeply embedded and entrenched in the laws and policies of the state and which I believe must be dismantled in order to end the War on Terror. My definition of *institutionalized Islamophobia* is as follows:

Institutionalized Islamophobia is a phenomenon whereby officially constructed hate and fear of Muslims are built into structures of the state and society for the pursuit of power and for the justification of war and repression. Islamophobia is based on the social construction of Islam as violent, barbaric, uncivilized, and opposed to normative democratic values. Islamophobia positions Muslims as existing outside of the moral boundaries extended to other communities such that their dehumanization results in consequences ranging from prejudice and discrimination to detention and even death. Intersectional identities of Muslims along various racial, ethnic, cultural, and linguistic lines make the source of Islamophobia difficult to distinctly isolate. However, Islamophobia represents a particular type of oppression that is rooted in anti-religious animus and, based on a Muslim's particular background, intersects with anti-Blackness, racism, cultural racism, nationalism, and xenophobia. Islamophobia is maintained and perpetuated by white supremacy, which upholds notions of dichotomous ideological values between the "West" and Islam.

Internalized Islamophobia

The most potent weapon in the hands of the oppressor is the mind of the oppressed.

—BANTU STEPHEN BIKO[5]

This powerful quote illustrates one of the most important reasons to address internalized Islamophobia. In order to understand the bigger picture that explains how institutionalized Islamophobia thrives, this book also addresses *internalized* Islamophobia and how it works in tandem with institutional Islamophobia to further the oppression of Muslims. It is for this reason that I grapple seriously with this concept. My definition of *internalized Islamophobia* is as follows:

Internalized Islamophobia refers to the phenomenon of Muslims absorbing dominant narratives and tropes about Islam and Muslims that suggest that they—the religion and its followers—are inherently violent and terroristic, uncivilized, backwards, repressive, uniquely patriarchal and oppressive of women, and opposed to normative democratic ideals. Manifestations of internalized Islamophobia include uncritical acceptance of these and other tropes and advocating the need for particularized interventions that address Muslims' exceptionally problematic behavior. Internalized Islamophobia is also expressed through efforts to overcompensate for and condemn acts of violence committed by Muslims on the basis of collective responsibility, while at the same time denying, minimizing, and otherwise erasing Muslim victimhood.

Internalized Islamophobia is manifested institutionally through the perpetuation by Muslims of harmful laws and policies that are rooted in the aforementioned problematic and demonizing narratives of Islam and Muslims.

As is the case with institutionalized Islamophobia, one does not exhibit internalized Islamophobia simply by critiquing Islam and/or Muslims. Rather, internalized Islamophobia is based on acceptance of dominant tropes that single out Islam and Muslims as exceptionally problematic without any comparative evidence or context to situate these claims.

PART I

NARRATING THE WAR ON TERROR

*It was as if Chile didn't have its own 9/11—
September 11th of 1973—when the U.S. government
overthrew the democratically elected Salvador
Allende and replaced him with the brutal dictator,
Augusto Pinochet. No, our 9/11 was different. It
involved Americans as the victims of terror, not as
perpetrators.*
—Roberto Sirvent and Danny Haiphong[1]

*All I need is a sheet of paper and something to write
with, and then I can turn the world upside down.*
—Friedrich Nietzsche[2]

Language is a powerful tool. It can start wars, sustain them, change their
course, or end them. In the War on Terror, the power of language to shape
and guide the public will has been leveraged to predetermine innocence and
guilt, to define who counts as human and who is merely a faceless enemy
or collateral damage, and to justify the sovereign's control over who gets
to live or die.

It is important to understand how language shapes our perception
of the world if we want to challenge the narrative of the War on Terror.
In the years since 9/11, language has been used to construct a particular
story about terrorism—about what it is, how we should fight it, and, most
crucially, with whom we associate it. In fact, the rhetoric of the War on
Terror has been so effective in shaping a particular perception of the group
responsible for acts of terrorism that we have been primed to accept different explanations about Muslims versus non-Muslims implicated in the
same form of violence.

In the aftermath of the 9/11 attacks, the US adopted various rhetorical
strategies that allowed it to assume a hegemonic posture of victimhood,
almost immediately exceptionalizing its suffering and seeking to create
a world divided on the basis of "us" and "them." The resulting narrative

1

framework positioned the threat terrorism posed to the US as a global concern, opening the door for the US to pursue its foreign policy objectives ruthlessly under cover of the imperative to defeat terrorism at any cost.

Language, when carefully curated to enlist the people's support, makes war possible while at the same time making impunity almost inevitable. As the vocabulary and rhetorical approach of the War on Terror developed in the immediate aftermath of 9/11, the absence of competing narratives gave the state more control in defining what language to feed the population. This is important because, in the words of sociologists John Collins and Ross Glover, "the more control the state has over the language a population hears and the images it sees, the easier it is to develop 'democratic' consent."[3] In other words, the consent of the governed to wage war is not automatic but is malleable and deliberately shaped by the linguistic structures chosen by the state.

Moreover, the official narrative that emerged to manufacture support for the nebulous and sprawling War on Terror would also serve as a basis to justify its worst abuses, eventually becoming so accepted that it operates invisibly in the background. For many Americans, their first exposure to mass violence was the 9/11 attacks. The US government took advantage of this national trauma to cultivate the public's natural fear and uncertainty and channel it into unquestioning support for an as-yet-unconstructed tapestry of illegal and abusive laws and policies. By selling a story about good and evil—with Muslims cast as the ill-defined enemy irrationally driven to destroy everything Americans held dear—the George W. Bush administration was able to essentially write itself a blank check to wield state violence however and wherever it determined necessary to vanquish the evil of terror, operating outside of normal channels for accountability. Subsequent administrations built on this foundation.

1.

REMEMBERING 9/11 AND CREATING THE WAR-ON-TERROR NARRATIVE

> *Whether we bring our enemies to justice, or bring justice to our enemies, justice will be done.*
> —PRESIDENT GEORGE BUSH, SEPTEMBER 20, 2001[1]

> *Looked at objectively, it is clear that the overwhelming majority of civilian deaths resulting from political violence are produced by what should be understood as "state terror." Terrorism also serves as an excuse to avoid diplomacy and the peaceful resolution of conflict.*
> —RICHARD FALK[2]

In the course of researching this book, I spoke with Perla,[3] a Muslim American PhD seminary student. One of the memories she recalled with respect to the 9/11 attacks was of her professor asking her class if any of the students remembered where they were when the attacks happened. Every single student in the class raised their hand. According to Perla, the 9/11 attacks were a traumatic event akin to the assassination of John F. Kennedy. For a large population of Americans, it was the first time they understood what violence of such a magnitude looked like.

Many Americans remember where they were in the moment of the 9/11 attacks, even if they don't remember everything that followed. In a book examining how 9/11 has been memorialized in the American mind, British author Lucy Bond explores different ways of understanding memory and the forces that shape it.[4] Far from being an objective reflection of the past, our experience of memory is in fact shaped by a variety of factors across different dimensions, including economic, cultural, and political power. Further, memory is neither static nor permanent and can change as different versions of history are asserted, contended with, and challenged.[5]

3

One of the fundamental goals of this book is to unpack the official narrative that has shaped public thought and memory in the aftermath of the 9/11 attacks and throughout the War on Terror. This is because the largely singular story told about the 9/11 attacks and their aftermath excludes significant mention of Muslims and Muslim Americans—unless it pertains to their criminalization and demonization. Insofar as this is the case, memory is not just about who gets to tell the story, but about who gets justice and who doesn't. An examination of the government's narrative is also a necessary step in understanding, and therefore challenging, the harmful policies with which it is intertwined and which it serves to justify and reinforce.

President George W. Bush's rhetoric in the immediate aftermath of 9/11 sought to link the attacks to key American values that could explain them for a country seeking answers. According to Bush, one of the primary reasons the United States was singled out for attack was its proud commitment to freedom. In his 2002 State of the Union address, for example, he said, "Freedom is at risk and America and our allies must not, and will not, allow it."[6] This type of statement served dual rhetorical purposes. On the one hand, Bush was promoting an intentionally narrow explanation, seeking to eliminate any alternative rationale for the 9/11 attacks by framing them as part of a fundamental conflict between freedom and the terrorists' hatred of it. On the other hand, he was positioning the war as a global struggle, particularly for Western countries who saw themselves as similar to the US and therefore susceptible to the same threats.

One of the reasons Bush was able to successfully frame the War on Terror in this way was that it fit into an existing narrative about Islam and civilization—read "Western civilization." In an address to an anti-terrorism summit of Central and Eastern European leaders held in November 2001, Bush warned of the dangers the terrorists posed, making the assertion that "given the means, our enemies would be a threat to every nation and, eventually, to *civilization* itself."[7] While Bush was obviously using the language of civilization to draw in Western leaders of "civilized" nations, the United States was also operating with the presumption that it was the apex of civilization. This presumption has served to justify unilateral action by the United States not just because it was targeted by terrorists, but also based on the assertion that its very survival as a country manifesting the highest form of civilization was at risk.[8]

It was no accident that Bush relied heavily on the language of civilization to frame the War on Terror. The 1996 book *Clash of Civilizations and the Remaking of World Order*, by political scientist Samuel Huntington, profoundly influenced the discourse around global conflict. Huntington argues that the struggle between opposing cultures—not disputes between nations—will fuel future conflict. In particular, he asserts that the clash of civilizations between the West and Islam is inevitable because the values underlying the two cultures are fundamentally opposed. Huntington wasn't a neutral observer—he came down firmly on the side of Western civilization, and to this end, he was speaking to the supposed "clash" from the perspective of how and why Islam was a problem. Huntington also wasn't shy about generalizing all of Islam, stating, "Islam's borders are bloody and so are its innards. The fundamental problem for the West is not Islamic fundamentalism. It is Islam, a different civilization whose people are convinced of the superiority of their culture and are obsessed with the inferiority of their power."[9] Huntington's theory put an intellectual gloss on the Islamophobia that has always existed in American thought and pop culture. Since 9/11 his theory has been relied on consistently in the official rhetoric. It has perhaps been most useful in raising the stakes of the War on Terror by cementing endless war as necessary to providing ongoing protection of civilization and the civilized.

Huntington's book fits snugly into the context of another, related theme that has animated American thought, as well as the way the country has interacted with the larger world since its founding. While there have been numerous iterations of the myth of American exceptionalism, with the language and focus evolving to adapt to changing circumstances and differing narrative needs, certain thematic threads can be seen to run throughout its history. Political scientist Joanne Esch focuses on three core elements. For Esch, the foundation of the myth is the idea that America sees itself as a "chosen nation," unique in the world for its dedication to freedom and equality. The second element follows from the first and asserts that because of this unique status as a beacon of virtue, America has a "calling" or "mission" that requires it to enter the world in such a way that shapes it in accordance with American values. Finally, the mythic structure and language of American exceptionalism strongly imprint the idea that in answering that calling, America represents the forces of good against evil. More dramatically, it is characterized as *inherently* good—so much so that it can never be thought to have questionable motives. This American story is so embedded in the public imagination that the use of lexical cues invoking its mythic framework has become a powerful rhetorical tool.[10]

The mythic language of American exceptionalism is threaded throughout the official discourse of the War on Terror, and it is especially insidious in the way it facilitates state violence by couching it in palatable, even inspirational, terms. Rooting the rationale for its unprecedented global war against terrorism in this familiar narrative framework, the United States has positioned itself as having a duty to spread its values, particularly freedom. This burden is not presented as a typical responsibility, however, but rather as a moral imperative deriving from the United States' supposed superiority relative to the rest of the world. Former president George W. Bush exemplified this rhetorical strategy in a 2004 press conference on the subject of Iraq and the US's role in Iraq becoming a free country: "I also have this belief, strong belief, that freedom is not this country's gift to the world. Freedom is the Almighty's gift to every man and woman in this world. And as the greatest power on the face of the earth, we have an obligation to help the spread of freedom."[11] This "unique" responsibility is, in reality, less about what other countries need and more about the political imperatives of the United States, and what violence it needs to disguise.

The continuing sway of the myth of American exceptionalism has consequences that ripple out far beyond the borders of the United States. It has had a profound influence on the way the US engages with international law in general, and with the international human rights regime in particular.

Historian Michael Ignatieff notes three particular ways in which this dynamic plays out. First, the United States signs on to international human rights and humanitarian law conventions and treaties and then exempts itself from their provisions by explicit reservation, nonratification, or noncompliance. Second, the United States maintains double standards, judging itself by more permissive criteria than it does its enemies. Third, the United States denies jurisdiction to human rights law within its own domestic law, insisting on the self-contained authority of its own domestic rights tradition.[12]

All three of these elements are on display in the way in which the myth has been employed in the context of the War on Terror. Because the United States, in this narrative framework, is inherently superior and uniquely situated to promote virtue, it is free to exempt itself from human rights requirements it endorses for the rest of the world, both directly and by the use of double standards in terms of actual practice. As I will explore in more detail later, this is also reflected in the way in which the US views its human rights obligations within its own borders, refusing to be beholden to international standards.

These narrative threads espousing the superiority and exceptionality of the United States as the pinnacle of civilization have served to reinforce the perception of American innocence and to justify interventions that focus solely on the need for others to change—or perhaps to be changed by brute force. Bluntly acknowledging this outlook in a Pentagon briefing on military responses to terrorism, then secretary of defense Donald Rumsfeld asserted, "We have a choice—either to change the way we live, which is unacceptable; or to change the way that they live, and we chose the latter."[13] Given the United States' violent interface with much of the world, this position might not have come as a complete surprise, but the latitude that the government would claim in enforcing its will without question across legal contexts and across the world through the mandate of its War on Terror is unique and relies on the evergreen message that the beacon of virtue in the world can never do anything wrong. To reinforce this, official War on Terror discourse relies heavily on the metaphor of war—while refusing to be bound by international *rules* of war—by elevating the terms to a mythical battle between good and evil.

Despite the harm they cause, political myths like American exceptionalism and civilization versus barbarism are incredibly difficult to challenge. This is because they use a shared vocabulary and set of cultural references to resonate emotionally with their audience, rather than having to introduce and defend a novel argument that could be pinned down and refuted. In addition, these myths are always shifting, with different elements emphasized or deemphasized as they are repurposed to meet different needs—and the more they are used to justify and explain, the more they reinforce themselves. Scholar Joanne Esch describes political myths as a kind of work in progress that operates outside of critical reasoning.[14] Rather, they are a cognitive device that uses social cues to activate systems of thought that are mostly invisible, taking advantage of the human brain's preference for categorical shortcuts. Putting it another way, she quotes social theorists Chiara Bottici and Benoît Challand: "Political myths cannot be falsified because they are not scientific hypotheses as to the constitution of the world or astronomical almanacs that foretell its future: they are determinations to act that always reinforce themselves."[15]

When Bush characterized the War on Terror in its earliest days as a fight for nothing less than history itself, his statements were firmly rooted in an intellectual tradition of American moral superiority, especially with respect to the Muslim world. And setting the stakes so high made the War on Terror seem necessary, urgent, and inevitable. In his 2002 State of the Union address, Bush expressed this urgency, saying, "History has called America and our allies to action, and it is both our responsibility and our privilege to fight freedom's fight."[16] Reiterating the quest for freedom, this statement made the US's "call" to history an imperative, and one the average American could feel they played a part in by supporting the War on Terror. Further ingraining the idea that the US's War on Terror was about creating and shaping history, Bush followed up on this theme a year later: "Whatever the duration of this struggle and whatever the difficulties, we will not permit the triumph of violence in the affairs of men; free people will set the course of history."[17] Contextualizing it in this way presented listeners with only one choice—support the War on Terror, or you will be holding history back. Enlisting the American people in making history also served to justify certain inevitable "minor" rollbacks on rights for some.

Bedtime Stories for Patriots

In the days after the events of 9/11, the Bush administration built the narrative framework that would launch a war and form the basis to support an unprecedented expansion of American military influence and would centralize power in the office of the president at the expense of the checks and balances normally imposed by Congress and the judiciary—both long-term conservative political goals. His successors, predictably, opted to retain, and expand, this power. The continuity of the War on Terror reveals a fundamental fact about the power of narrative: that it is both self-reinforcing and adaptive to changes in approach and circumstance. Although subsequent administrations differed in rhetorical strategy, they perpetuated and expanded the policies Bush began, basically unchecked. This was possible because although official language changed superficially, it retained the underlying mythic structure—the scaffolding on which the narrative of the War on Terror was constructed. This structure can be loosely divided into three core elements. The first, as we have seen, was built against the backdrop of existing American myth systems and served to manufacture a rationale for the breadth and depth of the US government's response to the 9/11 attacks by framing it as exceptional and ahistorical.

By presenting the attacks as not mere criminal acts but as a unique national tragedy representing a brand-new global threat, the government's narrative positioned them as exceptionally grievous and a prime symbol of American suffering.[18] This narrow frame—of the US as the singular victim of an attack unlike any other—created and sustained the impression that the September 11 attacks changed everything, that the whole world, in fact, had entered a new historical era. The common mantra of "Everything changed after 9/11," however, obscures the important fact that it was the US's response to the attacks, not the attacks themselves, that altered the global landscape. The willingness of the American people, and of our foreign allies, to support and participate in that response was not a spontaneous or inevitable reaction to the events of 9/11, but rather the result of a shared, mythologized conception of their significance.[19] The meaning attached to the attacks, in other words, is far from a simple recollection of objective fact. It is the result of a layered and complex narrative that arose from the desire of ordinary Americans to find significance in the wake of national trauma, and from the desire of their government to justify state violence.

An important effect of crafting the narrative in this particular way is that it serves to preempt or eclipse competing narratives. For example, take the use of the term *Ground Zero* to refer to the site of the collapsed twin towers, which replaced its previous usage for the devastation wrought when the United States dropped atomic bombs on the Japanese cities of Nagasaki and Hiroshima. Appropriating a phrase synonymous with American aggression for the purpose of positioning the United States as a victim on the world stage was a transparent attempt by the government to erase history.[20] The exceptionalizing narrative of US victimhood also paved the way for the justification of America's aggression in the War on Terror, and minimized the consequences for any subsequent abuses, such as the horrific treatment of Iraqi prisoners at Abu Ghraib. Any pushback on its policy that the United States might have gotten because of such abuses was deflected by the assertion that nothing could conceivably compare to the atrocity of 9/11.[21]

The narrative that emerged post-9/11 was designed to cue the American public regarding the right questions to ask, the right answers to these questions, and anything in between that would justify the US's War on Terror and the interventions it entailed. This rhetorical tactic was already apparent in a speech President Bush gave nine days after September 11, in which he stated, "Americans are asking 'Why do they hate us?'"[22] Whether or not most Americans had actually asked this question, they were being cued to think that this was the first question they would have naturally asked and that raw emotion—in this case, hate—was the driving force behind the attacks. Thus, Bush's reasoning was that not only were the terrorists motivated by simple hatred; the hatred could not be linked to anything rational.

Bush's statements also illustrate that the state was eager to utilize frameworks of trauma through which revenge would be seen as a legitimate response to the normality that had been disrupted and torn.[23] They also demonstrated how the state sought to disrupt any self-reflection by producing rhetoric designed to convince Americans that warfare was a reasonable and necessary starting point to obtain justice. Moreover, this rhetoric manipulated the psychological impact of the 9/11 attacks on the American public to advance military and political agendas—or what one scholar refers to as the "White House 9/11 trauma defense."[24]

Keeping the boundaries of the 9/11 story narrow, Bush characterized the War on Terror in strictly dichotomous terms, presenting the struggle between terrorists and the United States as one between good and evil. This language not only allowed the United States to maintain its image as an innocent actor; it also gave it permission to define whole groups of actors as summarily evil. President Bush wasted no time employing this black-and-white division in his language, stating in a speech on the day of the attacks, "Today our nation saw evil, the very worst of human nature."[25] Triggering Christian theological conceptions of good versus evil, this language served to transform a complex political context into a simplistic and predetermined equation. Further, Bush spoke of the terrorists as mere embodiments of essentialized characteristics, rather than as complex human actors, in order to provide a definitive explanation for their actions that was based on inherent violent tendencies. Terrorists, in other words, "did what they did because it is in their nature to do so—they murdered because that is what evil, demonic terrorists do."[26]

Bush's fixation on the terrorists' essentialized characteristics is threaded throughout his rhetoric. He described the terrorists variously as those who "embrace tyranny and death,"[27] who "are violently opposed to democracy," and who have an "ideology of terror and death" and a "dark vision of hatred."[28] Rather than providing an explanation for why the United States had been attacked, the goal of such vague but emotionally resonant descriptions of the enemy was to elicit diffuse, irrational fear, uncoupled from rational understanding, that would eventually give the United States government the license it needed from Americans to inflict massive and unfettered violence on a global scale. Bush and other official messengers used this essentializing language to obscure the scope and scale of the threat posed by the 9/11 attackers, casting them as the villains in an inevitable struggle, the boundaries of which remained conveniently hazy.

The second core element in the formation of the official narrative underlying the War on Terror is cementing the idea of the terrorist enemy in people's minds so firmly—and affixing it equally firmly to Muslims and Islam—that they come to be seen as completely other and not quite human. This involves a rhetorical strategy that essentializes the characteristics of not just the conflict but the enemy, allowing for a kind of dehumanization by metaphor that is emotionally powerful, but vague and amorphous enough to be expanded to fit the changing needs and targets of the War on Terror. President Bush often referred to the terrorist "enemy" in terms that suggested something less than human, bolstering the underlying narrative that drummed up public support for a conflict in which the goalposts were constantly shifting. For example, on September 12, 2001, he described the enemy as one who "hides in the shadows and has no regard for human life," and as "an enemy who preys on innocent and unsuspecting people, then runs for cover. This is an enemy who tries to hide."[29] Four days later, he called on other countries to participate in the War on Terror, citing the need to "eliminate the terrorist parasites who threaten their countries and our own."[30]

Bush continued on this theme in a radio address on May 17, 2003, stating, "From Pakistan to the Philippines to the Horn of Africa, we are hunting down Al Qaeda killers."[31] This statement demonstrates how boundless the War on Terror had become while utilizing language reminiscent of killing animals to describe the search for the terrorists. Beyond simply portraying the terrorists who attacked the United States as the most vicious in history, Bush's metaphors dehumanized them, eliminated the possibility that there could have been any rational explanation for their violence, and cemented the idea that warfare and militarism were the only appropriate courses of action.

This use of animalistic metaphors to provide rhetorical cover was not limited to the Bush administration or the immediate aftermath of 9/11 but has continued throughout the War on Terror. For example, in President Barack Obama's 2015 State of the Union address, he, like Bush, stressed that the United States would continue to "hunt down terrorists."[32] Then, a year later in his 2016 State of the Union address, Obama said, "We just need to call them what they are—killers and fanatics who have to be rooted out, hunted down, and destroyed."[33]

President Donald Trump did not hesitate either in using animalistic metaphors and reductionist language to minimize the humanity of those deemed terrorists or supportive of terrorism. Rhetorically, he went much further than his predecessors, exposing the naked Islamophobia of the War on Terror by "saying the quiet parts out loud." For example, in his remarks in a Joint Address to Congress in February 2017, Trump said the Islamic State of Iraq and Syria (ISIS) was "a network of lawless savages that have slaughtered Muslims and Christians, and men, and women, and children of all faiths and all beliefs."[34] In October 2019, a proud Trump boasted about killing Abu Bakr al-Baghdadi, the leader of ISIS, twice repeating, "He died like a dog. He died like a coward." In the same speech, he said of terrorists in general, "These savage monsters will not escape their fate, and they will not escape the final judgment of God."[35] Besides being dehumanizing, Trump's reference to the judgment of God here is reminiscent of President Bush's frequent references to God, clearly rooted in Christianity, which served to essentialize the Muslim enemy and position the War on Terror as a struggle between good and evil.

Don't Tell Anyone We Destroyed Iraq and Afghanistan

The final major component of the government's narrative justifying the War on Terror is the theme of American benevolence. Like the previous two elements, this one involves essentializing language that relies on social cues to mythic structures to do most of the work of communicating. To be convincing, the rhetoric around America's righteousness relies on a continuous construction of righteous conflict with a savage enemy, and it is developed in language that stands in stark contrast to these other thematic elements. This rhetorical strategy is designed to draw attention away from the self-interested foreign-policy objectives of the United States, for example, and redirect it into an image of a powerful country interested only in using its power to ensure the well-being of others.

The operation of this narrative is most apparent in the language surrounding the wars in Iraq and Afghanistan. For example, when it came to Iraq, Bush stated that "Iraqis are assuming more responsibility for their own security and their own future."[36] If you didn't know the context or the time frame in which Bush said these words, it would seem that the US's involvement in Iraq was out of pure benevolence. But the reason Iraq needed to build itself back up was because the United States had bombed it. This detail, however, was left out in order to erase the gravity of the United States' violence.

In a later statement on Iraq, Bush again referred to supporting Iraqi security forces, saying, "As those forces become more self-reliant and take on greater security responsibilities, America and its coalition partners will increasingly be in a supporting role. In the end, Iraqis must be able to defend their own country, and we will help that proud, new nation secure its liberty."[37] Again, the United States was absolved from any responsibility in creating the conditions that Iraqis faced, and in this case, the US and its coalition partners were positioned as innocent actors simply interested in Iraq's well-being.

This theme is often expressed in paternalistic tones, such as when Bush positioned the United States as the world's babysitter: "America is committed to keeping the world's most dangerous weapons out of the hands of the world's most dangerous regimes."[38] In addition to suggesting that the United States gets to decide which countries are the most dangerous, this narrative implies that we apply such enforcement across the board. Of course, this is completely false; it is well known that the US selectively targets countries while excluding others such as Israel, which has nuclear programs that go publicly unacknowledged despite the fact that it is an "open secret."[39]

In the run-up to the Afghanistan war, Bush's form of paternalism focused on the generosity of the United States. To this end, Bush asserted, "At the same time, the oppressed people of Afghanistan will know the generosity of America and our allies. As we strike military targets, we'll also drop food, medicine and supplies to the starving and suffering men and women and children of Afghanistan."[40] Rather than describing generosity, Bush's statement sounded more like the relationship between an abuser and their victims. In this type of relationship, the abuser causes harm while at the same time making the victim dependent on the abuser's help to remedy the harm the abuser caused.

Obama also was no stranger to the language of paternalism, especially when it helped disguise the United States' own violence. For example, in his 2010 State of the Union address, Obama asserted that "we stand with the girl who yearns to go to school in Afghanistan" and that "America must always stand on the side of freedom and human dignity, always."[41] But saying the United States must do something is different from saying it has done something or will do something. When it comes to standing on the side of freedom and dignity, the United States' record suggests that in most countries in the world, it has done the exact opposite.

In his last State of the Union address, in 2008, President Bush said, "Our foreign policy is based on a clear premise: We trust that people, when given the chance, will choose a future of freedom and peace."[42] This paternalistic quote served the dual rhetorical purpose of diverting attention away from US violence and further entrenching the idea of freedom as justification for that violence. This rhetorical stance was clearly intended to extend beyond the current moment, giving the United States a kind of blank check for future acts of violence against those it portrayed as needing help. It has also served to distance the US from whatever situation was causing violence and instability in the first place, positioning the US as an almost abstract, benevolent force.

However, the United States has always had objectives of its own in the region; it has never come to the table as a neutral party. The official discourse of the War on Terror vigorously and deliberately discourages any approach to understanding the 9/11 attacks that views them as part of an historical pattern, rather than a singular, momentous event. But this ahistorical framework conceals the legacy of US-led Empire in the Middle East that motivated Al-Qaeda to violence in the first place. In the words of Boise State professor Michael Blain, the effect of the government's narrative around terrorism and the 9/11 attacks was that "historical background of empire was disassociated from the memory of the event."[43]

The Resilient Narratives of Empire

Because the 9/11 attacks occurred in the early days of Bush's presidency, it was his narrative approach that largely shaped the framework through which the War on Terror came to be understood. Although Presidents Obama and Trump would each display seemingly divergent language, and were certainly very different from each other in tone, it was this underlying framework that they were modifying. And it was in support of the same policies, pursued relentlessly and unrestrained by any meaningful checks on the power of the executive from the public or the other two branches of government.

One of the central roles Bush played in launching, expanding, and sustaining the War on Terror was to "sell policies he linked to the counterterror effort such as civil liberty–abridging legislation and wars abroad."[44] Bush's narrative also sought to demonize certain leaders, selectively considering them state sponsors of terror and implying that the violence of Saddam Hussein and Muammar Qaddafi, for example, against their own people was somehow indicative of their propensity and desire to conduct attacks against the United States. More concretely, in his 2002 State of the Union address, Bush referenced an "Axis of Evil" that included Iran, Iraq, and North Korea.[45] The Iraq War ended up posing a conundrum in Bush speak, because he had initially campaigned on the lie that Iraq had weapons of mass destruction. When the weapons failed to materialize, the administration's narrative shifted to frame the Iraq War as a campaign for freedom and democracy.[46]

When Obama came into power, his emphasis was initially on retracting the excesses of the War on Terror and making an "ideological change."[47] For example, he largely abandoned the term *War on Terror* in order to give it less weight on his foreign-policy agenda. Where Bush exaggerated the terror threat in his public language, Obama sought to downplay it. With less emphasis on terrorism overall in his speeches, Obama also moved to directly address the threat in concrete terms. For example, instead of making broad-brush descriptions of the terrorist threat as evil, barbaric, and so on, Obama would name a group directly.[48] The specificity in Obama's language—and the implication that this would make military interventions more precise and targeted—stood in contrast to the Obama administration's actual pattern of launching indiscriminate drone strikes on mostly Muslim countries.

Despite a softer rhetorical approach overall, Obama did display a willingness to pivot to the brute language of war and power. For example, after the failed bombing attempt in Detroit at the end of 2009, which involved a Muslim man who put bombs in his underwear, Obama stated, "We are at war. We are at war against al Qaeda, a far-reaching network of violence and hatred that attacked us on 9/11, that killed nearly 3,000 innocent people, and that is plotting to strike us again. And we will do whatever it takes to defeat them."[49] Other threats revealed Obama's tough-on-terrorism approach in language as well as in action. For example, although he initially dismissed ISIS as a sort of light terrorism, in November 2014, when he could no longer ignore the threat, Obama stated bluntly that the goal of the United States would be to "degrade and destroy" ISIS.[50] Most chillingly, in 2011, Obama reportedly said to a journalist in regard to drone warfare that it "turns out I'm really good at killing people. Didn't know that was going to be a strong suit of mine."[51]

Because Bush had already established support for the underlying narrative and many of the policies that composed the architecture of the War on Terror, Obama was able to speak far less about it. Gabriel Rubin, Associate Professor of Justice Studies at Montclair University, reasons that the difference in the frequency with which Obama addressed the terror threat compared to Bush "speaks to the fact that Obama did not have to sell policy as Bush had already done the policy selling for him."[52] While Obama did attempt to roll back excesses of the previous administration, in practice his record on counterterrorism proved that beyond rhetoric, he was more than willing to execute the war that Bush started.

Though operating with slightly different priorities than Bush—for example, in his deemphasis of the war in Iraq and treating it as a distraction in the fight against Al-Qaeda—Obama maintained his commitment to challenging the terrorist threat through his narrative, utilizing the same understanding of the 9/11 attacks as Bush had.[53] As well, although he committed outwardly to aligning the values of the United States with fighting the War on Terror, Obama was deeply embedded in Bush's war in terms of policy—with the exception of drone warfare, which he expanded dramatically. Ultimately, Obama can be described as "Bush lite" because Obama didn't veer off the course set by Bush, but instead mostly preserved his predecessor's policies. Because Bush had done most of the policy selling and Obama could simply "adopt" his War on Terror, the latter had far less to sell and therefore gave far fewer speeches.[54]

The most obvious rhetorical difference between President Trump and his predecessors was his open embrace of Islamophobia, specifically in linking Muslims as a whole to terrorism.[55] In addition, his narrative tied immigration to terrorism, which resulted in policies rooted in Islamophobia, such as the Muslim Ban. This is not to dismiss the targeting of Muslims under both Bush and Obama, but instead to highlight the fact that Trump chose a rhetorical strategy that directly attributes social problems to essentialized characteristics of Muslims and other marginalized communities.

Before becoming president, Trump notoriously stated that "Islam hates us,"[56] and called for "a total and complete shutdown of Muslims entering the United States until our country's representatives can figure out what is going on."[57] After becoming president, Trump singled out Muslims, directing vitriol to Muslim congresswomen Rashida Tlaib and Ilhan Omar. In a series of tweets taking a shot at them in addition to the other two initial members of "the squad," Alexandria Ocasio-Cortez and Ayanna Pressley, he wrote that it was "so interesting to see 'Progressive' Democrat Congresswomen, who originally came from countries whose governments are a complete and total catastrophe, the worst, most corrupt and inept anywhere in the world (if they even have a functioning government at all), now loudly and viciously telling the people of the United States, the greatest and most powerful Nation on earth, how our government is to be run."[58]

While Obama's speeches focused less on terrorism than did Bush's, Trump reversed this course. In the first two years of his presidency, Trump made eighty-two speeches on terrorism, compared to the 135 that Obama made during his entire eight years as president. Trump also rolled back the terminology around terrorism, choosing to refer to "radical Islamic terrorism" and to the enemy as "evil."[59]

Unsurprisingly, Trump showed almost no tolerance in his rhetoric at all for Muslims and Muslim Americans—only mentioning tolerance toward them in 5 percent of his speeches.[60] In comparison, his predecessors rhetorically demonstrated tolerance toward Muslims and Muslim Americans far more—Bush in 13.5 percent of his speeches and Obama in 29 percent of his speeches. Trump displayed so little regard for Muslim life that even after the New Zealand massacre that resulted in the killing of fifty-one Muslims, he refused to acknowledge the identity of the victims, simply saying that he was "offering condolences to the nation of New Zealand."[61] The discrepancy between the frequency of his language criminalizing Muslims and that showing tolerance illustrates just how reliant Trump was on frankly hateful and oppressive tropes as a way to scapegoat Muslims and immigrants and deflect criticism of his policies.

To take another example, Trump's focus, both during his campaign and after taking office, on the now infamous Muslim Ban nakedly manipulated fears of immigrants from regions he believed, or purported to believe, exported terrorism.[62] The implementation of the Muslim Ban was an intervention that both was rooted in Islamophobia and served to short-circuit any analysis that might explain the San Bernardino attack of 2015, as well as attacks in Europe, in a way that reached beyond a predisposition to terrorism harbored by Muslims. In other words, Trump directly tied his narrative to a particular policy intervention in order to allow for only the explanation of radical Islamic terrorism to survive.

By analyzing the narratives used throughout the War on Terror, we can clearly see the power of language in making state violence on the part of the United States seem benign. Moreover, this language determines who the unequivocal protagonists and antagonists are. The United States has held steadfastly to the narrative that it was and is the ultimate victim and that no action on its part could undermine its status as such. However, when all is said and done, perhaps it's possible that "America projected an image of itself onto terrorists; alternatively, one might argue the thirst for revenge among Americans led the country to embody the very terrorists they hated."[63] Absent self-reflection, the US will continue to see itself as somehow different from the terrorists, regardless of what the mirror reflects.

2.

SETTING THE WAR'S RHETORICAL TERMS

*But the state lies in all the tongues of good and evil,
and whatever it may tell you, it lies—and whatever
it has, it has stolen.*

—Friedrich Nietzsche[1]

*Increasingly, questions are being raised about the
problem of the definition of a terrorist. Let us be wise
and focused about this: terrorism is terrorism. . . .
What looks, smells and kills like terrorism is terrorism.*

—Sir Jeremy Greenstock, British Ambassador to the
United Nations, in post–September 11, 2001, speech[2]

A core facet of the government's ability to control the development of the narrative framework supporting the War on Terror involves its capacity to claim the moral high ground from a position of power. Government speech is more powerful in shaping and manipulating public opinion because of the inherent coercive power of the state, its ubiquity due to the number of potential speakers, and the amplifying effect of speech from non-government sources such as the media, which inevitably will at least repeat the assumptions contained in official speech regardless of the particular stance taken by any given outlet at any given time. From the very earliest days after the attacks of 9/11, the Bush administration leveraged this power to construct a version of public morality in which the US and its national security needs would always be shifted into the place of good, despite the underlying factual context. This element of the narrative structure of the War on Terror is a powerful tool that Bush and his successors in office have utilized to preempt alternative explanations for terrorism that are based on root causes, and to preemptively block criticisms of the US's behavior that are based in morality.

The first step for the government in crafting its narrative around the ethical questions raised by terrorism and counterterrorism was to lay claim to the definitions that govern the terms of debate. The quote that opens this chapter represents a common refrain among American government officials and leaders of the coalition of states led by the US in the War on Terror. Of course, the definition of terrorism that Greenstock offers is circular and deceptive in its apparent simplicity. To claim that the definition of terrorism is not debatable because it is simply anything that "looks like terrorism" begs the question, What does terror look like? Are there any boundaries for what can be considered terrorism? Greenstock's quote deliberately answers none of these questions, but it does provide a clue to understanding the dynamic at play in how the official narrative post-9/11 has shaped our basic understanding of terrorism, the threat it poses, and what responses are seen as necessary to meet that threat.

The use of tautologies to define terror in particular political contexts is a common rhetorical tactic. For example, take the following statement from Dutch representative to the United Nations Dirk Jan van den Berg: "But 'ground zero' has made it painfully clear that terrorism in its true manifestation defines itself."[3] But a word cannot define itself, and it is impossible to identify a true manifestation of a thing that is undefined. Moreover, because terrorism as a concept is inherently value laden, it cannot be defined in a way that would speak to an objective reality.

At the root of these tautological definitions is this basic formula: "'Terrorism' is what 'terrorists' do. And 'terrorists' are those who commit 'terrorism.'"[4] Although terrorism has come to be presented as if it is somehow self-defining in this way, there are always underlying assumptions at play about what the term means based on the context and power dynamics. The "definitions" offered by the dominant narrative are actual socially constructed agreements to perceive similar actions in different ways depending on the actor. In particular, they serve to draw a bright line between state violence on the one hand and non-state-actor violence on the other and to define them only relative to each other so that the definitions can shift and adapt, erasing the factual underpinnings of any given instance or pattern of violence so the priorities of the more powerful—the state—are always seen as just.

Leaving terrorism amorphously defined in this way allows the United States to maintain its innocence by simply asserting that it does not "do terrorism." But it also operates on another level: leaving the question of who terrorists are technically open allows the content of the dominant narrative to fill in the definition by a side door, so to speak. In the language of the War on Terror, these discussions nearly always contain strong, if not direct, allusions to a particular group—Muslims. Labeling only violence inflicted by Muslim actors as terrorism—regardless of how clearly, or not, the term itself is defined—is deeply rooted in Islamophobia and has served to render the caricature of the Muslim terrorist a cover for state violence. It is important to note here that many use this fact to advocate for terrorism legislation that would be universally applied to perpetrators of violence including white nationalists. However, like all things related to terrorism, such a change would indelibly and only impact Muslims and other marginalized communities.

The question of definitions here is a crucial one because when counterterrorism policies are presented as a simple and direct response to terrorism, whether or not it lacks clear definition, it is easier for the state to evade moral judgment and questions about the legitimacy of its actions. Just the word *counterterrorism* limits the possibility of accountability, since the state itself determines what it believes is a reasonable response to terrorism. These linguistic choices functionally define the boundaries of what is considered legal versus illegal conduct. As scholars have pointed out, in contrast to Greenstock's glib dismissal, "terrorism" is not a thing that exists objectively in the real world, but rather a label applied to events based on an interpretation of those events and their causes.[5] The people doing the interpreting are not neutral observers, but rather are biased by their own interests in manipulating perceptions in order to achieve concrete political goals. Further, power dynamics make it nearly impossible to challenge these labels—for example, to see the state's violence as state terrorism—unless the new labels are supported by powerful third parties (e.g., the United Nations). Of course, political entities generally do not challenge each other's actions on the basis of neutral moral principles, but rather respect each other's constructed definitions of violence based on power dynamics. This doesn't alter what is actually objectively true— that if the same violent acts were committed by non-state actors, they would be labeled terrorism. However, they do not apply these underlying principles universally and their shared construction of reality is not grounded in empirical fact—that if the same violent acts were committed by non-state actors, they would be labeled terrorism.

This discrepancy, and others like it, can be explained by the social construction in policy design framework that was developed by policy professors Helen Ingram and Anne Schneider. Ingram and Schneider argue that the way particular populations are characterized and the way these characterizations are absorbed by the wider culture have a powerful influence on policy goals and design.[6] In general, groups constructed positively receive policy benefits and groups constructed negatively receive policy burdens. However, the relative power of the group constructed also impacts whether they are the recipients of policy benefits or burdens. So, groups with a positive social construction and a high degree of power can expect many policy benefits and few policy burdens, but groups with a similarly positive construction but a lesser degree of power may see little of either. Those with little political power and a negative social construction, of course, can expect the most policy burdens and the fewest policy benefits.

Ingram and Schneider are also concerned with how public-policy design impacts democracy. Policy sends clear messages not only about the socially perceived deservedness and undeservedness of different groups, but about what sort of policy outcomes can be expected in the future on the basis of each group's social construction. This in turn signals whether a group is encouraged to engage in or withdraw from the system. While social constructions of different target groups can change over time, they can also be deeply entrenched and hard to change. Just as group construction and power impact the creation of policy, policy reinforces these social constructions, creating a self-perpetuating cycle.

Social construction in policy design theory gives us a concrete tool for explaining the disparate impacts of the policy choices that are directly relevant to understanding the War on Terror and how deeply embedded the social constructions of Muslims as terrorists have been in the design and policies of the War on Terror. For as long as the War on Terror has been in existence, Muslims have been constructed as terrorists. This construction has been thoroughly embedded in the design and implementation of post-9/11 policies, overtly and covertly, domestic and external—including through the almost immediate profiling and detention of Muslim men after the 2001 attacks, the National Security Entry-Exit Registration System, the use of the Guantánamo Bay prison to house Muslim men, the domestic surveillance program Countering Violent Extremism (CVE), and numerous other programs and practices.

Once the underlying assumptions of the dominant narrative become as deeply embedded in policy as they have over the two decades since the events of 9/11, they become much more difficult to dislodge from the imagination of a public who accepts the reality of this political landscape as a matter of course, a public who has come to see as natural the way the War on Terror describes and shapes the world—so natural that the narrative itself operates invisibly, in the background.

A Question of Moral Equivalencies

> *You could hardly begin . . . to analyze political con-*
> *flicts involving Sunnis and Shi'is, Kurds and Iraqis,*
> *or Tamils and Sinhalese, or Sikhs and Hindus . . .*
> *without eventually having to resort to the categories*
> *and images of "terrorism" and "fundamentalism,"*
> *which derived entirely from the concerns and intel-*
> *lectual factories in metropolitan centres like Wash-*
> *ington and London. They are fearful images that*
> *lack discriminate contents or definition, but they*
> *signify moral power and approval for whoever uses*
> *them, moral defensiveness and criminalization for*
> *whomever they designate.*
>
> —EDWARD SAID[7]

Once the dominant narrative claimed control over definition setting, it was able to go further and argue, again tautologically, that any actions of the state in response to acts of terrorism, or its own arbitrary perceptions that such threats may arise in the future, are inherently just—or, if not quite just, justified—while the actions of those constructed as the "enemy" inherently *cannot* be just because they have no basis in reason nor can they be rooted in any legitimate system of ethics.

The narrative tactic of denying that moral equivalencies exist between state violence and non-state-actor violence is a heavily utilized rhetorical device that has served to legitimize the United States' violence in the War on Terror across many dimensions. This strategy is employed to accomplish four goals: (1) to define for the public who the United States is and what it stands for in comparison to the terrorists; (2) to entrench the notion that certain groups are inherently prone to violence; (3) to legitimize state violence and preserve embedded notions of victim and perpetrator; and (4) to preclude the possibility of the US being blamed for the standing or condition of another country or group.

At the core of this narrative structure is a simple set of associations that the official discourse has caused to be ingrained in the conversation around terrorism through constant repetition and recourse to emotionally laden social cues that are primed with existing stereotypes and mythic forms: namely, that the violence of the US is reasonable, necessary, and in any case a just and proportionate response to violence, real or imagined, perpetrated against it or its interests. In contrast, the threat posed by those constructed as the enemy other, again real or imagined, represents the polar opposite. It is blind, unreasoning, destructive—and it always takes the form of aggressor, never reacting to external forces. One consequence of this categorical demonization is that any meaningful distinction between different acts of violence committed by different groups is erased, resulting in the broad condemnations of all groups. Crucially, this posture also precludes the possibility of developing interventions that deal with root causes—located in many cases in historical or ongoing US state violence. At the same time, it allows the state to justify increasingly violent tactics because the terrorists are deemed to be an irrational force with whom political bargaining is impossible.

It is often the case that violence committed by oppressed groups is presented by those in power as incomprehensible and inexplicable, and it is not difficult to see that such characterizations serve to preserve the positions of the powerful and promote their interests. These types of constructions preclude the discursive possibility that the violence of oppressed groups could ever be seen as rational when the particular context of the conflict and its historical origins are taken into account.

A crucial dimension to the question of moral equivalence is the difference in how state violence versus non-state-actor violence is defined or framed. Sociologists Scott Poynting and David Whyte write that "the political violence of the oppressed is always represented as pathological and inhuman; it may be understood in rational terms but can never be conceded as rationally explicable, let alone as a rational response to the historically transmitted, material context of conflict."[8] Of course, groups designated as terrorists do sometimes commit indiscriminate acts of violence that target the innocent. However, the context under which their violence emerges is often negated and left unaddressed. One consequence of this absolute demonization is that it allows for the negative characteristics ascribed to terrorists to be seen as inherent to them, inviting a broader application to people and groups who are considered similar but are not violent. Crucially, this posture also precludes the possibility of developing interventions that deal with root causes, located in many cases in historical or ongoing US state violence. In addition, the terrorist threat is being framed here "as a force that cannot be politically bargained with,"[9] leaving violence as the only viable response.

Close analysis of President Bush's post-9/11 speeches reveals an overarching narrative of the enemy in which they are ascribed inherent characteristics, tactics, and motivations for committing acts of terrorism. One of the starkest examples of this is Bush's quote that "Al Qaeda and its followers are Sunni extremists, possessed by hatred and commanded by a harsh and narrow ideology. Take almost any principle of civilization, and their goal is the opposite. They preach with threats, instruct with bullets and bombs, and promise paradise for the murder of the innocent."[10] Here, he reiterates the now familiar notion that the enemy possesses certain inherent characteristics, that they are Sunnis of a particularly narrow-minded type who hate the West and the United States and whose violence has nothing to do with external circumstances or conditions.

Describing the terrorists' actions as motivated by hatred and rage is a tool designed to draw a bright line between state violence on the one hand (acceptable and even necessary to promote liberal values) and non-state-actor violence (terrorism). For example, Bush stated, "To prevail, we must remove the conditions that inspire blind hatred, and drove 19 men to get onto airplanes and to come and kill us."[11] This echoes the assertion that terrorists are not motivated by anything other than raw emotion. But hatred isn't the reason more than two million Muslims have died in the course of the War on Terror, nor is it the reason there are close to eight hundred US military bases around the world.[12] More than that, it isn't even the actions of those targeted in the name of fighting the War on Terror at all that have caused their victimization, but the ability of the massively powerful United States to link them in any tenuous way to a perceived threat to its national-security interests.

The narrow framing of questions of moral culpability in the government's narrative obscures the disproportionate breadth and scope of the US's response to specific acts of terror and seeks to absolve it from any accountability that might be independently inferred by examining its actions. When President Bush was signing the USA Patriot Act, he stated that it would "help counter a threat like no other our Nation has ever faced. We've seen the enemy and the murder of thousands of innocent, unsuspecting people. They recognize no barrier of morality. They have no conscience. The terrorists cannot be reasoned with."[13] By constructing the (undefined) "enemy" as completely irrational and completely lacking a moral compass—of course with the implication that this stood in stark opposition to the United States—Bush justified the restrictive and sweeping domestic law he was putting into place, which would be weaponized to the detriment of Americans themselves.

Bush administration officials didn't shy away from using the strategy of denying moral equivalencies even when the US's wrongdoing was indisputable and widely condemned. One example of this is Donald Rumsfeld's response to the Abu Ghraib scandal. Rumsfeld addressed accusations that his policies played a role in the torture that occurred there, graphic images of which had just been revealed to the public, by comparing the military's treatment of prisoners to beheadings by terrorists, asking, "Does it rank up there with chopping someone's head off on television? It doesn't."[14] Capitalizing on the construction of terrorism as an exceptionally brutal form of violence allowed Rumsfeld to insinuate that no act of state violence could ever be worse or less moral—that, in fact, the actions of the United States, no matter to what extent they trample over notions of decency and human rights, cannot even be considered in the same broad category. By using an example of violence by the enemy considered worse than that of the US, Rumsfeld also sought to make conduct that wasn't justifiable on its own—the torture at Abu Ghraib—justifiable in comparison.

Two years later, at a press conference in September 2006, President Bush was questioned about a statement made by former secretary of state Colin Powell expressing the fact that other countries had become skeptical of the War on Terror's moral footing. Bush responded by saying, "If there's any comparison between the compassion and decency of the American people and the terrorist tactics of extremists, it's flawed logic. It's just—I simply can't accept that. It's unacceptable to think that there's any kind of comparison between the behavior of the United States of America and the action of Islamic extremists who kill innocent women and children to achieve an objective."[15] This response desperately clung to the logic of moral equivalence and went so far as to preclude any critique of US actions at all. Moreover, it was in this way that Bush could give the US cover for its actions, regardless of how egregious, even preemptively.

In his State of the Union speech in 2016, President Obama echoed the same sentiment: "The American people should know that, with or without congressional action, ISIL will learn the same lessons as terrorists before them. If you doubt America's commitment—or mine—to see that justice is done, just ask Osama bin Laden."[16] In this particular case, though, context allows us to define "American justice" more precisely. In his statement, President Obama is speaking about the extrajudicial, targeted assassination of al-Qaeda leader Osama bin Laden the year before. The inclusion of this form of justice, untethered from the actual American judicial system and its principles, reveals the moral flexibility of the term the previous president deliberately left vague. Obama did not make a direct comparison between the US's actions and those of Al-Qaeda, but his words celebrating extrajudicial violence—violence that in fact defines the label of terrorism—suggest there is one to be made.

With the US's war stage barely visible, the beheading of American journalist James Foley by ISIL (an alternate name for ISIS) in 2014 emerged as an especially stark example of the group's enduring violence. The visibility of Foley's murder by ISIL, perhaps the opposite of what the group had intended, provided a convenient cover for the US's violence, allowing it to reject moral equivalencies that would call US conduct into question. To this end, President Obama responded to Foley's death by saying, "Jim was taken from us in an act of violence that shocked the conscience of the entire world. . . . Now, Jim Foley's life stands in stark contrast to his killers. Let's be clear about ISIL. They have rampaged across cities and villages killing innocent, unarmed civilians in cowardly acts of violence."[17] Here again, what makes the rejection of moral equivalencies so salient is the fact that the violence attributed to ISIL could have just as easily described the actions of the US.

The perpetual rejection of moral equivalence between the violence of the United States and that of the enemy during the Bush and Obama presidencies emboldened an already unabashed President Donald Trump. In Trump's 2020 State of the Union address, he said of the US's assassination of General Qasem Suleimani in the first few days of 2020, "Our message to the terrorists is clear: You will never escape American justice. If you attack our citizens, you forfeit your life."[18] Not only does his statement leave vague the meaning of "American justice"; it also allows the US to claim that anyone who is killed vis-à-vis its counterterrorism tactics is a terrorist. There's no need to explain any deaths because the logic affords the deduction that if someone is killed, they must have been a terrorist. Moreover, if someone is killed, it must also be justice. Trump's statement here applies a broad approach to the rejection of moral equivalencies—though in reverse order.

Another aspect of the War on Terror that has drawn the rejection of moral equivalencies into focus involves subjective assessments in which different modes of death are constructed as more or less moral depending on the actor. In an op-ed titled "Beheadings v. Drone Assassinations," former Federal Bureau of Investigation (FBI) agent Coleen Rowley starts with the question "Why do Americans hate beheadings but love drone killings?" in order to address the popular American perception that assassination by beheading is more gruesome than assassination by drone—the former generally attributed to non-state actors and the latter used by the US in its War on Terror.[19] She argues in part that the discrepancy between reactions to the two types of violence has to do with racism, such that drones are seen as acceptable to use on the other, as well as the visibility of beheadings versus drone strikes in the media and the invisibility of the destruction caused by drone strikes. Drone strikes are not more accepted merely because they impose physical distance between the act of violence and its human consequence, as the story is often told. They are also seen as less brutal because of another layer of distance imposed—the dispassionate distance of indifference that is enabled by seeing the target of the brutality as undeserving of moral concern.

Another, related element of analyzing comparisons of violence and what the US does or does not engage in is the use of the term *collateral damage* to obscure the gravity and gruesomeness of civilian deaths. What if collateral damage was actually described according to what the damage looked like—for example, with the use of drones? Then there would have to be recognition that "'collateral damage' is a far cry from acknowledging the blown-off limbs, the punctured eardrums, the shrapnel wounds, and the psychological horror that are caused by heavy bombardment."[20] Given the way it has adapted to excuse much more publicly visible atrocities such as Abu Ghraib, however, even this may not be adequate to dislodge the power of the government's narrative enough to make space for the kind of automatic public compassion that Americans feel when one of "their own" is the victim.

By constantly reiterating their comparative moral superiority, American political leaders on both sides of the aisle have shown their unchallenged commitment to the idea that no act of state violence—whether torture, extrajudicial killings, the devastation of civilian populations in Muslim-majority countries, or the targeting of Muslim Americans for state surveillance—could ever conceivably compare to the violence inflicted by terrorists—read: Muslims. Any and all harm to Muslims, on the other hand, is justified on the basis of the claimed superiority of America's moral position, which rests largely on the characterization of Muslims as the faceless, menacing enemy confronting all that is good in the world. Underlying this entire circular structure is one fundamental fact about the maintenance of state power: to retain legitimacy, and therefore the consent of the governed, the government needs to create a monopoly on what is considered "acceptable" violence. To do this, it leverages its inherent position of discursive power to shape narrative so as to gain a monopoly on the underlying script about morality and ethics.

Moral Exclusion

From the very first days and throughout the course of the War on Terror so far, Muslims and Muslim Americans have been indelibly linked to terrorism in the government's narrative, which has been so absorbed into the public imagination that its assumptions are now largely invisible to critical examination. Muslims and Muslim Americans have been dehumanized in the government's story, reduced to playing the role of shadowy villain. A direct real-world result of this is that the post-9/11 legal and policy landscape has been characterized by the constant scapegoating, demonization, and criminalization of Muslims and Muslim Americans. Even the most egregious abuses on the part of the state have been presented by both the state and its allies as justified. It is worth examining how this misrepresentation has come to be accepted from all angles.

Social psychologist Susan Opotow's theory of moral exclusion provides one way into understanding how these abuses can occur. According to Opotow, "Moral exclusion occurs when individuals or groups are perceived as outside the boundary in which moral values, rules, and considerations of fairness apply. Those who are morally excluded are perceived as nonentities, expendable, or undeserving. Consequently, harming them appears acceptable, appropriate, or just."[21] The concept of moral exclusion provides a way of understanding widespread support for policies such as the Muslim Ban, racial profiling, and even torture (or "enhanced interrogation techniques" in the parlance of the War on Terror) that single out Muslims for differential treatment.

This type of treatment toward Muslims and other similarly situated groups occurs when there is a feeling of disconnection toward that community coming from the dominant group. The consequences of feeling disconnected from another individual or a group can result in the triggering of negative attitudes, destructive behavior, and discriminatory responses.[22] In Opotow's theoretical framework, several psychological mechanisms are at work in the process of moral exclusion. Those most relevant to Muslims and Muslim Americans include biased evaluation, derogation, dehumanization, fear of contamination, and euphemisms.[23] Each of these processes plays a particular role in the demonization of Muslims. For example, biased evaluation leads to highlighting the inferiority of Muslims as compared to the in-group (in this case, white Americans); derogation and dehumanization, to seeing them as less human and therefore less deserving of compassion; and fear of contamination, to the mental positioning of Muslims as a threat to the well-being of their communities. Euphemistic framing of the issues involved further enables in-group acceptance of their harmful impact by masking its true moral nature (e.g., referring to torture as "enhanced interrogation"). To understand the difference in consequences between those who are considered in or outside of a moral community, Opotow writes, "Although both those inside and outside the moral community can experience wrongful harm, harm inflicted on insiders is more readily perceived as injustice and activates guilt, remorse, outrage, demands for reparative response, self-blame, or contrition. When harm is inflicted on outsiders, it may not be perceived as a violation of their rights, and it can fail to engage bystanders' moral concern."[24] Opotow also notes that there is a range of impact depending on the degree of moral exclusion and that it can make anything—from discrimination to genocide—possible.

An article by Muneer I. Ahmad, who served as an attorney for a former juvenile prisoner at Guantánamo named Omar Khadr, demonstrates the consequences of moral exclusion, although he doesn't call it that. In this article, Ahmad addresses the power of rights claims in the context of belonging to a community. According to Ahmad, a rights claimant has to belong to a community that has consented to their membership in the group. The problem that rights claimants at Guantánamo face is that the rights community—in a broad sense, the United States, and, more narrowly, the US legal system—never admitted them as members. In fact, the community did the opposite: casting out prisoners physically and metaphysically, as far away as possible.[25] Framed by the conceptual lens of moral exclusion, this example demonstrates the concrete implications of being morally cast out.

In the discourse and practices of the War on Terror, Muslims have been thoroughly excluded from moral consideration. Even when the government is forced to respond to some atrocity, usually because a particular incident is too visible to be ignored, it is invariably presented as a mistake or an anomaly, leaving the underlying narrative of the US's righteousness untouched. In these cases, the victimization of Muslims at the heart of the matter is simply left unaddressed—an omission allowed because of the way Muslim Americans and Muslims abroad have been construed as moral outsiders.

As we have seen, the mythic language of "good vs. evil" and the familiar narrative structure that relies on existential conflict between two irreconcilable sides—"us" and a deliberately vaguely defined "them"—has been critical to the process of defining moral boundaries in the War on Terror discourse, offering to larger society cues about whom we should see as part of our community and whom we should see as outside of it. Even when Muslim Americans are morally included in the official discourse, it is usually done in a way that makes their membership in the community contingent on fighting terrorism and agreeing to be partners in the War on Terror. Any Muslim who refuses to participate or who rejects the problematic notion on which this demand is built risks their inclusion being revoked, revealing it as having been an empty promise to begin with.

3.

DENYING MUSLIM HUMANITY
IN THE WAR ON TERROR

*Because if you need me to prove my humanity, I'm
not the one that's not human.*

—SUHAIYMAH MANZOOR-KHAN[1]

In 2004, when the Abu Ghraib scandal broke out, conservative commentator Rush Limbaugh responded by saying, in reference to the Iraqis who were tortured, "They are the ones who are perverted. They are the ones who are dangerous. They are the ones who are subhuman. They are the ones who are human debris, not the United States of America and not our soldiers and not our prison guards."[2] Although Limbaugh was widely viewed as extreme throughout his political career, this quote highlights the extent to which Muslims have been dehumanized in the War on Terror—as evidenced by the torture they were subjected to in the first place. Limbaugh's quote also speaks to a broader pattern in the way that Muslim victimhood is denied even when they are obviously and very visibly victims of the worst of the US's violence. Because they have been caricatured as inherently "dangerous" and "subhuman," Muslim suffering can be easily dismissed. Here, this rhetoric operated alongside wide dissemination of graphic images depicting the torture the prisoners endured. If a picture is worth a thousand words, then these pictures communicated just how inconsequential Muslim bodies are, and their constant circulation put the prisoners' humiliation on display over and over again. For Muslims like me, viewing these images was especially horrifying, not only because of the violence on display, but because the humanity of the Muslim victims was absent from the story that was told.

When atrocities of state violence like the prisoner abuses and torture at Abu Ghraib are witnessed too widely to allow for plausible deniability, it is inevitable that the narrative of "a few bad apples" will be put forward to explain them. Former president Bush, for example, relied on this well-worn trope to communicate that such behavior was not representative of the conduct of soldiers in Iraq generally and did not reflect any policy imposed from the top. Others in the commentariat leaped to analyze the tragedy in terms of human psychology[3] and the innate propensity to inflict violence that surfaces when social constraints are removed. The conversation that ensued about who should be held accountable treated what had happened as a deviation from the norm, a tragic but anomalous incident, and ignored the backdrop of state violence that continued unabated.

The narrowing of the question of accountability in these cases to the actions of the perpetrator alone serves to deflect attention away from the state and its patterns of inflicting violence. This dynamic operates on two levels. Even on the surface, the state's recourse to the tired argument about "a few bad apples" is not very convincing. After all, the lesson this common idiom is meant to instill isn't that a couple of bad apples are a random coincidence that has no relevance to the overall operation. The full sentence is, "A few bad apples *spoil the bunch.*" By the logic of apple farming, a system that is riddled with rot should be abandoned—and it is clear, smoke-screen idioms aside, that the abuses of the War on Terror are not limited to a few bad seeds. This points to the more structural problem with the official response to bad publicity. Acknowledging wrong actions only to turn around and excuse them as an aberration is another way in which the US uses its influence on the discourse to avert meaningful criticism—criticism based on the systemic abuse that is inherent in the entire apparatus of the War on Terror. The shocking photos of obvious atrocity, the ones that make it into the press, are just the tip of the iceberg of state violence, which is perpetrated against Muslims and Muslim Americans across sociopolitical dimensions that run the gamut from foreign wars to domestic surveillance and everything in between.

Crucially, the way in which the dominant narrative functions to preclude or, when necessary, deflect criticism of the state also serves to obscure the humanity of the War on Terror's real victims. Thus, for example, the stories of the Iraqis who were tortured at Abu Ghraib were completely lost in the conversation around the scandal. That this performance of accountability allowed the US to conduct business as usual in Iraq despite heightened public scrutiny is emblematic of the way in which the humanity of Muslims has been degraded and erased. The US has proven again and again since the inception of the War on Terror that it is willing to run roughshod over any notion of human rights and the rule of law—and the extent to which this has been allowed is a testament to the power of narrative to facilitate the creation of real-world systems and the resiliency that same narrative power displays in adapting to evade responsibility for the human cost of the systems it supports.

A particularly heart-rending example of how basic humanity has been denied to Muslim victims of the War on Terror involves the absolute control that officials at the infamous, but still operational, Guantánamo Bay Prison in Cuba have wielded over literal life-and-death decisions related to the prisoners—many, if not most, of whom were detained without charge and with little to no actual evidence of involvement in terrorism. On June 10, 2006, three different prisoners at Guantánamo, two from Saudi Arabia and one from Yemen, died by suicide after hanging themselves.[4] It is not difficult to imagine how a person, isolated and indefinitely detained in a prison rife with abuse, would feel an overwhelming sense of desperation and a need to escape. However, the reaction of Guantánamo officials was startlingly unempathetic. Rear Admiral Harry B. Harris Jr., the camp commander at the time, declared, "They are smart, they are creative, they are committed. . . . They have no regard for life, either ours or their own. I believe this was not an act of desperation, but an act of asymmetrical warfare waged against us."[5] This callous mischaracterization of a desperate act was not an exception. In fact, even earlier in 2003, when twenty-three prisoners attempted suicide, military officials described their attempts as "manipulative, self-injurious behavior" that they coordinated solely to disturb the prison's operations.[6]

As these examples illustrate, Muslims' humanity in the War on Terror has been denigrated to the point where their suffering cannot be seen as such—it has to be seen through the lens of the construction of Muslims as unreasoning terrorists bent on nothing more than destruction. In the most desperate moments of their existence, and even in their deaths, Muslims continue to be seen as fairy-tale monsters whose lives are irredeemable. At the same time, the dehumanization of Muslims allows, for example, the authorization of drone attacks with no genuine consideration of whether their target is a threat, instead murdering Muslims merely because they happen to fall within an appropriate age range. In both cases, Muslim lives are pawns in service of demonstrating that the United States is winning the War on Terror. It is a cruel irony of the United States that death can arrive in an instant to a civilian family in Iraq for no reason at all but the decision to end one's own life is denied to those for whom it is their only escape from constant violence with no end in sight.

Muslim Rage

In 2007, a Kashmiri man named Shakeel Bhat, who was a frequent pro-
testor in support of social justice issues, captured the attention of two
bloggers from the US, Buckley F Williams and Potfry (assumed names).
Dubbed "Islamic Rage Boy" by the bloggers, they turned the image of
Bhat into a cartoon of him protesting, seemingly yelling and with one
of his arms raised.[7] Bhat's cartoon image has been put on everything from
beer mugs to Valentine's cards, and even worse, the bloggers copyrighted
it. Although the bloggers claimed the image they produced was not solely
based on Bhat, but was instead a composite representation of a subgroup
of Muslim protestors described as "perennially angry," the image closely
resembles the Kashmiri activist. Though Williams claimed that the goal of
the cartoon was to facilitate debate and to highlight that Muslims are not
inherently a problem, the reliance on a well-worn trope in the form of a
caricature of a Muslim for comic relief is at odds with this goal, especially
insofar as it served to further normalize the trope that Muslims harbor
inexplicable rage.

Like other negative tropes of Muslims, that of inexplicable and irrational rage has consequences. Muslim rage has been strategically weaponized, not only to absolve Western states from violence inflicted on Muslims
in the name of counterterrorism, but to insist that because of their limited
capacity for reason, the only realistic way to engage is by meeting perceived violence with violence, often preemptively.

Not limited to bad action films, the caricature of Muslims as one-
dimensional and animated by rage alone carries the stamp of intellectual
approval as well. One of the more well-known early examples is a 1990
piece by British American historian Bernard Lewis that appeared in the
Atlantic, titled "The Roots of Muslim Rage: Why So Many Muslims Deeply
Resent the West, and Why Their Bitterness Will Not Easily Be Mollified."[8]
Without bothering to establish the factual basis for the ubiquity of "Muslim rage," Lewis goes through a litany of possible reasons for it, including
American support for hated regimes in Muslim countries, racism, colonialism, and imperialism. But for each of these explanations, Lewis has
a counterargument that denies their seemingly rational basis—American
support for hated regimes isn't that frequent, the US is working on its
racism, colonialism ended, and Muslims are only upset about imperialism
because they are governed by "infidels." If none of these things actually
captures the roots of Muslim rage, then what does? For Lewis, the only

argument left standing is that rage is inherent to Muslims, and this rage should be doubly frightening to the world because it can't be explained and therefore can't be mitigated by, for example, addressing the problem of resentment caused by US policies. Of course, Lewis intended these potential concerns to be straw-man arguments, which he would then quite easily knock down in order to "prove" his original biased assumption.

The intellectual gloss figures like Lewis put on the trope of Muslim rage so common in popular culture, not to mention the many reports purporting to address it as a serious issue coming from right-leaning think tanks and policy centers, are examples of how the government's discursive power is amplified beyond its own speech. The way in which this social construction has been adapted to meet the particular needs of the War on Terror narrative, however, is very much in support of concrete governmental interests. In this context, it serves four related purposes: (1) to allow the US to posture concern for understanding its roots, though only insofar as this concern justifies illegal and violent policies; (2) to ensure that political unrest and the legacy of violence perpetrated by the United States are seen as irrelevant to understanding the anger expressed by Muslims; (3) to absolve the US and other Western countries of any responsibility for actually addressing the root causes and social consequences of widespread rage; and, finally, (4) to deny Muslims justice, because justice is not for those whom we refuse to understand, those whose emotional responses and actions we refuse to grant the same room for nuance we leave for people "like us."

It did not take long for the trope of Muslim rage to evolve into its current form as justification for the policy choices of the War on Terror. Approximately three weeks after the 9/11 attacks, for example, so-called public intellectual Fareed Zakaria wrote an article in *Newsweek* titled "The Politics of Rage: Why Do They Hate Us?" Zakaria not only conflates Arabs with Muslims, he paints Muslims in broad strokes, arguing that theirs is a culture of fanaticism that fuels terrorism, and that there is essentially no context where Muslim behavior could be seen as rational.[9] The purpose of Zakaria's argument is twofold: to isolate Muslim responses to grievances as exceptional, and to double down on the notion that there is no explicable reason for Muslim rage.

In 2002, *New York Times* op-ed columnist Thomas Friedman took a stab at understanding Muslim anger in a piece called "The Core of Muslim Rage." Friedman wrote, "I have long believed that it is this poverty of dignity, not a poverty of money, that is behind a lot of Muslim rage today and the reason this rage is sharpest among educated, but frustrated, Muslim youth. . . . This is not to say that U.S. policy is blameless. We do bad things sometimes. But why is it that only Muslims react to our bad policies with suicidal terrorism, not Mexicans or Chinese?"[10] Because of how deeply entrenched the trope of Muslim rage is, Friedman is able to shrug it off as a problem of dignity while also isolating the Muslim response to violent acts of the US as unique. Of course, he conveniently left out details of the "bad things" the US does, because that's not the problem; according to his logic, characteristics inherent to Muslims are the only relevant factor in this analysis.

To take another example out of the many in existence, in September 2012, *Newsweek* published an article by Ayaan Hirsi Ali, titled "Muslim Rage and the Last Gasp of Islamic Hate."[11] The focus of Ali's article was on Muslims protesting a YouTube video called "The Innocence of Muslims," which mocked the Prophet Muhammad. Ali writes that "Islam's rage reared its ugly head again last week," implying that rage is inherent to the faith and, as she elaborates later in the article, that Muslims can be redeemed if they renounce their faith. Though Ali places the locus of rage in the religion as opposed to its adherents, the nuance yields little difference for the unredeemed Muslims who become acceptable targets of Western intervention all the same.

Ali's article would perhaps have drawn far less attention had it not been for the cover image on the issue in which it was published. The image, devoid of any context, was of Muslims angrily protesting, which was used to cue and reinforce the trope of irrational Muslim rage. To add insult to injury, after publishing the article and photo, *Newsweek* asked readers to use the hashtag #MuslimRage to discuss the cover. Though many, including Muslims, responded with humor to this hashtag, the possibility of legitimate rage was ignored.

While the aforementioned approaches seek to decontextualize and delegitimize any conceivable explanation of Muslim rage, others have addressed this question from a seemingly benign (at least to the outside world) and genuine curiosity. For example, in 2011 Steven Kull, a psychologist and international survey researcher, published a book called *Feeling Betrayed: The Roots of Muslim Anger at America*. Similar to other inquiries about Muslim rage, the author's starting point is 9/11, which automatically precludes from the beginning any potential of understanding the long legacy of the US targeting Muslims both in the United States and abroad. Moreover, the title implies a monolithic Muslim community and one whose anger real or perceived has still and yet to be understood. Notably, the US Department of Homeland Security supported the National Consortium for the Study of Terrorism and Responses to Terrorism (START) at the University of Maryland, which provided support to the author with different parts of the research.[12] Both institutions have an obvious interest in obscuring US state violence and perpetuating the notion of the Muslim threat.

In order to understand the driving force behind Muslim rage, Kull uses a combination of research methods including focus groups and in-depth surveys. Although Kull says that the narrative Muslims espoused at first was one focusing on the harm that the US has caused to the Muslim world (an overly broad term), he writes that with more time, what Muslims revealed was a sense of betrayal. This betrayal, he says, stems from the actions of the US and the incongruence with its projected values, at least insofar as the values were used to build amicable relationships with Muslims. Congruent with the narrative of Muslims as uni-dimensional beings with few feelings other than rage, Kull seems to express surprise at the nuances in responses, noting that they "turned out to be complex and layered."[13]

Like other writings that position Muslims as uniquely supportive of terrorism, Kull is concerned with terrorist groups' ability to operate more easily and recruit more members when the feelings they express align with those present in the broader society. If/when this becomes the case, he asserts, "the United States is not simply dealing with the problem of those terrorist groups, but with a larger system that encompasses the society as a whole."[14]

At a later point in the book, Kull addresses the perception that the United States coercively dominates the Muslim world. He writes that "benign rationales for the presence of U.S. forces in the region—that they are a stabilizing force or that they are there to fight terrorism—are roundly dismissed. Thus, there is widespread support for getting all U.S. military forces out of Muslim countries. In this sense majorities see themselves as aligned with al Qaeda."[15]

In the context that Kull is describing, alignment with Al-Qaeda seems meant to imply a more general agreement of their goals and tactics, instead of the possibility that the two groups might have the same or similar feelings because they are both exposed to the harm of US state violence. Regardless, the insinuation is intended to tether all Muslims to terrorism in order to stonewall any analysis that goes beyond that—especially anything pointing to the United States.

While much else can be said about the book and its contribution to the angry Muslim trope, what is most problematic is that the opinions expressed by Muslims are treated as subjective realities with no basis in objective actions by the United States. Once again, nothing rational can ever explain Muslim anger.

A Note on Rage and Infra-Humanization

The perpetuation of the trope of irrational Muslim rage not only helps to obscure US state violence, it also operates to facilitate the dehumanization of Muslims. The theory of infrahumanization describes a hierarchy of emotions separating humans from non-humans. Nick Haslam and Steve Loughnan assert that the theory of infrahumanization "recognized that humanness can be denied to others in subtle and commonplace ways, rather than being confined to blatant denials in killing fields and torture chambers." Haslam and Loughnan also note that the theory of infrahumanization operationalizes a definition of what humanness means and what specifically makes humans distinct from other animals.[16]

While Muslims have been stripped of their humanness overtly and explicitly, this theory helps to explain how the particular narrative of inexplicable Muslim rage leads to a demoted status of Muslims as less than human. This is important in considering the direct impact of problematic and violent narratives, especially insofar as they pave the path for human rights abuses.

Infrahumanization theory separates humans from those who are less than human or not human altogether, such as animals. In particular, the theory suggests a hierarchy of two sets of emotions—primary and secondary. Primary emotions which are shared by human and non-human animals include those such as sadness, fear, surprise, and anger. Secondary emotions include pride, remorse, or admiration and are only present among those considered fully human. Groups who are constructed as only having primary emotions and not secondary emotions are "conflated with non-human animals and become less than human,"[17] as a result.

This is relevant and applicable to the construction of Muslim rage and the existence of this feeling as primary and an almost singular one that defines Muslim existence. Like other groups who are only thought to have primary feelings and which are raw animalistic ones, Muslims effectively become less than human.[18]

Not a Dent in the Narrative

The greatest thing about this man is he's steady. You know where he stands. He believes the same thing Wednesday that he believed on Monday, no matter what happened Tuesday. Events can change; this man's beliefs never will.

—STEPHEN COLBERT ON GEORGE W. BUSH[19]

The consequences of the official narrative the United States has created and nourished, casting itself as the locus of reason and morality and Muslims as terrorists motivated by blind hatred, are stark. Because of its commitment to promoting this story, no matter what kind of conduct the US engages in or how egregiously that conduct offends moral decency, it will bend over backward to correct the image of itself and cast the behavior as the exception, preserving the sense of moral superiority that allows continued intervention around the world. A close examination of US conduct during the War on Terror makes it extremely difficult to sustain the claim that there can be no moral equivalence between terrorist acts of violence and acts of violence committed by the US. Nonetheless, it is this basic framework that continues to animate discourse around the War on Terror.

When the United States took control over Abu Ghraib prison in Iraq, in place of a portrait of Saddam Hussein they hung up a sign saying, "America is the friend of all Iraqi people."[20] This was a violent sign to put up especially because of what the world would come to know about the treatment that Iraqi prisoners endured at the hands of the United States. As I mentioned briefly before, in 2004 photos emerged of some of the most egregious torture of prisoners at Abu Ghraib—the most well known of which involved the use of dogs to discipline and intimidate the detainees. A later report produced by Major General Anthony Taguba would painfully enumerate the depth of the misconduct there, which included physical and sexual abuse.[21]

When the horrific images of this abuse came out initially, President Bush was interviewed by Al Hurra television and was asked, among other things, what the US could do to "get out of this." He replied, "First, the people in Iraq must understand that I view those practices as abhorrent. They must also understand that what took place in that prison does not represent the America that I know. The America I know is a compassionate country that believes in freedom. The America I know cares about every individual. The America I know has sent troops into Iraq to promote freedom—good, honorable citizens that are helping the Iraqis every day."[22] Far from expressing any semblance of accountability, the president's statement served to reiterate and center the narrative of the United States as a fundamentally benevolent country. As such, it was also a declaration of privilege—the privilege of the US to maintain its exceptional identity no matter what the challenge to it. This example also underscores a fundamental discrepancy of the United States between "normative commitments and actual state practices."[23] As we have seen, one of the most common rhetorical techniques used to minimize the contradiction between the values of the US as stated—the ones it purports to be defending—and its own apparent disregard for the same values in practice, is to present the perpetrators of any given incident as merely "bad apples," and the situation as isolated and unrelated to policies from the highest levels of the government. This strategy relies on the enduring power of the dominant narrative to cue associations between the United States and its purported values automatically and to preempt criticism by relying on the underlying assumption that anything the US does—even disregarding those values—is in service to them.

On another occasion, when the Bush administration was responding to the Abu Ghraib photos, Rumsfeld wielded the violence to promote the United States' democratic values, saying, "Our openness about [the prison abuse] is a lesson about the rule of law."[24] What Rumsfeld failed to mention was that preserving the rule of law meant a lot more than acknowledging a violation of it. Uplifting US governance in spite of the Abu Ghraib scandal, Bush highlighted his leadership, saying, "A dictator wouldn't be answering questions about this."[25] While Bush apparently found cause to celebrate his style of leadership using the lowest threshold possible, he intentionally ignored the anti-democratic practices that his administration had engaged in to sanction torture.

On May 17, 2004, Colin Powell gave a commencement speech at Wake Forest University in which he addressed the Abu Ghraib scandal. Eager to highlight the glory of the United States, Powell pridefully stated, "Watch America. Watch how we deal with this. Watch how America will do the right thing. Watch what a nation of values and character, a nation that believes in justice, does to right this kind of wrong. Watch how a nation such as ours will not tolerate such actions."[26] Earlier that day, however, Powell was on *Meet the Press*, where he admitted that Iraq had not had weapons of mass destruction, while essentially justifying the Iraq war by saying that despite not finding any stockpiles, Iraq had historically used these weapons.[27] Powell's commencement remarks, in which he gave a glowing image of the United States, compared to his acknowledgment that Congress and the public had been misled about weapons of mass destruction illustrated a more familiar logic in which the US's heroism came after the violence that it had caused and that necessitated its heroism. Thus, although the United States might have come onto the Abu Ghraib scene wearing a hero's cape, it was a cape drenched in blood. If the Bush administration's response to Abu Ghraib allowed us to watch anything, it was the use of official rhetoric to disguise the violence.

In 2005, a year after the Abu Ghraib scandal, several marines killed twenty-four Iraqi civilians in Haditha, including women and children and a man in a wheelchair.[28] Responding to the massacre, in 2006 Bush stated that "the Marine Corps is full of honorable people who understand the rules of war," and followed up by saying there would be punishment for anyone found guilty of breaking the law.[29] While the typical narrative for addressing war crimes by the US government wasn't utilized, the statement that offending marines would be punished promoted the idea that there was accountability for crimes in the War on Terror, by implying that because accountability was theoretically possible in this case, any and all crimes committed by the US were being appropriately dealt with. Nothing could be further from the truth. Moreover, this particular narrative allowed the government once again to slither out of the fact that these abuses and others like them were the product of a systemic problem and, in fact, representative of the US's never-ending imperialist violence. In the Haditha massacre, one marine received a reduction in rank, while the cases of another six were dismissed and one acquitted. The twenty-four civilians who were killed by US marines were buried in Martyrs' Graveyard, a cemetery in Iraq. Left on the deserted home of some of the deceased was a graffiti message that said, "Democracy assassinated the family that was here."[30]

In 2012, during the Obama administration, a marine posted a video of himself and three other marines urinating on the dead bodies of Taliban members. Similar to the case of Abu Ghraib, these acts were quickly condemned by officials in the US government, including former secretary of defense Leon Panetta and former secretary of state Hillary Clinton. Responding to the incident, Clinton stated, "It is absolutely inconsistent with American values, with the standards of behavior that we expect from our military personnel."[31] This was not a particularly surprising response, but aside from the fact that American values are spoken about but not actually practiced in any meaningful way, the standards of behavior she was referring to cannot be separated from the fact that they came out of an institution whose sole purpose is to conduct state violence. Moreover, after this condemnation, her statement quickly shifted to the United States' commitment to helping Afghans build and support a democratic Afghanistan, thus turning attention away from the egregious conduct of the marines and restoring the myth of the US's heroic and benevolent leadership.

In the same year, 2012, sixteen villagers were massacred in Kandahar, Afghanistan, by a US soldier. Reacting, then president Obama focused on bringing US troops home from Afghanistan and didn't mention the victims. His comments on the massacre were that "it appeared you had a lone gunman on his own," and that "in no way is this representative of the enormous sacrifices that our men and women have made in Afghanistan."[32] But sacrifices for whom? The Afghans who were killed or the ones who survived to watch the United State destroy their country? Obama's words erased the Muslim victims of a horrific slaughter and doubled down on the narrative trope that the US was fundamentally benevolent. In stark contrast were the words of Haji Najiq, an Afghan shop owner who lived in Kandahar and stated, with respect to the massacre, "We have benefited little from the foreign troops here but lost everything—our lives, dignity and our country to them. . . . The explanation or apologies will not bring back the dead. It is better for them to leave us alone and let us live in peace."[33] Until at least the time of this writing, the US has refused Afghanistan this much, not only because it continues to perpetuate the idea that it's helping the US, but also because of the continuous and embedded narrative lie that somehow brutality and violence are neither systemic nor American.

In 2013, Obama gave a speech at the National Defense University, addressing US military action abroad, detention and torture at Guantánamo Bay Prison, and white supremacist violence in the United States. On Guantánamo, Obama asserted,

America is at a crossroads. We must define the nature and scope of this struggle, or else it will define us. . . . Imagine a future—ten years from now, or twenty years from now—when the United States of American is still holding people who have been charged with no crime on a piece of land that is not part of our country. Look at the current situation, where we are force-feeding detainees who are holding a hunger strike. Is that who we are? Is that something that our Founders foresaw? Is that the America we want to leave to our children?[34]

Although Obama framed his questions as points of reflection, it is clear that like his predecessor, he believed that the United States is an exception, and thus, the answer to the question of whether our behavior in this instance represents who we are is meant to be a resounding no. Therefore, Obama's faux reflection, rather than addressing the reality of the ongoing abuses in the War on Terror, was instead meant to vindicate the United States from its own self. With this logic, just as Muslim victims cannot be identified by the injuries they suffer—because they have been predefined as the enemy—the United States after all cannot be defined by the sum of its actions, but only through the myth of certain values and principles that the US is thought to have been built on. In this way, actual accountability becomes nonexistent, and the obvious pattern of violence continues unacknowledged.

When the Senate Select Committee on Intelligence released their 2014 study of the Central Intelligence Agency's Detention and Interrogation program, commonly referred to as the Torture Report, Obama's initial remarks focused on how important intelligence agencies were for protecting American lives. Justifying the actions conducted by the US post-9/11 in pursuit of Al-Qaeda, Obama stated, "Our nation did many things right in those difficult years. At the *same* time, some of the actions that were taken were contrary to our values."[35] Naturally, Obama avoided the opposite of the word *right*, refusing to call anything the US had done wrong. Even a six thousand–page report that meticulously documented Central Intelligence Agency (CIA) torture wasn't sufficient to convince the government that the United States was really in the wrong. Moving on, Obama reiterated that he had "banned torture," yet he described the contents of the report as "enhanced interrogation techniques," despite the fact that it clearly documented nothing short of torture.[36] Lost in Obama's words was any mention of the victims. Moreover, this example demonstrated that nothing, absolutely nothing, could apparently get the US government to address its violence in any meaningful way.

As the examples above demonstrate, both Bush and Obama maneuvered the focus away from the victims of US violence toward mention of what the US had done or was doing right, thus minimizing or erasing the victimization of Muslims in an effort to sanitize the War on Terror and any attempt to examine violence by the US in a systemic way. President Trump, on the other hand, said the quiet part out loud: his blatant Islamophobia and nationalistic fear-mongering laid bare the narrative that had been operating in the background during his predecessors' administrations, openly glorying in brutality and offering no justifications other than the assumed superiority of the United States—morally, economically, and, most significantly, militarily—in contrast to every other country in the world. To take a stark example of his rhetorical style, when the United States dropped the "mother of all bombs" in Afghanistan in April 2017, Trump showed pride in how large a hole the bomb created and how much sound it made.[37]

In November 2019, President Trump pardoned two former soldiers, Army Lieutenant Clint Lorance and Major Mathew L. Golsteyn. Lorance was convicted of second-degree murder for ordering soldiers to shoot a group of Afghan civilians, leading to the murder of two civilians.[38] Golsteyn was charged with killing an unarmed Afghan man who he claimed was a bomb maker, and whose body he and two soldiers brought back to the base and burned in a pit reserved for trash.[39] Trump also ordered the restoration of Navy SEAL Edward Gallagher's rank.[40] Gallagher had been court-martialed for mortally stabbing an Afghan detainee and posing for a photo with the corpse, in addition to allegedly threatening other SEALs who reported him.[41] Gallagher was acquitted of murder, and the only penalty he received was demotion in rank.[42]

On Fox News, host Pete Hegseth from *Fox & Friends* shared that he had spoken to Trump about the three servicemen, and that Trump believed that "the benefit of the doubt should go to the guys pulling the trigger."[43] Echoing this sentiment of unconditional support for the servicemen, a White House statement said, "As the President has stated, 'when our soldiers have to fight for our country, I want to give them the confidence to fight.'" The statement also said, in regard to the pardons, that "the President, as Commander-in-Chief, is ultimately responsible for ensuring that the law is enforced and when appropriate, that mercy is granted."[44] Unfortunately, mercy here was granted to those who murdered civilians and desecrated corpses, but denied to civilians who were killed in a split second because military personnel are allowed to act on a mere whim in confidence that their actions will be justified by the racist narrative that defaults to the assumption that Muslims, even civilians, are terrorists.

Keep Your Eyes on the Prize

The narrative that sustains support for the vast military and political apparatus of the War on Terror has been remarkably static over the twenty years it has been operating. The way that the US has evaded accountability again and again for even the worst and most public atrocities done in the name of counterterrorism seems to indicate that no act of violence can disrupt or challenge the country's image of itself as innocent and fostering goodwill, and of Muslims as inherently the opposite. Throughout three (as of the time of this writing) seemingly very different presidential administrations, the basic structure has remained robust. When deviations from the script written by the Bush administration in the aftermath of 9/11 do occur, such as Obama's softening of the language around torture in order to signal a departure from Bush-era tactics, or Trump's amplification of the Islamophobia inherent to the narrative to drive support for extreme policies like the Muslim Ban, an examination of surrounding context reveals them to be functionally minor tweaks to the story.

Similarly, the two administrations that followed Bush in office took free advantage of the expansions of executive power and absence of any mechanisms for ensuring transparency and accountability or regulating the range of acceptable actions that the original narrative facilitated. Both Obama and Trump largely maintained the legal and policy structures of the early War on Terror—or expanded their reach, in many cases. Indeed, the impunity with which both administrations consistently enforced their will on the world under that same grant of authority reveals the fundamental flaw in allowing myth and propaganda to form the basis for power being concentrated in the hands of an essentially unchecked executive. That these three men had different political orientations and particular policy interests made no difference in terms of their willingness to use and abuse power.

A few days into 2020, President Donald Trump announced the killing of top Iranian general Qasem Soleimani, who spearheaded Iranian military operations in the Middle East. Although Soleimani had long been a thorn in the side of the US military and was responsible for much that should be condemned, his assassination was unexpected and sparked widespread alarm. The general was not a terrorist in the plain meaning of the word but the second-highest-ranking official in the Iranian government, and the unilateral action taken by the United States in killing him could easily and fairly have been interpreted as an act of war. According to Trump, however, the United States "successfully executed a flawless precision strike that killed the number-one terrorist anywhere in the world."[45] What Trump was describing in an almost surgical way was a targeted killing. The bland language he used was not accidental but was instead meant to obscure the possibility of seeing the target as human. Even if Soleimani as an individual wasn't owed any empathy, the impact of the dehumanizing language used in his case extends far beyond him—setting the general rule that Muslims have no human value or at least none worth preserving.

Another upsetting implication carried in this sanitized description of Soleimani's death is the suggestion that such "precision" strikes are de facto legal, as though not having murdered anyone else in the process somehow justifies extrajudicial killings.

A few months earlier, in October 2019, Trump had used similar language in announcing the successful strike against ISIS leader Abu-Bakr Al-Baghdadi, describing his killing as demonstrative of "America's relentless pursuit of terrorist leaders."[46] In the same speech, Trump pivoted to lamenting the deaths of two Americans at the hands of ISIS, journalist James Foley and humanitarian worker Kayla Mueller, and the violence committed by Al-Baghdadi in general—with the underlying implication being that any violence committed by the United States cannot have been at this level or with such brutality. Like the statements made by both Bush and Obama rejecting any moral equivalence between the US's actions and non-state-actor violence, Trump's statement served to deflect potential criticism by presenting the targeted killing as obviously justifiable in light of the heinous acts committed by Al-Baghdadi and ISIS. During his remarks announcing the killing of Al-Baghdadi, Trump also reminded his audience that his administration had killed Hamza bin Laden, whom he referred to as "the very violent son of Osama bin Laden." What Trump's language about both targeted killings does by constructing the enemy as outright evil is to make the illegalities of their deaths seem unimportant. The clear implication is that any similar extrajudicial action could also be justified under the banner of fighting terrorism.

This same dynamic was at play during the administration of Barack Obama, who was no stranger to targeted killings. In the most high-profile example, President Obama gave a late-night address to the nation on May 2, 2011, announcing that Osama bin Laden had been killed. In it, he said, "A small team of Americans carried out the operation with extraordinary courage and capability. No Americans were harmed. They took care to avoid civilian casualties. After a firefight, they killed Osama bin Laden and took custody of his body."[47] The juxtaposition between Obama's words "no Americans were harmed" and "they took care to avoid civilian casualties" is an example of the US's continued use of the tactic of emphasizing *American* lives saved in order to justify and minimize the deaths of Muslim civilians in the countries targeted.

Under the Bush administration, the prized death was that of Saddam Hussein. While the United States itself did not carry out the execution of Hussein, US forces captured him in December 2003 and handed him over to the Iraqis for his trial in 2006. Though painted as part of the War on Terror, the US campaign against Saddam Hussein was instead a campaign spearheaded by Bush for revenge and by deceit—including the lie that Iraq had weapons of mass destruction. This context is important, considering Bush's statement on the execution: "Saddam Hussein's execution comes at the end of a difficult year for the Iraqi people and for our troops. Bringing Saddam Hussein to justice will not end the violence in Iraq, but it is an important milestone on Iraq's course to becoming a democracy that can govern, sustain, and defend itself, and be an ally in the War on Terror. . . . Many difficult choices and further sacrifices lie ahead. Yet the safety and security of the American people require that we not relent in ensuring that Iraq's young democracy continues to progress."[48]

President Bush's words almost completely erased the context of the US's war in Iraq, couching the execution in value-laden terms while also laying the groundwork for the justification of the US's continued presence in the country by stressing that the violence wouldn't end with "justice" done—in the form of having deposed Saddam Hussein and seeing him executed. This willingness to condone and even celebrate violence while cloaking it in the language of benevolence is characteristic of the US's approach to promoting its military tactics in the War on Terror.

A similar dynamic is at play in the official language surrounding the relationship between the US and Islam. In the same speech in which he announced the strike that killed Osama bin Laden, Obama addressed this relationship, asserting, "We must also reaffirm that the United States is not—and never will be—at war with Islam. I've made clear, just as President Bush did shortly after 9/11, that our war is not against Islam. Bin Laden was not a Muslim leader; he was a mass murderer of Muslims. Indeed, al Qaeda has slaughtered scores of Muslims in many countries, including our own. So his demise should be welcomed by all who believe in peace and human dignity."[49]

Although this language was seemingly meant to dissuade Muslims and others from believing they were being targeted, this idea rested on the assumption that the only indication Muslims would have had of being targeted was the assassination of bin Laden and his like, instead of, for example, the ongoing bombardment of their countries with drones. This is perhaps why, in one last valiant act of deflection, Obama made sure to assert that Obama bin Laden was a mass murderer of Muslims—a statement presumably meant to distract from and minimize the fact that so, too, was the US. Finally, Obama made sure to absolve the United States of responsibility for any of the violence it had waged by remarking that "the American people did not choose this fight."[50] It's not hard to imagine

Pakistani civilians in the country where bin Laden met his fate thinking the same—that they had not chosen this fight either.

One especially striking example, the assassination of Muslim American citizen Anwar Al-Awlaki, neatly encapsulates the way in which the US has acted with impunity under the auspices of the mandate provided by the War on Terror. On September 30, 2011, nearly five months after President Obama announced the killing of Osama bin Laden, he announced the news of a successful strike against another target—Al-Awlaki—at the retirement ceremony of Admiral Mike Mullen.[51]

Al-Awlaki was born in the United States and was a US citizen at the time of his death,[52] but his story, according to different accounts from his family, community, and the US government,[53] has many twists and turns, beginning with his increasing politicization in college and culminating in his eventual self-imposed exile in Yemen. Though he had initially been identified by the government as a "moderate" Muslim who could be an acceptable spokesperson for the Muslim community after 9/11, the more invested and angered he became about the treatment of Muslims, the more run-ins he had with government authorities. Complicating the question of Al-Awlaki's exact relationship to the government was that it seems he served briefly as a government informant, getting involved in an operation that landed a fellow Northern Virginia community leader in prison.

Whether or not the US government had reason to suspect Al-Awlaki of involvement in Al-Qaeda in the Arabian Peninsula, as they later claimed, the government persistently surveilled him from shortly after 9/11 until his death, and at one point he was arrested by the Yemeni government at the behest of the United States. What is also clear is that over the same years he was being surveilled, Al-Awlaki became increasingly strident in his condemnations of the US's interventions in the Muslim world, and his expressions of anger extended to publicly praising terrorist attacks. Sometime in 2010, it became common knowledge that the US government was actively trying to kill him.

Asserting in his announcement of the successful murder that Al-Awlaki was responsible for planning and directing plots to murder innocent Americans, Obama said, "Awlaki and his organization have been directly responsible for the deaths of many Yemeni citizens. His hateful ideology—and targeting of innocent civilians—has been rejected by the vast majority of Muslims, and people of all faiths." Despite these claims, there was in fact little to no evidence that Al-Awlaki had been involved with Al-Qaeda or, if he had been in the past, that he was operational at the time.

Concluding the portion of his speech pertaining to Al-Awlaki's assassination, Obama asserted, "Working with Yemen and our other allies and partners, we will be determined, we will be deliberate, we will be relentless, we will be resolute in our commitment to destroy terrorist networks that aim to kill Americans, and to build a world in which people everywhere can live in greater peace, prosperity and security."[54] Absent from Obama's speech altogether was one inconvenient fact: Al-Awlaki was an American citizen. For the purposes of legitimizing the extrajudicial killing of an American citizen, not in combat, and without even any pretense of due process, it was apparently enough for the president to portray his death as a "success" in fighting terrorism. Later, during the Trump administration, Al-Awlaki's daughter would be killed in a drone strike—a powerful image in opposition to the lie that the US military in the War on Terror brings peace and stability to the people in the countries it targets.

Constructing Muslims as evil, demonic, and irrationally full of rage has been central to the narrative work of justifying the reach, destruction, and inevitable abuses of the War on Terror. And it has been successful. By explicitly and implicitly stripping Muslims of their humanity, the state has claimed for itself broad power to execute whatever interventions it deems necessary, especially when it comes to responding to Muslims' "irrationality." Because these constructions play an important role in sustaining and perpetuating the War on Terror, any attempt to dismantle the war's infrastructure necessarily relies on deconstructing these harmful narratives and tropes.

Muslims as a Means to Our National Security Ends

In a different context, in 2015, Obama gave a speech on terrorism after the San Bernardino shootings. Similar to other speeches he had given in this vein, this address reiterated that the United States was not at war with Islam. However, he went on to say, "ISIL does not speak for Islam. They are thugs and killers, part of a cult of death. And they account for a tiny fraction of more than a billion Muslims around the world, including millions of patriotic Muslim-Americans who reject their hateful ideology. . . . If we're to succeed in defeating terrorism, we must enlist Muslim communities as some of our strongest allies, rather than push them away through suspicion and hate. That does not mean denying the fact that an extremist ideology has spread within some Muslim communities. It's a real problem that Muslims must confront without excuse."[55]

There's nothing particularly extraordinary in this speech in terms of how Obama addressed terrorism, but because this speech was meant to address the aftermath of the San Bernardino shootings involving a married couple, one a US citizen and the other a permanent resident, Obama sought to draw the moral line between inclusion and exclusion of Muslims in general. His speech does the dance between condemning ISIL, distancing Muslims from ISIL, then calling on Muslims to confront extremism—not quite coming full circle, but close. Per his speech, Muslims are given a directive about how or when they will be morally included or excluded. Obviously, ISIL terrorists exist outside the US's moral community, but the conditions stipulated here by Obama base the inclusion of Muslims and Muslim Americans on whether or not they agree to become willing participants in the fight against terrorism. Their inclusion is also contingent on accepting the idea that radicalization is a widespread problem unique to the Muslim community.

Despite being widely associated with the original formation of the Islamophobic narrative that helped launch a global War on Terror, President Bush also frequently made gestures of conciliation toward Muslims, including by going to great lengths to assert (albeit without much evidence) that America was not at war with Islam. A characteristic example of his approach is seen in the following remarks released by the White House for the occasion of Eid al-Fitr, December 5, 2002: "America treasures the relationship we have with our many Muslim friends, and we respect the vibrant faith of Islam which inspires countless individuals to lead lives of honesty, integrity, and morality. This year may Eid also be a time in which we recognize the values of progress, pluralism, and acceptance that bind us together as a Nation and a global community. By working together to advance mutual understanding, we point the way to a brighter future for all."[56]

Though the relationship between the US and Islam was repeatedly addressed by both Bush and Obama, the dynamic they spoke to (1) is nonsensical, because a state cannot be at war with a religion; (2) is an empty sentiment that doesn't preclude being at war with Muslims in the form of specifically targeting those identifying as such; and (3) ignores the fact that many Americans practice the religion of Islam, so it is impossible to separate the United States from Islam in any meaningful way. In any case, rhetoric seeking to reconcile the underlying Islamophobia of the official narrative with the US's professed respect for the religion itself flounders quickly when it runs up against a factual account in plain language of the impact the War on Terror has had on its Muslim victims.

PART II

INSTITUTIONALIZED ISLAMOPHOBIA

Post-9/11 Law and Policy

In the bowels of the CIA, there is a sign that reads
EVERY DAY IS SEPTEMBER 12TH.

—BEN RHODES[1]

Our response involves far more than instant retal-
iation and isolated strikes. Americans should not
expect one battle, but a lengthy campaign, unlike
any other we have ever seen.

—PRESIDENT GEORGE W. BUSH[2]

In a speech before Congress on September 20, 2001, then president Bush referred to his administration's response to the 9/11 attacks as a "war" for the first time, saying, "Our war on terror begins with Al Qaeda, but it does not end there. It will not end until every terrorist group of global reach has been found, stopped and defeated."[3] Bush was clearly signaling his administration's intent to treat this conflict as something other than a traditional war, which would have had set objectives and boundaries of time and geography. There are three core issues with the approach introduced in this speech, the talking points of which would be repeated many, many times in the months and years to follow: (1) even if it were possible to identify and defeat every terrorist group on the planet, the US has no right under international law to unilaterally declare war on, potentially, the entire planet, nor to unilaterally decide which groups or governments amount to a terrorist threat on the basis of only American national security interests; (2) in a domestic context, any congressional authorization of a war on the basis of these incredibly open-ended remarks would essentially give the president a blank check for endless war, bypassing the check that Congress is meant to provide on the power of the executive, and with it whatever limited opportunity the American public has to meaningfully exercise its political will; and (3) perhaps most importantly, Bush's language about a war on terror versus a war on any particular nation or people suggests that the only impact of the violence would be the destruction of terrorists, not the deaths of millions of civilians and the normalization of state violence targeting Muslims at home as well as abroad on a massive scale.

The trajectory of the War on Terror has been toward the logical extremes of the problematic approach to combating terrorism post-9/11 that was laid out in the speech above and in many other, similar public statements made by government officials and their allies in the media. An entire infrastructure of state violence has been built on the basis of the story sold by the Bush administration in those early days after the attacks, and the objectives and attitudes of counterterrorism have since become so deeply entrenched within the formal structures of law and policy that the underlying assumptions are rarely questioned and the true reach of the War on Terror has, in a sense, been rendered invisible.

Popular conversation around the War on Terror tends to assume that it is primarily or wholly defined by warfare overseas, beginning with Afghanistan and Iraq and expanding from these conflicts to other parts of the globe. Although this association is natural given the language and metaphors of war utilized by the US government, the truth is that military operations abroad are merely one of the arenas into which this "war" has been extended, and it has profoundly impacted Muslim communities both domestically and abroad. In fact, the sheer scope of the War on Terror, as well as the way its public-facing fronts have been normalized as necessary to protect the US's national security, can make the state violence perpetrated by the US in its name difficult to conceptualize. In order to make the domestic and foreign aspects of the War on Terror's apparatus more visible, therefore, I propose five broad areas of policy and law in which the violence manifests, and will examine their structure separately. These five dimensions, or pillars, correspond with how the War on Terror is reflected in law and policy based on a broad overview of the surrounding research and literature, as well as the impact of these legal and political structures. The pillars are (1) militarism and warfare, (2) draconian immigration policy, (3) surveillance, (4) federal terrorism prosecutions, and (5) detention and torture. It is my hope that by elaborating on these five dimensions, I can paint a picture that encompasses the full extent of the state violence that has been facilitated by the monstrous apparatus of the War on Terror.

One common understanding of what constitutes a state, versus a group of people, is that a state has a monopoly on legitimate violence. The corollary of this widely accepted definition, of course, is that all other forms of violence are illegitimate. In the context of the War on Terror, the United States has used the power conferred by this construction not only to fight "terrorism," but as implicit support of the idea that the tactics it employs are inherently legitimate forms of violence. Because of this, many critiques of the US's state violence are limited to what amounts to a surface-level evaluation of the violent tactics employed, and never reach the question of whether it is even legitimate at all. This flawed premise about monopolies on violence prevents the United States from being seen as an agent of terror when it commits acts that would be clearly considered terrorism if any other actor were responsible.

Philosopher Jeremy Waldron highlights the problem posed by this loophole in Western political theory, recognizing that "although states may sponsor terrorism by non-state actors, states or state officials acting in this role can't themselves be terrorists. But no one denies that states can be terrorizers."[4] To this end, I define state violence as the following:

State violence is the illegitimate use of governmental authority to sanction, coerce, control, and repress in order to inflict and normalize harm and suffering including torture, murder, and genocide on individuals and communities.

As a disclaimer, my use of the word *illegitimate* is not meant to suggest that there is a form of legitimate state violence. This definition is merely meant to build on other literature that takes issue with the fundamental notion of state violence as inherently legitimate.

The five structural dimensions of the War on Terror provide a road map to understanding how its objectives have been implemented in law and policy. This analysis should be undertaken with an eye toward fully understanding not just how they work, but how state violence is institutionalized within each of these structures. State violence manifests in many different forms because there are many different aspects of the power of the state to exercise control. Typologizing modes of state violence allows a way in to understanding its true ubiquity, by breaking down how the government's differing types of control over different aspects of social and political life determines the form of the state violence inflicted in that area or areas.

The modes of violence embodied by the five dimensions of the War on Terror are, in corresponding order, corporeal, bordered, panoptic, juridical, and carceral. Further explanations follow:

1. Corporeal violence as part of militarism and warfare: The state exercises its control of the means of violence directly, through the infliction of both psychological and physical harm, as well as death, including by the military.

2. Bordered violence via draconian immigration policy: This is also a direct exercise of state power in terms of sovereignty, but here control of physical borders is leveraged against targeted groups through coercion, such as by restricting immigration or conditioning status on cooperation with state objectives.

3. Panoptic violence using surveillance: The state uses its power to surveil in order to control targeted groups by denying them the autonomy inherent in the ability of a person to conduct a private life with the certainty that the state, at least, is not a threat to their safety.

4. Juridical violence, including but not limited to federal terrorism prosecutions: In this context *juridical* refers to the procedural power of the state to deny its victims legal recourse, including by barring access to the justice system altogether or by wielding the judicial process against them.

5. Carceral violence in the forms of detention and torture: Here, *carceral* refers to the state's physical control over the bodies of its victims, which facilitates the ability to inflict harm in various ways—from the psychological harm of being detained, often indefinitely and without cause, to the use of torture (there is obviously some overlap between this mode and corporeal violence).

Even a cursory examination of the modes of violence inflicted by the state across the five dimensions of the War on Terror reveals the truly terrifying extent to which the threat of violence hangs over the heads of those it has singled out and targeted—Muslim and Muslim Americans. Supported by the underlying Islamophobia of the post-9/11 government narrative around terrorism, the laws and policies implemented by the Bush administration and perpetuated by Obama and Trump primarily target, directly and indirectly, Muslims and communities racialized as Muslim. Critically, any serious analysis of the War on Terror and how it can be dismantled must include how deeply embedded and institutionalized Islamophobia is in its massive infrastructure and the fact that the Muslim religious identity has served as a precondition to being targeted. For Muslims, the violence in these and other contexts is twofold in that it includes the direct harm inflicted, in addition to the knowledge that Muslim identity translates into disposability and a lack of accountability.

To understand how the War on Terror has expanded to the magnitude it has, sociologists have coined the concept of "political moral panics."[5] The concept of moral panics was initially developed to explain why some social problems seem to generate much more concern than others relevant to their actual impact. The process of creating moral panic is one of social construction: a threat to individuals comes to be seen as a moral threat to the entire social fabric through exaggeration of the threat posed and an overbroad definition of who poses the threat. Because it is socially constructed, the response will both reflect and shape political and cultural norms and goals. An example would be the outrage over the largely nonexistent phenomenon of so-called "welfare queens" in the eighties and nineties.

Political moral panics operate by making attainable policy goals that are not achievable through normal political systems. The threat, in the case of the War on Terror, is that of terrorist attacks such as what occurred on 9/11. Although such attacks are relatively rare, the threat has been exaggerated to make the public feel they are an imminent danger—enough so that rolling back certain political rights and freedoms is seen to be not only justified but absolutely necessary. At the same time, the definition of *terrorist*—that is, a category that includes all potential enemies—has expanded to include vast swaths of the world, as well as Muslims in the United States. In the official narrative, the "enemy" is an otherworldly, nebulous threat used to justify the use of extraordinary measures in a wide range of contexts. This amplification and expansion of the threat of terrorism has allowed the executive to consolidate power outside of the ordinary legislative process and evade oversight and accountability, from both the public and the judiciary.

There is a common misconception that the excesses of the War on Terror were the direct result of the Bush administration's overreaction to 9/11. However, the War on Terror has allowed for the creation of an ever-expanding arsenal of anti-democratic policies and tactics, operating outside the reach of partisan politics and normal rules of international relations. Because the War on Terror is not even close to ending, and because national security policies and laws often enjoy bipartisan support, the war's apparatus is ripe for deployment whether the United States is led by a Republican or a Democratic administration.[6] Moreover, the violence of the War on Terror has become so normalized and absorbed into so many facets of political life that it is difficult to imagine how any one person could successfully reverse it.

As of the time of this writing, the United States is far from winding down its War on Terror, but rather is now engaged in combating terrorism in eighty countries—40 percent of the world.[7] Moreover, the US's approach in the War on Terror has served to empower countries such as the Philippines and Israel to use similar rhetoric and repressive tactics based on the same claims of fighting terrorism.

In their book *Counter-Terrorism and State Political Violence: The "War on Terror" as Terror*, editors Scott Poynting and David Whyte ask, "Can we accept that counter-terrorism is indeed always conducted with the aim of eliminating or mitigating terrorism? Or is it deployed for another purpose—or a range of other purposes?"[8] If these questions had been posed and explored when the War on Terror was in its infancy, we could have avoided the death and destruction that the US caused across the globe. But two decades later, amid failed and never-ending wars, brutal immigration policies, unfettered surveillance, entrapment of Muslims, and indefinite detention and torture, we can conclude that the United States was never really interested in fighting terrorism, but rather in expanding the boundaries of existing structures to remove limits on the exercise of state violence and insulating itself from criticism.

4.

MILITARISM AND WARFARE

We Go to War for Peace

How can you have a war on terrorism when war itself is terrorism?

—Howard Zinn[1]

That's why we work so hard to extend our zone of security outward. So that our borders are the last line of defense, not our first line of defense. And that's why we built security measures that begin thousands of miles away.

—Tom Ridge, former US Secretary of Homeland Security[2]

Even before the identity of the 9/11 attackers was known, President George W. Bush made it clear that the United States would respond militarily. Alongside its use of the phrase *War on Terror*, the Bush administration almost immediately granted itself certain wartime privileges and rights, despite the absence of traditional hostilities.[3] This initial assumption that the law of war would apply was a departure from the norm in that there was no obvious locus of conflict or enemy other than the individuals who carried out the attack. This essentially laid the foundation for a "war" without end. As well, invoking the law of war allowed the Bush administration to operate outside the normal rules of international law, leading to egregious human rights violations.

One week after the 9/11 attacks, on September 18, 2001, Bush signed into law the Authorization for the Use of Military Force (AUMF), which gave the president the power "to use all necessary and appropriate force against those nations, organizations, or persons he determines planned, authorized, committed, or aided the terrorist attacks that occurred on September 11,

2001, or harbored such organizations or persons, in order to prevent any future acts of international terrorism against the United States by such nations, organizations, or persons."[4]

Although the AUMF was presented to Congress and the public as a limited authorization to target Al-Qaeda and the Taliban, in reality its vague and sweeping language has proven almost endlessly open to interpretation and to an expansion of scope. Since its passage, the AUMF has provided legal cover for the United States to use military force without obtaining prior congressional approval again and again. Ironically, however, Bush's 2002 State of the Union speech criticizes the enemies because they "view the entire world as a battlefield"[5]—a critique made about five months after the AUMF was signed into law. Presidents Bush, Obama, and Trump relied on the AUMF for justification in over forty operations in almost twenty countries.[6] Underscoring how far the interpretation and use of the 2001 AUMF has strayed from its original purpose of containing the threat of the specific terrorist groups responsible for the 9/11 attacks is the fact that this tally includes groups that did not exist at the time of its passage. However, this didn't stop Obama or Trump from using the AUMF against groups that were not responsible for the 9/11 attacks.

In addition to the AUMF, John Yoo, deputy assistant attorney general in the Office of Legal Counsel, authored a memo dated September 25, 2001, and titled *The President's Constitutional Authority to Conduct Military Operations against Terrorists and Nations Supporting Them*. The memo gave the president the authority to attack not only individuals involved in terrorism activities, but also foreign states that were harboring said terrorists. To this end, Yoo argued the following:

> We think it beyond question that the President has the plenary constitutional power to take such military actions as he deems necessary and appropriate to respond to the terrorist attacks upon the United States on September 11, 2001. Force can be used both to retaliate for those attacks, and to prevent and deter future assaults on the Nation. Military actions need not be limited to those individuals, groups, or states that participated in the attacks on the World Trade Center and the Pentagon: the Constitution vests the President with the power to strike terrorist groups or organizations that cannot be demonstrably linked to the September 11 incidents, but that, nonetheless, pose a similar threat to the security of the United States and the lives of its people, whether at home or overseas.[7]

The unbounded mandate of the AUMF, combined with the Bush administration's assumption of wartime rules of conduct, practically guaranteed the total lack of accountability we have seen in the way the global War on Terror has been fought. President Bush and both administrations that followed him relied on the expansive authority granted by the AUMF to bypass the constitutional power granted to Congress to declare war, eliminating any participation or voice, however slight, that such process gives the American people. This has allowed the War on Terror's global military footprint to expand exponentially—rippling out from the initial conflicts in Afghanistan and Iraq to touch nearly 40 percent of the entire world.[8] The US has been able to conduct its military interventions not only without any checks on its power, but with a secrecy that has allowed it to go largely unchallenged—by Congress or the public. The ever-expanding mandate of the War on Terror has led to endless war and, with it, a massive devaluing of human life around the globe.

Underlying both the way the Bush administration laid down the framework for interpreting the war mandate of the AUMF and the pattern he set for pursuing new interventions is a philosophical approach to global conflict that is deeply rooted in the narrative framework of American exceptionalism discussed in chapter 1. Often referred to as "the Bush Doctrine," this approach sees terrorism not just as criminal acts but as an ideology that has risen to prevalence in areas of the world that do not follow Western democratic norms. This ideology is not rooted in any positive principles but is animated by hatred and opposition to the West, particularly America. In order to truly protect itself from acts of terror, therefore, the US must root out and destroy the ideology that supports them. In keeping with how it sees itself as a beacon of freedom and democratic values in the world, then, the best way to do this is to "promote" Western democracy in the dark parts of the world that haven't freely chosen it. There are two problematic elements to this philosophy of national security. First, it legitimizes preemptive war. If it is backwardness that fosters terrorist ideologies that then lead to terrorist acts, the only way to fight terror at its root is to correct the backwardness—usually, during the War on Terror, with military intervention. Under this system, the war mandate becomes almost endlessly broad because there is no need to identify a particular threat or group and then connect it to a country—the Muslim world itself is the problem.

The broad mandate provided to the Bush administration in the wake of 9/11 and the approach to war that underlies how they put it into practice are not mere philosophical or legal considerations. They are tools that the executive has wielded in pursuit of concrete goals, whether economic or based in conquest. To take just one example of how these patterns of lack of accountability to Congress and the American people and a double-standard–based approach to international law have played out in the War on Terror, in both Iraq and Afghanistan the United States has utilized not only traditional armed forces but military contractors and mercenaries who are not subject to congressional oversight and whose violence has largely been unaccounted for. In 2007, contractors from the company then known as Blackwater and now known as Academi killed seventeen civilians in Nisour Square in Iraq.[9] Despite the numerous abuses by military contractors, the US government continues to rely on them as a way to expand wars and avoid putting service members at risk, which carries the risk of political backlash. This insertion of explicitly profit-motivated actors into the equation creates an even greater incentive for the violence not only to continue but to expand in scope. In 2020 President Trump pardoned the Blackwater operatives responsible for the massacre, making it clear that even when consequences are sought and attained for human rights abuses, it will not be enough to trigger true accountability.[10]

Afghanistan

The broad-brush approach that the US would take in fighting the War on Terror—that is, by targeting much more than the individuals involved or even the network that supported them and acting preemptively if necessary—was put into place quickly. On October 7, 2001, President Bush announced that military strikes had begun in Afghanistan, saying that "more than two weeks ago, I gave Taliban leaders a series of clear and specific demands: Close terrorist training camps. Hand over leaders of the Al Qaeda network, and return all foreign nationals, including American citizens unjustly detained in our country. None of these demands were met. And now, the Taliban will pay a price."[11] The United States would be going to war with Afghanistan, though the stated enemy was not the nation-state itself but the network of individuals responsible for the 9/11 attacks—a category that would expand from the original, stated target, Al-Qaeda, to include "every terrorist group of global reach."[12] This flexible mandate would allow for the US to continue to be involved militarily in the country, without being subject to fresh congressional scrutiny, even as the nature and identity of the terrorist threat shifted over the next nearly two decades.

It also meant, of course, that the borders of Afghanistan would not define the borders of the War on Terror.

The initial name of the military operation in Afghanistan was Operation Enduring Freedom—an ironic name given the continued occupation of the country after twenty years.[13] In the initial phase of the war, Osama bin Laden fled to Pakistan, and the Taliban was largely expelled from their stronghold in the city of Kandahar. However, the number of US troops increased from 1,300 to 2,500 by December 2001. Despite achieving victory early on in terms of diminishing Al-Qaeda and the Taliban, the Bush administration remained in Afghanistan to "help stabilize" the country and prevent terrorism from again taking root. Subsequently, the United States' efforts turned to nation-building, including taking on the training of Afghanistan's national police force.

On May 1, 2003, Secretary of Defense Donald Rumsfeld announced that major combat operations in Afghanistan had ended. Hamid Karzai, who had been the country's interim leader since 2002, was formally elected president in October 2004. Karzai's reelection in 2009 raised corruption concerns, and corruption would continue to plague the country, but President Obama decided to stay silent about it. Instability also continued in Afghanistan with periodic resurgences of the Taliban presence in the country—and subsequent increases in US troops, which went up to twenty-five thousand by 2007 and one hundred thousand in 2009, thanks to a surge sent in by the Obama administration.

Later in his first term, in 2011, Obama began holding initial peace talks with Taliban leaders. Operation Enduring Freedom officially ended in 2014, but the United States' presence in the country continued. The rebranded Operation Freedom's Sentinel began, which involved the US carrying out special counterterrorism operations with local Afghan support. By the end of Obama's second term, there were about 8,400 American troops in Afghanistan, which under Trump increased to about 13,000. In 2017, Trump also dropped what is referred to as "the mother of all bombs" on Afghanistan, targeting ISIS. In early February 2020, the US and the Taliban signed a peace deal, and near the end of 2020 Trump began withdrawing troops.

The consequences of the war in Afghanistan are vast, especially because the war has continued for so long: nearly twenty years as of this writing—the longest-running war in US history.

One of the biggest consequences of the war in Afghanistan has been the staggering loss of civilian lives, for which the United States has shown little to no regard. The Bush administration set the stage for apathy toward civilian deaths in the earliest days of the war, and this detachment from the human consequences continued through the two subsequent administrations. To take a representative example of what that callousness sounded like, in a Department of Defense briefing on October 29, 2001, Donald Rumsfeld stated the following in response to a question about minimizing civilian deaths:

> As a nation that lost thousands of innocent civilians on September 11th, we understand what it means to lose fathers and mothers and brothers and sisters and sons and daughters. [. . .] We did not start the war; the terrorists started it when they attacked the United States, murdering more than 5,000 innocent Americans. The Taliban . . . started it when they invited al Qaeda into Afghanistan and turned their country into a base from which those terrorists could strike out and kill our citizens. So let there be no doubt; responsibility for every single casualty in this war, be they innocent Afghans or innocent Americans, rests at the feet of Taliban and al Qaeda.[14]

Rumsfeld's logic of culpability blamed any and all US actions on the Taliban or Al-Qaeda, seemingly indefinitely. This rhetorical tactic that Rumsfeld used to emphasize the United States' victimhood also served as a way of diminishing the country's "moral responsibility for civilian deaths."[15] But even if the administration wanted to overlook and deny civilian casualties as proof that the war wasn't being won, that doesn't mean no one was counting. A study by the Watson Institute for International and Public Affairs estimates that between October 2001 and October 2019, there had been over forty-three thousand civilian deaths in Afghanistan. This number, as high as it is, does not capture indirect deaths, such as those that occurred because people lacked access to food, water, and/or health care, among other things.[16] Consequently, the real number of civilian deaths as a result of the United States' intervention in Afghanistan is much higher than the official tally, and many more ordinary Afghans who have not died have nonetheless suffered from the destruction the war has caused.

None of this stopped the US from feigning concern for the Afghan people in order to gain support for the war. One of the specific ways this was accomplished was by framing the war in Afghanistan as necessary in order to free its people—and, in particular, Afghan women—from the grips of the Taliban. First Lady Laura Bush played an important role in promoting this additional moral imperative in support of the war. Because of her advocacy, the war in Afghanistan grew to be seen as a virtuous battle to free Afghan women from their oppression under Islamic rule. Making explicit the link between the freedom of Afghan women and the use of military interventions, she stated, "Afghan women know, through hard experience, what the rest of the world is discovering: the brutal oppression of women is a central goal of the terrorists."[17] Laura Bush's statement was presented in the terms of a "heroic narrative"[18] that drew the average person into a mythical story that allowed them to see themselves as heroes. Rather than representing a genuine interest in the fate or daily reality of Afghan women, though, this sentiment represented nothing more than a cynical attempt to legitimize the US-led war by repositioning it as a just and moral endeavor.

Iraq

Although it would go on for two more decades, the war in Afghanistan was partially eclipsed by the launch of a new US-led war in the region—the war on Iraq. In his 2002 State of the Union address, Bush addressed what he called the "axis of evil," referring to Iraq, Iran, and North Korea.[19] Also, in 2002, at the request of the Bush administration, Congress passed a second AUMF to authorize the War in Iraq. The administration claimed that Iraq had weapons of mass destruction and was therefore in violation of United Nations (UN) Security Council resolutions. This claim was backed by no evidence and turned out to be completely false.[20] Nevertheless, Bush administration officials successfully built on the narrative of the War on Terror, expanding the definition of the terrorist enemy to include Saddam Hussein's Iraq. Bush was direct in this effort, saying explicitly, for example, "You can't distinguish between Al Qaeda and Saddam when you talk about the war on terror."[21] The argument for moving to invade Iraq quickly despite the shaky foundation of evidence is encapsulated in then national security advisor Condoleezza Rice's statement that "there will always be some uncertainty about how quickly [Hussein] can acquire nuclear weapons. But we don't want the smoking gun to be a mushroom cloud."[22] Only one member of Congress, Representative Barbara Lee, a Democrat from California, voted against the authorization of the war in Iraq.

In order to build global momentum for the war on Iraq, Bush went before the United Nations General Assembly, threatening military action if Iraq failed to disarm itself of weapons of mass destruction according to UN resolutions. As a result, Resolution 1441 was passed by the UN Security Council, giving Iraq the last chance to comply with disarmament obligations. Even though the UN's Monitoring, Verification and Inspection Commission, in seven hundred inspections over a period of five months between November 2002 and March 2003, found no weapons of mass destruction, that didn't stop the United States from pressing on for war. The US, along with UK allies, proceeded with plans to wage war on Iraq, ultimately ignoring UN processes and giving Saddam Hussein and his sons forty-eight hours to leave the country. Two days prior to the beginning of hostilities, Bush proclaimed, "Should Saddam Hussein choose confrontation, the American people can know that every measure has been taken to avoid war, and every measure will be taken to win it."[23] On March 20, 2003, the United States launched Operation Iraqi Freedom, ignoring rising and vocal public opposition to war in Iraq. The euphemistic campaign name couldn't have been further from the truth.

Shortly after the US and its coalition forces invaded Iraq, the Saddam Hussein regime was toppled, and on May 1, 2003, Bush delivered a speech claiming victory in Iraq in front of a banner that read "Mission Accomplished."[24] That same day, Rumsfeld spoke from Kabul, declaring that major combat operations in Afghanistan were over.[25] Saddam Hussein was arrested on December 13, 2003, by US soldiers and was assassinated a little over three years later, on December 30, 2006.

Despite Bush's declaration of "Mission Accomplished," the war in Iraq was far from over. From the beginning, sectarian divisions and conflicts had been exacerbated and now continued unabated, with periods of calm few and far between. A full account of American military involvement in Iraq and the associated upheaval there is beyond the scope of this book, but none of the three administrations since the invasion has been able to say truthfully that the conflict is over.

Most retrospective looks at the situation in Iraq divide the conflict into three phases. The first phase is characterized by the US's invasion, deposing the government of Saddam Hussein and installing a new regime in its place, and then the resulting insurgency. The US as an occupying force took two actions in particular that paved the way for destabilization in Iraq by creating power vacuums: outlawing Hussein's ruling Ba'ath party, and disbanding the military. In place of the previous government, the US installed one that was mainly Shi'a—a majority population in the country that had previously been locked out of power—and created a semi-autonomous Kurdish region. This led to increasing religiously based sectarian tensions, a fact that was exploited by Al-Qaeda–led Jihadi forces.

In an attempt to stem the rising tide of violence and unrest, the Bush and Obama administrations surged troops into the country during the second phase, 2007–11. After attempting, with limited success, to facilitate cooperation between the Shi'a and Sunni contingents against the insurgents, President Obama declared an official end to combat operations in Iraq on December 18, 2011.[26] He was widely criticized for leaving the country mired in political crisis.

The next phase of American involvement in Iraq was characterized by the rise of ISIS, a threat that Obama largely dismissed in 2011. In 2014, with the establishment of an Islamic State government seat in the city of Mosul, the US was forced to respond, and the level of troop presence has ebbed and flowed between then and the time of this writing. President Trump in particular had been uneven in his priorities, resulting in troops being withdrawn from the country haphazardly—a situation that did nothing to decrease the violence unleashed by the US's invasion.

The Iraq war has had a significant death toll. According to the Watson Institute for International and Public Affairs at Brown University, between March 2003 and October 2019 there were between 184,382 and 207,156 civilian deaths.[27] In addition, the war in Iraq has resulted in negative health impacts in the civilian population, such as birth defects and cancer—a result of depleted uranium munitions that the US has continued to use despite such grave consequences.[28] This devaluing of the humanity of Muslims abroad is perhaps the most striking characteristic of the way in which warfare has been waged post-9/11.

Beyond its human cost, the flimsy moral and legal justifications that were accepted as the basis for the Iraq War fostered a confidence in the power the office of the president had to act unilaterally. This in turn set the stage for a regime of endlessly expanding global warfare that would play out in the mushrooming of military interventions around the world, none of which required the executive to petition Congress for a fresh authorization, thereby triggering at least nominal accountability.

Syria

The free rein that the government was given in Iraq and Afghanistan post-9/11 emboldened the Bush administration to continue to extend the mandate it had claimed to expand militarily where and how it determined with impunity. Syria became a target of the United States as early as 2002, when then undersecretary of state John Bolton declared it "beyond the axis of evil" but still a nation seeking to develop weapons of mass destruction.[29] Both the Bush and Obama administrations imposed sanctions on Syria on the basis of this claim that its Bashar al-Assad regime had ties to terrorism and was actively working to develop a nuclear program as well as other weapons banned by international law.

The United States' involvement in Syria escalated steadily after 2011, when uprisings against the government there prompted the Assad regime to respond with violent crackdowns. In the early part of then president Obama's second term, the US mostly aided the Syrian rebels indirectly, sending "non-lethal" aid openly and authorizing CIA arms shipments to opposition forces more covertly. Obama threatened US military involvement as early as 2012, warning that any use by the Assad regime of chemical weapons such as sarin gas would cross a "thin red line," but he was prevented by Congress from launching military attacks. After 2013, however, the administration's focus shifted to the threat posed by the recently established ISIS, defined as a terrorist organization, and airstrikes against the group began in 2014. Appealing to the familiar narrative of the War on Terror was effective in mobilizing support for military intervention where the rhetoric of humanitarian concern had not been. This is an example of both the reach and the flexibility of definitions that have become embedded in the course of the War on Terror.

Airstrikes against Syria continued under the Trump administration, and Trump also introduced troops on the ground to support Kurdish forces in the country armed by the US. However, in October 2018 Trump claimed that ISIS had been defeated,[30] and two months later, in December 2018, he announced that all of the two thousand troops would be withdrawn—effectively abandoning the Kurds he had armed. President Trump's total lack of concern for the humanitarian aspect of the conflict in Syria was also reflected—starkly—in his actions blocking any Syrian refugees from entering the United States.

Another aspect of the Syrian conflict is its status as a proxy war. Although the intersections of global power and interests in that country and region are complex, the United States has a clear interest in challenging nations whose relative power or global support would otherwise put them out of reach.

Yemen

Consistent with its pattern of complicity regarding atrocities in the Arab world, the US has supported Saudi Arabia and the United Arab Emirates' war in Yemen throughout the War on Terror.[31] This, however, complicates an already problematic relationship between the United States and Yemen. Drone strikes on Yemen by the United States have been so frequent that a Yemeni graffiti artist, Murad Subay, painted a portrait of a Yemeni child with his back to the viewer, writing out the question "Why did you kill my family?" in English and Arabic in blood-red below a picture of a drone with the words "US Drones" on it.[32] This mural sits next to three others in Yemen's capital city, Sana'a, a visual condemnation of the US's drone strikes in Yemen.

The current conflict in Yemen began during the Arab Spring of 2011, when Ali Abdullah Saleh was overthrown after leading the country for thirty-three years. The ensuing instability led to a fragile and weakened central government, a situation that allowed Houthis, who reside in Yemen's northwest region and identify as Zaydi, to become more powerful. After Saleh was overthrown, Abu Rabbu Masour Hadi was put in power as a result of an agreement that was brokered internationally. Hadi was responsible for forming a unity government, and when he did, it excluded Houthis. As a result, the Houthis moved to depose Hadi, thus birthing the civil war in Yemen in 2014.[33]

Less than a year later, the Saudis formed a coalition of Arab countries with Sunni majorities interested in restoring the Hadi government. Saudi Arabia had initially and enthusiastically stepped in on Hadi's request because of Houthi hostility toward Saudi Arabia and because they received support from Iran—with which Saudi Arabia has long been at odds.[34]

Since 2015 the United States has been involved in the Saudi-led military campaign in Yemen,[35] which has included refueling Saudi warplanes bombing rebels.[36] Not only has the US provided military and logistical support; it has also provided intelligence. Despite the fact that the United States claims its support of Saudi Arabia is in part to try to reduce civilian casualties, there is no evidence in the slightest that the US involvement has accomplished this. Even worse, the US's "no strike" lists provided to Saudi Arabia have been frequently ignored. In 2017, despite the fact that American officials urged the coalition to include sites such as hospitals and refugee camps in their "no strike" list, a 2018 UN report found that not only did Saudi Arabia not consult the list; it actually kept striking these sites instead.[37]

Because of the war in Yemen, Yemenis have faced internal displacement, a cholera epidemic, famine, and poverty, with 80 percent of the country needing humanitarian aid.[38] In November 2017, the House of Representatives passed a resolution, 366–30, condemning US military assistance to Saudi Arabia that was aiding the country in its war in Yemen. Unfortunately, however, the resolution fell short of actually ending American support.[39] Two years later, in April 2019, Trump vetoed a bipartisan congressional resolution to finally end the US's involvement in the Yemen war.[40]

Africa

> *Some people believe that we are establishing AFRICOM solely to fight terrorism or to secure oil resources or to discourage China. This is not true. Violent extremism is a cause for concern, and needs to be addressed, but this is not AFRICOM's singular mission. Natural resources represent Africa's current and future wealth, but in an open-market environment, many benefit. Ironically, the U.S., China, and other countries share a common interest—that of a secure environment in Africa, and that's AFRICOM's objective. AFRICOM is about helping Africans build greater capacity to assure their own security.*
>
> —THERESA WHELAN, DEPUTY ASSISTANT SECRETARY OF AFRICAN AFFAIRS, DEPARTMENT OF DEFENSE[41]

Just as the War on Terror did not stay confined to Afghanistan or Iraq, the reach of its military apparatus is not limited to the Arab world. "A light and relatively low-cost footprint" was how Commander Stephen Townsend of Africa Command (Africom) described the US's presence in Africa in a hearing in January 2019.[42]

Established on October 1, 2007, and activated in October 2008, Africom, according to then president Bush, would "strengthen our security cooperation with Africa and help to create new opportunities to bolster the capabilities of our partners in Africa."[43] The idea that the United States was simply interested in Africa's security stood in direct contradiction to other statements by US officials, including one made by then Africom commander general Carter Ham in a speech in June 2012. According to Ham, the reason the US needed operations in Africa was because "the absolute imperative for the United States military [is] to protect America, Americans, and American interests; in our case, in my case, [to] protect us from threats that may emerge from the African continent."[44] Thus, like other alleged threats to the United States in the context of the War on Terror, the US used this excuse to intervene militarily and plant its tentacles of imperialism and neocolonialism once again.

Africom's mission statement, as quoted in a 2012 article in the *Guardian* was to "[contribute] to increasing security and stability in Africa—allowing African states and regional organizations to promote democracy, to expand development, to provide for their common defense, and to better serve their people." Painted as a benevolent endeavor by the United States, this conquest of Africa, like past ones by Western powers, was about control of the continent. Africom was largely a response to the US's declining influence over Africa in light of increasing investment by China. Moreover, in contrast to the paternalism embedded in the mission statement, positioning Africom as a benefit to and in service of the African continent, the institutionalization of Africom has focused on getting access to Africa's wealth. This has not even been a hidden agenda on the part of the United States. For example, at a conference in 2008, Vice Admiral Robert Moeller, describing the purpose of Africom, stated that it was about preserving "the free flow of natural resources from Africa to the global market."[45]

Many African countries initially opposed the US's presence vis-à-vis Africom, forcing the United States to operate the effort from Germany at first. One of Africom's strongest opponents was Muammar Gaddafi, who tried to block Africom from coming to Africa. In the wake of the uprisings in Libya in 2011, Africom played a lead role in the US-NATO alliance's bombing campaign, which killed tens of thousands of Libyans, though it was carried out under the guise of humanitarian assistance. Africom was also central to the implementation of a no-fly zone over Libya, approved by the Security Council to protect civilians.[46] After the US and NATO intervened in Libya and facilitated the assassination of Gaddafi in 2011, Africom was able to move full steam ahead, having been relieved of one of its greatest contenders.[47]

To date, Africom has twenty-nine bases in Africa across fifteen countries or territories. After over a decade, not only has the number of US military personnel in Africa increased by 170 percent; there has also been an exponential rise in everything from military missions and activities to programs and exercises.[48] Additionally, Africom has a military presence in fifty-three out of the fifty-four countries on the continent.[49] Demographic data also sheds light on another element of the US's interest in Africom operations, which is that it is overtly Islamophobic. More than 25 percent of the world's Muslim population lives on the African continent, which is home to twenty-one of the world's Muslim-majority countries.[50] The United States has focused its Africom activities heavily in those Muslim-majority areas—for example, escalating drone strikes in Somalia, ostensibly targeting the insurgent group Al-Shahab—but with little care for the cost in civilian lives. In addition, the US's only permanent Africom military base is located in Muslim-majority Djibouti.

Of course, many have leveraged critiques against Africom and, in particular, against the US's intention behind its creation. For example, organizations such as the US-based Black Alliance for Peace argue that the purpose of Africom is to "use U.S. military power to impose U.S. control of African land, resources and labor to service the needs of U.S. multinational corporations and the wealthy in the United States."[51] After operating for more than a decade in Africa, perhaps the light footprint isn't so light after all.

While much has been highlighted in this chapter about the United States' military interventions in Muslim-majority countries, the true scope of what has been made possible by the War on Terror is far vaster than what can be captured in this book. This unbridled warfare, both direct and by engagement in proxy wars—and unchecked by defined goals and targets or by regard for civilian lives—has cost the United States $6.4 trillion between 2001 and 2020.[52] Despite the costs of the war, whether in terms of civilian casualties or finances, it shows no sign of abating.

Drone Warfare

Drones are a tool, not a policy. The policy is assassination.
—JEREMY SCAHILL[53]

One of the most destructive examples of the way the United States has obscured the true extent and impact of its violence is the institutionalization of drone warfare. The US started using drones as a means of surveillance in the 1990s and, never one to shy away from adapting technology to make state violence more efficient, integrated their use as a weapon into the War on Terror almost immediately after the 9/11 attacks.[54] Drone technology facilitates the immense reach of the global War on Terror by allowing the military to mobilize to strike nearly anywhere—thousands of miles away from any "battlefield"—with very little investment in traditional tactics like troops on the ground. The US's extensive and ongoing use of drones also serves to obscure its most violent excesses by imposing literal distance between the actions of the military and their human cost.

Drone warfare has been sold as a better, cleaner tactic that will keep American soldiers safe. However, this concern for American lives does not extend to the people living in the countries the US has targeted. Instead, those targeted live in a state of constant fear. As a drone survivor whose family members were killed in northern Pakistan told the Center for Civilians in Conflict, "We fear that the drones will strike us again. . . . My aged parents are often in a state of fear. We are depressed, anxious, and constantly remembering our deceased family members. . . . It often compels me to leave this place."[55]

Passed just a week after the 9/11 attacks, the 2001 Congressional Authorization for Use of Military Force (AUMF), which gave the Bush administration broad discretion in fighting Al-Qaeda and the Taliban, is also the legal basis underlying the government's claimed authority for its drone warfare operations. As mentioned earlier, the 2001 AUMF gave the president permission to use "any and all necessary and appropriate force against those nations, organizations, and persons he determine[d]" to have been responsible for or involved with the events of 9/11, or any entity he deemed to be harboring those responsible.[56] This open-ended language has facilitated increasingly broad interpretations of its scope, which have evolved over time to essentially allow the US to treat the world as a battlefield—the definition of battlefield having been expanded to mean anywhere the enemy is. The Bush administration flexed the boundaries of this mandate by using drones to strike well outside of Al-Qaeda's reach, Afghanistan's borders, or indeed any actual fighting hot spots.

The use of drones has proliferated in the course of the War on Terror, with no slowdown in their use between administrations. The Bureau of Investigative Journalism estimated that the Bush administration launched fifty-seven strikes, mostly by drones, in Pakistan, Somalia, and Yemen. In contrast, Obama ordered 573 strikes, mostly by drones, in these same countries during his administration.[57] Given his reliance on and preference for drone warfare in the War on Terror, it's perhaps unsurprising that Obama ordered his first drone strike seventy-two hours, or three days, after he was inaugurated.[58]

It was also during the Obama administration, which so aggressively pursued the drone warfare program, that the scope of the AUMF's mandate was fleshed out and significantly expanded. In a 2009 brief submitted to the Supreme Court during a case challenging the government's latitude in detaining terror suspects without due process, the administration argued that the AUMF's grant of authority extended to "associated forces" of Al-Qaeda and the Taliban.[59] Despite the lack of actual language to this effect in the AUMF, the Supreme Court, allowing the executive branch wide discretion, placed its stamp of approval on this interpretation. Later, Obama administration lawyers would argue that this should be expanded to include targets whose terrorist activities were merely analogous to those of Al-Qaeda and the Taliban, allowing the military to target groups, such as ISIS, that didn't even exist at the time of the 9/11 attacks.[60] This interpretation, too, passed muster in courts that were extremely deferential to determinations made by the executive branch in waging the War on Terror.

Drone warfare has been waged in countries with which the United States is not technically at war, including Pakistan, Somalia, and Yemen. Because of the government's general lack of transparency and accountability in the War on Terror, data on civilian casualties has been significantly downplayed. For example, between January 2009 and the end of 2015, the Obama administration reported killing 2,436 people across four countries, including Pakistan, Yemen, Somalia, and Libya. Of those killed, the government claimed that only 64–116 of the deaths were civilians. In contrast, the Bureau of Investigative Journalism found that 2,753 people were killed during this same period, including a figure for civilian deaths that was six times higher than the number of civilian deaths reported by the government.[61]

In 2013, Obama made the following statement defending the tactics and scope of the War on Terror: "Moreover, America's actions are legal. We were attacked on 9/11. Within a week, Congress overwhelmingly authorized the use of force. Under domestic law, and international law, the United States is at war with al Qaeda, the Taliban, and their associated forces. We are at war with an organization that right now would kill as many Americans as they could if we did not stop them first. So this is a just war—a war waged proportionally, in last resort, and in self-defense."[62]

In the same speech, Obama referenced a set of presidential policy guidelines purporting to limit the use of drones, which was finally released three years later, in 2016. According to these guidelines, a strike could only be approved upon the determination that a lawful target was present—although this designation was made after the target had been killed. The policy guidelines mandated that drone strikes had to be conducted ensuring, with as much certainty as possible, that noncombatants would not be injured or killed.[63] However, not only were there no consequences to violating these guidelines, but "all military-age males in a strike zone [were considered] combatants, unless there [was] explicit intelligence posthumously proving them innocent."[64]

As Obama's presidency was close to ending, the White House released a "Report on the Legal and Policy Frameworks Guiding the United States' Use of Military Force and Related National Security Operations." In a section titled "Definition of 'Associated Forces,'" the report stipulates the following parameters:

> First, the entity must be an organized, armed group that has entered the fight alongside al-Qa'ida or the Taliban. Second, the group must be a co-belligerent with al-Qa'ida or the Taliban in hostilities against the United States or its coalition partners. Thus, a group is not an associated force simply because it aligns with al-Qa'ida or the Taliban or embraces their ideology. Merely engaging in acts of terror or merely sympathizing with al-Qa'ida or the Taliban is not enough to bring a group within the scope of the 2001 AUMF. Rather, a group must also have entered al-Qa'ida or the Taliban's fight against the United States or its coalition partners.[65]

Despite this last-minute attempt by President Obama to limit the definition of "associated forces," there have been no consequences to anyone involved in drone warfare, either before or after the report was released. Rather, this largely symbolic measure was intended, at best, to provide post hoc legal cover for the administration's actions, not to mandate distinctions between groups in any meaningful sense. Moreover, whatever legal gymnastics the Obama administration pursued to appease critics concerned by the expansion of the AUMF to include "associated forces," drone survivors who have lost family members tell a different story. In one case documented by the Center for Civilians in Conflict, drone strikes killed five members of the family of Malik Gulistan Khan, a tribal elder and member of a peace committee supporting the government. Khan lamented, "We did nothing, have no connection to militants at all. Our family supported the government and in fact . . . was a member of a local peace committee."[66] To add insult to injury, drone survivors are often stigmatized by members of their community, who believe that their being targeted by the United States is an indication of militancy.

Under President Donald Trump, the use of drones escalated even further. While Obama launched a drone strike approximately every 5.4 days, Trump launched them every 1.25 days.[67] Chillingly, Trump's induction into drone warfare happened on the day he was inaugurated, when he oversaw his first drone strike.[68] Revealing how flimsy the legal limitations implied in various Obama-era legal briefs and policy memos truly were, Trump also eliminated the (albeit mostly symbolic) accountability measures put in place during the previous administration. Trump's refusal to submit to even these minimal standards for transparency had the side effect of making the true extent of his use of drone warfare nearly impossible to measure.[69]

The military recognizes three categories of drone strikes, generally based on different levels of targets. Personality strikes target a specific target about whom intelligence is collected, while signature strikes involve individuals targeted based on patterns and characteristics associated with terrorists. Finally, double-tap strikes target those who appear on the scene after an initial strike has occurred, often including first responders and others attempting to rescue the injured while also removing the bodies of the dead. In one case, double-tap drone strikes were used to kill family members and friends of a group of people who had been targeted by an initial drone strike while they were eating.[70] Responding to the fear of double-tap drone strikes, a victim who lost a leg stated, "We and other people are so scared of drone attacks now that when there is a drone strike, for two or three hours nobody goes close to [the location of the strike]. We don't know who [the victims] are, whether they are young or old, because we try to be safe."[71] Although double-tap strikes are the most obviously horrific, all types present moral challenges.

In a potent symbol of how the free rein claimed under the AUMF has led down the path of murder without accountability, Obama's legacy included the use of what came to be known as "kill lists" to determine targets of drone strikes. In 2012, the *New York Times* reported that Obama and officials in his administration met weekly behind closed doors—on what became known as "Terror Tuesdays"—to determine the fate of those on the kill list.[72] At these meetings, there was a nomination process of proposed targets. While some of the targets were known to be operatives, others were nominated on the basis of loose associations with an actual target. Yet others were nominated simply based on where they resided in a particular country. In some cases, the alleged propensity to commit a future act of violence against the United States could be used to legitimize their murder. Obama even went as far as to authorize the killing of people whose identities were not even known—using the acronym TADS, which stands for "Terrorist Attack Disruption Strikes," as a label for this category. According to Jeremy Scahill, journalist and author of the book *Dirty Wars*, "By 2010, there were at least three entities within the US government that were maintaining kill lists: the National Security Council, which Obama dealt with directly during weekly meetings; the CIA; and the US military."[73]

American citizens have not been spared being killed by drone strikes, despite the obvious conflict between this form of extrajudicial killing and the due-process rights guaranteed by the US Constitution.[74] While Obama acknowledged the existence of due process for American citizens, his administration argued at the same time, "when an American has made the decision to affiliate himself with al Qaeda and target fellow Americans, that there is a legal justification for us to try and stop them from carrying out plots."[75] Specifically addressing due process, then attorney general Eric Holder asserted, "'Due process' and 'judicial process' are not one and the same, particularly when it comes to national security."[76] In practice, of course, this framing amounted to an evasion of responsibility—providing cover for the government to simply assassinate citizens with suspected links to terrorism without even the pretense of a fair trial. Holding unrestrained power and authority to kill US citizens, Obama responded in the review of the proposed assassination of Anwar Al-Awlaki as a target, according to William M. Daley, his chief of staff in 2011 that "this is an easy one."[77]

Indeed, less than three years later, in 2014, a Department of Justice white paper was released that legally sanctioned the extrajudicial assassination in Yemen of American citizen Anwar Al-Awlaki without due process of any kind.[78] Among the rationales included in the white paper for using lethal force without due process against a US citizen residing outside the United States, and who the government believes is planning attacks against it, is the determination by high-level officials that: (1) the target poses an impending threat of violence against the United States, (2) the target cannot be captured or their capture is deemed unfeasible, and (3) an operation against the target is executed in alignment with relevant law-of-war principles.[79]

Perhaps more striking is the death of Al-Awlaki's sixteen-year-old son, who was killed in a drone strike about two weeks after his father in 2011. When asked to justify Abdurrahman Al-Awlaki's death, former White House press secretary Robert Gibbs said, "I would suggest that you should have a far more responsible father if they are truly concerned about the well-being of their children. I don't think becoming an al Qaeda jihadist terrorist is the best way to go about doing your business."[80] In other words, the rationale of collective responsibility extends even to minors if they are Muslim—and can literally justify their deaths. And, as mentioned before, Al-Awlaki's eight-year-old daughter was killed in 2017—just days after Trump was inaugurated—during a US commando raid.[81] Like the ties that bind the family, there are ties that bind state violence across administrations.

The War on Terror has seen the US unleash catastrophic violence on wide swaths of the globe in the name of ensuring its security. The number of countries that have been involved in some way in the US's counter-terrorism war amounts to 39 percent of the world's nations, according to the Watson Institute for International and Public Affairs' Cost of War Project.[82] Involvement includes everything from a country training its forces in a different country, to hosting US service members who are fighting on the ground, to allowing the US to launch drone strikes from within a country's borders.

The United States has leveraged its considerable influence to center its own national security throughout the War on Terror. This framing of US aggression has often served to obscure its true, underlying interests in particular regions. It also obscures the tragedy of its millions of victims, a majority of whom are Muslim. In the language of the War on Terror, these civilian victims become simply "collateral damage," or are rolled in with "the terrorists" and are seen as not so much human beings but as an existential threat to US national security. Far from being incidental, the victims' Muslim identity is precisely what facilitates this reframing of reality. Muslims as a group have been set apart and demonized by the state and its allied voices so that almost any violence perpetrated against them appears justified. In the War on Terror, accountability has been buried along with the bodies of the dead.

5.

IMMIGRATION

This Land Is Our Land, This Land Is Our Land

Far from preventing violence, the border is in fact the reason it occurs.

—Harsha Walia[1]

By invoking the state itself as a victim, migrants themselves are cast as illegals and criminals who are committing an act of assault on the state. Migrants become prisoners of passage; their unauthorized migration is considered a trespass, and their very existence is criminalized.

—Harsha Walia[2]

On July 10, 2001, two months shy of the 9/11 attacks, then president Bush delivered remarks at an Immigration and Naturalization Service (INS) naturalization ceremony at Ellis Island in New York. Welcoming those who had become new Americans, he said, "Immigration is not a problem to be solved. It is a sign of a confident and successful nation. And people who seek to make America their home should be met in that spirit by representatives of our government. New arrivals should be greeted not with suspicion and resentment, but with openness and courtesy."[3]

Bush's stance toward immigration would dramatically shift after 9/11. With the advent of the War on Terror, immigration became one of the Bush administration's central policy priorities, characterized by a new, hardline approach that placed the issue at the nexus of national security. Although national security considerations in immigration policy were not entirely new, the fact that the 9/11 attackers held valid visas at the time of the attacks crystalized support for more intentionally focusing on this link. What ensued in the days, weeks, and months following the attacks made it clear that the distinction between national security and immigration enforcement would soon collapse under the weight of a slew of new policies criminalizing immigrants. Immigration enforcement would become integral to counterterrorism efforts and vice versa, with tactics being adapted to match this new orientation. As individuals and communities were increasingly targeted and torn apart because of this criminalizing paradigm of immigration, the specter of the state's violence was apparent not only in newly weaponized law and policy, but also in the construction and reinforcement of immigrant populations as "suspect communities."

Institutionalizing the connection between immigration and national security, President Bush signed the Homeland Security Act of 2002 into law, creating the Department of Homeland Security (DHS). The creation of the DHS involved a massive structural reorganization, subsuming different existing agencies, including the US Immigration and Naturalization Service (INS), and creating others. The INS, for its part, became three separate institutions: US Customs and Border Protection (CBP), US Immigration and Customs Enforcement (ICE), and US Citizenship and Immigration Services (USCIS).[4] The DHS was formed with an eye toward several objectives, including "effective control of US borders and the expansion of a 'zone of security' beyond US borders, enforcement of immigration laws, strengthened screening of travelers/workers and streamlined lawful visitor admission, and improved security by denying immigration benefits to 'dangerous individuals.'"[5]

The use of the word *homeland* was significant because it symbolically linked the domestic and international fronts of the new War on Terror, forming the foundation for a new landscape of global war without boundaries—whether spatial or temporal. The use of *homeland* also suggested "a rooted notion of racially white, timeless belonging to the United States,"[6] where borders—symbolic, invisible, and/or physical—became weapons in and of themselves, even before any enforcement. The purpose and language of the new immigration structure formalized in the creation of the DHS, with its implicit and explicit emphasis on the superiority of an imagined white America, both strongly signaled that the war on immigrants would be yet another battlefield from which the War on Terror would be fought.

Policy in the Aftermath of 9/11: Registration, Detention, and Removal

The Bush administration hit the ground running in cementing the idea that immigrants were a threat to national security and would be treated as such almost immediately after 9/11. A cascade of early policies and directives that targeted Muslims in the United States set the stage for the criminalization of immigration. These early policies began by targeting non-citizens, the least protected group in terms of public sympathy as well as law.

Among these early enforcement policies that targeted non-citizen Muslims present in the United States was the Alien Absconder Initiative, which was implemented in January 2002 with the stated goal of removing individuals in the United States who were in violation of deportation orders.[7] At the time of the initiative, 314,000 people from a wide variety of backgrounds were already classified by the government as "absconders." However, the government was quick to specify its intended targets. To this end, a memorandum from the Office of the Deputy General stated, "While the INS will ultimately deport all 314,000 from the United States, there are several thousand among that group who come from countries in which there has been Al Qaeda terrorist presence or activity. We want to focus our initial efforts on these priority absconders as we believe that some of them have information that could assist our campaign against terrorism."[8] Ultimately, this policy focused on six thousand individuals from predominantly Muslim and Arab countries—a fact highlighting the selective application of the initiative.[9]

In addition to singling out Muslims for special treatment in enforcing immigration violations, the Bush administration created policies that targeted non-citizens who were lawfully present in the United States, including by requiring immigrants from suspect communities to register with the government. The National Security Entry-Exit Registration System (NSEERS) was put into place by the Department of Justice in 2002 and was folded into the DHS in 2003. The program required non-citizen males sixteen years and older from twenty-five countries—all Muslim-majority nations with the exception of North Korea—to register with the government. Not only did this involve fingerprinting and photographs; it also involved intrusive interrogations.[10] Approximately eighty thousand men registered, and not a single one was charged with a crime. The NSEERS program had effectively ended in 2011. The regulation was not fully eliminated, however, but was instead simply delisted by the DHS.[11] In 2016, afraid of how then President Trump and his administration might utilize the infrastructure built to execute NSEERS, many rights organizations advocated for the Obama administration to dismantle NSEERS altogether, which he did.[12]

The post-9/11 immigration landscape also included special-interest detentions that rounded up hundreds of non-citizen immigrants, mostly Muslim men subject to racial and religious profiling, and held them in harsh conditions in a detention facility in Brooklyn, New York.[13] Similar to what has continued to happen elsewhere in the War on Terror, those detained were not charged, but their detentions were extended because the FBI claimed they had to make sure they had no terrorist connections. The men were held under new rules put in place specifically for this "special interest" category of people in custody, which dictated, for example, that they could be held up to forty-eight hours, rather than the normal twenty-four hours, without being charged. Several of those in detention were deported for visa violations.[14] According to the Center for Constitutional Rights (CCR), the remaining men were detained as terrorism suspects and held in brutal detention conditions for the many months it took the FBI and CIA to clear them of any connection to terrorism. Not only were some of these men's cases closed to the public; the Department of Justice (DOJ) also issued rules permitting eavesdropping on a client and their attorney if there was cause for suspicion that the conversation would "further or facilitate acts of terrorism."[15]

The CCR filed a lawsuit on behalf of these men as a group in 2002. The suit named Attorney General John Ashcroft, FBI Director Robert Mueller, and several others individually, and sought compensatory and punitive damages for their unlawful detention and the conditions of their confinement. The resulting case, *Turkmen v. Ashcroft* (eventually renamed *Ziglar v. Abbasi*), reached the Supreme Court, where the plaintiffs lost. The case turned on whether the special interest detainees would be able to exercise their rights under the Bivens doctrine, a long-standing constitutional precedent that allows civil rights claims to be brought against government officials. In a 4–2 decision, the Supreme Court ruled that non-citizen detainees did not have a right to sue government officials for constitutional violations that occurred while they were in custody if the government demonstrated their detention was necessary in the course of pursuing legitimate national security objectives. The rationale in denying the plaintiffs the ability to have the facts of their case heard in court was that "because those claims challenge major elements of the Government's response to the September 11 attacks, they necessarily require an inquiry into national-security issues."[16] The judiciary, in other words, was signaling that it was on board with the post-9/11 shift in immigration and related policy to a counterterrorism paradigm, enough so that they were willing to consider it outside of established constitutional standards, giving the executive significant space to target Muslim populations with impunity on the basis of vague, unchallenged national security objectives.

Crimmigration and Law Enforcement

As the War on Terror progressed, the criminalization of immigrants and immigration became more aggressive. In 2005, the DHS and DOJ implemented Operation Streamline, which created "zero-tolerance" zones along the US-Mexico border and instituted consequences for violations that included criminal prosecution, prison sentences, deportation, and removal—turning what previously would have been a civil matter into a criminal one.[17] A year later, in 2006, the Secure Fence Act provided authorization for the construction of seven hundred miles of fencing along the US-Mexico border.[18] This was not only a literal way of blocking entry into the country, but also a powerful symbol of just how immigration and national security had become inextricably linked in US posture and policy. Consistent with other War on Terror narratives, a fence or wall is meant to silently impart two messages: the sheer and undefeatable strength of the United States and, at the same time, the United States as a victim of other countries' failure to enforce their own borders. The idea that a physical structure embodies or symbolizes a particular narrative by virtue of visual and other cues is what I call "narrative physicality."

In 2008, the Bush administration instituted the Secure Communities program, with the goal of enabling law enforcement to enforce immigration laws. Though the collusion of law enforcement with immigration enforcement wasn't solely a product of the post-9/11 era, new protocols were developed to further facilitate information sharing. Under the typical circumstance of an arrest, local law enforcement would share fingerprints with the FBI. However, if the fingerprint data was from a jurisdiction where the Secure Communities program was in effect, Immigration and Customs Enforcement (ICE) would receive fingerprint data too. The DHS would then check the data against a database with information on over ninety thousand individuals and, among other things, look for immigration violations. If violations were found, ICE was authorized to make detainer requests, which meant that immigrants could be held for forty-eight hours after the designated time for their release. This effectively meant that ICE had free rein to target immigrants. In the absence of much scrutiny, detainer requests were made indiscriminately, thus resulting in the fact that "U.S. citizens, non-deportable Lawful Permanent Residents, and persons without any criminal convictions ended up getting caught in the dragnet."[19]

The Secure Communities program was theoretically designed to get "'convicted criminals' off the street and into deportation hearings."[20] In practice, it resulted in many immigrants being deported for minor offenses, such as traffic violations.[21] Aside from the extensive and direct damage caused to many immigrant communities, one of the lasting impacts of the Secure Communities program was the creation of a massive surveillance system that fed into ICE databases—which provided infrastructure for Trump's mass deportation agenda.[22]

President Obama ended the Secure Communities program in 2014, replacing it with the Priority Enforcement Program (PEP). The focus of PEP was narrowed to concentrate on undocumented immigrants who posed a threat to "national security, border security, and public safety."[23] While PEP also relied on data-sharing among agencies, it narrowed the purview of DHS and ICE from that of the Secure Communities program. Though PEP was intended to fix some of the problems with the Secure Communities program, superficial changes in the new program did not fundamentally alter the structure and premise of Secure Communities. Thus, constitutional issues raised by the earlier program, rather than being resolved, were instead exported to the latter.[24]

Signaling his opposition to even moderate reforms of hardline immigration policies, incoming president Donald Trump reinstated the Secure Communities program and signed an executive order titled "Enhancing Public Safety in the Interior of the United States."[25] Trump sought to make the scope of the reinstated program as broad as possible in order to further criminalize immigration. Thus, the order specifically included

> aliens who have been convicted of any criminal offense; have been charged with any criminal offense, where such charge has not been resolved; have committed acts that constitute a chargeable criminal offense; have engaged in fraud or willful misrepresentation in connection with any official matter or application before a governmental agency; have abused any program related to receipt of public

benefits; are subject to a final order of removal, but who have not complied with their legal obligation to depart the United States; or in the judgment of an immigration officer, otherwise pose a risk to public safety or national security.[26]

In addition, under the Trump administration, individual ICE agents were given broad discretion "about whom to detain and deport, under what circumstances, and for what reasons."[27]

Targeting Muslims with Impunity

Using the broad legal discretion granted to post-9/11 immigration policy implementation and enforcement decisions, the government has used current events to suspend immigration further at various times during the War on Terror. For example, in the wake of the Paris terror attacks in 2015, the Visa Waiver Program Improvement and Terrorist Travel Prevention Act was implemented, ending travel privileges for citizens of any country on the Visa Waiver Program (VWP) list who were dual citizens of Iraq, Syria, Iran, and Sudan.[28] In addition, if a citizen of a country on the VWP list visited any of these countries after March 1, 2011, they were prevented from obtaining a visa waiver. This new program was an alteration to the existing VWP, which was initially created to allow nationals and citizens of certain countries to travel to the United States for ninety days or less, for either business or tourism, without a visa. In 2016, Libya, Somalia, and Yemen were added to the list as countries of concern. Unlike Iraq, Syria, Iran, and Sudan, the restriction on dual nationals was not applied to Libya, Somalia, or Yemen, though it still stood for anyone who had traveled to any of the three countries since March 1, 2011.

At the same time, the US government has sought to restrict citizenship for qualified non-citizens. For example, under the Controlled Application Review and Resolution Program (CARRP), which began in 2008, numerous individuals experienced serious delays in the naturalization process because of their Muslim identity and the fact that they were considered a "national security concern."[29] The CARRP program defined a "national security concern" as "an individual or organization [that] has been determined to have an articulable link to prior, current, or planned involvement in, or association with, an activity, individual or organization described in the security and terrorism sections of the Immigration and Nationality

Act."[30] In addition to this overly broad definition, CARRP used the Terror Watchlist, a list with hundreds of thousands of names, to determine who should be deemed a "national security concern." The Terror Watchlist, still in use at the time of this writing, not only includes people arbitrarily but provides no mechanism for those on the list to contest their placement on it.[31]

The Terror Watchlist developed out of one of the earliest immigration-related counterterrorism measures implemented after 9/11, which was the Terrorist Screening Center (TSC) created in 2003. The TSC was designed to facilitate the sharing of terrorism information after the 9/11 Commission's Report identified the lack of cross-agency sharing of counterterrorism information as an issue. The TSC "is a multi-agency center administered by the Federal Bureau of Investigation and is the U.S. Government's consolidated counterterrorism watch-listing component responsible for the management and operation of the Terrorist Screening Database, commonly known as 'the watchlist.'" The Terrorist Screening Database contains identifying information for those "who are known to be or reasonably suspected of being involved in terrorist activities."[32] As of 2017, the watchlist had about 1.2 million people on it, including 4,600 American citizens or lawful permanent residents in the US.[33] Among the many reasons the watchlist is problematic is that there is a total lack of transparency with regard to who is on the list and how they got there.

One recent attempt to challenge the watchlist is *Elhady v. Kable*—a case brought by the Council on American Islamic Relations (CAIR) in 2016. In September 2019, the judge in this case ruled that the watchlist was a violation not only of the Due Process Clause, but also of the Administrative Procedures Act. The judge's decision stated in part, "The vagueness of the standard for inclusion in the TSDB [Terrorist Screening Database], coupled with the lack of any meaningful restraint on what constitutes grounds for placement on the Watchlist, constitutes, in essence, the absence of any ascertainable standard for inclusion and exclusion, which is precisely what offends the Due Process Clause."[34] Though CAIR declared the decision a "complete victory," the judge in the case, Anthony Trenga, did not declare the list itself unconstitutional, but merely the way in which the list was implemented. Though the judge initially ordered both parties, CAIR and the government, to submit possible remedies, he declined to require implementation of the specific changes CAIR had recommended, instead ordering the government to devise remedies that would make the watchlist compliant.[35] As of this writing, the government has appealed the case in the Fourth Circuit.

Because Muslim Americans, a community with theoretical rights as citizens, were making these claims, there was an embedded hierarchy in the rights of citizens versus non-citizens. Unfortunately, as I wrote in *Newsweek* in 2019, this could potentially risk "the ultimate creation of what could amount to two Watchlists for two classes of people. One for U.S. citizens, including notice, the opportunity to rebut one's listing, and whatever other procedures the court deems appropriate; and a second Watchlist that is not bound to any of those procedural requirements for all non-U.S. citizens, who, at any given point in time are not on U.S. soil."[36]

One of the lists derived from the Terror Watchlist is the No-Fly List. Placement on the No-Fly List prevents travelers from boarding planes that travel across or through the United States.[37] The list has far fewer names on it than the Terror Watchlist does, but the government has concealed most of its details, including the criteria for inclusion. One indication that these criteria are overbroad is that the No-Fly List has included names of dead people—because of the possibility, according to the government, that someone else might try to use their identity.[38] According to the American Civil Liberties Union (ACLU), the only recourse for those who are placed on the list wrongfully "is to file a request with the Department of Homeland Security's Traveler Redress Inquiry Program (DHS TRIP), after which DHS responds with a letter that does not explain why they were denied boarding. The letter does not confirm or deny whether their names remain on the list, and does not indicate whether they can fly."[39]

In October 2020, the Supreme Court heard the case of *Tanvir v. Tanzin*, a case based on the No-Fly List that challenged numerous government agencies, including the FBI, the Department of Justice, and the Department of Homeland Security. The plaintiffs, Muhammad Tanvir, Jameel Algibhah, and Naveed Shinwar, all American citizens, are Muslim men whom the FBI attempted to coerce into becoming informants and surveilling Muslim communities. When they refused, the plaintiffs were placed on the No-Fly List. Previous lawsuits challenging the No-Fly List have resulted in minimal changes to it, such that there is only a limited process for individuals to find out if they are in fact on the list, and no way to challenge placement on the list. The consequences of placement on the list for the plaintiffs included job loss, being stigmatized in their communities, and emotional and financial suffering.[40] In this case, the plaintiffs were informed that they were no longer on the list just days before trial, at which point the judge dismissed the rest of their suit, which sought damages for the financial and emotional harm caused by their years spent on the list. After an appeals court reinstated the suit seeking monetary damages from the FBI agents involved, the Trump administration appealed the case to the Supreme Court. In December 2020, the court ruled unanimously that federal officials, in an individual capacity, can be sued for monetary damages because of violations of the Religious Freedom Restoration Act, allowing the plaintiffs' quest for justice to go forward.[41]

The Muslim and African Bans

The restrictions on entry and travel primarily affecting Muslims that we've explored became more draconian than they had been with the election of Donald Trump, who as a presidential candidate had proudly asserted, "Donald J. Trump is calling for a total and complete shutdown of Muslims entering the United States until our country's representatives can figure out what is going on."[42] As president, Trump stayed true to his word, and within a week of his inauguration, on January 27, 2017, he signed an executive order implementing the policy that became known as the Muslim Ban, prohibiting citizens from Iraq, Syria, Iran, Libya, Somalia, Sudan, and Yemen from entering the United States for an initial period of ninety days. The order also put an indefinite stop on the admission of Syrian refugees, and a four-month stop on acceptance of any refugees at all. There was, however, an exemption for religious minorities, effectively prioritizing Christian over Muslim refugees.[43]

Implementation of this first ban was blocked by nearly half a dozen US district courts days after it went into effect. The matter subsequently went to the Ninth Circuit Court of Appeals, which ruled against reinstatement of the ban. In March 2017, Trump put a new ban into effect, in which entrants from the same list of countries, with the exception of Iraq, were banned for ninety days. No group of refugees was explicitly singled out, but all refugees were banned for 120 days. US district courts in Maryland and Hawaii blocked its implementation, and in May the Fourth Circuit Court of Appeals ruled against it, noting its intent to discriminate against Muslims specifically.[44]

With unrelenting fervor, Trump signed a third Muslim and African Ban into effect in September 2017, adding Chad, North Korea, and Venezuela to the list of restricted countries. Because of already-existing restrictions, in the case of Venezuela this was only applicable to government officials and their families, and in the case of North Korea was wholly unnecessary, raising questions about whether these non–Muslim-majority countries were added in good faith or to obscure the continued focus on targeting Muslims. Slightly different restrictions were placed on Iran, Libya, North Korea, Somalia, Syria, and Yemen, though most immigrant visas were suspended for a majority of entrants, and for countries such as Syria and North Korea, all nonimmigrant entry was banned as well.

The Supreme Court allowed the third ban to go forward. The court's majority held that it was within Trump's presidential authority to decide the scope of the ban as long as a country's inclusion was or could reasonably be connected to a "legitimate national security objective."[45] In granting such broad discretion to the government, the court declined to look beneath the surface to determine whether this latest version of the travel ban was, in effect, still a targeted effort to specifically exclude Muslims.

The Mouth of a Shark

While the details and rhetoric have varied slightly, twenty years and three administrations of the War on Terror have produced an immigration agenda that relentlessly elevates national security interests over human ones. This agenda has been pursued with a total lack of reflection on the root causes of migration, which include dislocation as a result of US economic and military intervention in other countries. As a result, much of the official narrative on immigration has tended to focus on the US's generosity and to extend to constructions of "good" versus "bad" immigrants.

The underlying notion of the US's welcoming generosity, coupled with false notions of the permeability of US borders, is a narrative that has also been used to justify certain measures. Another theme expressed is the use of brute force to curb immigration, and a pattern of unwillingness to entertain any other kinds of intervention. For examples of the consistency with which this script has been adhered to throughout the War on Terror, consider the following quotes from, respectively, Presidents Bush, Obama, and Trump in their State of the Union addresses:

> Extending hope and opportunity in our country requires an immigration system worthy of America—with laws that are fair and borders that are secure. When laws and borders are routinely violated, this harms the interests of our country. To secure our border, we're doubling the size of the Border Patrol, and funding new infrastructure and technology. (Bush, 2007 SOTU)[46]

Real reform means strong border security, and we can build on the progress my administration has already made—putting more boots on the Southern border than at any time in our history and reducing illegal crossings to their lowest levels in 40 years. (Obama, 2013 SOTU)[47]

For that reason, we will soon begin the construction of a great, great wall along our southern border. (Applause.) As we speak tonight, we are removing gang members, drug dealers, and criminals that threaten our communities and prey on our very innocent citizens. Bad ones are going out as I speak, and as I promised throughout the campaign. (Trump, 2017 SOTU)[48]

In the first quote, Bush personifies the United States as if it has divine values separate from the people who are ruling the country, suggesting that "illegal immigration" is an afront to the country rather than to the people who live within its borders. Moreover, Bush's statement positions the United States as a victim of "illegal immigration," which requires extreme intervention. Obama's statement adds the dimension of immigration reform—something he consistently pushed throughout his tenure as president. However, as his wording suggests, "reform" under his leadership amounted to essentially the exact same measures as under Bush, with changes designed not to challenge the underlying agenda but to carry out its aims more effectively.

Trump's language brings brute force to the forefront. He articulates in the most explicit terms possible what post-9/11 policy has in fact been designed to do all along: criminalize immigrants and leverage fear to gain momentum in support of state action that perpetuates violence against them. Trump emphasizes the essential criminality of immigrants through juxtaposition with the United States' "very innocent citizens"—a characterization clearly meant to extend to the United States itself and the impossibility that it could be guilty of any violence.

All three quotes make clear that in the US agenda, borders are a site of violence and, if framed the right way, justified violence. It's important to note, however, that the visible violence employed at borders is replicated in other ways that are less visible. For example, the Muslim and African Ban has everything to do with violent borders, but because the violence begins and ends abroad, it makes the human toll outside the US border almost invisible.

In the words of "Home," by Somali poet Warsan Shire:

no one leaves home unless
home is the mouth of a shark[49]

This speaks to one of the greatest perils of the US's immigration system—an inability and unwillingness to examine root causes of migration—which directly implicates the US in the humanitarian consequences.

Closing Words

In August 2020, several news outlets, including the *Chicago Tribune,* announced the forthcoming publication of *Out of Many, One,* by George W. Bush. Bush's book of forty-three portraits of immigrants was released on April 20, 2021, alongside his exhibit on immigration by the same name at the George W. Bush Presidential Center. Those who don't know much about Bush's violent legacy, particularly when it comes to immigration, might commend him for using art to illustrate and contribute to the narrative of an inclusive and tolerant United States where immigrants are celebrated. However, immigrants who were abused, detained, and deported by his order and under his watch have much different stories to tell—stories that may not be featured in fancy exhibits, but stories that will forever haunt the myth of the US as a nation of immigrants.

6.

FEDERAL TERRORISM PROSECUTIONS AND SURVEILLANCE

The FBI uses a method to turn a person to become an informant. That method is called MICE. It's an acronym. M stands for money. Using money to bribe them to become an informant. I, use their ideology to turn that meaning, in this case, to be religion. C, compromise, meaning some kind of information that makes that person vulnerable. E is ego.
　　　　　　　　　—CRAIG MONTEILH, US GOVERNMENT INFORMANT[1]

The government lost, f***ed up many cases. And I go there to fix it. This is my job. The closer.
　　　　　　　　　　　　　　　　　　—ELIE ASSAD[2]

Don't Hide and We Won't Seek

In the aftermath of the insurrection at the US Capitol on January 6, 2021, Black and brown communities in the United States watched as the FBI solicited help from anyone who could identify the rioters. Despite footage of the insurrection scrolling daily on various news channels, with numerous rioters' faces, clothes, and symbols in plain view, the FBI continued making appeals for help with IDs. Those unfamiliar with the FBI's history and its white supremacist origins may have perceived their efforts as genuine and demonstrative of their desire to hold rioters accountable. For others, particularly Black and brown Muslims, there was cruel irony in the FBI's pleas for help finding the white rioters, considering how this same institution over the years didn't so much find Muslim perpetrators of violence as it did create them. Put front and center, though not visible to all, was the fact that an institution rooted in white supremacy could not exercise violence against a manifestation of itself, but it could do so with others. In the post-9/11 context, these others have been Black and brown Muslims, who are treated as inherently violent and suspect—and who don't even have to have committed a crime to be charged and convicted.

While the Bush administration was seeking out the nebulous enemy on battlefields abroad, the government turned domestic courtrooms into battlegrounds for fighting federal terrorism prosecutions. Though individuals' lives and communities were being torn apart by federal terrorism prosecutions, including in the earlier years of the War on Terror often using informants, the US government showed no signs of slowing down. Through federal terrorism prosecutions Americans could have a visible enemy to grasp, one that could provide "evidence" that the US was winning the War on Terror.

In his study of terrorism prosecutions, legal scholar Wadie Said identifies two troubling ways in which terrorism prosecutions differ from regular criminal cases. The first is the adoption of a preemptive approach by the government, allowing the FBI to surveil and investigate targets even when they have not committed any crime and where there is no factual basis for suspecting they intend to commit one. In contrast, in the pre-9/11 context, individuals would only be charged with terrorism if an act actually occurred.[3]

The second element is the expansion in terror trials of the material-support statute, which has its origins in a 1996 law that was intended to focus on the provision of contributions such as money, weapons, and equipment to support the violent mission of foreign terrorist organizations.[4] From its inception, the law did not spare anyone; thus, even if an individual's motivation for providing support was based, for example, on charitable concerns, they could be and often were prosecuted. Post-9/11, however, the application of the material-support law was expanded dramatically. For instance, in *Holder v. Humanitarian Law Project*, the Supreme Court ruled that even protected speech could constitute material support for terrorism, thus taking it out of the sphere of protection.[5]

Tying these two differences pertaining to terrorism prosecutions together, Said states, "Taken in tandem with the preventive mindset of law enforcement and the proactive use of informants and provocateurs, which has seen the government create the threat it subsequently thwarts and prosecutes, the material ban goes further and allows the government to criminalize charity, solidarity, religious practice and speech."[6]

The civil rights issues that Said identifies with post-9/11 terrorism prosecutions have had grave consequences for the Muslim community. Several studies provide in-depth analysis of the problematic aspects of federal terrorism prosecutions since 9/11. For example, according to a Human Rights Watch report titled *Illusion of Justice: Human Rights Abuses in US Terrorism Prosecutions*, 50 percent of the convictions in federal terrorism cases involved the use of informants, while 30 percent were sting operations.[7] It is often the case that those targeted are vulnerable in some way, such as being disabled and/or impoverished.[8]

Don't Call It Entrapment

One reason, perhaps, that the government can claim to be successful in uncovering terrorist plots on US soil is that the preventive approach allows the FBI to target individuals without any suspected wrongdoing, a reflection of the War-on-Terror trope that Muslims are inherent terrorists. Adopting this preventive approach, however, has meant that if law enforcement wants a case to prosecute, they must take an active role in fostering the conditions that lead to the commission of an actionable offense. In practice, then, the FBI doesn't so much uncover terrorist plots as manufacture them, using "fishing expeditions" and outright manipulation. Treating all Muslims as suspects has given the government license to penetrate deeply into their communities, conversing with many different people until they identify someone whose viewpoints (they claim) make them susceptible to targeting. They then employ various tactics against the targeted individual to push them into being willing to commit violent action. For instance, the informant might manipulate them into voicing anger and make them more prone to at least entertain committing acts of violence by showing them graphically violent images or videos of Muslims being abused.

One such case involved a young man named Shawahar Matin Siraj, who was working at his uncle's bookstore when a New York Police Department informant befriended him. The informant, Osama Eldawoody, tried to convince Siraj that it was acceptable to return the violence of those who inflicted it on Muslims. In order to move him toward acceptance of this idea, Siraj, writing from prison, said that the informant

> showed me grotesque abuses of the Muslim prisoners at Abu Ghraib and added his emotional voice as to not wanting to die without a purpose, of cancer. Then while I was inflamed with emotions at work, he would give me websites that I should visit when I got home to keep me insighted [*sic*] overnight. On one occasion I was given a site

where a young Iraqi girl was being raped by an American [*sic*] guard-dog. She was terrified and it was a very inciteful [*sic*] experience to see that before retiring at night. There were articles and photos of children mangled or decapitated or burnt alive.[9]

Instead of pursuing cases that actually warrant attention, the informant targeted an innocent man, showing him material clearly designed to showcase egregious violence against Muslims, in order to provoke him to anger. Furthermore, the United States claims to be fighting terrorism, but is instead using the abuse of one group of Muslims to help criminalize another group of Muslims.

Siraj's case also demonstrates the extent to which the FBI will go to target especially vulnerable Muslims. In Siraj's case, a forensic psychologist who conducted an assessment of Siraj determined that he had "impaired critical thinking and analytical skills, and diminished judgment."[10] Nevertheless, he received a thirty-year prison sentence in 2007 for conspiring to plant bombs in a New York City subway. According to Human Rights Watch's "Illusion of Justice" report, at least eight of the defendants in the cases they reviewed presented with or showed serious signs early on that they struggled with mental or intellectual disabilities.[11] These cases, among others, demonstrate the lengths to which the government will go to criminalize the Muslim community, particularly Muslims who are already on the margins.

In cases such as Siraj's, where an informant is used to induce a targeted individual to commit or plan to commit a crime, an entrapment defense would appear warranted. However, alongside the post-9/11 shift to preventive tactics in terrorism investigations and prosecutions, courts have changed their approach to the issue of entrapment: if a defendant in a domestic terror case raises this defense, the prosecution must prove that the defendant was predisposed to committing the crime, such that the actions of the informant merely hastened the inevitable. But disputing the prosecution's claim of predisposition is nearly impossible for domestic terror defendants because the claim relies on character judgments that are subjective in any case, and especially so where the context of preemptive enforcement means that the construction of Muslims as inherently violent has already been accepted.

The Fort Dix Five

Another case involving the use of informants was that of the Fort Dix Five. This case started after five men—Mohammed Shnewer, Dritan Duka, Shain Duka, Eljvir Duka, and Burim Duka—took a trip to the Pocono Mountains. While there, they recorded a video of themselves at a public shooting range firing guns while saying, "Allahu Akbar." When one of the men took the video to a Circuit City store to have a VHS tape converted into a DVD, a store employee called the police to express concern. The call launched an FBI surveillance operation that lasted more than a year and employed two informants, both with serious criminal records and financial incentive to obtain information leading to conviction at all costs. Shnewer, three of the Duka brothers, and a fifth man named Serdar Tatar would eventually be charged and convicted of a terrorist conspiracy to attack Fort Dix in New Jersey.

Shnewer, nineteen at the time, was befriended by a forty-year-old man named Mahmoud Omar, whom the FBI had found in jail and recruited to be an informant. Omar encouraged the young man in a violent direction, at first obtaining and watching jihadist videos and lectures with him, and gradually becoming more specific and manipulative. For example, when Shnewer suggested prayer and charity as solutions to the injustices faced by Muslims, Omar pressed him to think more concretely, suggesting nearby Fort Dix as a potential target for taking action against the US military. Eventually he was able to convince Shnewer to go to the base to surveil it, and to approach Tatar, an acquaintance whose father owned a local pizza business that delivered to the base, about obtaining a road-access map. When Omar pressured Shnewer to take further action, however, such as practicing bomb making and making additional surveillance trips, the young man refused. For his part, Tatar actually approached the police with concerns about the request for maps.

Meanwhile, the Duka brothers were growing closer to another informant, fellow Albanian immigrant Besnik Bakalli, who used their long talks about religion, which he secretly recorded, to push them toward jihadism. No evidence was ever presented that the Duka brothers even knew about the supposed plot against Fort Dix, let alone participated in it, and in fact, the informants testified to this effect at trial. Even so, they were picked up by law enforcement for illegally purchasing firearms that Bakalli himself had provided to the Dukas. Although hundreds of hours of conversation between Bakalli and the Dukas were presented as evidence, no recordings existed for crucial moments such as any talk surrounding the gun deal. Despite this fact, they were charged as terrorists and convicted in December 2008, along with Shnewer and Tatar, of conspiracy to harm military personnel. All four of the defendants who had been subject to entrapment by the FBI received life sentences, with Dritan and Shain Duka getting an additional thirty years for the weapons charge. Serdar Tatar was sentenced to thirty-six years, and is the only one of the five not currently being held at a maximum-security facility for inmates considered a particularly dangerous threat to national security. Despite sustained public attention, all attempts to appeal the 2008 decision have been denied, including a 2016 retrial request to which the judge wrote that he was denying their "sole remaining claim." For their part, informants Omar and Bakalli walked away with six-figure paychecks.[12]

The Newburgh Four

I like the work I do. I enjoy the work I do. That's why I do it.
—SHAHED HUSSAIN, FBI INFORMANT, NEWBURGH FOUR[13]

Perhaps the most egregious example of entrapment via the use of informants is the case of the Newburgh Four.[14] Between 2007 and 2009, Masjid al-Ikhlas in New York State was being monitored by the FBI, which sent paid informant Shahed Hussain to infiltrate the community and uncover, or stir up, terrorist activity. Hussain had an extensive criminal record and had begun working with the FBI originally to avoid being deported following a fraud conviction. In 2008, he met and targeted James Cromitie, a struggling Walmart employee and outspoken anti-Semite. Cromitie, however, displayed no interest in radical Islam or terrorist action against the United States and initially resisted Hussain's efforts to coax him into plotting an attack. It was only after he lost his job at Walmart that he gave in and agreed to help carry out a plot developed by Hussain—which, of course, was fake—to plant bombs at a nearby synagogue and attack a US air base. To this end, Cromitie recruited three others to serve as lookouts, all of whom were struggling—with addiction, financial woes, and family medical issues—and one of whom lived with schizophrenia. All four were offered substantial monetary compensation in return for their involvement, with Hussain outrageously promising Cromitie $250,000 cash, a BMW, and a vacation. As in the Fort Dix case, although Hussain recorded conversations extensively, crucial interactions were missing, including the moments when the plot itself was being executed. At trial, the word of Hussain, a known fraudster, was accepted as evidence even when the tapes had been switched off. The Newburgh Four were convicted on a range of charges including, but not limited to conspiracy to use weapons of mass destruction within the US and conspiracy to acquire and use anti-aircraft missiles. These convictions were made despite ample evidence that their motivation was purely financial and the plot itself was staged and entirely planned by the informant Hussain. On appeal, the Second Circuit Court denied the argument that the conditions for legal entrapment were met, because the men believed the plot to be a true one even though they displayed no ideological commitment to it. By the logic of this ruling, the US government essentially has free rein to pre-convict Muslims of terrorism, targeting Muslim communities and manufacturing the necessary conditions.

Though the FBI directly targets Muslims to secure terrorism convictions, they also recruit them to become informants.[15] One of the ways Muslims have been pressured to become informants is through the exploitation of their immigration status. Specifically, the threat of deportation is made to coerce Muslims into spying on their own communities. The FBI also sometimes threatens to prevent family members of the person targeted from coming to the United States. Those who refuse to become informants pay a steep price as they become direct targets of the FBI themselves.

The Holy Land Five

The ubiquitous reliance in domestic terrorism prosecutions on the Antiterrorism and Effective Death Penalty Act of 1996 that banned material support for foreign terrorist organizations reflects and reinforces the preventive approach in investigation. The concern motivating the original law was that foreign organizations that were threats to national security were being supported from within the United States under the guise of charitable giving. In the post-9/11 landscape, however, the ban has become an infinitely flexible tool in the government's toolbox for prosecuting individuals who have been singled out via contemporary preventive methods, a kind of catch-all for making terrorism charges stick despite the conduct of the FBI or the tenuousness of the connection between that individual and any foreign terrorist organization.

One of the most prominent cases early in the War on Terror is paradigmatic of how sweepingly the material-support doctrine would be employed in domestic terror trials. The Holy Land Five case was the largest terrorism-financing case in history. The Holy Land Foundation was a charitable organization created in 1989 to support Palestinians in countries across the Middle East, in addition to refugees and war victims in or from countries such as Bosnia and Kosovo. The so-called Holy Land Five were accused of using the organization as a front operation that used zakat committees, a group of charities in the West Bank and Gaza, to divert funds to Hamas.[16] (Not so ironically, the United States Agency for International Development [USAID] was using the same zakat committees for resource distribution, and continued to use them three years after the Holy Land Foundation was shut down.)

No direct connection between the Holy Land Five and Hamas was ever established, and in fact, the US government backed off of this claim, arguing instead that *all* of the zakat committees were operating in coordination with the charitable arm of Hamas, essentially criminalizing all Muslim charities in the region. Moreover, the court decision in the case of the Holy Land Five extended beyond all reason a theory that says money is fungible, meaning that cash donations need not be directly connected to criminal aims because the receiving organization may use money for any purpose. Money sent for charitable activity, then, essentially frees up organizational resources for things like acquiring weapons, so such a donation still constitutes material support of terrorism. The court in the Holy Land case took this logic one step further, finding that although it did not fund terror directly *or* indirectly by freeing up resources, the charitable giving in this case enhanced the reputation of Hamas in the region and therefore constituted material support. The first trial of the Holy Land Five ended in a mistrial, but a year later, they were recharged. The second trial resulted in a material-support conviction and sentences of fifteen to sixty-five years in prison for each of the five men.

Tarek Mehanna

Tarek Mehanna is a pharmacist born in the United States, a devout Muslim, and a critic of US foreign policy.[17] Mehanna was very vocal about his belief in the right of resistance for Muslims in occupied countries, and he participated in rigorous dialogue along these lines.[18] In 2004, Mehanna traveled to Yemen, a trip he said was for religious and language training.

However, the government would later argue that he went there to join a terrorist training camp, and that he also translated a text called "39 Ways to Serve and Participate in Jihad."

The FBI started monitoring Mehanna in 2005, and he was charged in 2008 with providing false information to the FBI and in 2009 with providing material support for terrorism. Mehanna believed his arrest was based on his refusal to serve as an informant for the FBI.[19]

Despite a lack of evidence from the government proving that Mehanna had translated material at the behest of Al-Qaeda, that he intended to cause harm, or that he wanted to encourage imminent criminal behavior, "the speech-as-material-support theory," argues law professor and scholar Amna Akbar, "appears to have turned largely on his attempts to convince and 'inspire' others to support opinions the United States government finds objectionable."[20]

At his sentencing hearing on April 12, 2012, Mehanna delivered a powerful statement:

> It was made crystal clear at trial that I never, ever plotted to "kill Americans" at shopping malls or whatever the story was. The government's own witnesses contradicted this claim, and we put expert after expert up on that stand, who spent hours dissecting my every written word, who explained my beliefs. Further, when I was free, the government sent an undercover agent to prod me into one of their little "terror plots," but I refused to participate. Mysteriously, however, the jury never heard this. So, this trial was not about my position on Muslims killing American civilians. It was about my position on Americans killing Muslim civilians, which is that Muslims should defend their lands from foreign invaders—Soviets, Americans, or Martians. This is what I believe. It's what I've always believed, and what I will always believe. . . . The government says that I was obsessed with violence, obsessed with "killing Americans." But, as a Muslim living in these times, I can think of a lie no more ironic.[21]

Mehanna was convicted of conspiracy to provide material support to Al-Qaeda, providing material support to terrorists (and conspiracy to do so), conspiracy to commit murder in a foreign country, conspiracy to make false statements to the FBI, and two counts of making false statements. His case makes crystal clear not only that critiques of foreign policy by Muslims should and will be criminalized, but also that speaking out against state violence is a more serious offense than committing state violence in the first place. In other words, the US should have the freedom to commit state violence while suppressing those who speak out against its crimes.

Manufacturing Terrorism

A particularly horrifying federal terrorism prosecution case was that of Ahmed Abu-Ali, a Palestinian American who went to study at the University of Medina in Saudi Arabia when he was twenty-two years old. On June 8, 2003, after he had been in Saudi Arabia for nine months, the Saudi Mabahith, the country's secret police, arrested him on suspicion of being part of an Al-Qaeda cell. On June 15, 2003, and following, the FBI and Secret Service were allowed to view an interrogation of Abu-Ali through a two-way mirror, based on a request from the US government.[22] Abu-Ali endured forty consecutive nights of torture, including beatings, whipping, and the threat of amputation by the Saudis. The Mabahith allowed the FBI and Secret Service to continue to observe and even direct interrogations. Eventually, Abu-Ali was coerced into signing a pre-written statement admitting his involvement with Al-Qaeda and confessing to supporting terrorist activity from within the United States, including participating in a plot to assassinate then president Bush. He was detained by the Saudi government for two years without charge.

The horror of Abu-Ali's case didn't end there. After his family filed a habeas petition on his behalf and was denied, he was extradited to Virginia to face charges of material support to terrorism, and other terrorism-related charges. Abu-Ali returned to the United States on February 21, 2005, and was made to appear in court the next day. The charges against him included material support for terrorism in addition to a conspiracy to assassinate President Bush.[23] After a trial lasting three weeks, in which the primary evidence relied on by the government was his "voluntary" confession, Abu-Ali was convicted of all the charges against him and sentenced to thirty years in prison. He appealed the decision and his sentence. The government counter-appealed, arguing that his sentence was inadequate. Unfortunately, the district court re-sentenced Abu-Ali to life in prison with no parole. Abu-Ali is being held under Special Administrative Measures (SAMs) at the US Penitentiary, Administrative Maximum Facility, located in Florence, Colorado.

Another federal terrorism case is that of Sami Al-Arian. Sami Al-Arian, a professor at the University of South Florida, had built a life in the United

States and was a prominent Palestinian civil rights leader. Al-Arian was no stranger to surveillance, as the government had been monitoring him since 1993, but it wasn't until 2003 that then attorney general John Ashcroft indicted him on terrorism charges. The case against Al-Arian was based on the allegation that he, along with eight other men, was a supporter of Palestinian Islamic Jihad, a group designated under Clinton as a foreign terrorism group. Cruelly, the government held Al-Arian in pretrial custody for almost three years. Throughout that time he was subjected to abuse. Despite massive amounts of supposedly incriminating evidence, Al-Arian was acquitted on eight of the seventeen charges against him. The jury remained deadlocked on the remaining nine charges. Subsequently, Al-Arian agreed to a plea bargain—forced to plead guilty to providing the Palestinian Islamic Jihad with "contributions, goods, or services."[24] Al-Arian's ordeal did not end there: instead of releasing him from prison and beginning the process of deportation, the government came after him again for refusing to testify in another case criminalizing a Muslim organization. His refusal resulted in another eighteen months in prison for civil contempt charges, after which time the government added criminal contempt charges. Al-Arian was put under house arrest from 2008 to 2014 while awaiting court proceedings for criminal indictment. After those six years, the government dropped all the charges against Al-Arian. He was deported to Turkey on February 4, 2015, saying at the airport, "I came to the United States for freedom, but four decades later, I am leaving to gain my freedom."[25]

Two decades after the War on Terror began, many Muslims feel unsafe attending the mosque or any other Muslim community gatherings out of fear that informants may be present. The goal of informants—to control Muslims' movements, associations, and speech, after which the targeted individuals are criminalized—has continued to be a problem. Among other reasons, entrapments are extremely problematic because the government continues to construct Muslims as inherently prone to violence. As a result, the entrapment defense has never succeeded.

Surveillance

> Under observation, we act less free, which means
> we effectively are less free.
>
> —EDWARD SNOWDEN[26]

Like members of other religious groups, many Muslims consider their mosques and other spaces dedicated to Islam to be sanctuaries—places where they can practice their faith freely. However, these private spaces have been invaded as they have become a focus for government surveillance programs. Post-9/11, national security concerns have been accepted as a legitimately central, overriding interest in the creation of government policy, and counterterrorism perspectives have become deeply enmeshed in our institutions. It is within this context that the belief that Islam itself plays a role in radicalization, and subsequent involvement with terrorist organizations, has been embraced by the American public and institutionalized into domestic policy. The authority and ability of the US government to surveil its citizens in general was greatly expanded in the aftermath of 9/11, and in the years since, large-scale domestic surveillance has been largely normalized. Specifically, this newly broad ability of the state to reach unseen into people's private lives has resulted in a web of government surveillance policies that target Muslim Americans, both in intent and in practice, disrupting community bonds as well as the security and confidence that stem from an individual having a reasonable expectation of freedom from observation. Even for Muslims who escape the government's carceral net, this gaze is ubiquitous.

Shortly after 9/11, the Bush administration capitalized on real and contrived fears of the "new" threat of terrorism to enact what is widely known as the Patriot Act: "Uniting and Strengthening America by Providing Appropriate Tools Required to Intercept and Obstruct Terrorism" (USA PATRIOT) Act. This act gave intelligence agencies sweeping new surveillance powers. For example, the act gave law enforcement the power to use secret wiretapping to obtain intelligence, as well as the power to surveil electronic communications, financial transactions, libraries and bookstores, and more.[27] It further allowed law enforcement and government agents to enter and search homes, offices, and other private spaces without notice. Section 215, called the "Business Records Provision," gave the government the ability to obtain secret court orders requiring companies, including phone companies, to turn over any metadata that may be relevant to international terrorism, counterespionage, or foreign intelligence investigations.[28] Reflecting its focus on counterterrorism, the Patriot Act also includes stiffer penalties for convicted terrorists and removes the statute of limitations for terror-related crimes.

One of the most significant aspects of the Patriot Act is that it expanded the definition of terrorism to include "domestic terrorism" as well as the international variety. The Patriot Act defines domestic terrorism as follows:

"A person engages in domestic terrorism if they do an act 'dangerous to human life' that is a violation of the criminal laws of a state or the United States, if the act appears to be intended to: (i) intimidate or coerce a civilian population; (ii) influence the policy of a government by intimidation or coercion; or (iii) to affect the conduct of a government by mass destruction, assassination or kidnapping."[29] Attempting to preemptively counter the idea that the Patriot Act's provisions were intended to disproportionately target Muslims, it also included a section titled "Sense of Congress Condemning Discrimination Against Arab and Muslim Americans." This section specifies that Arab Americans, Muslim Americans, and Americans from South Asia are entitled to rights equal to those of other Americans, that acts of violence directed at these communities should be condemned and those committed by American citizens punished, and that groups should not be held collectively responsible for the acts of individuals.

It's important to note that the Patriot Act did not create a new crime of domestic terrorism, but rather expanded the existing definition to increase the government's ability to investigate terrorism. Under this new paradigm, the types of conduct within the United States that the government was allowed to investigate under the umbrella of terrorism—as opposed to criminal investigations, which entail many more checks on the discretion of investigators—were greatly expanded. This broad new definition, with its vague language—"appears," "intended"—would reach, for example, the types of protest tactics used by many domestic activist groups, such as so-called radical environmentalists. These organizations could then be investigated for federal terrorism offenses, subject to other Patriot Act provisions such as civil forfeiture, and anyone subsequently charged would face its much stiffer penalties, along with standards of evidence that greatly favor the government.

Although its provisions and definitions are neutral on their face, and some other groups and individuals have been prosecuted under it, it is clear that the Patriot Act targets Muslims, both in intent and implementation. That the drafters of the act felt the need to include an entire section insisting the act is not discriminatory toward specific groups is itself evidence that they realized a common-sense interpretation of the act's intent would assume its primary targets would be Muslim. More importantly, the lion's share of the Patriot Act's impacts in practice have been on Muslim Americans and their communities.

Countering Violent Extremism

In September 2015, a Black Muslim adolescent in Texas named Ahmed Mohamed was arrested after he brought a clock that he built himself to school.[30] One of Mohamed's teachers called the police on him, believing that what he had brought was not a clock but a bomb. As a result, Mohamed was arrested, handcuffed, and taken to the police department. Support for Mohamed was immediate, and he was released on the day he was arrested, but he was still suspended from school the next day. Mohamed drew support from technology companies across the United States, and also received an invitation to the White House from President Obama, including this tweet: "Cool clock, Ahmed. Want to bring it to the White House? We should inspire more kids like you to like science. It's what makes America great."[31] Even though Obama's gesture was seen as a positive one, what it disguised at the same time was the reason Mohamed got targeted in the first place: Countering Violent Extremism (CVE). Considered a soft counterterrorism tactic, CVE has been incredibly successful at normalizing suspicion of Muslims, including youth and children.

Tracing the Trajectory of CVE

Although the United States continued to wage its War on Terror militarily, in Afghanistan and then Iraq, the use of brute force proved unsuccessful in subduing their targets. In fact, by 2005, the war in Iraq had led to an increase of Al-Qaeda activity in the country. In response to the US's failure to contain the threat posed by Al-Qaeda, the Bush administration adopted a new "strategy against violent extremism," which broadened the focus of counterterrorism policy to the perceived problem of "support in the Muslim world for radical Islam."[32] Initially, this strategy was more of an analytical approach than a set of specific policy programs. For example, in 2006 and 2007, respectively, the FBI and the NYPD produced internal reports on radicalization suggesting that certain religious expressions and behaviors, including those that were "subtle and non-criminal,"[33] could be used to identify individuals who were likely to be swayed to extremism.

This notion that increased religiosity makes individuals more susceptible to extremist ideologies, which in turn increases the likelihood that they will engage with terrorism, is unsupported by empirical evidence. Nevertheless, it is the theoretical basis for contemporary approaches to terrorism, allowing consideration of variables such as beard length, that otherwise would have been considered completely irrelevant to criminal investigations. The operationalization of this theory has consequences far beyond the purview of the FBI or NYPD. As Aziz Huq, Assistant Professor of Law at the University of Chicago Law School, has noted, "Investment in 'radicalization' modeling yields dividends in the form of legitimacy for policies of investigation and prosecution bottomed on the state's claim of expertise."[34] In the course of the War on Terror, the theory's conceptual basis linking increased levels of religiosity and propensity to commit acts of violence has facilitated the implementation of policies and tactics that explicitly target Muslim communities.

What was mostly a theoretical approach without much in the way of structure or teeth under the Bush administration was institutionalized into policy by the Obama administration via the program of Countering Violent Extremism (CVE). In his 2011 State of the Union address, months before the official plan for the CVE program would be unveiled, Obama stated, "As extremists try to inspire acts of violence within our borders, we are responding with the strength of our communities, with the respect for the rule of law, and with the conviction that Muslim Americans are part of our American family."[35] This sentiment would prove to be far from genuine, but it and others like it provided rhetorical cover for the extensive surveillance of Muslim American communities that would be ushered in with the introduction of CVE.

About ten months later, in December 2011, the Obama administration announced its plan, releasing a national strategy guide titled "Empowering Local Partners to Prevent Violent Extremism in the United States." On the opening page of the guide is a message from President Obama where he speaks to the threat of violent extremism facing the country. Although he says the government is concerned with different types of extremism, his remarks focus almost exclusively on Al-Qaeda and on enlisting the Muslim American community into the work of Countering Violent Extremism. Take the following example: "Protecting American communities from al-Qa'ida's hateful ideology is not the work of government alone. Communities—especially Muslim American communities whose children, families and neighbors are being targeted for recruitment by al-Qa'ida—are often best positioned to take the lead because they know their communities best. Indeed, Muslim American communities have categorically condemned terrorism, worked with law enforcement to help prevent terrorist attacks, and forged creative programs to protect their sons and daughters from al-Qa'ida's murderous ideology."[36]

By attempting to "empower" Muslims to take action to challenge violent extremism in their own communities, this statement clearly implies that Muslims are more susceptible to extremism. And, in contrast to Obama's State of the Union remarks from earlier in the year, this statement made it clear that Muslim American membership in "the American family" was in fact conditional. Thereafter, the Department of Homeland Security launched pilot programs in Los Angeles, Boston, and Minneapolis, all cities with large Muslim populations.[37]

If it wasn't immediately obvious from the design of the CVE program and the language surrounding its rollout that Muslims were its intended targets, this fact was confirmed when the Obama administration announced a grant awarding $10 million to groups working to counter violent extremism. Thirty-one awards were granted, and as the Brennan Center notes, "of the non-profit groups providing services to communities and individuals, groups focusing on Muslims were awarded approximately 80 percent of funding."[38]

The Obama administration consistently pushed CVE as a community-led program. This was at best a misnomer, considering the fact that government agencies such as Department of Homeland Security (DHS), US Attorney's Offices, the FBI, and state and local law enforcement agencies led, funded, and administered the program.[39] Moreover, to call CVE a community-led program would suggest that the Muslim American community had come to an agreement that extremism was an issue in their community, as opposed to the government telling the community what to do. In reality, the fact that CVE programming heavily targets Muslim Americans has not been seen by the government as a potential source of backlash against the program. Instead, any potential opposition is attributed solely to Al-Qaeda's efforts to "lure Americans to terrorism."[40] When it has been acknowledged, anti-Muslim bias has been presented as a problem insofar as it lends itself to the perception that the US is anti-Muslim or "against Islam," therefore giving fuel to the recruitment efforts of terrorists. Muslim Americans in this equation are supposed to be front-line defenders against violent extremism while at the same time shielding the United States from any negative perceptions regarding differential or negative treatment of their community.

During Obama's years in office, the intent and implementation of CVE had been consistently presented as neutral in terms of who its targets were. In practice, though, it had always been true that "CVE relies on religious, racial, and political indicators, such as mosque attendance, feeling religious discrimination, and frustration with U.S. politics, and uses Muslim-invoking dog whistles like terrorism, radicalization, and extremism to make it clear, but not explicit, who this is really about."[41] While the previous administration studiously avoided acknowledging this explicitly, and claimed that, for example, white supremacists would also be subject to investigation, Muslims have always been the true targets of CVE efforts.

When President Trump came into power, this careful stepping around the true purpose of CVE in order to maintain public perceptions disappeared. Not satisfied with dog whistles, his administration weighed the idea of renaming CVE "Countering Radical Islam" or "Countering Radical Islamic Extremism," to indicate a specific focus on Muslims.[42] The name change never materialized, but the Trump administration did explicitly and aggressively target Muslims via surveillance. For example, in February 2018, a DHS draft report obtained by *Foreign Policy* outlined a plan for long-term surveillance of Sunni immigrants, including those already legally residing in the US and permanent residents.[43] The report also broadly identified certain permanent residents and US citizens as "vulnerable to terrorist narratives." Those considered at risk in the report are Sunni immigrants who are young, male, and from "the Middle East, Africa, and South Asia."[44]

Late in the Trump administration, in 2019, the Countering Violent Extremism program was brought under the umbrella of the newly created Office of Targeted Violence and Terrorism Prevention (TVTP), under the jurisdiction of the Department of Homeland Security (DHS). A special section on the DHS website explains the rationale for the merger: "While the underlying rationales may differ, the threats of targeted violence and terrorism overlap, intersect, and interact with each other. Likewise, there is some alignment in the tools that can be applied to address them. Preventing targeted violence and terrorism focuses on the proactive measures that are aimed at building protective capabilities of individuals and groups. These prevention activities aim to empower communities and individuals to be resilient to violent messaging and recruitment while protecting and championing democratic responsibilities and values."[45]

Although this program appears to give jurisdictions a broader mandate to address "homegrown" threats, it bears noting that if the government had been truly interested in investigating white supremacist violence, there has never been a shortage of mechanisms available. In recognition of this fact, as well as the structure and wording of the grant program, organizations that have long advocated against CVE programs on the basis that they target Muslims believe that TVTP will amount to more or less exactly the same thing. Outlining these concerns, a group of over seventy civil rights and civil liberty organizations sent a letter to Acting DHS

Secretary Chad Wolf in June of 2020. A press release announcing the letter states, "TVTP replicates the agency's Countering Violent Extremism (CVE) program—a failed, anti-Muslim counterterrorism program based on the debunked assumption that certain communities are predisposed towards violence based on their race or faith, and allows privacy and civil liberty violations."[46]

The Panopticon Muslims

The word *panopticon*, which means "all-seeing," was originally coined by British philosopher Jeremy Bentham to describe an ideal condition of perfect surveillance, where the power of the state was constantly visible but its attention never verifiable. For Bentham, this was a positive—he imagined how orderly a society might be whose citizens never knew when they were being observed but were always aware that they might be. More recently, French philosopher Michel Foucault revisited the term in order to talk about discipline and the state. Foucault called the panopticon a "cruel, ingenious cage" and used the term to refer to the effects of constant surveillance on the individual mind—specifically, how the internalization of this sense of being watched is reflected in behavior. Articulating the impact of the panopticon, Foucault wrote, "The major effect of the Panopticon: to induce in the inmate a state of conscious and permanent visibility that assures the automatic functioning of power. So to arrange things that surveillance is permanent in its effect, even if it is discontinuous in its action; that the perfection of power should tend to render its actual exercise unnecessary."[47] In this way, the subjects of surveillance no longer need to be controlled externally, but will control themselves.

If any aspect of the War on Terror has rendered the panopticon's mechanism visible, it is the collaboration with, and leadership in, CVE programs by leading Muslim Americans and Muslim American organizations. For example, one of the organizations that was critical to the development of "community-led" CVE programs was the Muslim Public Affairs Council (MPAC). MPAC's signature CVE-inspired program that promoted surveillance of Muslim communities is called Safe Spaces Initiative (SSI). Developed in 2014, with an updated version released in 2016, the initiative was framed as a community-led alternative to the government's CVE program. The Safe Spaces page on their website states the following: "Safe Spaces is an alternative to both heavy-handed law enforcement tactics and government-led countering violent extremism (CVE) programs.

Rather than accepting the notion that the only way to deal with terrorism is through tactics such as widespread surveillance and the use of informants, Safe Spaces relies on community-led and community-driven programs that communities and mosques will benefit from beyond the national security context."[48]

This statement perfectly elucidates MPAC's faulty and problematic framework—namely, that what was worth disputing in regard to CVE programming was not the premise of Muslims as inherently more prone to violent extremism, but instead how the problem of terrorism should be addressed by Muslims.

Both versions of MPAC's SSI program have included models for addressing violent extremism in Muslim communities. The first, included in their 2014 toolkit, was their Prevention, Intervention, and Ejection (PIE) model; in the 2016 model, it was limited to Prevention and Intervention (PI). The premise of the SSI reflects the governmental shift to violent extremism that focuses on prevention and preemptive measures to combat the terrorist threat. The problem inherent in MPAC's application of this philosophy is that, like the government, the organization treats the Muslim community as if they have special access to information on Muslims who might be prone to committing an act of violence. One of the problems for which Ahmed Shaikh, a California-based Muslim leader, critiques the PI model is the idea that mosque programming should be conducted "with a view towards terrorism prevention." Further, Shaikh notes, in response to the MPAC model's push to use spaces of worship to root out violent extremism, that "places of worship are not extensions of the national security state."[49]

As much as MPAC tried to promote their initiative as being community-led, it was nevertheless rejected by Muslim communities who saw the program as nothing less than a conduit for government surveillance.[50] Although MPAC claimed that their Safe Spaces Initiative was not part of the federal government's CVE programming, the toolkit was hosted on the DHS website. Further, members of the organization were actively involved in the government's CVE programming, including participating in the first-ever White House CVE Summit and appearing in a video endorsing a model of CVE used in Los Angeles for use across the nation. Even though MPAC claims to "vehemently oppose any measure that singles out our community,"[51] their SSI model did just that, for many years.

As one of the few Muslim American organizations invited to the Obama administration's CVE summit in February 2015, MPAC stated, "MPAC came into the summit with the intention to discuss three specific goals:

that US Muslims are treated as partners and not suspects, that government CVE programs are ineffective and community-led initiatives should be supported, and that entrapment and broad surveillance are antithetical to our nation's values and erode the trust of communities."[52] Despite these goals, it was perpetually unclear as to how a surveillance program could be community-led when the impetus for the program in the first place was the constant government narrative that extremism is a problem unique to the Muslim community.

Moreover, by advocating for community-led CVE programming, MPAC's narrative made it easier for the government to narratively distance itself from a surveillance apparatus rooted in anti-Blackness, Islamophobia, racism, and xenophobia. In this way, MPAC set the stage for the government to outsource its work to Muslims who believe surveillance of the community is warranted. The last goal, though addressing the serious problems of entrapment and broad surveillance, treats both as problematic insofar as they contradict MPAC's ideas about the values the United States holds, not because they have devastated the Muslim American community. Thereafter, the president of MPAC, Salam Al-Marayati, is quoted saying, "While we are not responsible for violent extremism, we must take responsibility in leadership to counter violent extremism since the American public is scared from groups like Al Qaeda, ISIS and Boko Haram."[53] But if Muslims aren't responsible for violent extremism, why was Al-Marayati asking them to be responsible for addressing it? Because at this point, the panopticon was doing what it was supposed to do—internalizing surveillance among Muslims.

While the Muslim Public Affairs Council played and continues to play a detrimental role in promoting the surveillance of Muslims, other Muslim organizations, nonprofits, and religious institutions have jumped on the CVE bandwagon as well. Included is Masjid Muhammad, a historical mosque in Washington, DC. In 2016, the mosque applied to a CVE grant program the Department of Homeland Security created and was awarded $531,194. In their application for funding, specifically in the section addressing their technical merit, they wrote, "Throughout the world, counterterrorism experts are increasingly using the internet, specifically social media, to combat violent extremism. However, these efforts are often undertaken without the guidance and influence of reputable and notable American Islamic scholars, educators, psychologists and sociologists. The support, voice, and engagement of American Muslims are critically important to addressing this growing international security issue."[54]

The narrative used here to support the need for CVE measures builds off many problematic tropes, most notably that Muslims have unique knowledge and are privy to the potential acts of violence of other Muslims. Moreover, in the more drawn-out application, the locus of the violent extremism interventions includes mosques and other Muslim spaces, thus cementing the notion that there is a connection between the practice of Islam and one's propensity to commit an act of violence.

Using funding provided by the DHS, Masjid Muhammad developed a counternarrative initiative called "American Muslims Against Terrorism and Extremism" (AMATE) which, in part, involves a poster series where Muslims are condemning terrorism. The main text of one of a series of posters reads, "Dear God, tell them I'm not a terrorist," with subtext stating, "Muslims are an integral part of the American fabric and we oppose extremism in any form."[55] This statement is accompanied by a picture of a young Black Muslim girl wearing hijab and holding a Qur'an, who appears to be no older than ten years old. It's no surprise that the government funds this initiative because rather than dissuading an audience of the idea that Muslims condemn extremism, it actually does the opposite. This happens because of the text, which, instead of diminishing a connection between Islam and extremism, actually *makes* the connection in order for this very connection to be negated. In other words, Muslims have to be able to establish the connection to extremism or terrorism in the first place in order to convince others that they are opposed to it.

In another poster, the main text reads, "I oppose terrorism," and, like the previous one, the subtext states, "Muslims are an integral part of the American fabric and we oppose extremism in any form." Pictured in the image are two Muslims, one with a sign that says, "Terrorism has no religion," and the other with a sign that says, "#IAMMUSLIM." As with the other poster, the connection between Muslims and terrorism is being established, and in this particular poster, the idea that "terrorism has no religion" is completely negated by the fact that the only two people in the picture are Muslim. If the point was to convince people that terrorism really doesn't have a religion, then why would the picture only include Muslims?

In yet another poster, there's a picture of a Muslim woman wearing hijab with her hands toward her face in supplication, with text that says, "Extremism has no role in Islam," and the same subtext: "Muslims are an integral part of the American fabric and we oppose extremism in any form." If extremism doesn't have a role in Islam, then why would this statement even need to be mentioned? Similar to the other posters in the series, the statements that are meant to counter negative associations between Islam/Muslims and extremism/terrorism instead reinforce the connection that is already assumed to exist and that the US government has continued to perpetuate.

Fusion Centers and Joint Terrorism Task Forces

One of the more problematic aspects of the surveillance apparatus post-9/11 has been the sharing of data across federal law enforcement agencies. In 2003, the first National Criminal Intelligence Sharing Plan was issued to pool resources between local, state, and federal entities that were already doing surveillance in order to optimize these efforts—a dramatic shift from the level of coordination pre-9/11.[56] The impetus to further facilitate a sharing environment across agencies came out of the Implementing Recommendations of the 9/11 Commission Act passed by Congress in 2007. The act also established "fusion centers," funded by the Department of Justice (DOJ) and DHS, which serve to aggregate local and state counterterrorism information for the purpose of making the information searchable.[57] Military officials and private sector entities are sometimes included in this information hub.[58] Sharing data allows different intelligence bodies to inappropriately use it for their investigations and prosecutions. Examples include the Drug Enforcement Agency acquiring intelligence tips from the National Security Agency (NSA), and local law enforcement getting information from the FBI. Fusion centers also enable intelligence information to be shared among state, tribal, territorial, and federal agencies.[59]

The Department of Homeland Security's website defines a fusion center as "a collaborative effort of two or more agencies that provide resources, expertise and information to the center with the goal of maximizing their ability to detect, prevent, investigate, and respond to criminal and terrorist activity."[60] There are two types: primary fusion centers and recognized fusion centers. Both provide information sharing and analysis, though the former type is focused on entire states, while the latter focuses on major urban areas.[61]

Fusion centers are important to the National Suspicious Activity Reporting Initiative. Suspicious Activity Reporting (SAR), according to the Bureau of Justice Assistance of the US Department of Justice, is "official documentation of observed behavior reasonably indicative of preoperational planning related to terrorism or other criminal activity."[62]

It's not difficult to understand why there is significant concern around fusion centers and the corresponding SAR. In addition to issues discussed above, fusion centers are problematic in that they allow access to and share information that includes, for example, local criminal records, federal intelligence, unlisted phone numbers, driver's license photographs, and credit reports—all of which is irrelevant to accomplishing any anti-crime or anti-terrorism goals that fusion centers claim to address.[63]

The definition of "suspicious activity" is intentionally vague to allow for broad discretion as to what counts as such, which has led to racial, religious, and political profiling. This is due to weak standards and already-existing biases among those doing the reporting. Indeed, the "suspicious activity" definition is so broad that it "could result in the creation of government databases that store files on individuals who have no link to terrorism or any other criminal activity."[64] Unfortunately, this also means that law enforcement effectively has license to establish contact with anyone reported for suspicious activity regardless of the legitimacy of the report or the fact that there would have been no other reason to contact them.[65]

Joint Terrorism Task Forces (JTTFs) work closely with fusion centers, though the former "are FBI-led partnerships among federal, state, and local agencies whose primary mission is to detect, prevent, and investigate acts of terrorism within their jurisdiction."[66] There are numerous problems with JTTFs, including the fact that they often target noncriminal behaviors. When police officers are assigned to JTTFs, they sometimes face a conundrum because they are supposed to abide by state and local laws, while also being bound to FBI rules. In practice and because of the secrecy surrounding JTTFs, police officers may have no avenue through which to address any concerns they have, which leads to a lack of oversight—already a problem with law enforcement and intelligence agencies.

Given the climate of suspicion of Muslims post-9/11, the JTTFs have played a role in the targeting of Muslims. Almost immediately after 9/11, JTTFs arrested over a thousand Arabs, South Asians, and Muslims of other backgrounds in response to ninety-six thousand tips from the public.[67] In 2011, despite a reform pledge, the FBI's JTTF was reportedly using Islamophobic material to train new members. The training course included the following on Sunni Muslims: "Sunni Muslims have been prolific in spawning numerous and varied fundamentalist extremist terrorist organizations. Sunni core doctrine and end state have remained the same and they continue to strive for Sunni Islamic domination of the world to prove a key Quranic assertion that no system of government or religion on earth can match the Quran's purity and effectiveness for paving the road to God."[68]

Although different tactics of surveillance of Muslims have been outlined in this section, it is nothing new in the United States and has long been a strategy to main power and control of marginalized communities.[69] Since then, surveillance has significantly evolved, and the development of technological tools has made surveillance more intrusive and pervasive. Cultivating fear, as the Bush administration did after the 9/11 attacks, has been critical to implementing increasingly broad surveillance powers and authority. Perhaps most problematic, the post-9/11 surveillance apparatus has enlisted Muslims themselves to carry out the work of the state. In so doing, the War on Terror has allowed for the effective surveillance of Muslim communities through external mechanisms supported by law and policy, and through internal surveillance designed to relieve the state of the burden of policing a community it has defined as a threat to national security.

7.

WE DON'T TORTURE PEOPLE, AND OTHER AMERICAN MYTHS

> *Well, torture, to me, Chuck, is an American citizen on a cell phone making a last call to his four young daughters shortly before he burns to death in the upper levels of the Trade Center in New York City on 9/11.*
>
> —Dick Cheney[1]

> *We tortured some folks.*
>
> —President Barack Obama[2]

"We do not torture," then president George W. Bush asserted at a news conference in November 2005.[3] Bush was responding to reports on the CIA's secret prisons excluding what was unknown to most—namely, that almost immediately after 9/11, members of his administration were using legal and narrative gymnastics to make treatment otherwise considered torture seem much more benign. The pains Bush took to deny torture were not only disingenuous in terms of his execution of the War on Terror, but categorically false. Joseph Pugliese, Professor of Cultural Studies at Macquarie University, notes that the US's history of torture "has been a normative practice in the operation of the US nation-state in terms of its laws and its agents—both legal (for example, army and police) and extralegal (vigilantes and lynching parties)."[4] Post-9/11, the use of torture was distinguishable in two different ways: (1) efforts to legalize the practice, and (2) the almost exclusive use of torture on Muslim prisoners post-9/11 as the primary mode of punishment. The latter bears emphasizing because of the fact that the use of torture on Muslims has often been treated as coincidental, instead of consequential, even in the face of a thriving War on Terror rooted in Islamophobia.

"The object of torture is torture," George Orwell wrote in the book *1984*.[5] Though it was written as fiction for a different political context, Orwell's observation bluntly names the inhumanity at the heart of the US's policy and practice around torture during the War on Terror. This statement, of course, directly contradicts one of the central assumptions built into the US's narrative post-9/11—namely, that torture is an ugly but necessary means of timely extracting intelligence information that is vital to preventing further acts of terror. However, empirical data has shown over and over again that torture does not yield credible results in terms of intelligence, because the person subject to such extremes will say whatever they can to make the pain stop. And in fact, the US, like other oppressive regimes throughout history, has used torture and the threat of torture to coerce prisoners into confessing exactly what they want them to. Lending further support to the statement in Orwell's novel, the torture suffered by the detainees of the War on Terror went on for years, far beyond the time they could reasonably have been expected to have remotely current additional information. Even if it did yield credible results, torture would still be a decidedly inhumane and criminal approach to gathering intelligence. Moreover, the question of effectiveness further illustrates the demonization of Muslims, because it trumps, in these calculations, questions on the legality, ethicality, and morality of torture.

Throughout the War on Terror, torture has been used as a tool of power and control which, especially when accompanied by widespread imagery of damaged bodies, projects a perverse understanding of what winning the war looks like. The impact extends to the survivors' communities, who become indirect targets of the punishment endured by torture victims. A 2001 report by Physicians for Human Rights (PHR) articulates the goal of torture clearly and in a way that resonates in particular with the torture of Muslims post-9/11: "Perpetrators often attempt to justify their acts of torture and ill-treatment by the need to gather information. Such conceptualisations obscure the purpose of torture. . . . The aim of torture is to dehumanise the victim, break his/her will, and at the same time set horrific examples for those who come in contact with the victim. In this way, torture can break or damage the will and coherence of entire communities."[6] The spectacle of torture post-9/11 has caused fear in many Muslim communities.

Particularly important in the context of detention and torture post-9/11 is how quickly the US government led by George W. Bush moved to execute the War on Terror by implementing a complex infrastructure to sanction previously illegal tactics while at the same time mainstreaming a total lack of accountability, allowing the CIA, among others, to act with relative impunity. Within six days of the 9/11 attacks, on September 17, 2001, President George Bush signed a secret Memorandum of Notification authorizing the CIA "to capture and detain a specific category of individuals." This memorandum extended the CIA's powers to detain "specific, named individuals pending the issuance of formal criminal charges," and granted the agency almost exclusive power to decide who to detain, the reason someone would be detained, and for how long they would be detained.[7] This was just the beginning of what would become a global operation in which prisoners were tortured in secret prisons known as black sites.

As the Bush administration moved to set the parameters of this "new war" and remove them from scrutiny, officials behind the scenes were busy providing legal justifications to sanction indefinite detention and torture. A series of memos in early 2002, for example, sought to address the question of whether members of Al-Qaeda and/or the Taliban were entitled to Geneva Convention protections, in order to justify the use of brutal torture techniques against them. Memos from John Yoo to General Counsel Jim Haynes and from Donald Rumsfeld to the Joint Chiefs of Staff both concluded that the Conventions did not apply, although they differed slightly in their reasoning. Yoo's memo on January 9, 2002, included two alternate explanations for why the Geneva Conventions didn't apply: According to Yoo, because Al-Qaeda members were non-state actors existing outside of a state that was party to the Conventions, the Conventions didn't apply to them. On the other hand, even though Afghanistan is a state, he argued that because it was a "failed state," the Conventions did not apply when it came to the Taliban.[8]

On January 25, 2002, then attorney general Alberto Gonzales sent a memo to President Bush that provided legal reasoning as to why the Geneva Conventions on prisoners of war would not apply to Al-Qaeda and the Taliban. In the memo, Gonzales wrote that in his opinion "the new [war on terrorism] paradigm renders obsolete Geneva's strict limitations on questioning of enemy prisoners."[9] Bush's seal of approval on this legal rationale to deny Geneva Convention protections to Al-Qaeda and the Taliban came on February 7, 2002, when he signed a memorandum titled "Humane Treatment of Taliban and al Qaeda Detainees." In the memo, Bush said he accepted the Department of Justice's conclusion that Article 3 of the Geneva Conventions would not apply to either Al-Qaeda or Taliban detainees and that neither qualified as prisoners of war.[10] Deflecting the blame for this exceptional claim of authority to operate outside of international law, the memo stated in part that "our Nation recognizes that this new paradigm—ushered in not by us but by terrorists—requires new thinking in the law of war, but thinking that should nevertheless be consistent with the law of Geneva."[11] In a familiar rhetorical ploy, the Bush administration paid lip service to the standards of the Geneva Conventions while refusing to be bound by them. This disregard for the same rule of law the US expects other countries to adhere to was represented as an inescapable result of the acts of terrorists against an innocent United States.

Casting prisoners beyond the bounds of domestic and international law and standards by deeming them enemy combatants was one of the clearest signals for those so designated that any semblance of justice would be a mirage. Considering how superficial the logics of the War on Terror have always been, the label "unlawful enemy combatant" was enough to create fear, to establish a differential system of justice, and to normalize human rights abuses. This reality gave senior administration officials wide latitude in describing the war that was being fought, regardless of inconsistencies and contradictions. For example, in remarks by Alberto Gonzales in 2004, then counsel to President Bush, to the American Bar Association Standing Committee on Law and National Security, he asserted, "Under these rules, captured enemy combatants, whether soldiers or saboteurs, may be detained for the duration of hostilities. They need not be 'guilty' of anything; they are detained simply by virtue of their status as enemy combatants in war. This detention is not an act of punishment but one of security and military necessity. It serves the important purpose of preventing enemy combatants from continuing their attacks."[12] Gonzales's statement was nonsensical because the capturing and detainment of individuals in the first place was done on the presumption that they were members of Al-Qaeda or the Taliban—which automatically implied guilt. Like other administration positions, logic was embedded on such a shallow level that the obvious intent of dealing with and treating prisoners however they wanted to was often crystal clear.

Though there was some ambiguous idea about the general boundaries of the term *unlawful combatant* right away, it wasn't until years later that a definition was codified, in the Military Commissions Act (MCA) of 2006. According to the MCA, an unlawful enemy combatant is

(i) a person who has engaged in hostilities or who has purposefully and materially supported hostilities against the United States or its co-belligerents who is not a lawful enemy combatant (including a person who is part of the Taliban, al Qaeda, or associated forces); or

(ii) a person who, before, on, or after the date of the enactment of the Military Commissions Act of 2006, has been determined to be an unlawful enemy combatant by a Combatant Status Review Tribunal or another competent tribunal established under the authority of the President or the Secretary of Defense.[13]

In spite of the definition offered, what made the term meaningless, beyond its malleable boundaries, was the fact that it was constructed through the weaponization of law—the same law that was used to sanction it.

Legalizing CIA Torture

In the months and years following the 9/11 attacks, Bush administration officials, who were dissatisfied with the existing parameters on torture as specified in domestic and international law, determined the need to provide legal justification for tactics that went far beyond common understandings of torture. While these tactics were articulated for use on Al-Qaeda and Taliban prisoners, in the context of the larger War on Terror the tactics deemed "legal" were only and specifically used on Muslims. In this way, the real question the Bush administration seemed to want an answer to was how far they could go in torturing Muslims. This, of course, was dependent on how Muslims were constructed, so the legal strategy had to go hand in hand with the narrative strategy. Thus, the constant demonization of War on Terror prisoners and Muslims in general was necessary to quell any public backlash about the use of torture.

Eagerly seeking to legalize torture, the Bush administration drafted the torture memos, as they are informally known very early on in the War on Terror, and put them into practice less than a year after 9/11. In fact, two memos were released as early as August 1, 2002. One was titled "Interrogation of al Qaeda Operative" and specifically addressed what techniques would be legally permissible for use on Abu Zubaydah, the CIA's first detainee. Written by Jay S. Bybee, then assistant attorney general, to John Rizzo, the CIA's then acting general counsel, the memo approved the following techniques: (1) attention grasp, (2) walling, (3) facial hold, (4) facial slap (insult slap), (5) cramped confinement, (6) wall standing, (7) stress positions, (8) sleep deprivation, (9) insects placed in a confinement box, and (10) the waterboard.[14] According to the Senate Intelligence Committee Report on Torture, these techniques were thereafter referred to as the CIA's "enhanced interrogation techniques."[15]

Though this memo was supposed to apply only to Abu Zubaydah, it was used as a basis for the CIA to use "enhanced interrogations" on other prisoners detained at black sites.[16] Over the years the CIA's rendition sites were in operation, prisoners were often shuffled between countries. In fact, two prisoners considered high-value detainees, Ramzi bin Al-Shibh and Abd al-Rahim al-Nashiri (among others), were moved to secret sites at Guantánamo in 2004, only to be transferred out shortly after because of the CIA's fears that these prisoners might obtain legal representation and habeas corpus rights due to a pending Supreme Court decision.[17]

The second memo, dated August 1, 2002, also from Jay Bybee, was titled "Standards of Conduct for Interrogation under 18 U.S.C. §§2340–2340A." This memo, sent to then White House counsel Alberto Gonzales, outlined the scope of treatment permissible under the UN Convention against Torture and Other Cruel, Inhuman, and Degrading Treatment or Punishment, commonly referred to as CAT. According to the memo, which was actually written by John Yoo, an official in the Department of Justice's Office of Legal Counsel, in order for an act to be considered torture, "physical pain amounting to torture must be equivalent in intensity to the pain accompanying serious physical injury, such as organ failure, impairment of bodily function, or even death." It also limited what could be considered mental torture to acts that resulted in "significant psychological harm of significant duration, e.g. lasting for months or even years."[18]

In December 2004, a memo written by Daniel Levin, then acting assistant attorney, was released, superseding the 2002 Yoo/Bybee memo. The memo acknowledged that by the standards set forth in the Torture Statute that an act could be considered torture if it involved "severe physical suffering," but not "severe physical pain."[19] Moreover, the Levin memo upheld the definition of torture as defined in the Convention against Torture. Notably, the Levin memo did not push back on the arguments made in the 2002 memos that considered the president unbeholden to any congressional acts that would criminalize torture.[20] At the same time, however, a footnote in the new memo made it clear that earlier opinions regarding the treatment of detainees "would not be different per the standards set forth in this memorandum."[21]

Levin ended up leaving the Office of Legal Counsel soon after and was replaced by Steven Bradbury, who became the acting assistant attorney general. Bradbury subsequently sent two memos to John Rizzo at the CIA. The first was designed to address whether specific interrogation techniques would be in compliance with the Torture Statute. Bradbury's assessment of the permissibility of different techniques was based on the assumption that the CIA's Office of Medical Services would be performing medical and psychological evaluations to establish that the use of interrogation techniques on a detainee would not result in severe physical or mental pain or suffering. The memo reasoned that with certain limitations, safeguards, and procedures in place, when used individually, techniques such as dietary manipulation, nudity, attention grasp, walling, facial hold, facial slap, abdominal slap, cramped confinement, wall standing, stress positions, water dousing, sleep deprivation, and waterboarding would not violate the Torture Statute. Bradbury's second memo followed up, arguing that even if these techniques were combined, it was unlikely they would constitute severe physical or mental pain or suffering, and asserted that sleep deprivation and dietary manipulation could be used while a detainee was being waterboarded. Other techniques were not allowable for simultaneous use with waterboarding, although they could be used near the same time—for example, within the same day. In another memo, sent nearly three weeks after the initial two, Bradbury confirmed that the CIA's interrogation techniques were not bound by Article 16 of the Convention against Torture because its program was conducted outside of the United States.[22]

In a 2005 debate with torture memo author John Yoo, Notre Dame professor and international human rights scholar Doug Cassel asked Yoo if there was any law that would prevent the president from crushing the testicles of a child. Yoo responded, "No treaty." Then when asked a follow-up question about Congress passing such a law, which he had argued against in the 2002 memo, he answered, "I think it depends on why the President thinks he needs to do that."[23]

Euphemizing Kidnapping: The CIA and Rendition

The term *rendition* has been used by the United States to "describe its practice of transferring terrorist suspects to a foreign government in order to obtain information from them by interrogation methods that are morally and legally unacceptable in this country. In other words, rendition is a mechanism used to outsource torture to other governments."[24] Putting it more bluntly and violently, one official involved in renditions explained that the purpose of rendering suspects to other countries was to enable torture, saying, "We don't kick the [expletive] out of them. We send them to other countries so they can kick the [expletive] out of them."[25]

In order to legally sanction the transfer of members of the Taliban, Al-Qaeda, or other terrorist organizations held captive outside the US to other countries, Assistant Attorney General Jay Bybee wrote a memorandum to General Counsel for the Department of Defense William J. Haynes II on March 13, 2002, addressing the president's authority to transfer prisoners. The memo concluded that "the President has plenary constitutional authority, as the Commander in Chief, to transfer such individuals who are captured and held outside the United States to the control of another country."[26] Because of the president's earlier determination regarding the denial of prisoner-of-war status to Al-Qaeda and Taliban members, Bybee reasoned that Geneva Convention Article 3, which restricted enemy prisoners from being transferred, did not apply. Though the Convention against Torture was also acknowledged per transfer restrictions, Bybee reasoned that it "poses no obstacle to transfer" because "the treaty does not apply extraterritorially."[27]

The CIA's Detention and Interrogation (DI) program ran from 2002 to 2009. Far from operating alone, the United States enlisted a global network of at least fifty-four governments. Moreover, the CIA built and operated at least ten secret prisons. Secrecy and lack of accountability were the hallmarks of this CIA program, leading to gross abuses of power and manifold human rights violations, including torture.[28]

In building its network of black sites in countries such as Thailand, Poland, Romania, Mauritania, Lithuania, and Diego Garcia in the Indian Ocean, the CIA also relied on other countries for interrogation, such as Jordan and Morocco.[29] In addition, rendered suspects were sent to Syria, and in at least one prison facility, detainees were put into coffin-size cells.[30] Other countries complicit in the United States' rendition program included the UK, Canada, Italy, Germany, and Sweden. Assistance from these countries included capturing and surrendering suspects to US custody, providing interrogation and abuse assistance, and allowing CIA flights to make stopovers.[31] Additionally, Guantánamo's Camp Echo was sometimes used to detain prisoners in the extraordinary rendition program until 2004.[32]

The *Washington Post* was the first to reveal the existence of the CIA's clandestine global interrogation network, in a story on November 2, 2005. A few days later, Jose Rodriguez, then the director of the CIA's National Clandestine Service, ordered the destruction of videotapes from 2002 that captured the torture of two detainees. After publicly acknowledging the CIA's secret black sites in 2006, President Bush ordered the transfer of the fourteen remaining CIA detainees into military custody at Guantánamo.[33] A year later, on July 20, 2007, Bush issued an executive order reiterating the ban on torture and cruel and inhuman treatment per US law, while at the same time allowing the CIA to restart interrogation of detainees held in secret and incommunicado. Worse yet, the range of allowable interrogation techniques was kept classified.[34]

Never a Dull Day in the Violence of the CIA

> *As rectilinear bars of blackness, the redactions that*
> *score the state's declassified texts occlude the victim*
> *of state violence even as they neatly geometrize the*
> *disorder of torn flesh and violated bodies. The slabs*
> *of redaction encrypt the disappeared victim of tor-*
> *ture in their textual black coffin. They graphically*
> *exemplify the obliterative violence of law.*
>
> —JOSEPH PUGLIESE[35]

While the United States was aggressively pursuing Al-Qaeda suspects around the world, on March 28, 2002, in a US-Pakistani raid in Faisalabad, Pakistan, they captured Abu Zubaydah, a Palestinian man who was raised in Saudi Arabia.[36] He was the first suspect detained by the CIA post-9/11, on the false premise that he was the chief of operations for Al-Qaeda.[37] Describing his treatment at a black site set up in Thailand, Abu Zubay-dah recalled, "I was told during this period that I was one of the first to receive these interrogation techniques, so no rules applied. It felt like they were experimenting and trying out techniques to be used later on other people."[38] Speaking about Zubaydah's capture, then president Bush said, "The other day, we hauled in a guy named Abu Zubaydah. He's one of the top operatives plotting and planning death and destruction on the United States. He's not plotting and planning anymore. He's where he belongs."[39] Despite these claims, no subsequent evidence was ever given that proved Zubaydah was who Bush said he was. In fact, a report on torture, released in 2014, documented that the CIA had acknowledged in 2006 that Abu Zubaydah was not a member of Al-Qaeda.[40]

Zubaydah was also taken to black sites in Poland, Guantánamo, Morocco, Lithuania, and Afghanistan. According to the Senate Intelligence Com-mittee Report on Torture (addressed below), the CIA rejected having Abu Zubaydah held in US military custody directly out of security concerns and because they would then have to declare him as a prisoner to the Inter-national Committee of the Red Cross. In other words, they wanted him kept where they would be unconstrained by any human rights protections guaranteed by international law.

Abu Zubaydah endured being stripped, subjected to sleep deprivation, slammed into prison walls, and waterboarded eighty-three times, among other torture tactics. In addition, he was rendered seven times throughout the four-and-a-half years he was in secret detention. Because of how CIA interrogators treated Abu Zubaydah and their worry that the treatment might have been illegal, they told their supervisors he should be cremated if he died during an interrogation. If Abu Zubaydah managed to survive, the interrogators wanted reassurances that he would "remain in isolation and incommunicado for the remainder of his life."[41]

In December 2007, the *New York Times* reported on the destruction of the videotapes capturing Abu Zubaydah's torture.[42] The destruction of the videotapes prompted an investigation in 2009 by the Senate Select Committee on Intelligence into the CIA's detention and interrogation program. The report based on the CIA's DI program was complete by 2012, at 6,700 pages. Two years later, after internal battles with the CIA and the approval of the White House, a 525-page executive summary was released to the public. The report found that the CIA misrepresented the number of detainees in its custody, and that at one of the black sites, they kept poor records of the number of detainees and their identities.[43] The report also painfully detailed some of the most outrageous forms of torture, such as rectal feeding and rehydration, confinement in boxes, water dousing, water boarding, stress positions, sleep deprivation, forced nudity, beatings, and threats.[44]

The Torture Report was released in 2014 by the Senate Select Committee on Intelligence and documented 119 prisoners who went through the CIA's program. However, other non-governmental organizational reports on CIA torture estimated that the number was higher—with one report estimating 136 prisoners[45] and another estimating over 200.[46]

An investigation by the Rendition Project and the Bureau of Investigative Journalism produced a report titled *CIA Torture Unredacted* to fill in the details that were missing from the Senate Select Committee on Intelligence (SSCI) Torture Report. According to the Rendition Project's report,

Prisoners were held in complete darkness for months on end, chained to bars in the ceiling and forced to soil themselves. Continual loud music, combined with extended sleep deprivation, dietary manipulation and stress positioning were deployed to reduce men to a completely dependent state. Interrogations involved being severely beaten, and repeatedly slammed against walls. Some prisoners were placed, for hours at a time, in boxes so small they had to crouch.

Others were subjected to water torture which induced vomiting, hypo-thermia and unconsciousness. Men were raped, mutilated, and threat-ened with guns, drills and being buried alive. They were strapped to chairs and to tables. They were hung upside down and beaten. They were chained to the floor in ways making it impossible to stand or sit. They were deliberately, systematically dehumanised in an attempt by interrogators to exert complete control.[47]

Gul Rahman's case of torture was particularly horrifying. Rahman was an Afghan refugee in Pakistan who was taken by the CIA to the Salt Pit, a secret facility in Afghanistan, in October 2002. While detained, Rahman endured brutal torture such as sleep deprivation, forced standing for days, and being drenched with freezing water to the point of hypothermia. He was also kept completely naked, naked from the waist down, or naked except for a diaper. Rahman died nearly a month later on November 20, 2002, of hypothermia while shackled and partially naked. Unfortunately, Rahman's family didn't learn about his death in CIA custody for sixteen years, and they have been unable to receive any information about where his body is, never mind recovering it.[48]

The CIA contracted out the development of "enhanced interrogation techniques" to two Air Force psychologists with no experience in inter-rogation.[49] James Mitchell and Bruce Jessen were paid $1,800 per day to develop interrogation techniques for the prisoners in general and to devise specific tactics for select prisoners. Despite their complete lack of interrogation experience, they participated in interrogating prisoners such as Abu Zubaydah and other "high-value detainees," including Gul Rahman and the KSM, who is considered to be the mastermind of 9/11.[50] Following an unsuccessful attempt at criminal prosecution, the two psy-chologists who devised the enhanced interrogation techniques program were sued in civil court, and a settlement was reached with two prisoners and a deceased prisoner's family. The details of the settlement remain confidential.[51]

In the foreword to the SSCI report, Senator Dianne Feinstein wrote, "Pressure, fear, and expectation of further terrorist plots do not justify, temper, or excuse improper actions taken by individuals or organizations in the name of national security. The major lesson of this report is that regardless of the pressures and the need to act, the Intelligence Commu-nity's actions must always reflect who we are as a nation and adhere to our laws and standards."[52] The lesson that Senator Feinstein didn't mention was that, as with other incidents of massive and egregious state violence in the United States, no one responsible for inflicting the violence from the top down would have to face accountability. This remains true.

The story of one man in particular starkly illustrates the flimsiness of the US's claim to be acting in the necessary pursuit of national security, regardless of whether torture is ever justified. In the earliest days after 9/11 (November of 2001) a man named Ibn al Shaykh Libi was captured by Pakistani authorities and handed over to FBI agents at Bagram. Considering him a high-value detainee, the CIA took him into custody and held him on the USS *Bataan* before sending him on to Egypt, where he was interrogated and tortured by operatives seeking to obtain evidence linking Iraq to the 9/11 attacks.[53] As a result of brutal interrogation, he was forced into confessing that Al-Qaeda and Saddam Hussein were working together and that Iraq was supporting Al-Qaeda with chemical and biological weapons.[54] Libi subsequently recanted his confession, saying, "I gave you what you want[ed] to hear," and, "I want[ed] the torture to stop. I gave you anything you want[ed] to hear."[55] On February 6, 2003, in a speech to the UN focused on making the case for war on Iraq, Secretary of State Colin Powell said, "I can trace the story of a senior terrorist operative telling how Iraq provided training in these weapons to al Qaeda."[56] Libi was the "senior terrorist operative" he was referring to. The US launched the war on Iraq a little over a month after Powell's speech.

The 9/11 Five: Case Studies in Rendition and Torture

> *Yeah, we waterboarded Khalid Sheikh Mohammed.*
> *I'd do it again to save lives.*
> —GEORGE W. BUSH[57]

Khalid Sheikh Mohammed, a Pakistani national who is considered the mastermind of the 9/11 attacks, was captured on March 1, 2003, in Pakistan.[58] Prior to being transferred to Guantánamo Bay in 2006, Mohammed was detained in Pakistan, Afghanistan, Poland, Romania, and Lithuania. His story was one of brutal torture, including being subjected to waterboarding at least 183 times over the course of fifteen sessions. Mohammed was also subjected to other "enhanced interrogation techniques," such as standing sleep deprivation (with his hands at or above head level), nudity, and water dousing. Recalling his experience being tortured, he said, "I was told that they would not allow me to die, but that I would be brought to the verge of death and back again."

Mustafa al-Hawsawi is a Saudi national who was captured along with Khalid Sheikh Mohammed.[59] The US alleges that al-Hawsawi held a senior position in Al-Qaeda in addition to supporting different roles in the group's network. Al-Hawsawi was detained in Pakistan, Afghanistan, Morocco, Romania, Lithuania, and Afghanistan until being transferred to Guantánamo Bay Prison along with the other four men accused of the attacks in September 2006. Like the other four men detained by the CIA, al-Hawsawi was tortured, enduring treatment such as water dousing and rectal exams that left him with chronic hemorrhoids and a host of other health issues.

Ramzi bin Al-Shibh is a Yemeni man who accused by the United States of being a primary coordinator of the 9/11 attacks, as well as continuing to work with Al-Qaeda to coordinate additional attacks throughout the following year.[60] Bin Al-Shibh was captured by Pakistani authorities in Karachi, Pakistan, on September 11, 2002, was delivered into CIA custody, and subsequently was transferred to an unknown third country. Although accounts conflict about the exact timeline and locations, bin Al-Shibh spent four years in secret CIA detention sites in several different countries, where he was undeniably subjected to torture. It is clear from the CIA's own accounts that he was detained in Morocco during late 2002 and early 2003, where he was tortured under interrogation technically conducted by Moroccan authorities, but CIA operatives were present and recorded parts of his interrogation, including "enhanced techniques." From Morocco, bin Al-Shibh was rendered to several other sites, where he suffered additional torture. According to Amnesty International, he spent at least twelve months in a Jordanian facility where he was subject to enhanced interrogation techniques including "electric shocks, long periods of sleep deprivation, forced nakedness, and being made to sit on sticks and bottles."

Eventually, he was rendered again, this time to a detention site in Poland, where he was subjected to "his most intensive period of 'enhanced techniques,'" according to an investigation by the Council of Europe's Commission for Human Rights. This was later corroborated by the US Senate Torture Report, which drew from the CIA's own records. According to the Senate report, the CIA's interrogation plan for bin Al-Shibh included "the use of near-constant interrogations, sensory deprivation, liquid diet, attention grasp, walling, facial hold, facial slap, abdominal slap, cramped confinement, wall standing, stress positions, sleep deprivation beyond 72 hours, and the waterboard. He was also threatened with the use of rectal rehydration." In addition, he experienced psychological torment such as being left shackled naked in the dark or subject to white noise and white light. This went on for four months, after which he was rendered several times to additional CIA secret sites. In 2006, he was sent to Guantánamo Bay Prison, along with other "high-value detainees," and was finally charged, in 2008, with conspiracy related to the events of 9/11.

Walid Mohammed bin Attash was another Yemeni national, captured in a raid in Pakistan on April 29, 2003, and rendered into CIA custody in Afghanistan.[61] He was accused by the US of being a bodyguard and lieutenant of Osama bin Laden and would spend three years at various secret CIA interrogation sites before being transferred to Guantánamo in late 2006 and charged with conspiracy in 2008. While he was detained in Afghanistan, bin Attash was subject to enhanced interrogation techniques including "facial grabs, facial insult slaps, abdominal slaps, walling and water dousing," according to the Senate report on the CIA's torture and rendition program. His own account of what he suffered in CIA custody in Afghanistan includes being left hanging in the dark shackled by his wrists above his head, and being interrogated in positions specifically designed for him, to put pressure on his artificial leg or on the stump where his leg was missing. He also describes horrific living conditions at the hastily constructed facility. Like al-Shibh, bin Attash spent time at the CIA facility in Poland, where he was subject to torture according to the blueprint laid out in al-Shibh's enhanced interrogation plan. In Poland, he was also subjected to degrading techniques designed to mock and offend his religious sensibilities, such as having female interrogators present during sessions while he was stripped naked.

Ammar Al-Baluchi, the nephew of Khalid Sheikh Mohammed, was captured in the same raid and held with bin Attash in Afghanistan, where he was subjected to the same degraded conditions and enhanced interrogation techniques.[62] Not much is known about his whereabouts after he was rendered out of Afghanistan, but he was subjected to egregious torture—so violent that not only have most of the details of his torture been censored, but the black site where he was held was destroyed. Al-Baluchi described his torture by the CIA:

> I wasn't just being suspended to the ceiling; I was naked, starved, dehydrated, cold, hooded, verbally threatened, in pain from the beating, and water drowning as my head smashed by hitting against the wall for dozens and dozens of times. My ears were exploding from

the blasting harsh music, which is still stuck in my head. Sleep deprived for weeks, I was shaking and trembling. My legs barely supported my weight as my hands were pulled even higher above my head after I complained that the handcuffs were so tight as if cutting through my wrists. Then my legs start to swell as a result of long suspension; [I] started screaming. And then the doctor comes. The doctor came with a tape measure, wrapped it around my leg and to my utmost shock, the doctor told the interrogators, no, that wasn't enough. My leg should get more swollen.[63]

Al-Baluchi was detained in a secret prison for three years before being transferred out of the CIA program and into military custody at Guantánamo Bay Prison in 2006, with the other four high-value detainees associated with the 9/11 attacks. In 2008, the men were formally charged with conspiracy related to that event. As of the time of this writing, they are still awaiting trial, although a date was recently set: August 2021. After so many years of delay, it's unclear if the trial will move forward as planned this time around.[64] All five are still being held at Guantánamo.

Guantánamo Bay

> *Prison is the only place where power is manifested in its naked state, in its most excessive form, and where it is justified as moral force.*
>
> —MICHEL FOUCAULT[65]

Shortly after the 9/11 attacks, the US war on Afghanistan made it Americans' first battlefield in the War on Terror. Afghanistan was also the "birthplace" of the US's detention and interrogation practices post-9/11.[66] When issues of capacity were raised by commanders in Afghanistan, the administration began searching for an alternative location to house prisoners. Guantánamo Bay, Cuba, was among the options and one that was attractive, considering the belief that detainees housed at the base would not be entitled to habeas rights.

On January 11, 2002, Guantánamo Bay Prison was opened to detain Al-Qaeda and Taliban suspects. Most of the prisoners who ended up at Guantánamo were captured in Pakistan or Afghanistan.[67] The culture of torture that was cultivated by the US government and practiced at Guantánamo was one of the reasons the prison gained notoriety, even in its early days of operation. Early on, visitors, journalists, and members of Congress who traveled to Guantánamo were made to go through Customs—a procedure designed to position Guantánamo as outside the United States both physically and, in order to deny detainees their rights, legally and symbolically.[68]

Before Guantánamo Bay Prison was even open for operation, in December 2001 the Office of the Secretary of Defense reached out to the Joint Personnel Recovery Agency (JPRA), the agency that oversees military Survival Evasion Resistance and Escape (SERE) training, for its use at the prison. The goal of SERE training is to teach American soldiers how to resist abusive interrogation techniques if they are detained by an enemy who disregards and violates the Geneva Conventions. Two months later, the JPRA provided training materials to Guantánamo interrogators; by the summer of 2002, psychologists working with interrogators at Guantánamo received materials on SERE tactics, including mock interrogation techniques. In the fall of 2002, Guantánamo personnel also received training by the JPRA, which included techniques utilized by SERE schools.

By the summer of 2002, the Department of Defense was pushing for more leeway in the interrogation of prisoners at Guantánamo beyond the Army Field Manual.[69] Later that fall, the SERE techniques that had been approved for use on Abu Zubaydah in CIA custody were also being used at Guantánamo Bay. The "success" of the CIA's program and its use of SERE techniques provided another rationale for their use at Guantánamo. The SERE techniques that were utilized included, for example, hooding, stress positions, sleep deprivation, temperature extremes, and psychological games to cause humiliation.

In September 2002, a group of senior administration officials including David Addington, who was the vice president's counsel, and Attorney General Alberto Gonzales traveled to Guantánamo. Major General Michael Dunlavey was selected by Secretary of Defense Donald Rumsfeld to command the new task force JTF-170 to run military interrogations at Guantánamo referred to as "policy constraints." Among the prisoners whose interrogation was discussed was Mohamed Al-Qahtani—the only person detained at Guantanamo whose abuse was defined as torture by a senior US government official.

A month later, in October 2002, Major General Dunlavey sent a memo to his superiors at US Southern Command (SOUTHCOM) asking for approval to use harsh interrogation techniques. The memo included a legal opinion written by Lt. Col. Diane Beaver, who argued that "enhanced interrogation techniques" would not violate the Torture Statute because "there is a legitimate governmental objective in obtaining the information necessary . . . for the protection of the national security of the United States, its citizens, and allies. Furthermore, these methods would not be used for the 'very malicious and sadistic purpose of causing harm.'"[70]

Lt. Col. Beaver's memo included three categories of interrogation to be used in successive and progressive order:[71]

a) Category I techniques:
   (1) Yelling at the detainee (not directly in his ear or to the level that it would cause physical pain or hearing problems).
   (2) Techniques of deception.
      (a) Multiple interrogator techniques.
      (b) Interrogator identity. The interviewer may identify himself as a citizen of a foreign nation or as an interrogator from a country with a reputation for harsh treatment of detainees.

b) Category II techniques:
   (1) The use of stress positions (like standing), for a maximum of four hours.
   (2) The use of falsified documents or reports.
   (3) Use of the isolation facility for up to 30 days.
   (4) Interrogating the detainee in an environment other than the standard interrogation booth.
   (5) Deprivation of light and auditory stimuli.
   (6) The detainee may also have a hood placed over his head during transportation and questioning. The hood should not restrict breathing in any way and the detainee should be under direct observation when hooded.
   (7) The use of 20-hour interrogation.
   (8) Removal of all comfort items (including religious items).
   (9) Switching the detainee from xxx to MREs.
   (10) Removal of clothing.
   (11) Forced grooming (shaving of facial hair, etc.).
   (12) Using detainees' individual phobias (such as fear of dogs) to induce stress.

c) Category III techniques:

    (1) The use of scenarios designed to convince the detainee that death or severely painful consequences are imminent for him and/or his family.

    (2) Exposure to cold weather or water (with appropriate medical monitoring).

    (3) Use of a wet towel and dripping water to induce the misperception of suffocation.

    (4) The use of mild physical non-injurious contact such as grabbing, poking in the chest with finger, and light pushing.

When the list of techniques reached Defense Secretary Donald Rumsfeld for approval, he was advised by General Counsel Haynes that all of the techniques were legal, although he recommended against the use of waterboarding and mock executions. Rumsfeld approved the use of Categories I and II, in addition to "mild, non-injurious physical contact" techniques from Category III. On the first page of the memo, Rumsfeld added a note that said, "I stand for 8–10 hours a day. Why is standing limited to 4 hours?"[72]

In the course of interrogation, as a 2006 report by the Center for Constitutional Rights found, Guantánamo prisoners were

- held in solitary confinement for periods exceeding a year;
- deprived of sleep for days and weeks and, in at least one case, months;
- exposed to prolonged temperature extremes;
- beaten;
- threatened with transfer to a foreign country, for torture;
- tortured in foreign countries or at U.S. military bases abroad before transfer to Guantánamo;
- sexually harassed and raped or threatened with rape;
- deprived of medical treatment for serious conditions, or allowed treatment only on the condition that they "cooperate" with interrogators; and
- routinely "short-shackled" (wrists and ankles bound together and to the floor) for hours and even days during interrogations.[73]

Other forms of psychological and physical torture at Guantánamo included the "going home" technique, which was designed to weaken prisoner resistance. This technique involved telling a detainee that he was going home; sending him to Camp 4, which was more relaxed—for example, with communal living; providing him with civilian clothes; then after a few days taking him to solitary confinement. This obviously had an impact on the prisoner's psychology especially as it made him feel he was essentially starting again from scratch. Another technique of psychological torture was called "frequent flyer," designed to punish the detainee or make him more compliant. This entailed taking a prisoner from one cell to another within the span of two to three hours for a period of time that would last between two to four weeks. JAG Defense Counsel Major David Frakt, whose juvenile client Mohamed Jawad had been subject to the frequent-flyer program, expressed surprise saying, "What I found was that he had been moved back and forth from one cell to another 112 times in a fourteen-day period. So, on average, less than every three hours, like 24–7. And I'm like, what is this exactly?"[74]

While Guantánamo was primarily a detention site for adult Muslim males, twenty-one juveniles have been held behind its bars. Omar Khadr, whose story follows in the next chapter, was age fifteen when he first arrived at the prison. During one of the interrogation sessions he was subjected to, while crying, Khadr lamented, "I lost my eyes, my feet, everything . . ." To this, the interrogator responded, "No, you still have your eyes and your feet are still at the end of your legs, you know. Look, I want you to take a few minutes. . . . I want you to get yourself together . . . relax a bit, have a bit to eat and we'll start again."[75] This example highlights a particular cruelty that has been inflicted on Muslim prisoners: in this case, a young boy who was clearly struggling mentally is asked to calm down and take a break in spite of knowing that what awaits him is further interrogation. In other words, the prisoner is asked to conform to a state of existence that the interrogator can work with, even though that means returning to a state of relative normalcy and a disposition that could have only been possible before his detention and torture. The impact of this trauma on Khadr as it was manifested in this instance of interrogation was the "violent truncat[ion of his] sensorium so that it no longer works to connect all the parts of his body to his sense of self as unified embodied subject in the world."[76] If Khadr's experience at Guantánamo exemplifies anything, it's the loss of self that is encouraged so that prisoners see themselves as the government does: as nameless, faceless individuals whose corporeal forms are only allowed to exist as means to the US's national security ends.

Abu Ghraib

> *The refusal to acknowledge the face of the victim*
> *guarantees their reduction to a subhuman status; in*
> *the denial of the face of the other is inscribed the*
> *violation and destruction of every ethical relation.*
> —Joseph Pugliese[77]

> *Abu Ghraib is the fully predictable image of what a*
> *torture culture looks like. Abu Ghraib is not a few*
> *bad apples—it is the apple tree.*
> —David Luban[78]

Abu Ghraib Prison was notorious for being brutal under Iraq's former president Saddam Hussein. This did not stop the United States from taking control of and reopening the prison in August 2003, five months after the US invasion of Iraq and the collapse of Hussein's government. What was previously used as a torture chamber governed by Saddam became a torture chamber governed by the US.

In September 2003, Guantánamo commander Major General Geoffrey Miller traveled to Iraq, and specifically to Abu Ghraib Prison. As an interrogation enthusiast who advocated for techniques such as twenty-hour interrogations, hooding, and sensory deprivation, Miller was sent to Iraq to convince the Combined Joint Task Force there to adopt the harsh techniques outlined in Rumsfeld's April 2003 memo.[79] Rumsfeld's memo, as mentioned earlier, included interrogation techniques such as dietary manipulation, environmental manipulation, and sleep adjustment. To this end, Miller reportedly told US military prison administrators in Iraq that they should "GTMO-ize" their detention facilities.[80] Importantly, this meant that interrogation techniques used on prisoners cast outside the bounds of Geneva Convention protections would now be used in the context of the US war on Iraq, where captured Iraqis were in fact entitled to Geneva Convention rights.[81] More than just exposing the brutality of the techniques on the global stage, the torture at Abu Ghraib demonstrated how little the US actually cared about the legality of interrogation techniques, in addition to how malleable legality proved to be. Although Guantánamo was seen as the gateway to the abuse and torture at Abu Ghraib, University of Wisconsin professor Alfred McCoy argues that the photos from Abu Ghraib and subsequent investigations "offer telltale signs that the CIA was both the lead agency at Abu Ghraib and the source of systematic tortures practiced in Guantánamo, Afghanistan, and Iraq."[82]

After Miller's visit, on September 14, 2003, the highest-ranking US general in Iraq, Lieutenant Ricardo Sanchez, issued the first CJTF-7 Standard Operating Procedures authorizing twenty-nine interrogation techniques, twelve of which went beyond the boundaries of the Army Field Manual and four of which risked falling outside of the Geneva Conventions.[83] The memo was in service of Sanchez's explicitly articulated goals to "create fear, disorient detainees and capture shock."[84]

The memo acknowledged that although the techniques proposed were based on those used in Guantánamo Bay, they were "modified for applicability to a theater of war in which the Geneva conventions apply."[85] Techniques authorized by this memo included the presence of dogs—a tactic designed to especially capitalize on Arab fears of dogs—sleep management, yelling, playing loud music, and controlling lighting in order to cause disorientation and prolong shock, making detainees assume stress positions, and false flags to trick the detainee into believing that their interrogator is not from the US.[86]

US Central Command made Sanchez rescind the September memo, and on October 12, 2003, he issued a new policy. A 2008 report from the Committee of Armed Services titled *Inquiry into the Treatment of Detainees in U.S. Custody* stated that although some of the harsh techniques had been removed in the subsequent policy, it "contained ambiguities with respect to certain techniques, such as the use of dogs in interrogations, and led to confusion about which techniques were permitted."[87]

By October 2003, about seven thousand Iraqis had been detained at Abu Ghraib, about 90 percent of whom were either mistakenly arrested and/or did not have any intelligence value.[88] The photographs that were released in April 2004 revealed the egregious torture that had been inflicted on detainees. The abuses captured included forced nudity, simulated fellatio, forced masturbation, being threatened with rape, leashing prisoners, pouring phosphoric liquid on detainees, beatings with broom handles and chairs, and blows to the head.

Among the prisoners detained at Abu Ghraib were some referred to as "ghost prisoners." Ghost prisoners were those held by the CIA in secret, whose identities were not recorded despite the fact that prisoner registrations are required by the Geneva Conventions. The reasons for prisoners' detentions were often unknown as well. One of the prisoners concealed by the CIA at Abu Ghraib was Manadel Al-Jamadi. Al-Jamadi was in military custody before he was brought to Abu Ghraib from the Baghdad airport, where the CIA and Navy SEALs allegedly beat him and doused him with cold water. He was subsequently taken to a shower stall, where a sandbag was put over his head, his hands cuffed behind his back, and his arms chained to a barred window about five feet off the ground in a posture known as the "Palestinian hanging"—all while he was being interrogated by the CIA.[89] Al-Jamadi died less than an hour later, bleeding profusely and exhibiting severe bruising on his face.[90] His autopsy recorded his death as a homicide that happened as the result of "blunt force trauma" and "asphyxiation."[91] Responding to Al-Jamadi's death, David Martine, then chief of the CIA's Detention Elicitation Cell in Iraq, made the decision to ice Al-Jamadi's body while military personnel and the CIA colluded to hide his death and smuggle the body out of the prison by taping an IV to the frozen corpse. Martine later said he referred to Al-Jamadi's corpse as "Bernie," a cultural reference to the movie *Weekend at Bernie's* in which friends of a deceased man march around with his body.[92] Among the Abu Ghraib photos released in April 2004 were those of Army Sergeant Charles A. Graner Jr. and Specialist Sabrina Harman with a thumbs-up and a smile next to Al-Jamadi's corpse, which was wrapped in ice with his bruised and puffy face exposed.[93]

A May 2004 report on the abuses at Abu Ghraib, known as the Taguba Report for its primary author, Major General Antonio Taguba, stated as fact that "between October and December 2003, at the Abu Ghraib Confinement Facility (BCCF), numerous incidents of sadistic, blatant, and wanton criminal abuses were inflicted on several detainees. This systemic and illegal abuse of detainees was intentionally perpetrated by several members of the military police guard force (372nd Military Police Company, 320th Military Police Battalion, 800th MP Brigade), in Tier (section) 1-A of the Abu Ghraib Prison (BCCF)."[94] The techniques of intentional abuse listed in the report include the following:

(1) Punching, slapping, and kicking detainees; jumping on their naked feet;

(2) Videotaping and photographing naked male and female detainees;

(3) Forcibly arranging detainees in various sexually explicit positions for photographing;

(4) Forcing detainees to remove their clothing and keeping them naked for several days at a time;

   (5)   Forcing naked male detainees to wear women's underwear;

   (6)   Forcing groups of male detainees to masturbate themselves while being photographed and videotaped;

   (7)   Arranging naked male detainees in a pile and then jumping on them;

   (8)   Positioning a naked detainee on an MRE box, with a sandbag on his head, and attaching wires to his fingers, toes, and penis to simulate electric torture;

   (9)   Writing "I am a Rapest" [sic] on the leg of a detainee alleged to have forcibly raped a 15-year old fellow detainee, and then photographing him naked;

  (10)   Placing a dog chain or strap around a naked detainee's neck and having a female soldier pose for a picture;

  (11)   A male MP guard having sex with a female detainee;

  (12)   Using military working dogs (without muzzles) to intimidate and frighten detainees, and in at least one case biting and severely injuring a detainee;

  (13)   Taking photographs of dead Iraqi detainees.[95]

One of the Iraqi prisoners who suffered from religious abuse gave testimony on his experience, saying, "They handcuffed me and hung me to the bed. They ordered me to curse Islam and because they started to hit my broken leg, I cursed my religion. They ordered me to thank Jesus that I'm alive. And I did what they ordered me. This is against my belief. They left me hang from the bed and after a little while I lost consciousness. When I woke up, I found myself still hang[ing] between the bed and the floor."[96]

On April 30, 2004, CBS aired photos of US soldiers abusing detainees at Abu Ghraib Prison. The horrific abuses photographed included a man standing on a box, covered, with wires attached to his hand and his arms extended. Other photos included detainees piled up naked on top of each other to form a human pyramid, while still others showed US soldiers leaning next to the bodies of dead Iraqis and smiling. The pictures also show detainees being forced to simulate oral sex, and detainees being threatened with dogs.

One of the compounding factors of violence of the Abu Ghraib photos was the fact that the Iraqis who were tortured already existed in a country being destroyed and occupied by their captors. Iraqi bodies could therefore be treated as "trophies of imperial conquest,"[97] with the pictures signifying "the deployment and enactment of absolute U.S. imperial power on the bodies of the Arab prisoners."[98]

Since their release, the Abu Ghraib photos have been viewed millions of times by audiences across the world. Many of them are reprinted in books, stored on websites, and depicted in artwork, thus turning audiences into bystanders of the prisoners' humiliation. The reproduction of the photos has also reinforced the spectacle of violence perpetrated against Muslims, turning it into a commodity for consumption—either to prove their inhumanity or to make visible their pain as proof that they have suffered.

Fundamental power dynamics are embedded in the relationship between the viewer of the photographs and the victim in the picture. Scholar Joseph Pugliese writes poignantly, "The victim that is being photographed is rarely allowed to stare back into the camera and, by implication, agentically address the voyeuristic gaze of the viewer; rather, the victim's gaze is entirely occluded by hoods or, alternatively, she or he is compelled to be photographed with an averted look that vitiates the power (a)symmetrically to return the gaze and thereby disrupt an unequal relation of visual power."[99] This dynamic is, unfortunately, perpetuated by the static images of the Iraqi bodies captured on film and reproduced, signifying until the current time the annihilation of justice past or present.

While complaints about torture had become widespread even in the early days of the US's War on Terror, the pictures from Abu Ghraib forced the US government to acknowledge the abuse instead of brushing it off as "allegations."[100] However, even when the US government acknowledged its own role in the torture, official responses sought to downplay the fact that the policy of torture came from the top and that torture was indeed systematic. For example, Secretary of Defense Donald Rumsfeld, who played a direct role in sanctioning brutal interrogation techniques, said that Abu Ghraib was "an exceptional, isolated" case.[101] Bush doubled down on the torture as isolated, saying he condemned the "disgraceful conduct by a few American troops who dishonored our country and disregarded our values."[102] In other words, torture came from the bottom up, and removing those at the bottom would obviously solve the problem. These performances of concern from the Bush administration only made them seem more disingenuous when considering the fact that while condemning torture at Abu Ghraib, they were conducting the CIA's interrogation program.

In 2006, Iraqis took control of Abu Ghraib Prison, and in 2014, they closed it. Eleven soldiers were convicted of abusing the prisoners at Abu Ghraib, yet no one at the top of the Bush administration's leadership received any punishment. Meanwhile, Abu Ghraib is still remembered as a torture chamber, first by Saddam Hussein and then by the Americans.

Little Gitmo

The detention of Muslim prisoners in the War on Terror has extended beyond Guantánamo and CIA black sites. For example, there are two prisons called communications management units (CMUs), one in Terre Haute, Indiana, and the other in Marion, Illinois, the former having opened in 2006, and the latter in 2008, without the requirement of public notice.[103] The Terre Haute CMU was repurposed from being a death row facility and was used to house inmates linked to "terrorist-related activity."[104] This was code for Muslim prisoners. The two prisons, nicknamed "Little Guantánamo" or "Guantánamo North," have populations that are over 60 percent Muslim, even though Muslims only account for 6 percent of the federal prison system. Rather than addressing the problem of obvious racial and religious profiling, "balancers," including environmental activists, sexual predators, and bank robbers, were moved into these prison populations.

The two CMUs operate under extremely harsh conditions, which include only thirty minutes a week of phone time, divided into two fifteen-minute segments, compared to three hundred minutes a month for many maximum-security prisoners, and less than ten hours of visitation a month from prisoners' immediate families, compared to up to forty-nine hours a month for those housed among the general prison population. To make matters worse, familial visits are no-contact and conducted through Plexi-glass, all while conversations between the prisoner and the family are monitored and recorded.[105]

The Law Protects Torturers, Not the Tortured

Muslim prisoners have had little recourse for the abuse they have experienced throughout the US's War on Terror, given the secrecy and the argument of national security that have effectively denied them access to any semblance of rights. In fact, with the exception of two civil suits against the CIA contractors who developed the agency's interrogation program, every case filed by detainees against the US has been dismissed.[106] In contrast, though far from sufficient, the UK awarded funds in the amount of £16 million to seventeen former detainees as part of a settlement agreement. Canada paid over $10 million to former Guantánamo child prisoner Omar Khadr and $10 million to rendition survivor Maher Arar. The European Court of Human Rights has also required reparation payments for two victims of the CIA's extraordinary rendition program, Abu Zubaydah and Abd al-Rahim al-Nashiri.[107]

Those who have sought accountability from the agents involved in abuses committed against them have relied on the Bivens doctrine, a measure created "by federal courts to provide a mechanism for civil redress for constitutional violations in the absence of a statutory remedy."[108] Two notable cases involve torture survivors who filed lawsuits against the US government: *El-Masri v. United States* and *Arar v. Ashcroft.*

El-Masri was a German citizen who was kidnapped in Macedonia and then transferred to the infamous Salt Pit facility in Afghanistan. He endured brutal torture and interrogation, only for the CIA to later admit that El-Masri was innocent. Because of everything El-Masri endured, he filed a lawsuit naming then CIA director George Tenet, ten unidentified CIA employees, and several others. Even though El-Masri's claim was against individual agents and not the US government, the US government was allowed to enter into the proceedings to make sure US interests were protected.[109] El-Masri's case was dismissed on the basis that his claims might expose classified information. This decision by the district court stated the following: "In the instant case, this question is easily answered in the negative. To succeed on his claims, El-Masri would have to prove that he was abducted, detained, and subjected to cruel and degrading treatment, all as part of the United States' extraordinary rendition program. As noted above, any answer to the complaint by the defendants risks the disclosure of specific details about the rendition program. These threshold answers alone would reveal considerable details about the CIA's highly classified overseas programs and operations."[110]

Denying El-Masri access to justice on the basis of this logic reveals how essentially illusory the promise of remedy is for those abused and detained unjustly in the United States' post-9/11 framework. In 2012, the European Court of Human Rights declared that Macedonia had violated the European Convention of Human Rights in their treatment of El-Masri, and he was awarded compensation in the amount of $74,000. Years later, in 2018, Macedonia formally apologized to El-Masri for detaining and torturing him.

Maher Arar was another victim of the extraordinary rendition program. A dual citizen of Canada and Syria, Arar was detained by the United States in New York while he was en route from a family vacation in Tunisia. Arar was subsequently rendered to Jordan and then to Syria. During his time in detention, he was brutally tortured. Thereafter, Arar filed a lawsuit naming then attorney general John Ashcroft, FBI director Robert Mueller, and other federal officials in pursuit of compensatory damages and declaratory relief.[111] Like El-Masri's case, Arar's was dismissed, denying his constitutional claims while also ruling that "Arar lacked standing to seek declaratory relief and there was no viable cause of action under the Torture Victim Protection Act."[112] Because Canada had provided the United States false information that triggered Arar's detention and torture, after a public inquiry into his case, he was awarded $10 million in compensation from the Canadian government.

Although other countries have since acknowledged and attempted to compensate for their culpability in the torture that El-Masri and Arar suffered, to this day, neither man has received any official acknowledgment of wrongdoing from the United States. The US's refusal to acknowledge and remedy harm is emblematic of its conduct in the War on Terror in general. More problematic still, rather than rendering justice to Arar and El-Masri, the US Constitution served as an obstacle to justice and a tool for promoting government impunity.[113] The fact that no one was held accountable in either case not only legitimized illegal conduct, but also promoted the idea that none of the perpetrators engaged in conduct that was illegal and wrong. This analysis underscores a key feature of the War on Terror and indeed much of the history of the legal system in the United States—namely, that the law can be and often is used as a tool of oppression.

The End of Torture?

On January 22, 2009, Obama signed an executive order on detention and interrogation policy requiring Guantánamo Bay Prison to be closed, and in the meantime for conditions at the prison to comply with Article 3 of the Geneva Convention.[114] The order also prohibited any government agency—military, CIA, FBI—from using any interrogation techniques outside the US Army Field Manual. In addition to ordering the closure of black sites and preventing their use permanently, this executive order barred any dependence on Department of Justice or other legal advice concerning interrogation that was issued between September 11, 2001, and January 20, 2009. Despite the order containing some positive developments, it still allowed the CIA to render suspects to third-party countries, albeit with the claim that the administration would seek assurances that individuals rendered wouldn't face torture and cruel treatment.

Before Obama became president, he made it clear that prosecution was off the table, saying with regard to torture that "we need to look forward as opposed to looking backwards."[115] At the same time, he provided a shield for future acts of torture by relying on a description of work ethic as opposed to involvement in abuse: "And part of my job is to make sure that, for example, at the CIA, you've got extraordinarily talented people who are working very hard to keep Americans safe. I don't want them to suddenly feel like they've got to spend all their time looking over their shoulders."[116] What Obama's decision not to prosecute anyone involved in the torture apparatus made clear was that there would not be accountability for the past or the future. That remained true throughout and until the end of Obama's presidency. At the same time, the Obama administration blocked all detainee civil suits by invoking the State Secrets Doctrine.[117] In the case of a Tunisian named Redha al-Najar, who was disappeared and tortured by the CIA, including hooding and sleep deprivation facilitated by interrogation at all hours of the day, rather than investigating al-Najar's allegations of torture, the Obama administration worked to bar his access to the courts and to prevent him from getting counsel.[118]

In response to the release of the Torture Report, Obama said, "One of the strengths that makes America exceptional is our willingness to openly confront our past, face our imperfections."[119] That was far from the truth, especially as the White House prevented the Senate Select Committee from accessing nearly ten thousand documents about the CIA's secret detention program.[120] With respect to the report, the Obama administration refused to declassify it in its entirety, thus making his claims of openness and transparency even more hypocritical.

Obama publicly maintained the façade that he objected to torture, even though under his leadership, torture tactics were still being used. One of the reasons for this was that the Army Field Manual, which he reinstituted as the standard for interrogation, actually includes tactics that could amount to torture. Under Obama, not only was solitary confinement used routinely, but prisoners on hunger strikes were also force-fed.[121]

Obama's successor, Donald Trump, was an outright torture enthusiast, and during the early days of his administration, he had planned to release an executive order titled "Detention and Interrogation of Enemy Combatants." The draft of the order that was published by the *Washington Post* showed that Trump planned to revoke President Obama's executive orders requiring the humane treatment of prisoners and the closure of Guantánamo Bay Prison. In 2018, President Trump signed an executive order titled "Protecting America through Lawful Detention of Terrorists." The purpose of this executive order was to keep Guantánamo Bay Prison open—which he announced at his State of the Union address. In his speech, Trump stated, "When necessary, we must be able to detain and question them. But we must be clear: Terrorists are not merely criminals. They are unlawful enemy combatants. And when captured overseas, they should be treated like the terrorists they are." His statement not only reiterated the notion that terrorism is a uniquely violent crime but also utilized the circular argument that a terrorist is a terrorist because they are a terrorist.[122] While the Trump administration didn't establish an official policy on interrogations or torture, there have been numerous accounts of abuse, including the practice of neglecting hunger strikers to the point of their almost dying. For example, in October 2017, Yemeni prisoner Khalid Qassim, who had then been detained at Guantánamo for fifteen years, wrote in an op-ed, "I started hunger strike because I was so frustrated, so depressed—I have been locked up here so far from my family for 15 years. I have never been charged with a crime and I have never been allowed to prove my innocence. Yet I am still here. And now Donald Trump says that none of us—the 26 'forever' prisoners who have apparently committed no crime, but merit no trial—will ever leave here so long as he is in charge."[123]

Another prisoner, seventy-year-old Saifullah Paracha, who complained about the mistreatment of his fellow prisoners on hunger strike (Paracha has never been able to hunger-strike because of his age), was, as a result, punished by being sent to solitary confinement. He told his lawyer, "We are getting collective punishment because of the hunger strike. . . . It felt like when we were brought in to Gitmo. Not since the beginning days of Guantanamo has it been like this. It's a hell."[124]

Conclusion

> Interrogation was another torture. . . . If you're not
> cooperating, they will put you in a long box, like a
> coffin, and they will close the door on you. There is
> no oxygen. It's completely closed. Stones are put on
> your top. You feel as if you're dying.
> —GHAIRAT BAHEER, CIA TORTURE VICTIM[125]

In 2006, Bush delivered a speech on terrorism and addressed CIA torture, saying, "This program has been and remains one of the most vital tools in our war against the terrorists. It is invaluable to America and to our allies."[126] Regardless of his confidence or projected confidence in the program, the CIA's DI program was as egregious as it was illegal. Nevertheless, no one in higher levels of government has been held accountable to this day, and we can assume, based on the US's practice of torture over the course of its history, that no one ever will be.

Torture is one of the most egregious forms of state violence practiced in the course of the War on Terror and one that has been visible and invisible at the same time. In an interview conducted shortly after the release of the pictures of Iraqis tortured at Abu Ghraib, a journalist asked Bush whether torture was ever justifiable. Bush responded, "Maybe I can be more clear. The instructions went out to our people to adhere to the law. That ought to comfort you. We're a nation of law. We have law on the books. You might look at these laws, and that might provide comfort for you."[127] What Bush didn't mention, of course, is that the "law" he was referring to was based on legal decisions made with the intention to legitimize torture and to roll back restrictions on an egregious form of state violence that has been widely condemned domestically and across the world. The question Bush's statement also raised is whether or not the state policy he was referring to was legitimate. Used in this context, state policy is legitimate when "it does not appear to contravene widely shared values, norms, and ideals."[128] In the context of the War on Terror, however, torture is an American value.

While there may be some lessons learned in terms of how the legal infrastructure post-9/11 has wielded so much abuse, it is important to remember how pervasive is the underlying Islamophobia that justifies it. Making slight and superficial modifications to interrogation techniques, for example, was clearly less about the boundaries of the law and more about how to get away with torturing Muslims. The legacy of US detention and torture in the War on Terror is a system of sanctioned state violence that is both systemic and deeply rooted. This must be acknowledged before it can be meaningfully addressed. In the meantime, it will live on in the bodies and minds of those who were so callously abused and tortured. They are still waiting for justice.

8.

GUANTÁNAMO BAY PRISON

They're living in the tropics. They're well fed. They've got everything they could possibly want. There isn't any other nation in the world that would treat people who were determined to kill Americans the way we're treating these people.
—DICK CHENEY COMMENTING ON
GUANTÁNAMO BAY PRISON[1]

The government and intelligence community have, since January 11, 2002, "sold" to the public the idea that Gitmo serves three related purposes: detention, intelligence gathering/interrogation, and prosecution.
—MATHEW SANDOVAL[2]

In November 2015, I went on a delegation to Cuba with Witness Against Torture to raise awareness of Guantánamo Bay prison and to call for its closure. I had only heard of Guantánamo in the context of the prison and had no idea that there was a city, Guantánamo City, with a vibrant social and cultural life completely detached from the naval base and the prison. As I came to know, two completely different worlds defined Guantánamo. Unfortunately, the Guantánamo that the US had created, a place of notorious brutality, has eclipsed almost everything else.

In his book *The Significance of "Gitmo" to National Security: Whether the Prison at Guantanamo Bay, Cuba Is Necessary as a matter of National Security*, 1st Lt. Jeffrey Mendoza writes, "The significance of 'Gitmo' to National Security was obvious back in 2001, on the heels of the 9/11 terrorist attacks. At that time, a place like Gitmo was absolutely necessary for purposes of national security. In the moment all Americans cared about was making sure that nothing like 9/11 ever occurred again."[3] Mendoza offers no elaboration on this assertion and, as such, wants the reader to take for granted that Guantánamo as an intervention was the most logical and sensical.

Further, Mendoza conflates the need for *an* intervention with Guantánamo as *the* intervention—one that disregards whose bodies will get sacrificed to ensure that certain Americans—white Americans—feel secure.

To the extent Mendoza and others like him still validate the prison as necessary nearly two decades since it opened under the guise of the War on Terror, it has come to symbolize the colonization and domination of Muslim bodies by the United States government—symbolism amplified by the condition of unknowingness that has rendered prisoners invisible as victims, but visible as perpetrators. Beyond its symbolism, however, Guantánamo is "a stand-in for torture, abandonment of the rule of law, and the general threat to civil liberties posed by the war on terrorism."[4]

One of the most inconvenient realities of Guantánamo's masquerade of justice is that all of its post-9/11 captives have been Muslim. This is not a coincidence, and is demonstrative of its place as one of the most visible sites of institutionalized Islamophobia. More than serving the theoretical purpose of detaining suspected Al-Qaeda and Taliban members, then, Guantánamo is a prison whose mandate has been to so thoroughly conflate Muslims with terrorists that it doesn't actually matter *who* is detained, but rather *that* they were detained. Further compounding the layers of oppression that Guantánamo has come to represent, the prison's faux legal structure based on the premise of guilty until proven innocent has cemented the prison as a place of differential justice for Muslims.

Of course, creating a differential system of justice for Muslims was by design. In fact, one of the reasons the US government chose Guantánamo for War on Terror prisoners was because of the past precedent of detaining Haitian and Cuban refugees in the 1990s, when the courts ruled that they were not entitled to constitutional protections because they were outside US borders.[5] In choosing a location to detain War on Terror prisoners, the assumption that they would also be denied constitutional protections was one of the compelling reasons Guantánamo was selected for use. When all has been said and done, what Guantánamo has effectively done is to establish a precedent for sanctioning the abuse of Muslims while also pushing the boundaries of what is deemed acceptable treatment of Muslims. Ultimately, what Guantánamo has contributed to is the normalization of practices such as indefinite detention, torture, and other forms of state violence against Muslims.

In this way, Guantánamo has always been about control, whether of the land the prison was built on or of literal bodies. Guantánamo is, what one writer articulates, an example of a "colonized [space] of exception."[6] This is because the US seized control of Guantánamo from Spain and has leased the territory since 1903 for use as a coaling station and naval base. The lease cannot be terminated unless both Cuba and the United States agree to its termination. Although Cuba has long protested US control of Guantánamo Bay, the US has refused to leave. In this context, the violence visited on the bodies of those who have been and continue to be detained at Guantánamo can be seen as stemming from the violent colonial legacy of the US, the land it occupies, and its relationship to Cuba's sovereignty.

The Journey to Guantánamo Bay Prison

If you followed the logic of the US government when it comes to post-9/11 detentions, the prevailing wisdom seems to be that if you treat a person like a terrorist, they become one. Once they are objectified as such, the US renders irrelevant actual guilt or innocence of the person detained, while priming observers to ask what they did, not whether or not they are culpable in the first place. Many of the initial photographs from Guantánamo without a clear view of prisoners' faces have served exactly this purpose.

After enduring a twenty-seven-hour flight to Cuba, shackled to their plane seats and refused use of the bathroom, on January 11, 2002, the first twenty prisoners arrived at Guantánamo, four months to the day after the 9/11 attacks. An iconic photograph of the first prisoner arrivals shows them in a fenced area, kneeling and shackled, wearing bright orange jumpsuits and blacked-out goggles.[7] When asked why the first prisoners were made to wear shackles, Richard Myers, then chair of the Joint Chiefs of Staff, responded, "These are people that would gnaw through hydraulic lines in the back of a C-17 to bring it down. . . . So these are very, very dangerous people, and that's how they're being treated."[8]

A total of 780 Muslim men and boys have been detained at Guantánamo,[9] most of them arriving between 2002 and 2004.[10] In 2006, however, fourteen prisoners who had been detained by the CIA through their Detention and Interrogation (DI) program arrived at Guantánamo. In addition, twelve more prisoners were brought to Guantánamo after being tortured in CIA secret prisons, putting the total number of prisoners transferred there from the CIA at twenty-six. In March 2008, Muhammad Rahim, whom the US government described as a "close associate" of Osama bin Laden, arrived at Guantánamo.[11]

Representing one of the only instances of the US government excelling in diversity, the men detained at Guantánamo came from over forty-nine countries. However, a large majority—75 percent—represent five countries: Afghanistan, Saudi Arabia, Yemen, Pakistan, and Algeria.[12] Magnifying the cruelty of detention at Guantánamo was the fact that the US government refused to reveal the names of the prisoners detained, leaving many families with no information about their whereabouts. This was a manifestation of the fact that the US government didn't actually care about the men's identities, as long as they had bodies they could label as terrorists. The lucky families were those who found out the whereabouts of their loved ones through the media.[13] It was only in 2006 that the government released the prisoners' names, not voluntarily but in response to a Freedom of Information lawsuit filed by the Associated Press.[14]

Since the prisoners were detained in countries outside of the United States, it was easy for the US government to claim that all the prisoners held at Guantánamo were apprehended while engaged in warfare on the battlefield. However, 86 percent were not captured on the battlefield at all, and only 5 percent of Guantánamo prisoners were captured by American troops.[15] The majority of prisoners were in fact sold to the United States for bounties in the amount of $5,000 per individual.[16] For example, one bounty flyer distributed in Afghanistan read, "Get wealth and power beyond your dreams." Another said, "This is enough money to take care of your family, your village, your tribe for the rest of your life. Pay for livestock and doctors and schoolbooks and housing for all your people."[17] Unfortunately, this encouraged Afghan and Pakistani soldiers to turn in Arabs in particular from outside the local community, in addition to whoever they considered tribal enemies.[18] Moreover, once this strategy of capturing Muslim men was revealed, it became clear that it didn't actually matter who the state was detaining as long as their bodies would serve as means to the US's national security ends.

Already marginalized and oppressed in their own country, twenty-two Uighur Muslims ended up in Guantánamo after being sold as "terrorists" in Afghanistan—a country where they were residing, ironically, to escape the repression of Muslims by the Chinese government.[19] Even though the United States determined that the Uighurs were not actually a threat to the US, it took many years for them to be released.[20] They could not be repatriated to China due to fear that they would be tortured and possibly executed. At the same time, resettlement elsewhere was difficult because of how powerful the Chinese government is and because other countries acquiesced to pressure from China not to accept any Uighurs. Additionally, because the US was preparing for an impending war on Iraq, it did not want China to intervene. China agreed not to interfere in the US's war plans on the condition that the US officially designate the Uighurs as terrorists.[21] As a result, the US released Uighur prisoners to third-party countries where they had no roots.[22] Although they were better off in a third-party country instead of China, the lack of support from the US government post-Guantánamo posed its own challenges.

Guantánamo as the Embodiment of Institutionalized Islamophobia

When it comes to the US's carceral state and the systematic targeting of an identity group, Guantánamo is not an exception. However, in earlier years of the prison's operation, the singular identity detainees shared—being Muslims—was treated as a coincidence instead of the result of a deliberate and intentional strategy of targeting Muslims. In contrast to other laws and policies of the War on Terror that appear neutral on their face, Guantánamo offered no such ambiguity in terms of whom it meant to target. Institutionalized Islamophobia at Guantánamo, however, has never been simply a matter of the identities of the men who come through the prison's doors, but of the treatment they are subjected to behind its ugly walls. This includes techniques of punishment and torture that specifically weaponize prisoners' religious beliefs.

For many of Guantánamo's Muslim prisoners, prayer was a time of peace, calm, and reflection. With the call to prayer, Muslims are reminded to join in reflection and surrender to God. But this was a calm rarely afforded them. Detained men reported interferences to the prayer call made by guards who deliberately broadcast English-language messages at the same time.[23] Even worse, officers also ridiculed the Muslim call to prayer by imitating it with mock Arabic and laughing. Where obstruction of prayer wasn't satisfying enough, those in charge of the prisoners kept the men disoriented and unable to pray, in addition to lying to them about the time and refusing information that would allow them to position themselves facing Mecca. Finally, to get the men to cooperate with interrogators, their prayer caps and beads were designated "comfort items" so they could be used for bribery.[24]

In 2002 and 2003, Guantánamo detainees reported abuses of the Qur'an, one of their most prized possessions, to FBI interviewers. Among the prisoners' allegations was that the Qur'an had been flushed down the toilet.[25] Further reports of abuse of the Qur'an in 2005 prompted an investigation by Brigadier General Jay Hood. Hood's investigation uncovered five cases of mishandling of the Qur'an, some intentional and others unintentional, which included "getting copies wet, standing on a Koran during an interrogation, and 'inadvertently' spraying urine on a copy." Beyond abuse by US personnel, Hood claimed to find fifteen cases of prisoners desecrating their own Qur'ans—a claim that, even if accurate, would seem to represent more about how prisoners were being treated, particularly with regard to psychological torture, than about any individual beliefs about Islam and the Qur'an. Moreover, this was likely due to mental duress, and in no way does this translate into translate into a license for Guantánamo personnel to do the same.[26]

Maintaining that "mishandling" the Qur'an was never condoned, Hood stated, "When one considers the many thousands of times detainees have been moved and cells have been searched since detention operations first began here in January 2002, I think one can only conclude that respect for detainee religious beliefs was embedded in the culture [of the task force] from the start."[27] Hood's downplaying of US personnel abusing the Qur'an was not surprising, given how numerous accusations of other abuse and torture were handled by the government. Perhaps misunderstood as an act of transparency, Hood's acknowledgment of US personnel abusing the Qur'an was actually a way of containing the allegations while projecting the idea that there were actual boundaries for how Guantánamo prisoners were treated. Moreover, his assertion that the detainees' religious beliefs were respected from the beginning hinged again on a lack of context, as if these instances of abuse of the Qur'an were isolated events. But if Guantánamo has stood for anything, it's the wanton abuse of Muslims rooted in demonizing Islam as a religion and their practice of it.

The abuse of the Qur'an weighed very heavily on prisoners—in some cases leading to suicide attempts. One prisoner stated, "As a result of the insult of the Holy Quran I decided to commit suicide. I tried to hang myself by the neck. . . . I was then taken to the hospital. When I was asked why I had done it, I said I couldn't tolerate the insult and desecration of the Holy Quran. . . . Afterwards when I was taken to Delta block [for mentally ill detainees] . . . I learned 28 more people had also tried to commit suicide like me."[28]

From November 2002 to September 2003, a Muslim chaplain named James Yee worked at Guantánamo. He has since described some of the abuses that occurred while he was there. According to Yee, there was an interrogation room that had a large circle on the floor. Yee described it as "a satanic circle, in which an interrogator would place the Muslim prisoner and attempt to force that prisoner to bow down and pray—like to prostrate in the form of the Islamic prayer." While prostrating, the prisoner was then subjected to the interrogator screaming, "Satan is your God now, not Allah."[29]

Adding insult to injury, in 2002 former secretary of defense Donald Rumsfeld authorized interrogation techniques such as removing facial hair and/or removing clothing—both sacrosanct to many observant Muslims.[30] One prisoner even recounted that an army barber left a cross-shaped patch of hair on his head.[31] Further, detainees were also subjected to forcible baptism in interrogation rooms if they refused to cooperate.

Knowledge about how many Muslims are reserved about gender and sexual relations led to prisoners being sexually taunted on many occasions.[32] This included being watched in the showers by female guards and being forced to urinate or defecate on themselves as punishment if they were found with "contraband."[33] Other examples of violations of prisoners' sense of modesty included forcing the detainees to urinate and defecate in front of a female guards and being punished for placing a sheet to cover themselves in the bathroom and shower so they would not be visible to guards or a security camera.

More specific examples of religious abuse at Guantánamo include the story of Mohamedou Slahi, one of Guantánamo's most well-known former prisoners, who had his head and beard shaved and was forced to wear a burqa. In addition, because Slahi believed music was impermissible in Islam, interrogators would taunt him by playing it. Slahi was also prevented from praying and fasting during the month of Ramadan in 2003. On one occasion, he recalled that a sergeant first class entered the room he was in, saying, "Stop the fuck praying! You're having sex with American whores and you're praying? What a hypocrite you are."[34] As a result of Slahi's refusal to stop praying, he was prohibited from performing prayers for an entire year. He was also force-fed as a way to prohibit his fasting during Ramadan.

In the case of Bahraini prisoner Jumah al-Dossari, a "female interrogator had his clothing cut off, then removed her own and stood over him. Just before wiping what she said was menstrual blood on his face, she kissed the crucifix on her necklace and said, 'This is a gift from Christ for you Muslims.'"[35]

Despite the multiple ways that knowledge of Islam was weaponized to abuse and torture Muslim prisoners, many nevertheless expressed how their faith helped them cope with life in detention. One prisoner relayed this, saying, "Islam teaches us a lot about patience and prayer. Be patient and God will take care of you, so my faith and prayer kept me going." Perhaps what the American government didn't realize was that while they were trying to break prisoners' religious beliefs and faith in God, they were in many cases strengthening them. Islam may have been the reason these Muslim men were detained to begin with, but it was also the reason why many survived Guantánamo.

Guantánamo in the Courts

If we can't bring them to trial, so be it.
—John Ashcroft[36]

The architects of Guantánamo never intended it to serve as a forum for truth-seeking—the guilt of the men detained there was assumed. Rather, it was designed to prevent the operation of justice by denying prisoners any real means to legally challenge their detention either through processes bound by the international law of war or through the United States justice system. Guantánamo Bay prisoners have, however, continued over the years to seek access to United States federal courts to claim their rights to be fairly tried. The Supreme Court has defined, in broad strokes, the boundaries of the constitutional and legal rights of the Guantánamo detainees in four landmark cases: (1) *Rasul v. Bush*;[37] (2) *Hamdi v. Rumsfeld*;[38] (3) *Hamdan v. Rumsfeld*;[39] and (4) *Boumediene v. Bush*.[40] Legally, the rulings handed down in these four cases serve to limit the inherent power claimed by the Bush administration in the early days of the War on Terror to detain indefinitely outside the reach of international law and constitutional protection. In practice, however, their effect on the ability of the Guantánamo detainees to obtain justice has been limited.

The first cases to reach the Supreme Court, in 2004, were decided on the same day. At question in *Rasul v. Bush* was whether a non-citizen captured in Afghanistan and detained at Guantánamo could access the US federal court system via the writ of habeas corpus. Overturning the ruling of the lower court and rejecting the executive's argument that this right should not extend to foreign nationals held outside US territory, a 6–3 majority of the court ruled that it did. Despite Cuba's sovereignty, the "complete jurisdiction and control" exercised by the United States over the Guantánamo facility was enough to trigger the defendant's right to challenge his detention in federal court.[41]

In *Hamdi v. Rumsfeld*, a case involving a US citizen accused of fighting for the Taliban in Afghanistan, the court was asked to decide whether Hamdi's due-process rights had been violated by his being held indefinitely without trial or access to an attorney. The Bush administration argued that the executive had absolute authority during wartime to designate someone as an enemy combatant and restrict their access to the US court system. A majority of the court ruled that detainees challenging their detention had the right to "receive notice of the factual basis for this classification [as an enemy combatant] and a fair opportunity to rebut the Government's factual assertions before a neutral decision-maker."[42]

Although it was technically a favorable ruling, the court's decision in *Hamdi* stressed that the conditions of ongoing conflict did in fact place a special burden on the government that may justify the special tailoring of habeas corpus proceedings. In broad language, Justice Sandra Day O'Connor, writing for the majority, outlined a suggested process loosely based on existing military proceedings for determining whether the conditions of the Geneva Conventions had been met, but allowing for, for example, hearsay evidence or even presumptions in favor of government evidence under certain circumstances. This language has since been relied on by lower courts in affirming the expansion of the government's authority to detain.

In response to the court's rulings in *Rasul* and *Hamdi*, the Department of Defense established Combatant Status Review Tribunals (CSRTs) within the military to make factual determinations regarding detainees' status as enemy combatants. But prisoners were de facto being designated as enemy combatants, thus having to fight this designation from the assumption of guilt. This was made all the more difficult because of how broadly *enemy combatant* was defined to include anyone who provided direct support to undefined "associated forces"—a leap from just Al-Qaeda and the Taliban.[43]

The CSRT process also raised substantial due-process concerns. Most significantly, although the detainees were allowed a personal representative, that person was not permitted to actually advocate on their behalf. In addition, the proceedings were private, and only redacted transcripts were released—and only for some of the detainees. This, combined with the fact that no time frame was set for release or repatriation should a challenge be successful, made the process ripe for abuse and political manipulation. In practice, the CSRTs operated to preserve the status quo. They were designed to give prisoners watered-down due-process rights while still permitting easy convictions by bypassing established legal processes such as habeas petitions.[44]

For its part, Congress reacted to the court decisions by passing the Detainee Treatment Act (DTA) of 2005,[45] which attempted to strip Guantánamo prisoners of their habeas rights legislatively. The Supreme

Court rejected this approach the following year with its ruling in *Hamdan v. Rumsfeld*. The court in *Hamdan* held that the executive's inherent power to detain is necessarily limited by Congress acting in proper exercise of its war powers *and* by the internationally established laws of war, making the due-process guarantees of the Geneva Conventions enforceable in federal court. The decision found that the tribunal that had tried *Hamdan* had violated his rights by denying him access to relevant evidence and parts of his trial.

In 2008, the Supreme Court finally put the question of federal jurisdiction over detainees' habeas corpus rights to rest with its decision in *Boumediene v. Bush*, ruling that the section of the Military Commissions Act (MCA) of 2006 dealing with habeas rights was a violation of the Suspension Clause of the United States Constitution, which says the writ of habeas corpus shall not be suspended except in cases of rebellion or invasion. In contrast, the MCA, designed to supersede the ruling in *Hamdan*, prohibited federal habeas petitions in all cases pertaining to detention, substituting the procedures outlined in the DTA. A majority of the court found the DTA's procedural protections to be an inadequate substitute for the habeas writ. Further, they ruled that detainees, including non-citizens, were not barred from invoking their rights under the Suspension Clause merely because they were being held at Guantánamo or had been designated enemy combatants.

Boumediene v. Bush was the last Guantánamo case to reach the Supreme Court, and on its face the ruling might appear to have been a major legal victory for the detainees. In addition to affirming rights advances from previous cases, the *Boumediene* decision seems to have settled the question of where future law in this area will emerge from—the judiciary—meaning that the constitutional guarantees obtained by detainees are safe from further incursions by Congress. However, the court in *Boumediene* left its decision in broad terms, declining to elaborate on what specific procedural or substantive elements would be necessary to make the military's legal process constitutional. By abdicating this role, the Supreme Court essentially signaled that the lower courts, specifically the DC Court of Appeals, would be responsible for determining the shape of things going forward. Importantly, none of the legal rights won by Guantánamo detainees in federal court prohibited the use of military commissions as the primary method by which prisoners were able to mount challenges to their detention.

Military Commissions

Despite the Supreme Court's rulings requiring consideration for the due-process rights of Guantánamo detainees challenging their status, legislation continued to be passed affirming the extrajudicial military commissions process that had resulted in so many rights violations. The Military Commissions Act (MCA) of 2006 explicitly authorized "trial by military commission for violations of the law of war, and for other purposes."[46] The MCA made its grant of authority subject to the creation of a tribunal process that implemented certain procedural improvements over the ad hoc system and provided a direct avenue for appeal. Unfortunately, many of the same issues that plagued the initial iterations of these military trials were preserved under the "improved" system, including the permission of coerced testimony. The MCA also expanded the list of crimes triable by military commission well beyond the scope of what would be considered a war crime under international law, making it applicable to "any enemy combatant," which included those accused of material support and conspiracy.[47]

Shortly after Obama took office, Congress passed the updated Military Commissions Act of 2009, which attempted to bring the process into line with the Supreme Court's decision in *Boumediene*.[48] The new act mandated additional procedural improvements such as allowing prisoners greater access to representation, tightening rules about the use of hearsay evidence, and prohibiting evidence obtained by coercion. However, the 2009 act left untouched some of the most significant pitfalls of its predecessor. For one thing, it applied only to foreign nationals accused of war crimes, making the law discriminatory on its face. It also continued to allow charges for conduct not considered war crimes under international law.

Whatever the value of the procedural improvements in the updated MCA, its due-process protections fall far short of those granted to defendants in US federal courts or to those accused of war crimes under the international laws of war. The military commissions inherently lack transparency and independence, making them particularly vulnerable to abuse, as the history of Supreme Court litigation bears out. Even if the government had demonstrated a legitimate interest in keeping these trials within the purview of the military, that could have been accomplished without creating an entirely new process ad hoc by utilizing the existing court martial system, which has the benefit of experienced judges and well-established rules of evidence and procedure that closely track those of the US federal court system. Crucially as well, the due-process rights afforded to defendants in other venues apply equally to citizens and foreign nationals.

Ultimately, the Military Commissions Act of 2009 was a weak effort at reform that represented a betrayal of then president Obama's campaign promise to close Guantánamo and reckon seriously with its legacy of injustice. Demonstrating his support for the military commissions, President Obama stated, "Military commissions have a history in the United States dating back to George Washington and the Revolutionary War. They are an appropriate venue for trying detainees for violations of the laws of war. They allow for the protection of sensitive sources and methods of intelligence-gathering; they allow for the safety and security of participants; and for the presentation of evidence gathered from the battlefield that cannot always be effectively presented in federal courts."[49]

In the same speech, Obama noted that twenty-one people were being held in Guantánamo for "no legitimate" reason. He believed their release was important because "the United States is a nation of laws, and we must abide by these rulings."[50] The driving force behind the creation and continued use of military commissions, however, is the government's desire for ease of conviction in spite of our laws—in addition to avoiding consequences for the government's use of cruel, inhumane, and degrading tactics on the prisoners at Guantánamo.[51] The commissions, in short, can be understood "not as a legitimate forum for trying war crimes, but as an avenue for short-circuiting legal processes that might hold us accountable for our wrongs."[52]

Compounding the due-process concerns baked into the entire system of trial by military commission is the fact that the DC Circuit Court has been consistently hostile to the rights of Guantánamo detainees. In the years following *Boumediene v. Bush* and the passage of the 2009 MCA, the DC Circuit Court has utilized its authority as essentially the last avenue of appeal to shape the law in a way that heavily favors the government. As recently as 2020, in *Al-Hela v. Trump*, a three-judge panel of the court ruled that a foreign national held outside the territorial bounds of the United States had no constitutional right to due process at all[53]—a ruling that would seem to bring the detainees back to square one in terms of their right to access justice. As of this writing, it is unclear what the future of the *Al-Hela* ruling or its impact will be, but even if it reaches the Supreme Court, it is likely to represent at least some measure of threat to even what limited rights the prisoners have won.

Even when the Muslim prisoners at Guantánamo have been successful in making rights claims, these have largely turned out to be hollow victories. Landmark decisions such as *Rasul* and *Boumediene* have had very little functional effect on the lives or prospects of the prisoners. These cases are perceived as great victories for the detainees, but in fact, what they have gained is very narrow and legalistic. As attorney Joseph Margulies, who was lead counsel in the *Rasul* case, puts it, "It is closer to the truth to say that they can file a lawsuit. They cannot, however, mount a serious challenge to their detention."[54]

Rights and Rightlessness

If you want a definition of this place, you don't have a right to have rights.
—Nizar Sassi, former Guantánamo prisoner[55]

As a function of being dehumanized, the men detained at Guantánamo have been forced to live in precarity. Detaining prisoners at that location specifically because the Bush administration wanted to deprive them of their rights has always been and still is based on the premise that they don't deserve any. While the court cases discussed above adjudicate this premise, they are demonstrative of the fact that prisoners have had to negotiate their rights from a point of deficit, starting with whether they have rights in the first place instead of how to protect and/or exercise the rights they are due. Nizar Sassi's quote above poignantly illustrates the extent of rights deprivations such that there is essentially no starting point from which to claim them. When Nizar Sassi was released in 2004, the prisoners he was leaving behind pled that he "tell the world what is happening here."[56] But what could Sassi have told the outside world to make Guantánamo make sense?

Professor A. Naomi Paik's theory of rightlessness explains what Sassi's situation made difficult to understand—namely, the particular way that prison camps such as Guantánamo Bay strip prisoners of their rights in such a fundamental way. More specifically, as Paik argues, because places like the prison at Guantánamo Bay exist outside of the boundaries of ordinary legal and civil rights, the people held there become rightless in the sense that they are cut adrift from any system that meaningfully confers human (and legal) rights. To be a rightless subject is to be "removed from the rest of the world to the world of the camp, where the protections that many of the rest of us take for granted do not apply."[57]

Though there is now a system in place to allow attorneys to visit their clients—a contrast from the early days of Guantánamo's operation—prisoners have nonetheless continued to be almost entirely cut off from their families and communities.

While prisoners were effectively rendered rightless, faux justice systems at Guantánamo cemented their status as such. For example, in the earlier years of Guantánamo's operation, Combatant Status Review Tribunals (CSRTs) were used to determine whether prisoners should still be designated as enemy combatants, a designation that was automatically imposed on them without process and by virtue of their being at Guantánamo. In other words, the adjudication process had nothing to do with rights and everything to do with arbitrariness that was only acceptable for those deemed rightless.

Complementing the violence of legal systems designed to affirm the status of prisoners as rightless is the violence embedded in making rightless subjects appeal for rights from the same system that renders their rights nonexistent. At the same time, rightless subjects have to face the violence inherent in recognizing that "claiming rights is one of their only means to resist rightlessness."[58]

Making rights claims, however, at a place like Guantánamo can be understood as resistance insofar as such claims expose the violence of the state, whether they result in any tangible benefit to the claimant or not. As Muneer I. Ahmad, former lawyer for juvenile prisoner Omar Khadr, argues, "The rights claim sought not to escape the violence of the state, but to make that violence more costly to the state." In other words, rights claims impose a burden on the state that leaves the state in the position of explaining that prisoners have no rights, instead of making the prisoner argue their rights' existence. Further, rights claims can turn the tables and shift power, such that the onus on the prisoner shifts from proving they've been harmed to making the state justify its violence.[59]

Rights claims are also powerful because they make the government engage in discourse that puts their violence on display. Further, as Ahmad notes, "The claim of rights itself may interpose a membrane between the state and the individual even if the right itself ultimately is found not to exist."[60] Even where rights are deemed nonexistent, rights claims as resistance provide an avenue through which prisoners can confront the state's violence and, in so doing, categorically reject "Guantánamo's dehumanization project."[61]

While rights claims may be useful in theoretical discussions on the rights of prisoners and in exposing the state, the benefits are often limited to that purpose. In the context of the discussion above, the provision and acknowledgment of prisoner rights would seem welcome—that is, if they can actually be exercised and if they manage to change a prisoner's status and condition. Jumah al-Dossari, a Bahraini prisoner who was detained for five years and who survived multiple suicide attempts, recalled the impact of the *Rasul v. Bush* Supreme Court decision on his case: "[One day] the military gave me a piece of paper that laid out the allegations against me. I had been in Guantanamo at that point for 2 ½ years. My lawyer later told me that I had received this paper as a result of a U.S. Supreme Court ruling that detainees were to be allowed to have court hearings. We never got the promised hearings; instead we went through military hearings at Guantanamo in which we were not shown any evidence or allowed to have lawyers. All we got was the piece of paper."[62] What al-Dossari's case makes clear is that the recognition of rights differs little from rightlessness when it comes to tangible outcomes for prisoners seeking reprieve from Guantánamo. Furthermore, cases like al-Dossari's highlight the fact that systems rife with and defined by deep injustice can render rights not only nonexistent but irrelevant to the whims of the state.

Prisoner Resistance at Guantánamo

> *To me, hunger striking is a way of holding my head high. It's a simple exchange: of pain for dignity.*
> —KHALID QASSIM[63]

When one is situated in a place of deprivation where one's proximity to life or death is controlled by the state, hunger strikes represent one of the few tactics a prisoner can use to protest conditions of injustice. Hunger strikes represent a prisoner's embodiment of existence as resistance, as they wield their lives as leverage against the state. Despite the clarity with which prisoners on hunger strikes communicate their reasoning for taking this action, some people wrongly assume that the end goal of a hunger strike is death, instead of life with dignity. Former Guantánamo prisoner Abu Wa'el Dhiab dispels this idea pointedly by asking, "Why do you think I am on hunger strike in the first place? If I die, it is not because I killed myself. The U.S. government killed me."[64] Even though participation in hunger strikes can be fatal, the prisoner takes this action as part of their decision to resist and refuse to take part in their own dehumanization.[65] This puts the state in the position of navigating the political calculus of dispersing justice or injustice, and life versus death.

Hunger striking as protest involves the "weaponization of life," which refers to "the tactic of resorting to corporeal and existential practices of struggle, based on the technique of self-destruction, in order to make a political statement or advance political goals."[66] In this sense the body becomes a "conduit of [a] political intervention." Sociologist Chris Yuill writes similarly of hunger strikes, "The body becomes a weapon, the means by which the prisoners strike back at the authorities."[67] Additionally, Joseph Pugliese, Professor of Cultural Studies at Macquarie University, says in regard to the poetics of self-harm, that they "contest the injustice of state violence" and that "the poetics of these acts reside in embodied articulations that are purposive and performative—precisely as they run the razor's edge between life and death."[68]

In hunger strikes, the body is political and becomes a place where the violence of the state is enacted and where negotiations of life versus death are carried out. This includes the "coexistence of oppression and resistance taking place on the prisoners' bodies."[69] Hunger strikes thought of in these terms can also be conceptualized as a tactic centered on prisoners asserting agency over their corporeal and spiritual bodies as a challenge to the government that has long tried to break them down in order to exercise absolute control over them.

In the context of Guantánamo prisoners in particular, who have been referred to as the "worst of the worst"[70] or "bad guys,"[71] hunger strikes offer a direct way of challenging political and public indictments through nonviolent protest—a message that seems hard to digest for those clinging to the notion of Muslims as terrorists. Hunger strikes are an appeal to the larger public to witness and make visible the injustice that has defined existence at Guantánamo. Over the twenty years that Guantánamo Bay Prison has been open, there have been multiple hunger strikes, including in 2002, 2005–6, 2013, and 2017.

In late February 2002, a military police officer triggered religious sensitivities by removing a prisoner's homemade turban during his prayer. The ensuing strike escalated over the course of two months, with prisoners protesting harsh living conditions, the lack of legal recourse, and religious degradations.[72]

Two years later, in June–July 2005, mostly facing the same predicament, prisoners went on a hunger strike again, with specific demands that included the following:[73]

- We need respect for our religion, including an end to the desecration of the Qur'an and religious discrimination;
- We need fair trials with proper legal representation;
- We need proper human food and clean water. We are not given adequate amounts of food and the food is often old and inedible. The water is frequently dirty and tastes contaminated;
- We need to see sunlight, and not be forced to go months without seeing daylight;
- We need to know why we are in Camp 5 for so long, in some case for over a year. What have the Camp 5 detainees done to be treated so much worse than the other detainees?
- We need basic human rights like everyone else in the world—including real, effective medical treatment;
- We need to be able to contact our families, and write to them and receive letters. Some prisoners have not received any of the letter sent by their families, their families have not received any of the prisoners' recent letters, and this is a widespread problem across the camp;
- We need the "level system" of the various Camps and privilege levels to be abandoned and everyone treated equally; and
- We need a neutral body to observe the situation and report publicly about the conditions at Guantanamo.

Most of the prisoners detained in Camp 5, which was designated for non-compliant prisoners held in solitary confinement, participated. At least 200 prisoners total, across different camps, joined in this hunger strike, though the government claimed a much lower number. During the summer 2005 hunger strikes, Colonel Mike Bumgarner reached out to prisoners to initiate a conversation about improving camp conditions. Bumgarner's efforts led to different meal plans, an abandonment of the tiered punishment and reward system that was often arbitrary, and the creation of a six-member council of detainees. The council was, however, short lived and was terminated because the detainee council members were passing notes to each other during the second meeting to conduct private communication. Thereafter, those who complied with camp rules were rewarded with snacks such as Gatorade and power bars, while those who continued to resist camp rules were met with tightened discipline. Shaker Aamer, who had been a member of the detainee council, was subsequently put in isolation.

In June/July 2005, a prisoner named Jarallah Al-Marri went on a hunger strike. Al-Marri was held in solitary confinement for over a year, confined to his cell for up to three weeks at a time, and subjected to light in his cell twenty-four hours a day, seven days a week. Al-Marri was subsequently hospitalized because of the hunger strike and because of a heart condition. During his hospitalization, as Al-Marri told his attorneys, a nurse made sexual advances toward him in order to get him to end his hunger strike. One of the only concessions by the government was to provide the prisoners with clean bottled water. This hunger strike ended on July 28, 2005.[74]

However, another hunger strike started just weeks later, in mid-August 2005, in protest of the government's failure to bring the camp into compliance with the Geneva Conventions as they had agreed to do during the previous strike. In addition to downplaying the number of hunger strikers in the August strike, the government tried to prevent legal counsel from accessing their clients. This included attorneys for a prisoner who had been physically assaulted and psychologically abused by military personnel.[75]

A year later, in 2006, restraint chairs were introduced to conduct force-feeding at Guantánamo as a response to continued hunger strikes. Should the prisoner refuse to eat, the chairs would restrain the prisoner's body at six points, including hands, feet, head, and torso. Through tubes inserted through the nostril, prisoners are force-fed a liquid nutrient and water solution. After the procedure, instead of allowing the prisoner to get out of the chair, they were sometimes left for two hours to ensure digestion.[76]

Like other punishments at Guantánamo, force-feeding is, and was meant to be, extremely painful. In 2013, a Guantánamo prisoner named Samir Naji al Hasan Moqbel wrote an op-ed in the *New York Times* about his experience being force-fed, saying, "I will never forget the first time they passed the feeding tube up my nose. I can't describe how painful it is to be force-fed this way. As it was thrust in, it made me feel like throwing up. I wanted to vomit, but I couldn't. There was agony in my chest, throat and stomach. I had never experienced such pain before. I would not wish this cruel punishment upon anyone."[77]

Lakhdar Boumediene, the plaintiff in *Boumediene v. Bush*, described his reasons for hunger striking: "I stopped eating not because I wanted to die, but because I could not keep living without doing something to protest the injustice of my treatment. They could lock me up for no reason and with no chance to argue my innocence. They could torture me, deprive me of sleep, put me in an isolation cell, control every single aspect of my life. But they couldn't make me swallow their food. And I knew they wouldn't let a detainee starve to death."[78]

Despite these statements and others similar to them by Guantánamo prisoners, prison officials routinely characterized force-feeding interventions as suicide prevention. This characterization served the purpose of legitimizing force-feeding by projecting the idea that prisoners went on hunger strikes because they wanted to die, not because they were trying to obtain political demands within the prison and, ultimately, freedom from Guantánamo. For example, when asked about hunger strikes at Guantánamo, at a media roundtable in June 2006, William Winkenwerder, assistant secretary for health affairs at the Department of Defense, responded, "There is a moral question. Do you allow a person to commit suicide? Or do you take steps to protect their health and preserve their life?"[79]

Although the government feigned concern for prisoners, the moral question of indefinite detention was apparently never asked—only the questions that would obscure the real issue as to why prisoners were in this predicament in the first place. Similarly, in a document on Standard Operating Procedure from the Joint Task Force Guantanamo Bay, Cuba Joint Medical Group, it states under the policy section that "the DoD and Joint Task Force Guantanamo (JTF GTMO) policy is to protect, preserve, and promote life."[80] Unflinchingly hypocritical, this statement demonstrates the cruelty of the government's efforts to "promote life" in order to subject prisoners to death-like conditions. Articulating this point similarly, one scholar refers to force-feeding as a form of "violent care." The scholar notes that the contradiction embedded in this term is highlighted by the fact that the attempt to preserve the life of a prisoner is pursued to the point of violence, temporary or permanent physical debilitation, and sometimes death.[81]

In a 2013 article on force-feeding for the *Atlantic*, author James Hamblin asked, "When does 'suicide prevention' become torture?"[82] Of course, the United States does not agree with this characterization of force-feeding, even though in the past, the UN Human Rights Commission said that force-feeding at Guantánamo was torture.[83] Hamblin also addressed the question of what actually qualifies as suicide prevention, quoting from a *New York Times* op-ed by Brian Mishara, professor of psychology and director of the Center for Research and Intervention on Suicide and Euthanasia at the University of Quebec in Montreal. Responding to the hunger strikes at Guantánamo in 2006, Mishara had written, "In the case of Guantánamo, intervening to save or prolong a person's life without trying to change the person's reasons for wanting to die cannot be considered suicide prevention. Suicide prevention would involve intervening to change the person's desire to die (despite his circumstances) or changing the situation that he feels is intolerable."[84] Of course, the state stood to gain by conflating hunger strikes with suicides—namely, "to conceal the occurrences of resistance to neutralize their reverberations, not only in Guantanamo but across detention centers and prisons around the globe."[85]

Abu Wa'el Dhiab, mentioned earlier, was one of dozens of Guantánamo detainees whose force-feedings were captured on video and who petitioned to have the videos preserved. In the case of *Dhiab v. Obama*, the legality of force-feeding was challenged, as was the government's refusal to release the videotapes. While the judge on the case, Gladys Kessler, condemned force-feeding, she left the practice intact. With respect to Dhiab, she stated, "The Court simply cannot let Mr. Dhiab die."[86] The obvious irony of this decision was articulated by Dhiab himself: "When I complain, they say 'we are protecting your life, we are protecting your health.' What kind of concern about my life and health is this, if they put me in such pain I am unable to sleep? I am peacefully demonstrating. Why are you torturing me?"[87]

Continuing the thread of the promotion of life, the messages coming from the US government across the board were really only about who gets to decide the prisoner's fate. In this way, the promotion of life is more properly conceptualized as control over death. The idea of "necropolitical sites of exception" illuminates what this form of living effectively looks like. "Necropolitical spaces are those sites of exception, such as the slave plantation, the colony, and territories under occupation, where populations are not killed but 'subjected to conditions of life conferring upon them the status of living dead.'"[88] Thus, rather than promoting life, interventions by government officials are simply about keeping the prisoners physically alive, even if they were effectively rendered living dead.

As prisoners continued to languish, some went on longer-term hunger strikes. In 2012, the suicide of prisoner Adnan Latif led the military to inflict collective punishment on the remaining men. On the pretext that Latif might have hidden pills in either the binding of his Qur'an or his genitals, authorities resumed an earlier practice of inspecting prisoners' Qur'ans—a practice that had been abandoned because of rampant abuse of the holy book by guards—and required genital inspections whenever a prisoner entered or left his cell.[89] In 2013, the prisoners began another mass hunger strike, but the government's response was to force-feed at least half of the 106 of them.[90] The strike and the force-feeding policy prompted renewed worldwide condemnation of Guantánamo. In response to criticism, President Obama maintained his support for force-feeding, saying, "I don't want any of these individuals to die."[91] Of course Obama wasn't actually concerned about the prisoners as human beings, because if he were, he would have made changes to the conditions and predicaments that caused the hunger strikes in the first place. That's also why his solution to the hunger strikes was pursuing federal terrorism prosecutions—not, for example, actually freeing the prisoners who the government knew were innocent all along.

In a 2019 article, British scholars Yasmin Ibrahim and Anita Howarth wrote of the force-feeding of hunger-striking detainees, "Blood and bodily waste are spilled endlessly in these rituals and become both a weapon of torture and humiliation and means to condemn and control these racial-ized bodies. The pain of the condemned body is not recognized, neither is it reserved any sympathy, but becomes a canvass to constantly test the thresholds of pain and its attendant humiliation and compliance. Within this necropolitics, death is not an option, but the body, mind and its religion become sites of violence and constant transgression to mark their posses-sion and submission to the imperial power."[92]

This quote powerfully captures the role of force-feeding—in particular, the true purpose it serves beyond false attempts to center a prisoner's well-being. Force-feeding is yet another means through which prisoners' dignity and autonomy are stripped from them. More insidiously, it is a way of send-ing prisoners the message that their calls for justice will only be met with violence.

In December 2013, Guantánamo officials produced a twenty-four-page document titled "Medical Management of Detainees with Weight Loss" outlining standard operating procedures for dealing with prisoners on a hunger strike—without once using the term. The term "long-term non-religious fasts" was used instead to describe and euphemize these prisoner actions.[93] Though the document says medical personnel should attempt to get consent from prisoners for treatment, it allows force-feeding (referred to as "enteral feeding") if consent is withheld, and it does not contain any requirements for minimizing the pain and suffering of the prisoner.

That same month, also in response to the hunger strikes, the US mili-tary announced that it would no longer publicly disclose hunger strikes at the prison. Explaining the decision, Navy Commander John Filostrat, of the military's Joint Task Force Guantánamo, stated in an email that "the release of this information serves no operational purpose and detracts from the important issues, which are the welfare of detainees and the safety and security of our troops."[94] In an interview at Guantánamo, Filostrat said, "It's been a self-perpetuating story. It's the strikers' desire to draw attention to themselves, and so we're not going to help them do that."[95] Outrageously, his quote sounded more as though the prisoners were being self-promotional instead of pleading with the world to care about their plight.

Like Obama, Filostrat was clearly evading an obvious discussion about why prisoners were engaging in hunger strikes in the first place, while feigning concern for prisoners' well-being. Filostrat's response also highlighted the paradox of preserving prisoners' lives in a system specifically designed to make them die slow deaths.

After yet another hunger strike occurred in 2017, under President Trump a new policy of not intervening in hunger strikes was adopted by a new medical officer at Guantánamo.[96] Eric Lewis, an attorney for Pakistani prisoner and hunger striker Ahmed Rabbani, described it bluntly: "The policy in a nutshell is, if you don't want to eat and you want to starve to death, go ahead."[97] Far from signaling respect for the bodily autonomy of the hunger strikers, this tactic of complete nonintervention was designed to minimize the power of the protest and send a message to the world that the prisoners wanted to die. If that were true, the government could easily absolve itself of responsibility by merely standing by and letting them wither and die. But again, death was not what hunger strikers are seeking—they're seeking justice.

Adnan Latif, the thirty-six-year-old Yemeni prisoner whose death by suicide in 2012 sparked mass hunger strikes, had described Guantánamo as "living in a dying situation."[98] Latif was cleared for release four times, yet was left to languish, waiting for justice in a prison whose very existence was antithetical to justice. Not quite two years before his death, Latif wrote to his lawyer,

> Hardship is the only language that is used here. Anybody who is able to die will be able to achieve happiness for himself, he has no other hope except that. The requirement is to announce the end, and challenge the self love for life and the soul that insists to end it all and leave this life which is no longer anymore called a life, instead it itself has become death and renewable torture. . . . A world power failed to safeguard peace and human rights and from saving me. I will do whatever I am able to do to rid myself of the imposed death on me at any moment of this prison.[99]

As Latif's story reveals, the Guantánamo prisoners live in a state of paradox and precarity—somewhere between life and death. This is because their lives and deaths, in an objective sense, mean nothing to the US government. Yet there is still contestation between the prisoner and the government about one thing: control over life, and thus over the narrative. Latif exercised what little control he had when he died by suicide—his narrative imparted through the remains of his lifeless body. With Latif's passing, whatever control the government attempted to exert over his story will have to contend with the haunting words he left behind.

Similarly, regardless of how the government handles hunger striking at Guantánamo, this form of resistance among the prisoners has solicited a call for answers and challenges to government policies. Perhaps more than that, it has telegraphed a powerful message: that the men detained at Guantánamo refuse to acquiesce to the abuses they have endured; that they are the ones who give their lives value, not the president, Congress, or anyone else. Whatever the US government takes from them, it can't take away their belief that they deserve something better, something humane, and something just.

Art and Erasure

"Approved by US Forces" is written on the back of any artwork leaving Guantánamo. Anyone seeing the poignant paintings produced by Guantánamo prisoners would see, instead of a national security threat, images of cityscapes, bodies of water, tubular telescopes meant to represent surveillance at the prison, in addition to images reflective of real life, such as a painting depicting Alan Kurdi, the three-year-old Syrian boy whose drowned body was found near the Greek island of Kos in 2015.[100] Another painting, called "Vertigo at Guantánamo," by Ammar Al-Baluchi, is meant to depict a brain injury he sustained as a result of torture by the CIA.[101]

The art program at Guantánamo started under the Bush administration "in an attempt to prevent prisoners from disintegrating into despair and resorting to self-harming actions (including suicide attempts)."[102] Yet art is not just powerful because of what it means to the artists, but because it can communicate messages to viewers in a way other modes of communication cannot.

With little to call their own, the men at Guantánamo would routinely give their attorneys their works as a show of gratitude or for safekeeping.[103] In the fall of 2017, thirty-six paintings, drawings, and 3-D objects produced by prisoners were displayed at John Jay College of Criminal Justice in an exhibit titled "Ode to the Sea."[104]

The exhibit was well received by the public, subsequently triggering attention from the government as well and prompting the Department of

Defense (DOD) to suspend the release of any artwork from Guantánamo, claiming it was property of the US government. Worse than holding on to prisoners' artwork was the threat from the government that it might destroy their creations. Though the DOD indicated concern about the sale of prisoners' artwork in terms of where the proceeds would go, the government seemed more apprehensive about the fact that the exhibit garnered so much media attention—and perhaps about what stories were being told to the outside world that might put a dent in the government's narrative. Moreover, through this exhibit, prisoners were able to take control of the problematic narratives the government ascribed to them, perhaps stoking the government's fears that prisoners could and would be seen as human—a perspective that could weaken support for keeping Guantánamo open.

To this point, M. Neelika Jayawardane, an associate professor of English at the University of New York Oswego, wrote the following in an op-ed reflecting on the art exhibit from Guantánamo: "We know that art can trigger far more complex conversations. It can reveal that which we would rather not know about, it can contradict the powerful who attempt to control what comes into our visible spaces, and it can move us out of our social and political inertia, and challenge us to take action."[105]

Guantánamo prisoner Djamel Ameziane expressed this point powerfully, writing to his lawyer, "For many years we Guantánamo prisoners were pictured by many US government officials as monsters, the evilest people on earth, the worst of the worst, and I am sure many Americans believed that. Displaying the artwork is a way to show people that we are people who have feelings, who are creative, that we are human beings. We are normal people and not monsters."[106]

Life after Guantánamo

> *We don't make apologies for having detained people lawfully.*
>
> —Lee Wolosky[107]

The injustice of being imprisoned at Guantánamo doesn't end once the direct abuse stops and the prisoners are freed. Not a single Guantánamo prisoner has received any apology or compensation from the United States government. Further, the stigma of being labeled a terrorist in a climate of global Islamophobia poses an additional challenge as these former prisoners bear the weight of harmful narratives in their efforts to rebuild their lives.

For example, former prisoner Airat Vakhitov said, "I consider the biggest humiliation I have suffered [to be] the stigma that the Americans gave to me. The life-long brand of terrorist, extremist, which I received in Guantánamo has stayed with me since being extradited to Russia." Another former prisoner, Hussein al-Merfedy, stated, "We thought we would be free when we left Guantánamo. . . . Instead, we went from the small Guantánamo to here—a bigger Guantánamo."[108] There is probably little if anything that will help these Muslim men heal from the terror and trauma that haunts them, especially in the global climate that has become so invested in a never-ending War on Terror.

Lutfi Bin Ali, a Tunisian citizen who spent thirteen years in Guantánamo before he was released to Kazakhstan, expressed similar sentiments. Despite the fact that Bin Ali was subjected to egregious torture at the hands of the US government, he's expressed an eagerness to return to Guantánamo rather than face the isolation in his host country, where he knows no one. "At least in Guantánamo there were people to talk to. Here I have nobody."[109] For Bin Ali, the hell he knew was better than the hell he didn't. Eventually, because Bin Ali was extremely ill, he was granted permission to move to Mauritania. He had held out hope that being in Mauritania would allow him to go back to his home in Tunisia and to get the medical care he so desperately needed. However, because he was unable to get critical heart surgery, he died before he could return to Tunisia.[110] Guantánamo might not have killed Bin Ali directly, but it put him on the path to imminent to death.

Younous Chekkouri, a Moroccan citizen, spent fourteen years at Guantánamo without being charged with a crime or facing trial. After six security agencies found no evidence to continue his imprisonment, he was released—only to be imprisoned again because Moroccan authorities claimed he had formed a militant group.[111] He served five months of a five-year sentence before being acquitted by a Moroccan appeals court. Years later, Guantánamo continues to haunt him; and even leaving home causes Chekkouri fear because he imagines the faces of Guantánamo Bay guards among people in the crowds. Chekkouri has lamented, "I'm living this kind of depression" and "I'm not normal anymore."[112] For former prisoners like him, a "normal" life may never be a reality especially since the US government has not vindicated any of the men nor provided any substantial or meaningful support to help them heal.

Mohamedou Ould Slahi is one of the most well-known former prisoners from Guantánamo. Slahi's ordeal began in 2001, when his own country of Mauritania detained him at the request of the United States. Slahi was subsequently rendered by the CIA to Jordan, then Afghanistan, and finally Guantánamo, all while enduring egregious torture such as sexual humiliation, death threats, and a mock kidnapping.[113] Slahi documented his experiences from the time he was arrested in Mauritania to his detention at Guantánamo Bay in his book *Guantánamo Diary*, which has reached audiences across the globe. Though Slahi was released to Mauritania in 2016 after fourteen years of detention, he was initially denied his passport—which made it impossible for him to leave the country for medical treatment needed for ongoing pain from a surgery he had at Guantánamo.[114] In 2019, Slahi finally received his passport, which had been caught in the crosshairs of a blame game between Mauritania and the US. The only country that has given him a visa is South Africa, where he was able to travel. However, his visa application to travel to Germany, where his wife and son live, has been denied as of this writing.[115]

As the many stories of Guantánamo prisoners reveal, the cruelty of the prison knows no bounds. This includes the detention of twenty-one children. Asked to comment on children at Guantánamo, former vice president Dick Cheney stated, "This constant refrain of the juveniles . . . these are not children."[116] Even when prisoners were considered juveniles or children, the narrative of former juvenile prisoner Omar Khadr as "terror's child" effectively "reinforc[ed] the notion of the Muslim terrorist suspect as constitutively monstrous, so much so that his children are natural-born terrorists."[117]

One of the more well-known cases of child prisoners at Guantánamo, Omar Khadr was detained in 2002 at the age of fifteen because the US government alleged that he threw a grenade that killed US Army Sergeant First Class Christopher Speer and injured two others in Afghanistan. While at Guantánamo, Khadr was subjected to sleep deprivation and solitary confinement, and was used as a human mop. Charged with five war crimes, he eventually pled guilty in order to leave Guantánamo, making him the first child to be convicted of a war crime since World War II.[118]

Concessions like these are at the heart of what US Colonel Morris Davis has referred to as the paradox of Guantánamo: "You have to lose to win. Those lucky enough to get charged and convicted of a war crime have good odds of getting out of Guantánamo, but those who are never charged could spend the rest of their lives in prison."[119] For his part, even after pleading guilty, Khadr was given an eight-year sentence by the US military commission—a widely condemned and discredited system of justice.[120]

Khadr was eventually repatriated to Canada in 2012, after spending ten years in US custody. However, when he returned to Canada, he had to spend another three years in detention before he was released on bail in 2015. In 2014, Khadr tried to have his war-crimes convictions overturned in a military commission appeals court, but without success.[121] Unlikethe majority of former Guantánamo prisoners, in 2015 Khadr received compensation in the amount of $10.5 million for "his ordeal abroad and any resulting harm"—not from the United States but from his country of citizenship, Canada.[122]

Two people taking issue with the compensation Khadr received are the widow of US Army Sergeant Christopher Speer, Tabitha Speer, and Sergeant Layne Morris, who was injured in the firefight that killed Speer. Together they sued Khadr in Utah, winning a wrongful-death judgment in 2015 in the amount of $134 million—a judgment they are still trying to get Canada to recognize at the time of this writing.[123]

Khadr's story reveals the many layers of injustice that former Guantánamo prisoners face, both because of the aftermath of the faux legal system at the prison and due to legal struggles after their release. Khadr's post-detention ordeals haven't stopped yet, but rather have included barriers to rebuilding his life, such as being able to find employment. As Khadr stated painfully, "A lot of times when I apply for work or volunteering I don't hear back from people. In the nursing program I applied and of course you have to do a criminal background check and of course when that comes back all the charges come up. So realistically for the time being I don't think that anybody is going to be willing to risk, like, people like me but are not willing to take that risk to employ somebody with a history as mine."[124]

There are many more stories of former Guantánamo prisoners, including some who have been able to successfully rebuild their lives. Nevertheless, what all these stories reveal is that even if Guantánamo closes, there will always be a piece of its haunting memory scattered across the globe, in those whose lives were stolen by the prison.

The Unknown Unknowns

In a 2002 Pentagon Briefing, Secretary of Defense Donald Rumsfeld was asked whether there was any evidence suggesting that terrorists had been supplied with weapons of mass destruction by Iraq. He responded, "There are known knowns; there are things we know we know. We also know there are known unknowns; that is to say, we know there are some things we do not know. But there are also unknown unknowns—the ones we don't know we don't know."[125]

The same slippery logic—we don't know what we don't know—has plagued efforts to end detention at Guantánamo. Regardless of who is in the White House, the threat of recidivism has been used to argue against closing the prison. Even if a prisoner is successful in challenging their detention, or if the government does not have enough evidence to convict them of a crime (or if that evidence has been tainted by torture), the argument goes that we can't know whether they will engage with terrorism if they are released. Lurking in the background of this argument, of course, is the unspoken fear that even an innocent man may very well have been radicalized after years of detention and abuse.

According to a government report from August 2020, 17.1 percent of former prisoners have been confirmed to have reengaged with terrorism, with an additional 14.3 percent suspected of reengaging.[126] These numbers are problematic for several reasons. For one thing, the information the government has relied on in making these determinations has not been independently verified. More troubling, the criteria for what constitutes recidivism include expressing anti-American opinions, including former prisoners sharing their stories with the outside world.

The fundamental problem with the specter of recidivism, however, is that it creates a cruel catch-22 whereby unjustly detained and abused prisoners are deemed too dangerous to release precisely because this treatment might (reasonably) lead them to harbor anti-American sentiments. In the words of Harvard professor Rebecca Lemov, the trap is this: "We cannot release you because, although you were once innocent, through your detention, we have decided, you risk potentially becoming guilty of unknown acts. In this potentiality, there is a kind of projected culpability of an unclear but undeniable sort. These men, accompanied by a massive dossier of information drawn from or about him, have nonetheless become unknown unknowns."[127]

Guantánamo Stays Open for Business

Guantánamo has become an institutionalized part of the War on Terror. Despite its being mired in legal and political problems, no serious attempt was made to close it by Presidents Bush or Obama, and President Trump expressed his enthusiasm for the notorious prison by issuing an executive order to ensure it would stay open indefinitely.

Though under President Bush's administration 532 prisoners were released from Guantánamo and he claimed he wanted to shut it down, he also lamented that it wasn't as easy as it sounded. In 2006, for example, he commented, "I'd like to close Guantánamo, but I also recognize that we're holding some people that are darn dangerous, and that we better have a plan to deal with them in our courts."[128] That same year, though, his attorney general, Alberto Gonzales, advocated against the use of the courts to fairly try Guantánamo prisoners, remarking before the Senate Judiciary Committee, "We must eliminate the hundreds of lawsuits from Guantánamo detainees that are clogging our court system."[129] Of course, Gonzales did not acknowledge that if there were hundreds of lawsuits, it probably meant something was fundamentally wrong in the system of "justice" they had established.

In his 2011 memoir, *Decision Points*, President Bush wrote, "While I believe opening Guantanamo after 9/11 was necessary, *the detention facility had become a propaganda tool for our enemies* and a distraction for our allies. I worked to find a way to close the prison without compromising security" (emphasis added).[130] In true fashion, Bush's statement absolved him, and the US, of any responsibility for establishing and operating an illegal prison designed to indefinitely detain and torture Muslim men. The problem of Guantánamo, for Bush, was not its existence but the reaction it provoked in the mind of the Muslim "enemy." Moreover, Bush's statement illustrated that after nine years of the prison's operation, and the lies that have upheld its physical and symbolic structure, when it comes to the destruction of Muslim lives, remorse is impossible.

While running for president in 2008, then candidate Obama made the closure of Guantánamo part of his policy agenda. Three days after his inauguration on January 20, 2009, President Obama signed an executive order to close Guantánamo within one year.[131] This ambitious timeline proved difficult, and at the end of his eight-year, two-term administration, the prison remained open. President Obama repeatedly blamed Congress for obstructing the closure of Guantánamo on the basis of the National Defense Authorization Act (NDAA), which prohibited funds from being used for detainee transfers to other countries. The only exception was in the 2010 NDAA, which limited funding for transfers. From the 2016 NDAA onward, the bill prohibited funds for detainee transfers not only to other countries but also to the United States. Although President Obama expressed concern about the Guantánamo regulations in the NDAA, he nevertheless signed the bill every year. As of this writing, both funding prohibitions remain in place.

In addition to the annual NDAA serving as a barrier to the closure of Guantánamo Bay Prison, President Obama put restrictions in place that barred certain prisoners from returning to their country of origin for security reasons. For example, Obama forbade Yemenis from being repatriated after the Christmas Day 2009 suicide bombing attempt because the bomber supposedly had links to Yemen.[132] In later years, Yemenis were also denied repatriation because of the unstable security situation in Yemen—one that the US contributed to. In addition to these challenges, many prisoners were deemed by authorities to be too dangerous to release and at the same time too difficult to prosecute (often because of evidence that had been tainted by torture).[133]

In his second term, Obama created the position of Special Envoy for the Closure of Guantánamo. Ambassador Lee Wolosky, who served in this position from July 2015 until January 2017, expressed the difficulty of transferring prisoners out, saying, "The fact that they have been labeled in a political discourse as the worst of the worst, which some of them are, but some of them aren't. And the ones we're moving out are not, but they're lumped in there. . . . That certainly makes the task of doing what we do, which is looking at each case and convincing our foreign partners to look at the facts of each case, more difficult, because of the labeling."[134] This concern was disingenuous, considering that the Obama administration did nothing to challenge the public image of the prisoners, even when they knew the vast majority of them were innocent of any charges.

Obama asserted in his final State of the Union address that he would "keep working to shut down the prison at Guantánamo: it's expensive, it's unnecessary, and it only serves as a recruitment brochure for our enemies."[135] Notably missing from this statement is any mention of the injustice perpetrated on the Muslim men detained there. And as with Bush, Obama's characterization of the prison as a "recruitment brochure" for terrorists reinforces the trope of irrational, angry Muslims, while evading all accountability for the horrors of Guantánamo.

Ultimately, the Obama administration released 197 men detained at Guantánamo. However, his failure to close the prison set the stage for incoming president Trump, an overt Islamophobe, to further institutionalize a facility designed to demonize and criminalize Muslims.

Even before Trump was elected, he expressed enthusiasm for keeping the prison open, saying, "Guantanamo Bay, which by the way, which by the way, we are keeping open. Which we are keeping open . . . and we're gonna load it up with some bad dudes, believe me, we're gonna load it up."[136] In January 2018, Trump signed an executive order to keep Guantánamo open—and to allow ISIS fighters to be transferred into the prison.[137] Notably, though many prisoners have been cleared for release, only one was released under Trump—months after he signed the executive order.[138] Several months prior, then secretary of state Rex Tillerson had cut the position of Special Envoy for the Closure of Guantánamo, making prisoner transfers out effectively impossible. In a crystal-clear signal of his intent, then President Trump's commanders were told to prepare for the prison's operation until 2043.[139]

Although no new prisoners have been sent to Guantánamo as of this writing, forty remain, with virtually no hope of leaving—a continued lesson in American justice.

An Open Letter

As I stated at the beginning of this chapter, in November 2015, I traveled to Cuba on a delegation with Witness Against Torture. Our goal was to get as close to the gates of the Guantánamo military base as possible in hopes that somehow the Muslim men who were detained would know of or at least feel our presence. We camped on a hill about twenty minutes outside Guantánamo City, waking up each day to conduct remembrances of the men detained and to imagine what their return home might look like. Even though we were mere miles away from the prison, we knew that the best chance of our message getting to prisoners inside was to get the media to pick up our story of solidarity. As a Muslim on the delegation, I remember the pain of being so close to my Muslim brothers, yet so far away. So I wrote a letter to the men, hoping that, one way or another, my message would reach them. I still hope it will.

To my dear Muslim Brothers detained in Guantanamo Bay Prison,

I want you to know that today I'm coming to you, that I'm walking to the naval base to find you. I want you to know that your lives transcend borders and that your spirits exist above law. I want you to know that my liberation is bound up in yours; that none of us are free until you are.

I want you to know that I've carefully looked through your pictures and read your stories; that I examined your pictures closely and tried to fathom your pain and suffering. That I tried to do so, in hopes of alleviating just a small piece of your torture.

I want you to know that I pray for you every day. That I can't wear the color orange without knowing and feeling that there exists, on the edge of a small country, a prison that tortures you.

I want you to know that I'm here until the end and until you are free. I want you [to] know that a journey of a thousand miles begins with a single step, but that I count none except those that bring you closer to freedom and justice.

I hope that one day, *Insha'Allah*, we will greet each other at the mosque, saying *Assalamu Alaikum*, knowing that you are my protector and that I am yours.

Until then, dear brothers, be well and rise up, knowing that you are not alone. We hear you, see you, and will never let your lives be in vain.

Your sister in Islam,

Maha

PART III
INTERNALIZING, CHALLENGING, AND LIVING ISLAMOPHOBIA IN THE WAR ON TERROR

The pressure of simply existing in a climate of Islamophobia cannot be overstated, and strategies for coping vary between individuals and groups. One of the burdens of existing in this oppressive context is the constant exposure to narratives that malign Muslims, which are embedded in almost every aspect of cultural, social, and political life. In the realm of the political, narratives exist both to preemptively support certain interventions and to justify them after the fact. In the context of the War on Terror, Muslim Americans have often been pigeon-holed into expressing their identities in relationship to the dominant narrative that constructs Muslims as inherently violent, barbaric, and uncivilized, among other tropes.

There are vastly different approaches that people take to existing in this reality. Some people internalize problematic assumptions about Islam and Muslims whether they are empirically based or not. This isn't always a conscious process or intentional, yet it has implications all the same. This influences their perceptions of themselves, of the broader Muslim community, and of the external-facing systems of power that impact their lives and communities. Others take the opposite approach of rejecting the dominant narrative about Muslims, putting in its place an understanding of the contours of Islamophobia and its fundamental assumptions. Still others embody aspects of each of the above approaches in that they can negotiate with the public perception, but without fundamentally changing or challenging the strategies that emerge from those with internalized Islamophobia. In order to develop a holistic picture of the Muslim American response to the War on Terror, it is critical to understand the range of ways in which Islamophobia is internalized, leveraged, challenged, and resisted.

Collectively, these responses can be contradictory, and when viewed from the vantage point of outsiders to the community, they may suggest that Muslim Americans are working toward different goals and in ways that are mutually exclusive. We can attribute part of this to the fact that Muslim Americans are not a monolith and do not have a singular animating purpose. However, it is important to assess whether the different strategies utilized can actually bring about positive change and whether these strategies lead to a logical end defined by a broad goal of obtaining equity, equality, and justice for Muslim Americans.

For many Muslim Americans and organizations addressing Islamophobia, the focus is most heavily on institutional, structural, and interpersonal Islamophobia. Frequently ignored or unacknowledged is internalized Islamophobia. Internalized Islamophobia is extremely important to address because of how those manifesting this form of oppression often participate in and strengthen institutionalized Islamophobia. Thus, it is imperative to examine internalized Islamophobia more closely, consider its strengthening effect on institutionalized Islamophobia, and address its impact beyond the individual and on the wider community.

One of the more harmful ways many Muslim American organizations have engaged with the problematic and dominant narratives has been to collude with and support them. Thus, for example, when acts of violence are perpetrated by Muslims, some of the more uniform responses focus on condemning the violence, attaching existing tropes to the characterization of the violence, and ultimately accepting the premise of collective responsibility. When Muslim Americans openly embrace rather than reject collective responsibility as a narrative strategy, they effectively give the government and the external community license to perpetuate the same.

Only a few organizations are examined in chapter 10, and it should go without saying that they are not representative of the larger Muslim community. Nevertheless, many insights can be gained by analyzing their leadership, their narrative strategies and responses, and how they align with the goal of gaining or restoring human and civil rights for Muslim Americans. Recognizing that obtaining rights is not an all-or-nothing matter, we will also analyze these organizational responses in order to understand the cost of inclusion in government decisions, including the extent to which rights and basic humanity are negotiated or compromised.

It's difficult to encompass the totality of the violence that has targeted and continues to target Muslims in the course of the War on Terror. One way to bring this violence to light, however, is by telling personal narratives that speak to the reality of Muslim life post-9/11. While the consequences of the US's War on Terror have touched every aspect of the globe and the lives of millions of Muslims, it is Muslim Americans who live at the heart of empire. This is a reality that impacts Muslim Americans' direct experiences in the United States, in addition to their position vis-à-vis the global war. The personal narratives included in the last chapter of part 3 are of Muslim Americans' "lived experiences"—a term that speaks to experience itself, but also to living through it. The inclusion of these personal narratives is important in documenting and building historical memory of how Islamophobia in the War on Terror has already impacted Muslim Americans. This documentation also serves the purpose of understanding how to move forward in a war—whether named or not—whose lack of a conceivable end has been normalized. The Muslim Americans interviewed for this book shared not only their lived experiences but also their vision of justice for Muslims. They are a reminder that there is another way forward.

9.

OPPRESSION FROM WITHIN

"I'm Muslim, but I'm not angry." "I'm Muslim, but I don't hate Americans." "I'm Muslim, and I'm a feminist." "I'm Muslim, and I'm descended from pilgrims on the *Mayflower*." These statements were made by Muslim Americans as part of a 2015 Buzzfeed video titled "I'm Muslim, but I'm Not . . ."[1] The two-minute video is split into two parts. The first part includes Muslims claiming their identities and what they're not (the "not" preceding a stereotype about Muslims). The second part starts with Muslims' affirmations of their identities—this time, with Muslims claiming what they are (a refutation of a stereotype about Muslims). While the video was intended to be an uplifting message about Muslim humanity, it exemplifies an approach to representation and visibility that is problematic. Whether by refuting a stereotype directly or by claiming a stereotype as a way of refuting it indirectly, these statements reinforce, rather than dispel, stereotypes about Muslims.

This narrative structure erases the possibility that Muslims can be nuanced individuals who articulate their ideas, thoughts, and beliefs with more complexity than what is desired in media soundbites. It also runs the risk of adding fuel to the fire of anti-Muslim associations by introducing new elements to the stereotypes. The statement "I'm Muslim, and I like Thanksgiving" exemplifies both of these pitfalls. Of the myths the video meant to refute, Muslims' attitude toward Thanksgiving was probably not at the top of the list—so this statement introduces a new, specific connection into the general trope of Muslim anti-Americanism. Speaking to nuance, there are valid reasons for Muslims, or anyone else, to dislike Thanksgiving—for example, because it amounts to nothing less than a celebration of Indigenous genocide. By positioning Muslim identity two-dimensionally in relation to stereotypes, this form of cultural communication ties it to the same negative tropes it is trying to combat.

Videos presented in this form are often widely celebrated; as of this writing, the one on Buzzfeed had over three million views, with numerous commenters (many seemingly Muslim, based on their names) celebrating the positivity of the message and repeating the particular phrases that reso-nated with them. Despite the affirming language, the undertone of the con-versation is that Muslim Americans have to prove themselves to be "real" Americans. In this case, proof means showing how their beliefs and behav-iors mirror and/or are identical to mainstream American culture. By present-ing in this way, Muslim Americans in the film and in the comments articulate the idea that "we are like you," or "we are like our oppressors." Regardless of the particular impetus for the making of this video, it demonstrates a com-mon pattern found in responses to current events by Muslim Americans who believe the onus is on them to humanize themselves and make Islam and Muslims more palatable to the US, and to the West as a whole.

The consequences of living with oppression as a member of a targeted group are more easily recognizable when they take the form of societal and state structures such as hardline immigration policies and incidents such as hate crimes. Less recognized is the impact of these formal and informal external oppressive forces when reflected internally, and how these internalized psychological and social structures shape Muslim responses to their oppression. In a book whose purpose is to capture as wide a view as possible of the impacts of the War on Terror on Muslim and Muslim American communities, examining how Islamophobia manifests internally is a core and necessary piece of dismantling the formal structures that institutionalize Islamophobia into law and policy. Though internal-ized oppression—specifically, internalized Islamophobia—manifests most directly in the individual, there are consequences on the larger group to which the individual belongs and with whom they share their stigmatized identity. Reinforcing negative tropes about Muslims and Islam that have been internalized, even implicitly, can and often does have a ripple effect into public policy. If this matter were left unaddressed, our explanation of how the underlying Islamophobia of the War on Terror has continued to thrive would be incomplete.

Internalized Oppression

While the focus of many marginalized communities operating in a policy/legal space has been on confronting and addressing the direct results of oppression, far less attention has been paid to the way external oppression impacts a person's sense of self. According to Scholar Hilde Lindemann, a person's identity becomes injured or damaged when a person in an oppressed group accepts the powerful social group's construction of their identity. The resulting devaluation of oneself as a member of the oppressed group is what Lindemann refers to "infiltrated consciousness."[2] This concept is helpful in understanding the process through which individuals become disempowered on the basis of the harmful ideas that are leveraged against them by those in power and which are subsequently internalized.

The concept of internalized oppression is concerned with the form that this oppression takes within an individual, the consequences of internalization in terms of how individuals view and relate to their community, and how this process ultimately promotes and perpetuates domination and subservience to the dominant society. In this book, I take it as a rule that internalized oppression "is an inevitable condition of all structures of oppression,"[3] such that its existence cannot be denied. If we are interested in truly recalibrating the power of marginalized communities within the dominant structure, then not only can the existence of internalized oppression not be denied, but it must also be contended with directly. Although the contexts in which internalized oppression has been examined vary, many definitions and ideas that recur throughout this body of literature are either directly applicable or readily modifiable to apply to internalized Islamophobia specifically.

As a starting point, a conceptual understanding of what exactly constitutes internalized oppression is required. Although there are many definitions, feminist scholar Gail Pheterson defines internalized oppression as "the incorporation and acceptance by individuals within an oppressed group of the prejudices against them within the dominant society. Internalized oppression is likely to consist of self-hatred, self-concealment, fear of violence and feelings of inferiority, resignation, isolation, powerlessness, and gratefulness for being allowed to survive. Internalized oppression is the mechanism within an oppressive system for perpetuating domination not only by external control but also by building subservience into the minds of the oppressed groups."[4] Many responses from Muslim Americans to institutionalized Islamophobia exhibit aspects of this definition, particularly when it comes to gratitude toward the oppressor for their survival. Though not included in this definition, it is important to note that internalized oppression benefits the dominant power directly not just because the oppressed perpetuate their own oppression, but also because the dominant power structure is relieved from exerting force to perpetuate the subjugation of a marginalized group.

There are three different ways that internalized oppression is manifested: intrapersonal, interpersonal, and institutionalized. The first manifestation, intrapersonal, is concerned with inferiorizing beliefs that one holds about oneself and how these beliefs are enacted on one's own self. Internalized oppression manifests interpersonally when these beliefs about inferiority are expressed toward others, generally members of one's own group. Finally, internalized oppression becomes institutionalized "when the same inferiorizing beliefs and practices become normalized—perhaps even to the point where social norms, policies, or laws are developed to legitimize them."[5] Although the focus of this book is on the institutionalized manifestation of internalized oppression, the three manifestations reinforce each other.

Another, more historically situated framework for understanding the different dimensions of internalized oppression is Frantz Fanon's theory of colonized minds. Fanon, a French-Martinican psychiatrist, was one of the foremost thinkers on the structures of colonialism, oppression, and internalized oppression. In his book *The Wretched of the Earth*, he presents four phases of colonialism from the entry of foreign colonizers to the exploitation of people and resources, the destruction of Indigenous culture, and the construction of the colonizers as civilized and the colonized as savage and therefore in need of reforming. The last and final phase is the establishing of a society built on institutions—including political, social, and economic ones—designed to benefit the colonizers and uphold the power dynamic of this group as superior, while the colonized are repeatedly and consistently subjugated.[6]

Fanon's model illustrates how insidious colonialism was and is, while underscoring a less acknowledged impact of colonialism on colonized groups: in addition to the brute force and domination they must bear, the violence of colonialism meant colonized groups absorbed the colonizers' constructions of themselves and their values as superior to those of the colonized.

In a similar vein, Albert Memmi, a French-Tunisian Jewish writer and essayist, offers another critical perspective on internalized colonialization. Memmi's concept of the "mythical portrait" speaks to how the colonized are negatively constructed by the colonizer in order to justify policing them. As a result, the colonized have to navigate complex feelings about their mythical portrait, including whether the colonizer has constructed their image correctly or not. To this end, Memmi writes,

> Constantly confronted with this image of [themselves], set forth and imposed on all institutions and in every human contact, how could the colonized help reacting to [their] portrait? It cannot leave [them]

indifferent and remain a veneer which, like an insult, blows with the wind. [They] end up recognizing it as one would a detested nickname which has become a familiar description. The accusation disturbs [them] and worries [them] even more because they admire and fear their powerful accuser. "Are not they partially right?" [they] mutter. "Are we not a little guilty after all? Lazy, because we have so many idlers? Timid, because we let ourselves be oppressed?" Willfully created and spread by the colonizer, this mythical and degrading portrait ends up being accepted and lived with to a certain extent by the colonized.[7]

Both Fanon and Memmi provide powerful conceptualizations of internalized colonialism that highlight just how detrimental this form of oppression is.

More contemporary scholars, seeking to understand the impact of colonialism on different ethnic groups, refer to a "colonial mentality," a form of internalized oppression that emerges out of long histories of colonialism, such that the colonized perceive themselves as ethnically inferior. The manifestations of colonial mentality include (1) denigration of the self, (2) denigration of one's culture, (3) discrimination against less assimilated members of one's own group, and (4) tolerance and acceptance of historical and contemporary oppression by the colonizer. These frameworks are directly applicable to the project of understanding the way Muslims have internalized their own oppression and how this dynamic plays out as a function of the War on Terror.

Theories of internalized oppression and colonialism aim to describe the full impact of dominant structures of power on the oppressed, including participation in or support of systems that perpetuate their own oppression. Though not articulated in the same terms, research on inequality and what allows for its reproduction is also instructive in identifying specific ways members of an oppressed group perpetuate their own inequitable treatment. To understand how internalized oppression functions through the lens of inequality maintenance, this book draws from a theory that identifies generic processes by which inequality is reproduced, including othering, subordinate adaptation, boundary maintenance, and emotion management. Each of these processes is composed of several subprocesses, which I explain in greater detail below.

"Defense othering" is a subprocess of othering that occurs when members of a subordinate group distance themselves from each other because of the stigma assigned to the group and/or because some want to distinguish themselves from other group members who embody something the dominant group finds undesirable.[8] The logic of the War on Terror, which operates on the basis of a government-constructed dichotomy between "good" and "bad" Muslim, has pitted Muslims against each other in this way.

One of the strategies the oppressed may use to cope with their subordinate status and what they are denied as a result of it is the trading of power for patronage. "Trading power for patronage" involves the acceptance of one's subordinated status while engaging with members of the dominant group in order to get compensatory benefits.[9] Though members of the subordinate group may feel empowered by virtue of proximity to power, this strategy offers little guarantee of shifting power between the subordinate and dominant groups. Thus, for example, a member might get a seat at the table but is prevented from speaking, or if they are permitted the opportunity to speak, they would likely be limited to speech that reaffirms the narrative of the dominant group. This dynamic, therefore, while appearing to offer some degree of power, is yet another way inequality is reproduced.

The last relevant process to reproducing inequality per this theory, as it pertains to Muslims, is emotion management. As a process, "emotion management" refers to the way emotions are shaped by culture—both symbolically and materially. As a subprocess of emotion management, regulated discourse creates the boundaries and rules "about what can be said, how it can be said, and who can say what to whom." The normalization of certain forms of discourse can also play a powerful role in reproducing inequality.[10] A narrative that has been accepted as the standard operates to regulate thought and emotion in addition to defining what can and cannot be said, and by whom. Unfortunately, those seeking membership in the dominant group or those seeking to be listened to may feel the need to resort to using the "master's linguistic tools," which reaffirms the dominant group's discourse.[11] Muslims operating according to these terms may end up repeating simplistic narratives, such as that Islam is a religion of peace, which respond to the dominant discourse instead of offering alternative and possible contradictory perspectives that would challenge the need for that response in the first place.

Expressions of Internalized Islamophobia

> *You must remember, the so-called Jihadis who are in reality, mentally unstable individuals run by Quranic fundamentalists, do not represent the whole Muslim population of the world.*
>
> —ABHIJIT NASKAR[12]

Like many others, Naskar, a world-renowned neuroscientist, repeats a tired narrative distinguishing the average Muslim from the "terrorists." His use of the word *remember*, however, signals an important detail—that it takes a conscious effort to accept that not all Muslims are terrorists. Instead of critiquing the embedded notion that Muslims should be held collectively responsible, he legitimizes it by essentially responding with "Not *all* Muslims." As is typical, Naskar ascribes the characteristic of being "mentally unstable" to the terrorists to eliminate the possibility that anything rational could be motivating their violence. This quote was not selected because it is somehow unique—indeed, it is emblematic of the way many Muslim Americans have responded to acts of violence perpetrated by other Muslims by accepting collective responsibility. Moreover, Naskar's quote also provides an example of what it looks like to perpetuate Islamophobia by using language similar to that of the state.

Twenty years into the War on Terror, the phenomenon of internalized oppression is crucial to understanding how Islamophobia from external sources can be challenged by the Muslim community. Its existence represents a deep conundrum for those organizing against institutionalized Islamophobia—namely, how to challenge Islamophobia from the external community and Islamophobia from the internal community at the same time. But because internalized Islamophobia emboldens and reinforces institutionalized Islamophobia, the two need to be addressed simultaneously. In the context of the War on Terror especially, the state has often weaponized internalized Islamophobia as a way of enlisting Muslims to do the work of oppression for it. To illustrate this phenomenon, the examples below examine the language used in writings by Muslim Americans that collude with the dominant narrative and demonstrate internalized Islamophobia.

A major way in which the narrative of the collective responsibility of Muslims is reflected in the public language of prominent Muslims themselves is through an outsized emphasis on the role of religion in radicalization or deradicalization. This is particularly the case when op-eds focus on responding to current events involving some act of violence by Muslims. To this end, an op-ed by Imam Suhaib Webb and Scott Korb, published in the *New York Times* on April 24, 2013, and titled "No Room for Radicals," was written in reference to the Boston Marathon bombers.[13] The launching point of the op-ed was a quote from Representative Peter T. King of New York, the Republican chair of the House Subcommittee on Counterterrorism and Intelligence, calling for more surveillance of Muslim communities. Instead of talking about how harmful surveillance is and has been to the Muslim community, critiquing the theory of radicalization as empirically unsound and mainly applied to Muslims, or naming the many other abuses that have happened in the course of the War on Terror, Webb and Korb focused narrowly on dispelling the myth that radicalization happens at American Muslim institutions, including mosques and community centers. Going through a catalog of these institutions, they argue, "Yet what's most obvious to anyone who has spent time in these communities is that whether they are devotional or educational, focused on the arts or on interfaith cooperation and activism, this mediating set of American Muslim institutions is keeping impressionable young Muslims from becoming radicalized." The picture painted in this op-ed is that whatever else American Muslim institutions do, their most important function is to perform the state's work of preventing radicalization. Furthermore, the narrative espoused in this piece suggests that, unlike other religious institutions, American Muslim institutions cannot exist solely to provide religious/spiritual guidance (outside the realm of radicalization, terrorism, etc.), social services, or community building.

The authors argue further, "Representative King and others have it exactly, completely wrong—the American Muslim community has actively and repeatedly, day in and day out, rejected such radicals on religious grounds: they do not know mercy." Where the authors go wrong here is in assuming that someone such as Representative King, with his long history of outright Islamophobia, might be moved to change his views. Because of this faulty assumption, they end up essentially answering a rhetorical question—Why don't Muslims condemn radicalization?—with a statement that serves no purpose but to perpetuate collective responsibility by accepting that the burden of challenging extremism lies with the Muslim community. Furthermore, the authors' rhetorical position is extremely vulnerable. What if in the future someone could be shown beyond doubt to have been radicalized at a mosque? By encouraging the hollow argument that mosques can and should be forces for deradicalization, the authors set themselves up to be disproved, purely based on numbers, as soon as someone inevitably points to a situation where the opposite happened. This strategy gives unnecessary fuel to Islamophobes seeking new information to buttress their bigoted beliefs in the minds of the public, not to change their minds. Even more troubling, it is easy to envision Webb and Korb's argument being used to justify the surveillance of the entire community. Given that it rests not on challenging what's actually problematic about Representative King's statement, but on making broad, unsubstantiated claims about the "purpose" of American mosques and other Muslim American gathering spaces—claims that cater to the notion of collective responsibility—it would seem the authors would have to accept that conclusion.

Other prominent Muslim Americans who often speak publicly on behalf of the whole community seem to feel there is a unique burden on them to condemn terrorism unequivocally and loudly. One example is Tarek El-Messidi, founding director of Celebrate Mercy, an organization whose mission is to educate Muslims and the general public about the Prophet Muhammad's (peace be unto him) life and character. In a 2015 interview where El-Messidi was asked about condemning terrorism, he stated, "The narrative is being defined for us, and we're being defined by these extremist acts and the poll numbers show that. . . . I personally do feel like condemning is an unfortunate necessity right now because our community is misunderstood. But I think that's partially the Muslims' fault because we're not changing the narrative. Condemning is just a Band-Aid solution. It feels like putting a Band-Aid over a tumor."[14]

Even though El-Messidi begins by acknowledging that American Muslims are beholden to an externally created narrative, he immediately signals that the blame should be placed on Muslims. In doing so, he disregards the fact that if the state had not been so diligent and successful in linking terrorism to Muslims and Muslims alone, the community would not find itself so occupied with condemning terrorism at every turn. Moreover, instead of challenging the root causes of why the Muslim community might be "misunderstood," he falls into the trap of accepting collective responsibility—twice. First, he accepts the burden of condemnation as a necessary evil. We have seen this before. And second, El-Messidi goes much further by blaming Muslims for the continued existence of the false narrative that places the burden of condemnation on them. Logically, this is counterintuitive—how can the responsibility for a story told about a people lie with the people whose identities are circumscribed by its telling? Does El-Messidi really believe that Muslims are on equal footing when it comes to promoting a particular narrative? Ultimately, his argument is circular; its internal logic depends completely on internalized Islamophobia. In adopting the "Band-Aid" solution of condemnation with its implicit acceptance of collective responsibility, the Muslim community abrogates its power over the narrative. You can't change a narrative you've adopted as your own.

Even more disturbing, El-Messidi demonstrated a full embrace of collective responsibility three years prior, in 2012, when he asked Muslims to write condolence letters to the family of Ambassador Chris Stevens, who was killed in Libya.[15] The project resulted in 7,700 letters, sent by Muslims from 115 different countries. Though it's unknown exactly what the contents of the letters were, since the goal was to offer condolences from Muslims, if a connection wasn't already established linking Muslims to the violence that killed the ambassador and holding them collectively responsible, El-Messidi's campaign sealed the deal. Internalized Islamophobia was therefore manifested through this project, which, regardless of intent, reduced all the other factors of the ambassador's murder to religious identity—in particular, Muslim identity.

Religious leaders such as Sheikh Hamza Yusuf have long manifested internalized Islamophobia; in his case, it has been demonstrated through collaboration with the US government. One of the most famous Muslim Americans in the world, Yusuf made headlines, including in a piece I authored,[16] when he accepted an invitation from well-known Islamophobe and secretary of state Mike Pompeo to serve as an advisor to the Commission on Unalienable Rights. Even after Yusuf received significant backlash, he provided no explanation as to how this position would benefit Muslims beyond getting a proverbial seat at the table.

This wasn't the first time Yusuf took to advising problematic presidents; in fact, he was called on by former president Bush to participate in an interfaith prayer event shortly after 9/11. More significantly, Yusuf is credited with persuading the Bush administration to change the name of the attack on Afghanistan from Operation Infinite Justice to Operation Enduring Freedom.[17] This suggestion was made on the basis of the assumption that Muslims would be offended by the name Operation Infinite Justice because justice is an attribute of God in Islam. What Yusuf ignored was the obvious possibility that Muslims would be more offended by being detained, tortured, and attacked with drones than by the name of the campaign under which this abuse happened.

In a June 24, 2016 op-ed titled "The Orlando Shooter Googled My Name. I Wish He Had Reached Out to Me," Hamza Yusuf pondered the possibility that Omar Mateen wanted to reach out to him for counsel prior to his shooting spree at the Pulse nightclub earlier that month rather than, as the FBI thought, because he wanted to harm Yusuf.[18] Seeking to describe the roots of violence such as Mateen's, he argued in the op-ed, "Much of the violence we are witnessing has more to do with political vacuums, disempowerment and self-determination movements that use religion as a rallying cry in parts of the world that are still deeply theocentric. . . . If we look at the places and people radicalized, certain commonalities emerge. Many of the places have been victims of violence for decades." Though Yusuf was critiquing the use of religion as a source of violence, he was, at the same time, leveraging his religious (not political) background as a sheikh to impose a particular understanding of violence—an understanding which, coincidentally, mirrors that of the state. In other words, Yusuf had no problem using his religious authority to give oxygen to the state's intentionally narrow explanation for acts of terrorism.

One of the most violent effects of internalized Islamophobia is its manifestation in Muslims who minimize violence against other Muslims, treating their victimhood as secondary to the problem of how to avoid terrorist recruitment. A prime example of this can be found in the testimony of Abdullah Antepli, a professor at Duke University who testified for the North Carolina Commission on the Inquiry of Torture (NCCIT). The NCCIT was established to examine North Carolina's role in the CIA's rendition program. To this end, the NCCIT held a public hearing November 30–December 1, 2017.[19] During the course of the hearing, Antepli was the only Muslim who gave testimony. Rather than use his testimony to highlight how Muslims—the sole known victims of the CIA's detention and interrogation (DI) program—were brutally tortured, how the tactics used were rooted in an understanding of what would most humiliate those who had been detained, and how Islamophobia in general allowed for the dehumanization and subsequent abuse Muslims faced at the hands of the CIA, Antepli's remarks framed the torture as a "mistake." In his testimony, he also considered torture through the lens of morality. While many have used moral arguments to understand state violence, whether justifying or challenging the practice of torture, this approach inherently centers state actors rather than their victims. In most cases this framing allows the state to be seen as redeemable. As well, exaggerated morality claims—especially when they are presented to suggest that the state is motivated by them—obscure the true goals of political and military domination.

In the course of his testimony, it became clear that Antepli viewed the problem of torture not primarily as the impact on victims and survivors, but rather as the ways in which terrorist groups use or will use examples of the US's abuse of Muslims to recruit new members. Under this premise, he stated,

> What the what kind of impact is happening for the Muslim community, both in the United States as well as in overseas, these kind of issues that the lack of response—ethical, moral response—lack of ethical, moral correction that torture issues are facing are a prime recruitment material for evil organizations like ISIS, al-Qaeda and otherwise, as those of us who are involved. I'm so happy to hear your voice as well. It is basically feeding the basic promise of these evil organizations because they know they cannot defeat us militarily because they know the primary aim of any terrorist or opposition by especially Muslim terrorist organizations who are active in many different parts of the world today.[20]

Antepli's words could not have done a better job of diminishing the need for justice for Muslims—a fact that is not surprising considering that he showed more interest in the perpetrators of torture than in its victims, who are all Muslim. Going deeper into this theme, Antepli asserted, "Torture will not destroy the victims of torture, but it will morally erode and destroy the perpetrator and his and her society, his and her community, his and her religion, his and her entire universe."[21] It's wholly unclear what Antepli was referring to when he stated that torture wouldn't destroy the victim, especially since he didn't indicate that he had spoken to a single one. But this sentiment is emblematic of a consistent theme in terms of whom Antepli is interested in supporting and redeeming: the United States—not anyone, including Muslims, who have been harmed by this country.

Antepli, from his platform as the sole Muslim invitee, reiterated the dominant narrative that the US, even when engaging in outright brutality, is somehow morally superior to the terrorist organizations whose violence it purports to oppose. This idea of moral superiority, infused with an ahistorical narrative of the United States, led Antepli to suggest that, unlike in other countries, US torture is somehow more devastating because it's not in this country's nature to engage in such behaviors. To this point, he stated, "If Egypt, if Turkey, if Myanmar is doing these kind of practices, it's almost expected of them because their foundational commitments, where they are as a society, their aspiration for all sorts of different reasons, not to put those people down, but it hurts more. It's morally more problematic that we are doing it, and we are doing it after many, many times after we saw these pitfalls."[22] Following this logic, the United States is called to address torture because it damages the perception of what this country stands for, not because torture is illegal and unethical or because of the destruction it causes survivors.

Also in 2017, an organization named Women's Islamic Initiative in Spirituality and Equality (WISE) hosted a conference in Washington, DC, with the title "WISE Up: Knowledge Ends Extremism." Complementing the conference was a report covering topics such as American Muslim identity, extremist ideologies and recruitment methods, and Muslims' civil and human rights.[23] There were over seventy contributors to the report, and though one of the stated goals was to decouple from the extremists' ideology, the framing of many of the pieces made it almost impossible to meet that goal.

In fact, the very inclusion of some of the writings in the *WISE Up* report directly reflected the internalized Islamophobia of the compilers. For example, a piece titled "Islamophobia and Domestic Security," by Major General Douglas M. Stone (Ret.), opened like this: "I want to begin with a single statement: Islamophobia makes our country less secure."[24] From the beginning, Major General Stone essentially communicates to the reader that the only reason Islamophobia should be addressed is to safeguard a nation-state from harm. Throughout the article, rather than condemning Islamophobia and the treatment of Muslims as an issue in and of itself, he repeatedly links it to national security. When mentioning Abu Ghraib, he says nothing about the brutal torture that occurred behind its walls, instead focusing on how the US would benefit from being able to resume the goal of winning the hearts and minds of Iraqis. Further, like many other government officials, addressing the harm caused to Muslim victims is a means to the US's national security ends. To this end, Stone asserts that "there is no denying that Abu Ghraib was—and still is—being used against us as extremist propaganda."[25] In other words, the US should not be worried that its soldiers committed war crimes in plain sight, but that the torture of Muslims makes us less safe. Muslims' humanity can easily be dismissed, especially when it comes to protecting American lives. Perhaps Major General Stone believed that his affirmation that collective responsibility should be abandoned was helpful, but like the rest of what he wrote, it came back to national security. Major General Stone concludes his piece with the following: "There is no middle ground on the issue of Islamophobia and domestic security. It is of utmost importance to treat American Muslims with respect and appreciation for the commonalities that we share. As I learned during my time in Iraq, building strong and trusting relations with the American Muslim community will greatly enable law enforcement to learn of potential early-warning indicators. I believe that our law enforcement agencies must lead the way in showing that the American Muslim community is their best ally in this united fight against extremism."[26] As one last hurrah, Major General Stone's conclusion positions Muslims as a means to the US's national-security ends.

The following example may seem unsurprising, given how many Muslims themselves minimize the humanity of other Muslims. In another *WISE Up* essay, titled "Modeling Partnership between Communities and Law Enforcement," the author, Salam Al-Marayati, argues in favor of community-driven responses to issues such as violent extremism.[27] While Al-Marayati feigns critique of law enforcement's attempts at interventions to violent extremism that do not allow for an "authentic" voice, he somehow overlooks the fact that it is the government that has told Muslims they have a violent-extremism problem, not Muslims who themselves have determined that they have this problem. Al-Marayati argues that Muslims should not be singled out as the sole group that has issues with violent extremism. But if Muslims shouldn't be singled out, it is unclear why *he* is singling them out as his case study, especially when he mentions specific acts of state violence that have had an indelibly negative impact on Muslims—violence that isn't directed at white extremists. Reading further into his essay, we see that Al-Marayati's only real concern with singling out Muslims is that leaders in the community will be hesitant to address threats of ISIS—as if they have to follow the government's violent-extremism agenda in order to be concerned about violence in their communities.

Attempting to explain why Muslims might view law enforcement negatively, he writes, "The fiasco at Guantanamo Bay, stories of rendition, sting operations and entrapment: all of these have played into the mindset within the community that law enforcement is part of the problem or is an obstacle to any solution."[28] Rather than acknowledge the objective harm that has befallen the Muslim community, he instead focuses on the impacts of these government actions on Muslims' perception or "mindset." Moreover, his statement suggests that the perception of law enforcement as problematic is worse than the actual violence law enforcement commits in the first place, and upon which Muslims' perspectives are based.

We'll Give You Our Blood

Muslim Americans are rarely celebrated in the public eye. One of the few ways that Muslim Americans gain recognition is through military service, though even this is limited. One such example is Khizr Khan, a Pakistani man who rose to prominence after speaking at the Democratic National Convention (DNC) in 2016 in support of Hillary Clinton. Khan is a Gold Star father whose son, Army Captain Humayun Khan, was killed by a car bomb in Iraq in 2004.[29] In his debut on the DNC stage, Khan condemned Trump for his bigotry and racism. He also showed gratitude for the freedom for which his son had fought. But it was no accident that it was Khan who was selected to speak in support of Clinton, who was largely considered a war hawk.

Khan, as expected, spoke about freedom through the narrow lens of US militarism. But his condemnation of Trump's obvious and over-the-top bigotry was, at best, a toothless argument, and his presence was merely symbolic. As a Muslim, he was a symbol of those who were the target of Trump's worst bigotry. As a Gold Star father, grieved but proud of his soldier son's heroic death, he was a symbol of what the United States imagines its military tradition to be—honorable. He leveled his criticism at the easy target Trump presented but posed no challenge at all to the status quo of militarism and violence, making him a safe choice for the no-less-complicit DNC. In a real sense, Khan and his family were deemed worthy of being celebrated because they were doing the work of the empire and showing pride in warfare. In her book *Islamophobia, Race, and Global Politics*, Nazia Kazi sums up the problem at the root of this symbolic performance: "Khan's speech positioned the loss of his son in a US war as a marker of legitimacy for American Muslims, issuing a reminder that Muslims too serve in the US war machine. This might explain the roaring applause. Service in the Iraq war has become another marker of legitimacy; support for the armed forces and their military incursions is a baseline credential for Muslims to prove their worth."[30] As a public figure, Khan has continued to perform this function for the interests behind the US's military empire.

A year after his speech at the DNC, Khan published a book called *An American Family: A Memoir of Hope and Sacrifice*. In the book, he writes, "I embraced American freedoms, raised my children to cherish and revere them, lost a son who swore an oath to defend them, because I come from a place where they do not exist."[31] Using his platform, this time as an author, Khan again embraced a theory of freedom rooted in war, never pausing to consider the impact of US wars in general or of the Iraq War in particular—one built particularly by the propagation of lies and the one that led to his son's death.

Neither did Khan's involvement with the Democratic Party end with the 2016 election. In 2020, he appeared in at least one video for the Democratic National Convention, and his name was used in multiple fundraising emails for Joe Biden's presidential campaign.[32] At the end of an email message in July 2020, Khan wrote, "Nowhere but in the United States is it possible that an immigrant who came to the country empty-handed gets to stand in front of patriots and in front of a major political party. . . . It is my small share to show the world, by standing there, the goodness of America."[33] But Khan was not celebrated for being an immigrant alone; he was celebrated because of his status as both a Muslim and a Gold Star military father. His immigrant status may have helped support the perception of a welcoming and diverse United States, but it is hard to believe that he would have been on the stage in 2016 if he weren't an enthusiastic supporter of US militarism. Would Khan be featured so prominently if he used the platform the Democrats gave him to denounce war in general and the Iraq War in particular since that's what killed his son? Of course not. He was not there to be a moral force against war. He was tokenized, his Muslim and immigrant identities co-opted to lend moral force to war, and to justify the loss of his son and so many others like him. Khan's role is that of a triumphant American who overcame his Muslim identity (at least politically) to embrace the greatness of the United States.

One of the most problematic aspects of legitimizing American identity as a Muslim through the lens of militarism is what happens when that identity is questioned and/or gets rejected. The fundamentally inaccurate assumption underlying American identity and citizenship for Muslims is that it will lead to acceptance that is permanent, not temporary and based on context. In an op-ed titled "I'm a Muslim U.S. Marine, but Am I American Enough?" Mansoor Shams talks about his experience coming to the United States from Pakistan when he was six years old. He recalls being surprised by a woman who helped him get on the escalator and later praises her for, essentially, not being racist toward him—a pretty low bar. Nevertheless, he laments, "I no longer am sufficiently 'American,' according to the definition some use today. And this is after I've served my country faithfully and honorably as a proud U.S. Marine."[34] But there is a fallacy behind this line of thinking, and it is the false promise that participating in American institutions, proudly defending American ideals, even to the point of being willing to give your life, has ever been all or even most of what *really* makes one an American. Shams seems to thoroughly miss this point, choosing instead to believe that the current moment (he wrote in 2018) was an aberration, that President Trump's hateful invective marked a fundamental break from an America where a stranger would help a child on an escalator. What he failed to understand is that Trump's declarations were not designed to target a specific subset within the Muslim community, but rather to vilify the community as a whole. In this way, they are wholly consistent with the Islamophobic narrative employed by the state since the onset of the War on Terror at the very least. Contextualized, it is painfully clear that Shams's military service cannot rescue him from being distrusted as an outsider, a member of a group that has been and continues to be vilified at all levels of American communication. In spite of this, the author says he tries "to rationalize the words of the president and . . . give him the benefit of the doubt." This was a hopeless project. Even if he were susceptible to such pressure, Trump could not be called back to a value system that never truly existed. While embracing national security through militarism and empire gained Khan a place at the DNC in 2016 and a consistent presence as a token of the Democratic Party in following years, Shams's reflection demonstrates that American identity, as constructed by white supremacy, does not have an open-door policy even for those who try to live up to its constantly changing demands. Shams, in other words, will likely continue to be seen as not "American enough."

In 2008, Colin Powell appeared on an episode of *Meet the Press* to endorse presidential candidate Barack Obama.[35] Powell gained praise for his forceful response to the baseless claim being pushed by a small but increasingly influential faction in the Republican Party that Obama was Muslim. He began by noting the fact that Obama was a Christian, something that had never really been in doubt, and then moved into a defense of Muslims rooted firmly in the military narrative of heroic sacrifice. He told the story of Kareem Rashad Sultan Khan, a US Army specialist who died in Iraq, recalling for the audience a picture of Khan's mother visiting her son's grave in Arlington National Cemetery. Describing Khan's gravestone, Powell commented, "And as the picture focused in, you could see the writing on the headstone. And it gave his awards. Purple Heart. Bronze Star. Showed that he died in Iraq. Gave his date of birth, date of death. He was twenty years old. And then at the very top of the headstone, it didn't have a Christian cross. It didn't have a star of David. It had a crescent and star of the Islamic faith. And his name was Kareem Rashad Sultan Khan. And he was an American."

Edward Curtis contends compellingly with this relatively new dynamic of inclusion of Muslim servicemen in the American story as it is told by the powerful. Curtis argues, "In the case of the fallen Muslim soldier, a different kind of story about Muslims in the United States was offered to displace the older myth of the Muslim beast. In this new liberal myth, Muslims would play the role of the heroic patriot, and, in exchange, the nation would owe them and all Muslim Americans social acceptance and an opportunity to become part of the multicultural melting pot."[36] This is exactly right. General Powell's remarks, and the praise he received for them, reveal the way in which these stories of Muslim servicemen, in particular those who have died, extend Americanness to Muslims only within a narrow purview based on a contingency agreement—what they will trade or compromise to be American. One aspect of this compromise is that they must be willing as Muslim Americans to fight and possibly kill other Muslims in support of the American military project. Even when they do, however, America does not keep its side of the bargain—as we have seen with the story of Mansoor Shams. In the new paradigm of praise, these servicemen are lauded for being Muslim, but only insofar as their identity serves to legitimize the wars in which they fight. As Curtis puts it, Muslim Americans are "valuable precisely because of their nearness to the enemy—Muslim American service members proved, by their blood sacrifice, that the US war on terror was just and right."[37] Despite their payment in blood, it is clear that the terms of the exchange even for Muslim soldiers—the promise of inclusion in American polity—have been at best selectively honored.

Muslim and American: A Contradiction?

Another way Muslims participate in the production of counternarratives that reiterate the premises of the dominant narrative is through answering the question of whether it is possible to be both Muslim and American without contradiction. To be clear, this question is set up with the premise of Islam as a problem because it cannot be integrated into what it means to be American. This, of course, ignores many factors, including the fact that there is no single definition of American identity. Though masquerading as a question that allows for actual consideration of what it means for a religion to be in contradiction with a nation-state, in reality it is often a prompt that American Muslims are coerced to respond to because of what silence might suggest. This is the case even as Muslims continue to be victims of the state.

This question has been responded to again and again by Muslims who treat its basic assumptions as legitimate. Thus, their responses include some form of an assertion that there is no inherent contradiction between these two identities. A representative example is public speaker Sami H. Elmansoury's *WISE Up* op-ed, "Defining Patriotism through Legacy." Elmansoury rejects the notion that there is a conflict between being Muslim and being American while also decrying "violent supremacist extremism" promoted by some Muslims. Referencing ISIS, Al-Qaeda, Boko Haram, and al-Shabaab, Elmansoury writes, "These groups are not representative of my beliefs, and they are likely not representative of most others. It is therefore in the best interest of the Muslim community to unapologetically ramp up its efforts to quell the scourge of global extremism that veritably exacerbates the lingering climate of mistrust within society at large, regardless of sideline discussions on cause and blame."[38] In responding this way, Elmansoury introduces extremism as a factor to consider in this conversation, which therefore legitimizes it as an idea to consider in whether a Muslim can also hold the identity of an American. Moreover, the end of his statement, "regardless of sideline discussions on cause and blame," takes incredibly important issues—the root causes of conflict and accountability—and trivializes both by using the word *blame*.

Additionally, if violence as a general principle is worth condemning as a Muslim, why isn't the United States' violence worth condemning as an American? Because of the power dynamics and the assumed value of being American versus being Muslim, the question of whether the *United States'* violence is consistent with *Islamic* values is one that cannot be meaningfully posed or answered as long as the reign of American empire continues.

Beyond the call to challenge extremism in the Muslim community, Elmansoury includes a list of suggestions that American Muslims can take in order to "stake their own claim to their new homeland." The suggestion of claim-staking in their new homeland excludes Muslims whose homeland has *always* been the United States. Elmansoury further adds that staking claim can "humanize their coreligionists abroad by actively participating in political leadership, in entrepreneurship, and in various constructive industries, by producing legislation or scientific achievements that benefit society at large and artistic works that are worthy of the Oscars and Grammys."[39] The standards on which American Muslims are judged are extraordinary and exceptional—a high price to pay for being accepted in the United States.

While some Muslims have dealt with the question of whether the two identities—American and Muslim—are in contradiction to one another, the reality of American xenophobia, racism, and Islamophobia means that the order of identities is a point of contention as well. In a piece titled "Muslim American or American Muslim. Does It Matter?" Yasmina Blackburn poses this question: "Am I more or less Muslim or American depending on the order of my labels?"[40] She concludes that the order of her identities does in fact determine how much she is of one or the other. She draws this response from a narrative guide titled "Talking to Americans about American Muslims," especially the guide's section on "promoting fairness," which indicates that listing one's identity as American Muslim is important to dispelling the idea that this group is "foreign," with different values. The author also refers to someone who responded to her by tweet, asking, "Why would anyone write Muslim before American . . . unless religion takes precedence over country? And this is what people condemn. IMHO."[41] But what if instead of precedence, the question was about which identity resonates more with a person's experiences and beliefs, especially when it comes to being Muslim in a country that marginalizes this identity? If being American means having a set of rights, and these rights have been stripped from many Muslims, what does it really mean to put American before Muslim if the former is the reason the latter is struggling?

Ultimately, the author believes that it is Muslims' responsibility to do their part to address misperceptions and the fear others might have of them. Like other narratives in this realm, the burden of Americans' oppressive beliefs is shifted onto the victims of these beliefs. Non-Muslim Americans are rarely asked to examine their biases; instead, American Muslims or Muslim Americans have to shift their behavior, identities, and so on to make themselves more palatable to the "average" American. These discussions also signal a larger problem, which is the rigid framing of political issues that do not, in reality, allow for any form of dissent. Thus, rather than asking if being Muslim is compatible with being American, the real question seems to be what Muslim Americans or American Muslims are going to do to accommodate themselves to Americans' intolerance and bigotry.

A few years earlier, in 2011, the Fiqh Council of North America released a resolution titled "On Being Faithful Muslims and Loyal Americans."[42] In their first sentence, they assert that there is "no inherent conflict between the normative values of Islam and the US Constitution and Bill of Rights." Much of the statement purports to instruct to Muslims—that they should participate in civic life in the United States, contribute to addressing social problems, and, perhaps for Muslims who think otherwise, recognize that there is in fact no contradiction between being a Muslim and being a loyal American. Though this statement is rooted in leveraging Islam to answer the question of identity, it also continues to problematize Islam insofar as this intervention is deemed necessary at all. Moreover, the Fiqh Council resolution introduces the element that Muslims must prove they are loyal in order to be considered fully American. It also presupposes a common understanding of what loyalty means and minimizes how it has been and continues to be weaponized to cast Muslims out of the American body politic.

Feisal Abdul Rauf, the imam at the center of the Park 51 Mosque controversy, responded to many of these same issues in "Five Myths about Muslims in America."[43] Among the myths he raises is the idea that "American Muslims oppress women." He disputes this myth by saying that Muslim American women are more educated than Muslim women in Europe and the average American, adding that Muslim American women lead many civic organizations. This is a demonstration of how narrowly these questions can be answered. In fact, any acknowledgment of women's oppression becomes a problem that all Muslim Americans, without exception, must account for.

Rauf also speaks to the myth that there is a problem of American Muslims becoming homegrown terrorists. He contradicts this myth using data from the Triangle Center on Terrorism and Homeland Security, which indicates that non-Muslims exceeded Muslims in the number of terrorist plots. Interestingly, after the backlash he received for the Park 51 Mosque, he states in response to this myth, "As an American Muslim leader who worked with FBI agents right after Sept. 11, 2001, I fear that identifying Islam with terrorism threatens to erode American Muslims' civil liberties and fuels the dangerous perception that the United States is at war with Islam. Policymakers must recognize that, more often than not, the terrorists the world should fear are motivated by political and socioeconomic—not religious—concerns."[44] Considering the fact that this piece was authored in 2011 and that Rauf worked with the FBI, it's unclear as to how he considered the erosion of Muslim rights still hypothetical. Rather than being based in reality, this instead seemed like a polite plea not to criminalize Muslims, even going so far as to not critique the damage that had already been done in order to be heard. This is indicative of how Muslims are supposed to concede and/or minimize their humanity in order to appeal to the coerced narrative of the state. What if, instead, Rauf had addressed the actual loss of rights for Muslims, demanded an end to the abuses, and critiqued the narrative that the state uses to solidify the link between Muslims and terrorism? Perhaps that would have put him more in tune with the reality of Muslim oppression post-9/11.

In all of these cases, the Muslim identity is problematized, while American identity—what it has meant and what it means now—is left without critique. Further, these cases reinforce a version of American identity that is conflated with white Christian identity, which necessarily excludes significant numbers of citizens of the United States. What does national identity then mean for a country built on exclusion, white supremacy, and anti-Blackness? National identity, in other words, is the problem because of who is able to claim an American identity and who isn't. If American identity, which has been exclusive since its inception, was never meant to include different communities, the individual who has a hard time adjusting shouldn't be problematized—the country that operates with mechanisms of exclusion should.

The Rhetorical Question That Keeps on Giving

Ask any Muslim who has lived through the War on Terror and they will inevitably have been asked the question, "Why don't Muslims condemn terrorism?" Muslims differ significantly on whether and how to answer this question. Some Muslims feel called to respond, while others reject the explicit rationale of collective responsibility embedded in the question. Regardless, the question has developed life of its own because it is not actually meant to be answered but rather to come back to the same initial conclusion: that Muslims condone terrorism. Thus, those asking the question already are not looking for any response that doesn't conclude that Muslims don't condemn terrorism, ever.

A website titled The American Muslim (TAM) lists hundreds of references to Muslims condemning acts of terrorism.[45] There's even a page that speaks to the selective use of such information when the question is still asked. One example of the selective use of information is an article by Thomas Friedman titled "If It's a Muslim Problem, It Needs a Muslim Solution."[46] Sheila Musaji, the TAM website's founder, references this article and asserts that Friedman makes an error when he says, "To this day—to this day—no major Muslim cleric or religious body has ever issued a fatwa condemning Osama bin Laden." Perhaps if Friedman had conducted any amount of research on this topic, he would have come across Musaji's website, which would have directly addressed his assertion. But the point of his assertion was not to obtain evidence, but to further cement the question of Muslims condemning terrorism as rhetorical, and therefore left unchanged regardless of the answer.

When it doesn't work to list numerous instances of Muslims condemning terrorists, some try appealing to the facts of the matter. Though there is a plethora of empirical data showing that the risk of Muslims committing acts of terror is actually far lower than for other groups, data is useless if the question is, functionally, intended to be rhetorical. In a *Huffington Post* piece titled "Muslims Are Not Terrorists: A Factual Look at Terrorism and Islam," Omar Alnatour writes about being fatigued by the expectation that he should condemn terrorism whenever Muslims are found responsible for a shooting or an act of terror.[47] Toward the beginning of the piece, Alnatour states, "As a Muslim, I am tired of condemning terrorist attacks being carried out by inherently violent people who hijack my religion." Interestingly, while critiquing the concept of collective responsibility, Alnatour directly mimics the discourse of the state in his description of terrorists—read "Muslim terrorists"—as *inherently* violent. He does so without accounting for the fact that this widely used and problematic trope is not limited to Muslim *terrorists* but extends to Muslims in general. Alnatour's assertion here communicates a desire to create distance between his Muslim identity and the terrorists whom the external gaze might otherwise confuse as being the same. Alnatour ends with an appeal: "As an American Muslim, I plead you all to deeply consider the facts mentioned here the next time you see a news headline about Muslims and terrorism." But Alnatour's plea cannot be answered because he's responding to a rhetorical question, which again allows for no response.

Breaking the Shackles of Internalized Oppression

> *Thus, the behavior of the oppressed is a prescribed behavior, following as it does the guidelines of the oppressor. The oppressed, having internalized the image of the oppressor and adopted his guidelines, are fearful of freedom. Freedom would require them to eject this image and replace it with autonomy and responsibility.*
>
> —Paulo Freire[48]

As this chapter has illustrated, internalized Islamophobia emboldens an already robust external system of institutionalized Islamophobia. With Islamophobia as pervasive as it is, it is not difficult to trace the roots of internalized Islamophobia. However, dismantling internalized Islamophobia is as important as dismantling other forms of Islamophobia, if not more so, because when an individual is free from internalized oppression, they can become an agent of change, not a participant in injustice. Paulo Freire's quote above begs an important question: Are Muslims afraid of freedom— specifically the freedom to reject categorically and unequivocally the assumptions about Muslims and Islam on which Islamophobia thrives? Then, some follow-up questions: What stories would we tell about ourselves without the pressure of responding to Islamophobic narratives that are imposed upon us? What will it take to eject the image of the oppressor? Hopefully this book provides food for thought.

10.

THE PROVERBIAL SEAT AT THE TABLE

Muslim American Organizational Responses
to Institutionalized Islamophobia

In 2019, then president Donald Trump hosted his second Ramadan iftar during his term in office. Invitees included ambassadors and diplomats from Muslim-majority countries, but no Muslim American leaders. Despite Trump's openly antagonistic stance toward Islam, some Muslim American organizations lamented their exclusion. For example, a staff member of the nationally prominent Muslim Public Affairs Council (MPAC) expressed frustration, telling Voice of America that the absence of Muslim Americans was indicative of "how the president does not see American Muslims as part of America."[1]

MPAC elaborated on its purported concerns in a press release, stating, "Many of those he did invite represent autocratic and repressive governments, regimes that routinely oppress innocent citizens and violate the rights of women, minorities and free-thinking people."[2] Their description of the Muslims in attendance seemed to ignore the fact that these types of leaders have always garnered favor, as well as financial and political support, as a function of the United States' desire for power and control over such countries. Had MPAC gone on to make this point, it would have been a useful critique. However, raising this concern in the context of lamenting exclusion was hypocritical. Finally, much of MPAC's characterization of the countries from which these leaders came could have easily been applied to the United States itself. However, rather than using this event to draw attention to the violence inflicted on Muslims domestically and to the violence of the Trump administration—including the symbolic violence of hosting an iftar in the first place—MPAC's concerns effectively boiled down to the fear of missing out.

Although no single organization represents the entire community, there are several national groups that have worked to normalize Muslim American engagement with the government and monopolize access to the political process. Though engagement with the government is not problematic in and of itself, what often is problematic is what that engagement looks like in terms of what values are presented, and what compromises are made. Perhaps most important is the question of whether the perspective that is presented represents the perspectives widely held in the Muslim community, and whether the engagement addresses their interests effectively. Before addressing specific problematic narratives embedded in the common responses of Muslim American organizations to oppressive, Islamophobic government actions and policy, it is useful to consider the role played by overarching forces of oppression in shaping the context out of which these responses emerge.

Outcomes of Oppression

"I hope the perpetrator isn't Muslim." This has been a common refrain among Muslim Americans in the aftermath of mass acts of violence. This response stems from the knowledge that being held collectively responsible is an ever-present reality, and the resulting fear of societal backlash has become all too common in the context of the War on Terror's constant demonization of Muslims. The consequences of living amid oppression has naturally had repercussions and implications for how Muslim Americans interact and engage with the external world. As we saw in the previous chapter, there is also an internal dimension to the ways in which members of this group enter the world that is a less direct result of the impacts of external oppression. For example, intragroup behavior may be policed on the basis of "restoring" the group's image to the outside world.

Although the Muslim American community is extremely heterogeneous and not very unified, there are commonalities in how they are impacted by forces of oppression especially in the aftermath of mass violence. For example, particularly in the aftermath of a violent act, stereotypes and negative judgments often arise against the group based on the actions of a single problematic individual—a concept referred to as "collective threats."[3] There are obvious consequences not only for the way someone who has absorbed these perspectives acts with members of their own community, but also for how they project or present the group's identity externally.

Stereotype threat theory provides another angle through which to view the impacts of oppression on the group level via the individual level.[4] Research shows that members of a stereotyped group often experience increased anxiety and elevated sensitivity to perceived threats, and respond to culturally embedded assumptions by acting in a way intended to disconfirm the stereotype. Indeed, individual group members may believe they have a responsibility to disconfirm problematic tropes about their group. By extrapolating from the psychological and social effects of such pressure on individuals, we can understand how it impacts group behavior as well. It's important to note here that an individual's mode of disconfirming a stereotype also has implications for the larger group—especially if, in the process of disconfirmation, a different stereotype is confirmed or an implied connection between the group identity and the stereotype or negative behavior is strengthened. For example, it is often the case that when Muslim Americans work to disconfirm the stereotype of Muslims as terrorists, their actions actually result in reifying the connection and, even worse, upholding the dominant narratives that create the pressure to disavow stereotypes in the first place. The more visible the individual is in public life, the more this becomes a group-level issue.

A final background frame for how the Muslim community is impacted by and responds to oppressive forces involves how they face threats to their identity. As we have seen, owing to collective guilt, Muslims are often faced with the question of how their collective identity is shaped because of the "bad" behavior of an individual Muslim. Part of this can be explained by understanding whether and how Muslims, as a stigmatized group, are responding to the stigma. More specifically, we might ask, How does group stigmatization impact Muslims' responses to situations where their religious identity is threatened?

One response to stigma is feelings of shame. In his dissertation, Dr. Hakeem Jefferson, a professor of political science at Stanford University, articulates the extent to which shame is felt in a group context: "Group-based shame goes beyond recognizing that what some member of the group has done is bad; it is an emotion that is evoked when one feels that, as a consequence of that transgression, the group is bad, and importantly, that others will make a judgment of the group's character based on the violation."[5] Experienced this way, shame might motivate some Muslims to react to stigma by distancing and distinguishing themselves from the offending Muslim(s), or in some cases, rhetorically stripping the perpetrator of their Muslim identity.

The Politics of Respectability

Just as it is helpful to consider the background forces of oppression and their impacts on groups generally, understanding the approach that some Muslim advocacy organizations take in responding to the oppressive structures of the War on Terror specifically requires exploring various concerns within the larger community and how they shape collective identity. One framework for exploring this phenomenon is the concept of respectability politics, a term first coined by historian Evelyn Brooks Higginbotham in a book titled *Righteous Discontent: The Women's Movement in the Black Baptist Church, 1880–1920*. Higginbotham's book focuses on the role of Black women in making the church an influential vehicle for facilitating political and social change within the Black community.[6]

For Higginbotham, "respectability politics" referred to a political strategy prevalent in the Black community and focused on promoting particular behaviors in order to counter the harmful stereotypes imposed on Black people by white people. Adhering to this code of behavior would, the women believed, enable the Black community to gain equality in society and the legal system. For these Black Baptist women, respectability politics centered public behavior as a measure of individual self-respect, which supported the elevation of the community as a whole.[7] In other words, the politics of respectability "emphasized reform of individual behavior and attitudes both as a goal in itself and as a strategy for reform of the entire structural system of American race relations."[8]

An important dimension of Black respectability politics that this points to is that its adherents had no intention of giving in to the demands and expectations of white supremacy or of abandoning their political aims. Rather, they believed that if the Black community constantly modeled "correct" behavior, it would show their moral superiority to whites and fundamentally challenge the social order.

Higginbotham's book focuses on the role of Black women in making the church an influential vehicle for facilitating political and social change within the Black community. Respectability politics, however, grew to be influential well beyond that context, with comportment and principled adherence to the behavioral values of the white bourgeoisie being insisted upon by early Black intellectuals such as W. E. B. Du Bois and Booker Washington. In the twentieth century, they played a central role in the strategies of civil rights leaders in advancing their claims of equal rights.

A primary critique of Black respectability politics comes out of the role it played in the civil rights movement and focuses on the way insistence on strict adherence to white middle-class standards sidelines the experiences and needs of the most marginalized members of the group. An example of this dynamic is the famous Montgomery Bus Boycott, in which Rosa Parks's refusal to give up her seat became the focus of nationwide attention. The success of Parks's political action followed earlier, similar events, but in those cases, the women involved—one of whom was pregnant and unmarried, and another whose father drank—were not deemed respectable enough to represent the movement.[9] Such division between, on the one hand, group members viewed as closest to the ideals of the dominant culture and, on the other hand, those furthest from such ideals is a direct result of accepting that the way to gain access to equal rights in a white system is to convince white society to see you as similar to them, and therefore deserving.

The experience of Black Americans with respectability politics has far-reaching and clear implications for other stigmatized groups seeking a foothold in mainstream American culture. One element of this is the focus on the individual as the locus for social change in respectability politics, which can be seen as an emphasis on worthiness. For example, immigration narratives often focus on how particular groups are more worthy of status by virtue of their members' commitment to adapting to mainstream American culture. Immigration scholar Angela Banks notes that immigration respectability narratives "seek to counter negative perceptions by showing that the excluded immigrant groups are culturally indistinguishable from mainstream Americans."[10] The application in this context highlights the fact that marginalized groups often have to compromise the rights of other groups or segments of groups in order to gain even limited inclusion in the dominant culture. In pursuing access as individuals to the rights and privileges automatically granted to those in a relatively more powerful social or political position in this way, marginalized groups sacrifice their ability to collectively challenge the conditions that created the power imbalance they are responding to.

Another, related pitfall of respectability politics as a strategy is that it focuses on the white gaze—or "white panopticon," to use a phrase that more completely captures the omnipresence of white supremacy and its narratives—and how to appease it.[11] The argument here is that the theory of respectability politics is fundamentally rooted in assimilationist thought, in that it starts with behavioral standards that are not only modeled on the norms of the dominant culture, but chosen because they are precise opposites of behaviors associated with negative stereotypes about the marginalized group. Modeling correct behaviors that are based on white culture's association of specific negative behaviors with a particular group, therefore, can actually reinforce and entrench the very stereotypes the group is trying to counter. In other words, assuming responsibility as individuals for countering negative stereotypes implies consent to the validity of these categories in the first place. Implications of this shortcoming for other marginalized groups such as immigrants include determining whose leadership is uplifted and whose is suppressed based on the extent to which their behavior conforms to the dominant culture.

The Dead End of Muslim Respectability Politics

The assimilationist approach to gaining access to equal rights is directly relevant to the landscape of Muslim American political responses to the injustices of the War on Terror. The primary form that respectability politics have taken in the context of responding to the injustices of the War on Terror has been the centering, on the national stage especially, of Muslim American "rights" organizations whose core political strategy is to promote adaptation and accommodation in order to engage in respectability politics, with the goal of gaining a proverbial seat at the table. Believing that problematic government policy structures are a function of insufficient Muslim representation in government, several prominent Muslim American organizations argue the necessity of reassuring the dominant culture that the community in general upholds American values and is therefore deserving of access. What is rarely recognized is the fact that the cost of getting a seat at the table often comes in the form of a significant amount of compromise of one's values, directly or indirectly.

In some cases where Muslim leaders accept responsibility for proving the humanity, and Americanness, of the community a seat at the table requires more—colluding with the state's harmful narrative by embracing the validity of its underlying themes and assumptions. For example, the narrative of Muslim criminality may be reinforced by highlighting the values of Islam and Muslims that are congruent with the mainstream culture and deliberately contrasting them with the criminal actions of individuals. Any positive social change achieved using this strategy is necessarily piecemeal and does little, if anything, to challenge systemic and institutionalized Islamophobia. Indeed, it often has the opposite result of entrenching harmful state narratives. Respectability politics also can result in behavioral policing, such that those seeking change outside the halls of government are ostracized and/or deemed too radical, regardless of any gains they make.

A paradigmatic example of the embrace of respectability politics comes from a blog authored by Sheikh Hamza Yusuf, a globally known Muslim leader (mentioned also in chapter 9) who has been embedded in many Muslim and Muslim American organizations. In an essay titled "We Shall Overcome," one week after Trump won the 2016 presidential election, Yusuf wrote, "Now is the time to realize that we have too much work to do, not protesting, not lighting fires, not saying, 'Trump is not my president.' He is, and that is how our system works: by accepting the results and moving on. Now we have to work to make sure our educational, political, and scientific institutions, which are some of the finest in the world, are protected and perfected. We are the majority, not the haters."[12] Considering the fact that the title of his blog referred to a popular song emblematic of the civil rights movement, his condemnation of protests—and his highlighting of institutions entrenched with inequality—was ironic, to say the least. Further, the vision of the United States projected in his statement makes it seem as though Trump is the only aberration of an otherwise perfect union. Engrossed in the politics of respectability, Yusuf's blog focuses on what internal changes can be made to conform to the reality of external injustice, instead of focusing on what external changes need to be made to promote justice. Finally, Yusuf's blog also demonstrates how problematic respectability politics can be when those relying on this political strategy have vastly different experiences of the external world than do other members of the same community, and the latter are expected to conform.

The ability of Muslims as a group to successfully leverage a strategy for acceptance based on respectability has been even further limited by the success of the underlying narrative of the War on Terror in reshaping the boundaries of what assumptions go unquestioned. From Dick Cheney's statement that Guantánamo prisoners were the "worst of the worst" to Trump's statement that "Islam hates us," demonizing tropes of Muslims are frequently used to preempt any civil rights claims. While it goes without saying that there is no single strategy for combating Islamophobia, it is at the same time impossible to claim that all strategies contribute toward reaching the same goal.

Because of this book's emphasis on the use of narrative by the state as justification for the War on Terror and its concomitant violence, the analysis that follows on Muslim Americans' organizational responses to events and policies post-9/11 focuses on those that support, affirm, and/or collude with the official narrative. Crucially, this analysis also considers how Muslims are positioned within these organizational responses, such as assuming blame or being erased altogether. More directly, this book critiques the idea that responses that buttress and/or affirm the state's narratives of violence can simultaneously challenge Islamophobia and promote Muslims' rights.

Betting on the Recognition of Muslim Humanity

In December 2016, leaders from several Muslim organizations, including the Council on American-Islamic Relations, the Islamic Society of North America, the Muslim Public Affairs Council, and the Islamic Circle of North America, sent a letter to President-elect Donald Trump to express their concerns about the policies he might promote under his administration.[13] The letter underscored the historical and present place of Muslims in the United States, addressed Muslim Americans' contributions across different fields, highlighted how their values align with those of other Americans, and emphasized that just like other Americans, they love the United States. Though the letter lamented a rise in hate crimes toward Muslims, they absolved Trump of any responsibility for that rise, instead giving him credit for denouncing these crimes on an episode of *60 Minutes*. Just days into Trump's presidency, it was clear that the letter had fallen on deaf ears. Not only did his hateful rhetoric continue, but President Trump signed an executive order putting his first Muslim Ban in place seven days after his inauguration.

Given the fact that Trump expressed rampant Islamophobia throughout his campaign—and that such behavior was considered a selling point to many Americans in the 2016 election cycle—no one should have been surprised. Indeed, the letter strategy was misguided and represents a problematic approach to advocacy within many Muslim American spaces. The letter focused heavily on Muslim Americans proving themselves worthy of basic respect, it gave Trump thanks for addressing a problem—hate crimes—that his rhetoric played a direct role in provoking, and it adopted the clearly false posture overall that Trump's Islamophobic words and actions were not, in fact, intentional.

In producing and publicizing this letter, these organizations cued others to believe that in order to demand accountability from the state, you must prove yourself worthy of the respect afforded automatically to members of the dominant culture. But Muslim Americans should be able to call for accountability without a litmus test of how American they are. Preempting questions of Muslim American belonging, values alignment, and loyalty with an answer gives the government license to treat these questions as legitimate, which is the opposite of accountability. In addition, rather than serving as an effective rebuke to the Trump administration, this letter and the lack of any positive outcomes stemming from it reveal how little political power mainstream Muslim organizations actually possess. This lack of power is reflected in interactions with the political system in general and is not limited to Trump or Republicans.

In July 2020, then presidential candidate Joe Biden addressed a virtual crowd of Muslim Americans at the Million Muslim Votes Summit, an event hosted by the political organization Emgage Action. Notably, at one point in his speech, he recited a hadith, or saying of the Prophet Muhammad (peace be upon him).[14] Because many Muslim Americans have never felt included in either the Democratic or the Republican Party, Biden's effort to engage with the community was, for some, a welcome gesture. During his address, the former vice president spoke to how he would, among other things, reverse harmful Trump-era policies such as the Muslim Ban, stating, "Muslim communities are the first to field Donald Trump's assault on black and brown communities in this country with his vile Muslim ban. That fight was the opening barrage in what has been nearly four years of constant pressure, and insults, and attacks against Muslim American communities."[15]

Biden's address also focused on the many issues that Muslim Americans, like other Americans, are impacted by, such as health care and economic inequity. Similarly, his campaign page dedicated to Muslim Americans stated, "Joe also understands the pain Muslim-Americans feel towards what's happening in Muslim-majority countries and countries with significant Muslim populations."[16] However, his platform was limited to the plight of the Uighur Muslims who are being abused, detained, and tortured by the Chinese government—even though the United States' War on Terror gave the green light to abuse Muslims on the basis of labeling them "terrorists."[17] At the same time, the fact that he didn't address the wars in Iraq and Afghanistan that the US directly waged in the earliest days of the War on Terror is demonstrative of the fact that the country will never acknowledge its own wrongdoing.

In contrast, one of the most concrete changes Biden's platform pledged to make was to reestablish White House Eid celebrations, which were a tradition largely abandoned in the overtly Islamophobic Trump years,[18] signaling that symbolic gestures such as these appeared to be more important to the incoming administration than restoring the constitutional rights of Muslim Americans. To the extent that more meaningful change was addressed in the platform, it seemed clear that it would be limited to restoring rights lost under Trump. A return to square one in the context of Muslim rights in the War on Terror is not progress, but like the symbolic respect of the White House Eid, reversing Trump's most outrageous actions costs nothing politically, and indeed is likely to be popular with liberal whites. This fundamentally hollow promise underscores just how easily Biden expects to be able to appease Muslim Americans. Rather than forging a legitimate path ahead by demonstrating an understanding of the violence of the past, Biden's speech, campaign platform, and general positionality served to further minimize the systemic and institutionalized Islamophobia of the War on Terror. By focusing on Trump as the starting point, Biden shone by comparison, but not by merit. The Obama-era War on Terror included increasing drone warfare exponentially in Muslim-majority countries such as Yemen and Somalia, implementing the Countering Violent Extremism program (which targeted Muslims almost exclusively), and ordering extrajudicial killings. Biden's failure, as of this writing, to address these policies almost ensures that they will continue—especially because ignorance is so widespread concerning how deeply entrenched the Obama-Biden administration was in Islamophobic state violence—unless there is a compelling political reason for changing course.

Even more concerning than the all-too-common occurrence of a politician evading history on the campaign trail is the way in which Muslim Americans cooperated, allowing Biden to sweep his own history under the rug without challenge. For example, Emgage Action endorsed Biden almost immediately after he became the presumptive nominee, effectively letting him off the hook in terms of working for Muslim votes.[19] Moreover, the immediate endorsement actually revealed the community's lack of political power (to the extent that Emgage claimed representation) because a politically empowered community wouldn't simply accept a candidate just because he wasn't Trump, especially considering the fact that state violence is bipartisan. The absence of political power was further manifested at the Million Muslim Votes Summit in the way Biden lacked transparent engagement, offering no reflection whatsoever on the abuses of the past or substantive promises of reform—because he wasn't asked to.

Do Muslim Americans Have Political Power?

The campaign to get a million Muslim votes represented an effort demonstrative of a community eager to leverage their collective power to effect change. By using Muslim identity to mobilize potential voters, the message to the community was that they should have a vested interest in participating politically—after all, how else would change come about? This underscores an important point about political power—namely, that in order to verify its existence, any change attributed to the power must be different from what would have been accomplished without the power.

How exactly is political power defined? The following is one definition:

> The ability to shape and control the political behavior of others and lead and guide their behavior in the direction desired by the person, group, or institution wielding the political power. . . . That is to say, political power is the ability of one political actor—e.g., an individual citizen, a family, an interest group, a political action committee, a political party, or the government—to effect a desired change in the behavior of other political actors, persuading or forcing the latter to act in a manner they would not act in in the absence of the former's impact on the situation.[20]

This definition is helpful in defining the functional boundaries of what constitutes political power and what falls within its purview. Practical and descriptive, it is a rebuke of the commonly accepted but rarely critically examined belief that access to decision makers in and of itself constitutes positive change. True evaluations of the presence or lack of political influence should focus on what positive developments, if any, are gained as a result of this access.

The Million Muslim Votes Summit, along with Biden's appearance at it, is emblematic of the way some Muslim American organizations have sought to build political power through the system. Muslim Americans who engage with government often seek to justify their actions by retorting, "If you're not at the table, you're on the menu." But what, short of not being eaten alive, is gained while at that table? What would have been different about the Million Muslim Votes campaign if Muslim Americans had measurable political power? As a starting point, they would have been able to critique Biden's history as Obama's vice president without fearing repercussions. Without a demand for acknowledgment of how the

Obama-Biden administration perpetuated and expanded the abuses of the War on Terror, engagement with Biden became an endorsement of the very apparatus in need of dismantling. Further, absent a common and specific goal for equity and justice, engagement with the government stands in contradiction to much of the work being done on the outside.

Although Muslim American engagement in the political system is deemed necessary by the mainstream of the community, some segments within it either have interacted with the system on their own terms (and less frequently) or have withdrawn from it altogether. In *Exit, Voice, and Loyalty: Responses to Declines in Firms, Organizations, and States,* A. O. Hirschman looks at two possible outcomes when individuals are faced with an institution's dysfunction or lack of utility: exit and voice (though they are not mutually exclusive).[21] Those who exit the system are not interested in its reform, nor in communicating their grievances, while those who choose voice, even if critical, are opting to stay engaged in the system in hopes of changing it. Hirschman notes that different conditions make the choice of one or the other strategy more appealing or possible, such as whether an alternative exists to the failing institution. Voice is adopted most often in the early stages, and even in the face of a failing institution, some remain committed to the voice option. Hirschman refers to these people as "loyalists." Those who don't exit, despite suffering, operate under the belief that things will get better, that the exercise of voice will cause institutional change.

Muslim American organizations that operate in the realm of government advocacy are, in Hirschman's terms, exercising voice. While some critical rights have been restored through the use of voice, manifested changes are not usually systemic, which inevitably prolongs the struggle to achieve any semblance of real equality and equity. A prescient question, then, is this: To what extent and for how long can voice over exit be sustained? For Muslim Americans who want to believe change is possible, voice may be the only option they consider. Viewing Muslim American politics through this lens is useful insofar as it establishes a different rationale through which to understand decisions made around government advocacy.

In the wake of 9/11, the Muslim American community looked to prominent advocacy organizations—both those that had already existed and those that were created shortly after—to be the frontline defenders of the larger Muslim community. Scholars Anny Bakalian and Mehdi Bozorgmehr, who studied several post-9/11 organizations, write that "Middle Eastern and Muslim American leaders shepherded their organizations by distancing and condemning terrorists, demonstrating allegiance to the

United States through outreach, and calling for the inclusion of Islam in America's mosaic."[22] Though published over a decade ago, Bakalian and Bozorgmehr's book describes political tactics that, rather than evolving, have almost entirely remained the same. And while other aspects of Muslim American organizational advocacy have become more sophisticated, there has been little effort to critically examine why these initial responses have not evolved to include a more nuanced discussion or any attempt to break away from this narrative deadlock. This is especially problematic because a few prominent organizations dominate the narrative space and, in many cases, perpetuate Islamophobia intentionally or unintentionally.

Case Studies in Accommodation

Although there are numerous Muslim American organizations, the national arm of the Council on American-Islamic Relations (CAIR National) and the Muslim Public Affairs Council (MPAC) are two of the largest and most well known. Both have typically been among the first to publicly respond to urgent and current national security issues since 9/11, such as torture, the Iraq War, and mass shootings. Because these groups are public facing and their work involves frequent engagement with narratives around Islam and Muslims, a close examination of the discursive structures that pattern their communication is instructive. Content analysis conducted on both organizations' responses to the aforementioned issues reveals several patterns and themes: (1) overemphasizing acts of violence perpetrated by Muslims as exceptional; (2) implicitly absolving the US government of responsibility by minimizing and backgrounding state violence; (3) repeating American mythological language and tropes; (4) assuming the burden of explaining violence perpetrated by Muslims; and (5) limiting or excluding altogether any mention of Muslim victims of the US's state violence. Some of the issues selected for this analysis go back to the beginning years of the War on Terror. However, the inclusion of later ones is meant to illustrate the organizations' strategies over time. As the examples below demonstrate, there were no visibly significant shifts in the approach taken in response to the dominant narrative.

Erasing and Minimizing Muslim Victimhood

As the second war launched by the United States since the War on Terror began, the invasion of Iraq in 2003 brought unspeakable atrocities upon the Iraqi people. Several Muslim American organizations felt compelled to respond immediately to the war in Iraq at its inception, as well as in the years following. Just as Muslim lives in general have been devalued in the War on Terror, the deaths of Iraqis were minimized, and the value of their lives discounted. One of the most specific reflections of this devaluation in the language of Muslim organizations is through quantifying the number of American lives lost with precision, while deaths of Iraqis are referred to with far less specificity, even if trying in some way to capture the gravity of the war for the people of Iraq. For example, in 2008 CAIR called for the US's withdrawal from Iraq, lamenting the four thousand American soldiers who had died by that point, while referring to the "uncounted thousands of Iraqi civilians" who had also died.[23] Not only was the discrepancy in the numbers left unaddressed, but the specificity in numbers for Americans and not Iraqis supported the narrative that American lives have more value than Muslim lives—a message that has been consistently reiterated by the US government. The anonymity of the deaths of Iraqis seems a clear signal that, given the reason for their deaths, they will remain "unrecognized within U.S. public forms of grief and remembrance,"[24] an erasure that is legitimized by Muslim organizations that parrot the narrative patterns of the US government.

As one of the most harrowing policies of the War on Terror, the CIA's Detention and Interrogation program, as examined in chapter 7, was executed exclusively on Muslim prisoners. The Torture Report, as it is informally called, was released in 2014 by the Senate Select Committee on Intelligence. Despite the fact that every known victim of the CIA's program was Muslim, responses from Muslim American organizations such as CAIR, MPAC, and the Islamic Society of North America (ISNA) made no mention of this fact.[25] Consistent with the government narrative that has consistently denied systemic violence against Muslims in the War on Terror, these supplementary narratives buttressed the government's narrative that treated the victims' religion as irrelevant.

Hand in Hand with the Narrative of the State

Another aspect of how some prominent organizations' speech harms Muslims involves direct or indirect support of the American mythology on state violence. For example, in March 2003, when the US decided to attack Iraq on the false premise that Saddam Hussein had weapons of mass destruction, there were massive protests all across the globe. Days before the attack, as the US was edging toward the war with Iraq, in a message to Saddam Hussein former president Bush said, "Should Saddam Hussein choose confrontation, the American people can know that every measure has been taken to avoid war, and every measure will be taken to win it."[26] Although the war on Iraq was a war of aggression on the part of the US, Bush's narrative consistently painted Iraq as the provocateur. Nevertheless, many around the world recognized the US as the aggressor, independent of an assessment of Hussein's leadership. Instead of joining the growing number of voices dissenting from this false narrative, less than a month later, and despite the ongoing critique of the US's war, MPAC echoed the Bush administration's propaganda blaming Hussein for a war that was clearly instigated by the US. To this end, the organization stated, "MPAC wishes Saddam Hussein had avoided this war by heeding our call, on December 21, 2002 at our annual convention, and other calls like it, to step down from power and spare innocent lives in a military confrontation. Unfortunately, Hussein decided to waste innocent lives in a vain attempt to uphold his dictatorship at any cost."[27] Rather than calling any attention to the fact that the US had launched this war with very little global support, MPAC, like the US government, attributed the onset of the war and its consequences solely to Hussein. This narrative effectively diminished US responsibility for the war both in the immediate aftermath and in the years that followed. The fact that MPAC endorsed this violent narrative is demonstrative of their consistent efforts to gain proximity to power.

Another example is the response to former president Obama's announcement of the assassination of Osama bin Laden on May 2, 2011. As in previous speeches, Obama reiterated the claim that the US was not at war with Islam, saying, "We must also reaffirm that the United States is not—and never will be—at war with Islam. I've made clear, just as President Bush did shortly after 9/11, that our war is not against Islam. Bin Laden was not a Muslim leader; he was a mass murderer of Muslims."[28] As if from an echo chamber of the US's narratives on its own state violence, CAIR released a statement that was almost identical to Obama's: "We join our fellow citizens in welcoming the announcement that Osama bin Laden has been eliminated as a threat to our nation and the world through the actions of American military personnel."[29]

Further reiterating and affirming the narrative about bin Laden and his death that was offered by Obama, that Osama bin Laden was not a Muslim leader or representative of Islam, CAIR's statement said, "As we have stated repeatedly since the 9/11 terror attacks, bin Laden never represented Muslims or Islam. In fact, in addition to the killing of thousands of Americans, he and Al Qaeda caused the deaths of countless Muslims worldwide."[30]

Similarly, an MPAC statement quoted the president of the organization, Salam Al-Marayati: "We hope this is a turning point away from the dark period of the last decade, in which bin Laden symbolized the evil face of global terrorism."[31] Senior MPAC advisor at the time Maher Hathout added, "We support President Obama's statement that bin Laden was not a Muslim leader, he was a mass murderer of Muslims."[32]

Both statements applied a familiar misguided formula—namely, that bin Laden was the only embodiment of terrorism—which absolved the US of reflecting on its own action as part of the continuous threat. By giving Obama's narrative on bin Laden air, CAIR National and MPAC gave the government affirmation and allowed it to claim unearned credit for caring about Muslim life, even while announcing a killing. Furthermore, by joining Obama in placing special emphasis on the lives lost as a result of bin Laden, shifting any blame for Muslim deaths away from the US, these organizations tacitly affirmed the idea that the many, many lives lost as a direct result of the US's actions post-9/11 are inconsequential and not worth mourning when compared to those killed by terrorists. Those killed by the US, by default, are excluded from post-9/11 frames of grief that elevate the significance of the loss of American lives.[33]

In the case of the oft-repeated government narrative denying a conflict between the US and Islam, CAIR National's statement reaffirmed it, saying, "We also reiterate President Obama's clear statement tonight that the United States is not at war with Islam."[34] Repeating the language about war between the US and Islam, in addition to challenging bin Laden's leadership, the Islamic Circle of North America (ICNA) responded to Osama bin Laden's death in nearly identical language: "We reiterate President Obama's statement that America is not at war with Islam and Osama bin Laden was not representative of Muslims."[35]

It is not clear what political objective MPAC, CAIR and ICNA sought to accomplish by parroting the narrative that the United States is not at war with Islam. Had Osama bin Laden's murder been the only instance of the US's violent targeting of Muslims, this narrative might have been believable. However, Muslims have been almost exclusively targeted in the War on Terror in all contexts—far beyond those considered to be terrorists by the US. Most importantly, the US does not have to be at war with a religion to violently target its adherents. Allowing this empty claim of tolerance to go unchallenged, and ignoring the Islamophobia inherent in the US's actions, compounds the harm done.

On December 9, 2014, Democratic senator Martin Heinrich gave a speech on the Senate floor reacting to the release of the executive summary of the Torture Report, saying, "Torture is wrong; it is un-American; and it doesn't work."[36] Similar sentiments were expressed by other members of the Senate, thus reiterating the popular myth and government narrative that the US's state violence is contrary to the values the country claims to hold. Echoing one of the central government narratives, CAIR stated in response that "torture is not an American value. We should not be questioning whether or not it worked, but why we ever used such brutal and illegal interrogation techniques."[37] Similarly, MPAC asserted, "The torture report will remain a stain in our history,"[38] as if to say that post-9/11 CIA torture represented an exceptional case. Finally, Dr. Sayyid M. Syeed, a representative for the Islamic Society of North America (ISNA), responded to the report, "The revelations about the use of torture have been a source of torture to many of us. We had taken pride in the fact that we have left behind many societies where it was a norm and that we had chosen to be part a nation that prided itself on its belief in human dignity and human rights."[39] This statement was particularly revelatory of the consequences of reiterating the government's narrative, not because US torture caused shock to this particular individual, but because of the way other countries' use of violence is used as a point of comparison with the intention that the United States can almost always prove its moral high ground. It is in the consistent construction of the US's essence and actions as moral that the government has been provided cover for its state violence, including for a long history of torture that has been almost completely normalized. Finally, the idea of torture as exceptional frames state violence as something accidental or done by mistake. Torture, however, is always a deliberate act.

Collective Responsibility

In addition to amplifying the devaluation of Muslim lives, collaborating with government narratives around the War on Terror further entrenches the paradigm of collective responsibility that is foundational to the power of these narratives. On April 23, 2013, Farea Al-Muslimi, a Yemeni writer and activist, testified at a congressional hearing on the targeted killing of terrorist suspects overseas. In providing his account of meeting with drone strike victims, he shared, "I have spoken to many victims of US drone strikes, like a mother who had to identify her innocent eighteen-year-old son's body through a video and stranger cell phone. Or the father who held his four and six-year-old children as they died in his arms."[40] Al-Muslimi shared many more stories of drone victims, illustrating just how brutal the US's drone warfare has been in Yemen.

Submitting testimony for the congressional hearing on drone warfare, after thanking members of the committee, CAIR said: "CAIR and the American Muslim community unequivocally condemn all acts of terrorism and support our nation's war against al-Qaeda and its allied forces."[41] The inclusion of this obligatory condemnation was problematic on many fronts, including the legitimization of the dominant narrative—in this case, falsely limiting the scope of those targeted. Moreover, by prefacing the substance of the testimony with this disclaimer, CAIR validated the idea that in order for Muslim voices to be taken seriously, they must participate in the self-flagellating act of collective responsibility. However, in using the collective responsibility strategy as a bargaining chip, CAIR's testimony provided legitimacy to the expectation that all Muslims should be prepared to defend the actions of other Muslims.

Continuing to fight the War on Terror domestically, Obama responded to the Boston Marathon bombings in 2013 by saying, "The American people refuse to be terrorized," and "If you want to know who we are, what America is, how we respond to evil, that's it: selflessly, compassionately, unafraid."[42] As usual, the official rhetoric delivered by Obama in this example referred to evil—a characteristic attributed solely to terrorists to signal that they were irredeemable. "As we come to terms with the actions of this past week, we must stand together in the face of this evil and unfathomable act."[43] The use of the word *evil* reproduced the War-on-Terror rhetoric pits the evil actions of the terrorists against the goodness of the US and its violence. Moreover, the use of the word *unfathomable* replicates the logic of the War on Terror that has allowed the United States to label non-state-actor violence as exceptionally brutal, while its own violence—state violence—is presented as inherently benign and thus without comparison to that of the terrorists.

While CAIR National joined in condemning the Boston Marathon bombings, they also called on the community to take specific action: "While spiritual measures can serve to comfort those in physical and emotional pain, we also call on Muslims and others in the Boston area to donate blood through the Red Cross as a concrete show of support for the bomb attack victims."[44] The suggestion that Muslims in particular should take collective responsibility for the attacks, and by giving literally of their own bodies, entrenched and projected their guilt even further. Adding to the list of condemnations of the Boston Marathon bombings, the Islamic Circle of North America expressed similar sentiments via then president Naeem Baig, who said, "All Americans including American Muslims condemn this heinous attack on civilians and pray for the quick recovery of the injured."[45]

The onus of the attacks imposed so deliberately on all Muslims by the government found a home in MPAC, CAIR, and ICNA's responses, although CAIR went further, seeming to believe that the only remedy to the blood shed on the day of the Boston bombing was to provide their own blood in service and sacrifice.

The Muslim American population is estimated at approximately 3.45 million people and is extremely diverse. Any claim to represent this varied community is extremely complicated. Nevertheless, several Muslim American organizations have occupied a sizable space in shaping narratives and policies that impact the entire community. The erasure of Muslim victims, affirmation of state violence and of the harm inflicted by the resulting policy choices, and the internalization of the prerogative of collective responsibility, are the costs of collaborating with the official discourse of the War on Terror. In leveraging respectability politics as a strategy for gaining inclusion in government and mainstream society, many Muslim organizational responses echo rather than challenge problematic government narratives and public discourses that demonize Muslims in the first place. This effectively preserves the power of the dominant narrative while undermining the possibility of a Muslim counternarrative.

However, for many Muslims, the Trump presidency inspired a deeper look into the systemic injustices that have long been a part of the United States, including in the War on Terror. As a result, there are now growing calls in the Muslim community to reject collective responsibility and respectability politics in favor of liberatory politics based on the unequivocal humanity of Muslims.

Political moments in the last twenty years have often triggered the assertion that the Muslim American community is at the crossroads. But how long can we be at a crossroads without moving forward? And what will shift the tide? We are now at a political moment in which Muslim Americans can and should reflect, because there are consequences to resuming self-flagellation and the practice of respectability politics. While the

Muslim American organizations mentioned in this chapter are certainly not representative of the vast and diverse leadership in the community, an analysis of the spaces and narratives they shape is far overdue. Recognizing as much is the first step toward radically reconfiguring the approaches Muslim American organizations take to state violence and is necessary if we are to meaningfully challenge the violent legacy of the War on Terror.

11.

LIVED ISLAMOPHOBIA

Muslim American Narratives Post 9/11

Despite the fact that Muslims have been the primary victims of the War on Terror, Muslim voices have been marginalized or invisibilized in post-9/11 narratives. When stories are told, they often lack nuance and focus on fitting interview responses into the framework the dominant narrative imposes. This might include, for example, asking Muslim Americans how they reconcile their two identities, to follow the notion that Muslim identity necessarily is a contradiction to American identity. This is not to say that powerful stories haven't been told of Muslims and Muslim Americans post-9/11, but to point out the need to address some of the most critical issues faced—many of which run contrary to mainstream narratives. Moreover, many of the existing narratives and stories of Muslims have been told by those outside the faith, particularly white non-Muslims. The perspective from which these narratives and stories are told matters.

As a long-time writer and researcher on institutionalized Islamophobia, I began conducting interviews with Muslim Americans in 2011–12 for my doctoral research. I interviewed seventy-five Muslim Americans over the course of nine months, using an extensive qualitative questionnaire that asked about their attitudes toward citizenship (both legal and cultural), if they had been directly impacted by the War on Terror, what they believed the purpose of the War on Terror was, if their political participation was impacted because of the laws and policies implemented, and several other questions. Those interviews were conducted during the Obama administration, but I expect that if I conducted the same interviews today, the responses wouldn't be much different.

Twenty years after 9/11, the War on Terror is complicated to fully address. So much of the War on Terror, at this point, has become normalized. Yet at the same time, nothing feels normal about being singled out, profiled, and targeted—all of which captures the Muslim experience in the post-9/11 context. This book gave me an opportunity to interview eleven Muslim

Americans to gain their perspectives on this era. Though participants were answering my interview questions in 2020, during the end of the Trump presidency, across the board they expressed an understanding of the War on Terror as part of a larger system of violence, not limited to a particular administration or even the last twenty years. The interviewees I spoke to for this study are from a range of ethnic/racial backgrounds and professional backgrounds. My goal was to select individuals from backgrounds that mirrored, at least to some extent, the different subgroups within Muslim communities. The interviews included Muslims who are African American, South Asian, Somali, Latinx, Arab, Afghan, and white. Participants' professions included a professor, a student, researchers, organizers, advocates, and others. Each is identified here as they felt comfortable.

It bears noting that those interviewed are predominantly women. This was not due to coincidence, but rather to my desire to uplift the many Muslim women who are engaged in the work of dismantling Islamophobia. It is Muslim women who have been fighting every step of the way in defense of our communities, and it is to them we owe our deepest thanks.

Buthaina: A Yemeni Advocate

The gravity and almost spectacular nature of the 9/11 attacks garnered different memories from the interviewees. Buthaina, a Yemeni American, recalled being at her grandma's house on 9/11, huddled together with her family. As they watched the destruction on TV, she remembered her grandma saying, "It's like watching back home." Buthaina recounted that her grandma didn't specifically mean Yemen; she was talking about the general turmoil in the Middle East. This illustrated an important juxtaposition with the ways in which the average American has been shielded from acts of mass violence in other countries, especially at the hands of their own country, the United States.

Like many Muslims, Buthaina felt the impact of the 9/11 attacks on her daily life almost immediately. When running a simple errand to buy groceries the day after, she was confronted by a man in the parking lot who told her to go back to her country. Then came the narrative that constructed the Muslim enemy.

From Buthaina's perspective, the world went from understanding Islam from an orientalist lens to understanding Muslims as mean, terroristic, and inherently violent—the latter shaped in particular by the Bush administration. For Buthaina, "the world changed because Islamophobia was just revamped and just manufactured to be this durable, sturdy mechanism to just push and spew hate."

I asked each interviewee what the War on Terror is and what it entails. Buthaina's understanding of the War on Terror was quite broad, encompassing not only what was happening domestically, but also abroad. For Buthaina,

> the War on Terror . . . is, I mean it's a mastermind—like whoever manufactured it. Here we are all these years later, twenty years. . . . Here we are almost twenty years later and we are still seeing children being bullied in schools, we're still seeing Muslim women that are observed [having their] hijab being pulled or [being] yanked by their scarves. In San Jose, which is a progressive city here in the Bay Area, San Jose police officers were making fun of the hijab, saying that they could tie it around the Muslim women's necks as a noose. So, the War on Terror has really justified all of these things, which include all these discriminatory immigration policies, endless wars in almost all of the Middle East and parts of North Africa.

Buthaina described a common problem: the inability to connect what was happening domestically with what has happened abroad. Buthaina was illustrating a frequent oversight in the Muslim community, which, in many cases in my view, shows up in the way Muslim organizations adhere to this artificial distinction in service of the state. The distinction between domestic and foreign matters reinforces the idea that Muslim immigrants who come from other countries should firmly disconnect what happens "over there" from what happens here in order to fit into the empire's assimilation project. As an advocate for Muslims abroad, she expressed frustration because of what she believed some Muslims were doing to silence these stories. For Buthaina, the only thing separating her from the fate of Muslims abroad was her citizenship, a privilege she uses to highlight stories from abroad. But she's also particular about telling these stories because "Muslim community apologists are really focused on, I hate to say erasing, but silencing them."

Ever since the US launched the War on Terror, attitudes have varied in the Muslim community about the way it continues to be perpetuated. For example, some Muslims have actively engaged in furthering or promoting counterterrorism policies, while others have rejected the notion that Muslims are inherently predisposed to committing acts of violence. Buthaina described more or less two groups of Muslims when it came to positions toward the War on Terror: Muslims who have internalized Islamophobia, and those who have adopted an apologetic approach toward any act of violence committed by Muslims. These differences are often manifested by Muslims working for the government in the realm of counterterrorism. "It is often the case that victims of Islamophobia are victimized twice over," Buthaina said, "because of the policies themselves . . . and because Muslims are working with these institutions and agencies to entrap our people. . . . So Islamophobia uses the protection of national security and then Muslim Americans use, you know, counteracting violent extremism or they use this preventing violent extremism."

Given how central the War on Terror has been in the lives of Muslims such as Buthaina, it is unsurprising that she rejected the common narrative that has declared the War on Terror over: "If we are going to talk about stopping or ending the War on Terror, then we have to talk about Yemen. We have talked about Libya, we have talked about Iraq, we have talked about Afghanistan, we have to talk about Sudan, we have to talk about Oakland, we have to talk about the airports, we have to talk about all these CVE programs. We have to talk about all of these things. So I think if we don't have all of those things on the table, then no one can say the War on Terror has ended."

Buthaina's experience as a Muslim living under the War on Terror highlights how problematic this apparatus has been and still is, whether because of the local-to-global connections, daily experiences as a visible Muslim, or the role Muslims play in the oppression of their coreligionists. Beyond simply addressing injustice, Buthaina also shared her vision of collective liberation, saying, "It means that Palestine is free from the hands of Zionist occupation. It means Islamophobia is eradicated. . . . MENA [Middle East North Africa] free of imperialism and militarism. Our mosques will be safe from monitoring and surveillance. Our youth will be safe from being entrapped and watched and profiled. It means that we can move freely in and out of airports without being treated as suspect, without being held with suspicion." Further, Buthaina added, "It'll mean that our brothers and sisters in the movement who are fighting their respective fights . . . will also be free from the shackles of this, you know, white supremacist machine, so police brutality will be not a thing anymore. . . . So I think collective liberation means justice for all of our fights. . . . Our liberation is bound together and I think it's almost impossible to gain liberation without incorporating intersectionality."

Bijan: An Afghan Advocate

Following the history of scapegoating in the United States, one of my interviewees, Bijan, who identifies as Afghan American, remembered 9/11 and his fear that the perpetrators would be identified as Muslim. Bijan was at school at the time of the attacks and recalls how one of his Indian American friends was concerned for his safety, though at the time he didn't think his identity would be a consideration in how he was treated. Two days after the attacks, Bijan wrote a letter to the editor for the local news-paper, calling for unity and saying the oft-repeated phrase "We're in this together." As an Afghan American, he added that he hoped there wouldn't be backlash against his community if the attackers were identified as Muslim. Despite his plea, a letter to the editor next to his likened Muslims to scorpions whose deaths could be condoned as revenge.

Bijan's identity as an Afghan became particularly salient for him, and he remarked, "You have to remember that being Afghan wasn't a thing before September 11; nobody had heard of Afghanistan." But this new visibility caused fear for Bijan's family, and his dad instructed him to stick to his American friends, which meant his white American friends. In the post-9/11 context, in which Afghanistan became the first military target in the War on Terror and the US invasion of Afghanistan has become the lon-gest war in US history, Afghans like Bijan moved from a lack of visibility to a hyper-visibility.

With the War on Terror building up, Bijan also noted an interesting digression in the narrative—one that supported going out and shopping. He remembered seeing shopping bags with American flags on them, a reflection of how the country was incorporating a capitalistic approach to counterterrorism tactics in the larger War on Terror.

Speaking to the War on Terror and what it entails, in Bijan's view "it just became a catch-all for anything the military wants to do. And it means nothing anymore." Thus, for Bijan the War on Terror was simply a means to unrestricted and unending violence without any clear purpose.

Bijan told me that his parents had become US citizens in 2000, and because he was under eighteen, he automatically became a citizen as well. As a citizen, Bijan felt that he could accomplish anything in this country, but his attitude changed after the events surrounding the Park 51 Islamic Center. Bijan had believed after 9/11 that people could be educated about Islam and that this would serve as a teachable moment. But Bijan told me that after seeing Park 51 incidents, he felt the reaction was different. "It was just pure hatred, it was just pure xenophobia, it was just pure Islamophobia, it went against everything I understood about freedom of religion, about, you know, who can be an American, about all of this stuff. And it made me really, really sad." This realization came with the understanding that challenging the oppression of Muslims would not, as he had thought earlier, happen through interventions that simply sought to correct people's misunderstandings of Islam and Muslims.

Bijan identified that one of the consequences of the War on Terror on the Muslim community was the fact that "it caused the big rift between respectability Muslims who wrap themselves in the American flag and, you know, invite the FBI to their mosques, and the ones who are poor and surveilled and scapegoated and then entrapped. This division has further reified the otherness of American Muslims, and especially the idea that we are not American."

One of the most poignant parts of the interview was when Bijan told me how his disposition has changed in his response to the War on Terror: "I grew up an optimist, and I always have been an optimist, but I'm not anymore. And I think it's because of the War on Terror. You know, I used to think, okay, give it another few years and Afghanistan will have peace, but no. I think it's just to permanently destabilize the country, because that's been happening for the past decade, two decades."

Nevertheless, Bijan expressed a vision of justice for Muslims that would include an official apology, in addition to Muslims "fighting for and getting what they deserve." Beyond justice for Muslims, Bijan's vision of collective liberation was one that would entail fighting for Black people, disabled people, the LGBT community, and other marginalized communities. "And I think it's especially important to fight for Black people, remembering that whatever the figures, that 40 percent were Muslims and they were the first Muslims here, and they were forcibly, brutally stripped of any rights."

Rosita: A Latina Advocate

With all the laws and policies that have been sanctioned under the guise of the War on Terror and that have specifically targeted Muslims, interviewees noted many different consequences. Rosita, an interviewee who identifies as Puerto Rican and Mexican, observed that after 9/11, many people were converting to Islam—something she identified as a positive benefit in the attacks' aftermath. But the myriad other consequences for her and other Muslims were far less positive.

The impact of the 9/11 attacks and what followed was felt by different people at different times. Because she wasn't a Muslim at the time of the attacks, Rosita initially believed she wouldn't be impacted by the aftermath, but the creation of the US Immigration and Customs Enforcement (ICE) agency changed that. Rosita's conception of the War on Terror was broader than ICE, however, and when I asked her what she thought the war was, she told me that it is a "campaign to demonize Muslims, not only nationally but also internationally. Specifically, internationally, the US always needs an enemy in order to justify the unnecessary budget that the Department of Defense has, in order to almost hype the American people, white American people, into believing they are, without question, the best nation on Earth. But this is a justification to spread American capitalist values across the world and it doesn't apply to us. So Islam is demonized as backwards because there's this underlying terror of separating Christendom from American values."

One of Rosita's struggles was proving to members of her family that Islam was a good religion after she converted. She stated, "I found myself having to go into politics to prove Islam was good to my family, and no new convert should have to be thrown into politics when they're just trying to better their connection with God." One of the most hurtful experiences she endured was discrimination from her own people, meaning others from Latin America. Though she didn't express this, it's important to note that the narrative criminalizing Muslims post-9/11 has been so pervasive that many communities of color have also internalized and subsequently harbor Islamophobic views. This is not an excuse but an illustration of just how normalized the narrative has become.

Another element of Rosita's "identity crisis," as she described it, was the feeling that she couldn't be Latina and Muslim. This made her feel like she was supposed to learn about Middle Eastern or South Asian politics, which was unsurprising given the way the dominant narrative, especially post-9/11, conflated Arabs with Muslims.

One of the stories Rosita shared with me was about her experience at a Latino Muslim conference. The FBI was given a platform to speak at the conference, and they specifically said they were looking for applicants for a job—one that she remembered as being along the lines of a liaison of some sort. For Rosita, this was very troubling, and she told me that she thought it was disrespectful to have the FBI there trying to recruit Latinx Muslims and have an FBI agent that spoke Spanish do the recruiting, but that his express rationale was:

> "many of you are converts and have studied this faith so you're able to discern what's right from wrong." . . . And so I'm just sitting there with my arms crossed like I cannot believe I'm listening to this and, you know, this is . . . because the War on Terror continues to target Latinx Muslims to use as informants. Just seeing that for the first time was really unnerving and made me really scared, to be honest. Now especially because we're the fastest-growing population converting to Islam.

Rosita also named the fact that Muslims within her community were living in fear, and because of this, they responded by trying to prove their Americanness. This was manifested in displays of the American flag and hesitance to wear traditional and/or cultural clothing. Essentially, many Muslims felt that they needed to "conform to the idea of what it means to be an American."

Rosita also spoke to the matter of Muslims internalizing Islamophobia, though she hesitated to describe how it manifests. Her example was of a Muslim who feels uncomfortable praying in a public place. "And that is internalizing Islamophobia by not feeling comfortable enough to pray during a break at a convening. You pray in a corner. You have every right to pray in that corner and nobody should judge you for that. That's your responsibility. Don't stop living the faith you proclaim to hold."

Was the War on Terror over? Rosita responded, "That's a lie. I would want to see no more recruitment for the military in Black and Latino communities. Remove these institutions and these policies like ICE. Remove these laws that randomly spring up in different states that require Black and brown people to prove their Americanness. Stop the zoning challenges that happen when people try to build or expand their Masjid and you know communities are against it because of their Islamophobic tendencies. The war will be over when we stop the intentional otherizing of Muslims."

When it came to collective liberation, Rosita was passionate about the need for different communities to work together and to realize that what affects one group impacts another group, even if it is manifested differently. "We all need to come together in order to fight and push back on the things and the powers-that-be that keep us separated from one another so we don't learn, but also struggling to make ends meet. . . . When Black people are free, it's a trickle-down effect. Starting off and realizing that Black liberation should be at the forefront of liberation for everyone and especially as Muslims—we should never side with the oppressor."

Perla: A White PhD Student

Perla converted to Islam in 1990 and was married to an Egyptian Muslim man. She remembers her husband, an avid news reader, on 9/11 watching TV coverage of the attacks on multiple channels over and over again. Perla heard about a mental-health number you could call, so she called, distressed over whether she would be considered a traitor because she was associated with Arabs and Muslims.

Because the Islamic school that her children attended received a bomb threat in the days that followed 9/11, it was closed the first few days after the attacks. When school did resume, Perla kept her children home, at least initially, and then for the first few Fridays after that, afraid that the school would be a target because of the significance of the day in Islam.

Though not immediately after the 9/11 attacks, Perla recalls that her daughter was harassed by a classmate who told her she was related to one of the 9/11 attackers, Mohammed Atta, because her name started with "Atta." Many years later, after the Boston Marathon bombings, someone told Perla's son he looked like one of the bombers. Daily consequences of the War on Terror for Perla's son also included self-censorship, including being too afraid to buy a pressure cooker online because he worried the government would target him as a bomb-maker.

One of the post-9/11 impacts Perla observed was the fact that Muslim conferences stopped. In addition, organizations advocating for and soliciting donations for Bosnia and Kashmir, which had been common before 9/11, disappeared. Moreover, Perla noted, the post-9/11 consequences of running such an organization, especially if the government accused them of wrongdoing, were much harsher—an observation matching significant crackdown on Muslim charities by the government particularly in the earlier days of the War on Terror.

For Perla, "the War on Terror, of course, was used to further the goals of the US empire like it has. And just like using [Japan's attack on] Pearl Harbor [as justification] to do things domestically and abroad, I think the War on Terror has been made to do that, and now twenty years later, it's still the same. You know, it advances and morphs like racism does . . . or, let's say, the War on Terror moves to a different phase as counterterrorism moves to a different phase as counter-extremism moves to a different phase." With this understanding of the War on Terror, its continuation seemed almost inevitable.

Perla's post-9/11 experience also included knowledge that not all Muslims were what they seemed. More specifically, she told me a story about an Iraqi man disappearing from the mosque she went to, only to end up in Iraq's interim government. The lesson she learned from this was that "you never know who's in your mosque listening, who's working for the government, who's going to sell out." Religious spaces in this case, for Muslims, were being polluted by the government so as to make communities feel unsafe at all times. But of course this relied on Muslim individuals within the community who were willing to work with the government.

One example of this, which we discussed earlier in this book, is Countering Violent Extremism (CVE). According to Perla, "CVE is one of the big things, and Muslims participate in it—totally participate in it and embrace that narrative that there is something inherently violent in Islam, and they need to make sure that people think their religion is x, y, and z and that they aren't violent; they're peaceful people. But again, that shows you that the narrative is central because they are acknowledging it and arguing against it."

Among the issues Perla raised in her interview was the way Muslims accused of crimes were dealt with, including the automatic assumption of guilt and believing the government's narrative of criminality without even a hearing or trial. This had consequences extending to death, such as how the Boston Marathon bomber who was killed was refused burial by many Muslim leaders. "First of all," Perla said,

> I think that Muslims have their burial rites and they have rights in the community, and we have to do that whether you think somebody is a terrorist or not—and again, he didn't have a trial. And even if he did, I still feel like he had a right to be buried; that's just my opinion. It's our job to just put him in the ground and bury him. If we can bury child molesters and murderers and all these other kinds of people, then you can bury these people . . . and it bothered me that no mosque would even take his body when it was dead.

With all of this said, Perla expressed belief that collective liberation would happen when "the oppressed collective gains the same standing and rights and justice as other groups, [when] every group exists with equity."

Armando: A Latinx Veteran and Advocate

Armando, another interviewee, identifies as Chicano and Mexican. Like several others I interviewed for this book, Armando was not Muslim at the time of the 9/11 attacks. Interestingly, however, he was in the Marine Corps. When the 9/11 attacks happened, he was in boot camp, and a supervisor woke him and the others in training to let them know the World Trade Centers had been hit and the US had been attacked. After watching TV and seeing the images that night, Armando was told "they" hate us and that they would be going to war.

Aside from being told they were going to fight, very few other details were communicated to Armando and his colleagues. But the little that was explained painted a picture that the United States was at war to fight back against "political acts of violence that terrorize us or our allies."

Asked about how Muslim organizations responded to the 9/11 attacks, he said, "We [had] to apologize . . . we [had] to say we're sorry collectively." But he told me there were efforts to move away from this response. The war in Iraq was presented as a war for the purpose of freeing Iraqis. But Armando recalled that when they entered Iraq, "people [were] fleeing and people were walking with other belongings they carried, like fleeing the cities. . . . And it was kind of just calm, but then like after a while you started to see . . . as we're driving to the cities, people were throwing rocks at us and bottles and stuff like that. And so then, at that point, there was this frustration when we realized we weren't here to free anybody and we're now just . . . doing this job that we hate and just trying to get through it to come back home."

Armando left the Marines in 2004 and converted to Islam. Embraced by a Muslim community that was predominantly Palestinian, Armando learned about the violence and terror they had experienced. Hearing their stories made him reflect on the fact that "[now I] was on the opposite end of what I was essentially involved [in] in Iraq."

Armando relayed to me an experience he had while teaching at school with me. A leader of a previously operating organization called the Bureau of American Islamic Relations called his school district and told them Armando was going to kill his students if Trump won the election. After an investigation, Armando was cleared and was able to go back to school. He told me, "The idea that because I'm Muslim or because of who I was as far as being willing to defend my community against these racists would warrant an attack to get me fired from a job was very troubling."

Armando described internalizing Islamophobia. When he first converted, he started growing a beard and wearing a kufi, but was discouraged from essentially looking too Muslim. Armando attributed this to the idea that "there are ever-watching eyes."

For Armando, the consequences of 9/11 and the War on Terror were how much destruction they brought to communities abroad, including Falluja in Iraq, where children have been born with birth defects as a consequence of the US bombing the city with depleted uranium.

Moreover, Armando didn't believe that the War on Terror was over. In response to this question, he explained,

> There's still 800 bases around the world. I think that in itself the War on Terror has already been being waged long before they officially started it or whatever, like it's the way it's commonly known as it being from like 2001 on or whatever. You know, I think the United States and its forces have been waging [war] and terrorizing communities for a long period of time, and I think that it doesn't look like it's gonna end anytime soon, in the sense of starting to pull back US militarism that is flourishing, like the weapons industry. . . . Yeah, I would be like, no, that's not finished. It's not over by a long shot.

But that was because of the idea they fed them: "Politics is politics; this is war."

"Nobody's free until everybody's free," Armando told me when I asked him what collective liberation meant to him. He added, "I love these revolutionary quotes that are Marxist or anarchist or communist or just, you know, antiracist—you know these quotes about collective liberation, and then being Muslim also, like when they talk about the ummah [the whole community of Muslims] is one body and everyone, you know, feels pain, and everybody feels like that's the ideal of something that we strive for . . . a utopia that we're endlessly working towards."

Armando said that part of this struggle includes justice for Muslims, which means that this community would have a voice to speak for themselves. This would mean "being fully empowered and capable of rising up, collectively and together."

Ryan: A White Researcher

Convert identity in the context of the War on Terror was brought up by another interviewee, Ryan, who identifies as white. Though she wasn't Muslim at the time of 9/11, she nevertheless remembered the explanation offered for why the US suffered this violence as "They hate our freedoms." Ryan converted eleven years after the start of the War on Terror, and she described how her family responded to this news in Islamophobic ways—for example, asking her if she was going to become radical and whether she was, as a result of converting, going to give up her rights, because that's what they understood about women in Islam. Though she couldn't say with certainty that it was solely the War on Terror that shaped her family's understanding of Islam in this way, she nevertheless felt they were operating with the backdrop of the state narrative of the 9/11 attacks.

One of Ryan's struggles was around internalized Islamophobia because of the fact that she was a white person who "had direct agency in upholding anti-Muslim rhetoric and policies." But for Ryan, this just meant she had to work on unlearning messages about Muslims—and that was something she was very committed to.

Conscious of her whiteness, she described how, as she learned about the War on Terror, she grew cognizant of the fact that in many cases a white-convert identity was used as a pretext for FBI informants. To this end, she said that "being a convert is used as a cover to infiltrate a community, and I don't have any hard and fast analysis in terms of a percentage of how many cases in which, and like a breakdown by race or ethnicity. But I feel like anecdotally, a lot of the cases I've come across—not all, but a fair amount, especially some of the most egregious cases—have been white Muslims, like that Craig Monteilh guy [a former FBI informant who made the news in 2012]."

But whiteness was not only relevant insofar as informants go, but also in the way the US operates the War on Terror generally. To this end, Ryan said, "I think of the War on Terror as another way in which the US, and by extension whiteness globally, is just trying to continually reassert, dominate, and control itself. . . . It is always something that white people do. . . . It has incredibly devastating material consequences, harm, and violence against predominantly Black, brown, Indigenous, Muslims, and poor people."

Muslims themselves were often part of the machine targeting other Muslims, according to Ryan. This happened, for example, with Obama's Countering Violent Extremism program. What drew Muslims into this paradigm, she said, was the framing the Obama administration used to convince Muslims that Islam was not the problem. Ryan further described the framing as promoting the idea that the government wants to help Muslims help themselves. Ryan added, "You know, I feel like a lot of us, a lot of Muslims bought into it as a much safer, a much nicer alternative. But again, it's so dangerous because it's like . . . diverting the conversation from 'all cops are bastards' to, well, you know, how helpful it is to have a school resource officer at the school, just to make sure everyone's safe. I mean, it's just such a slippery slope. I just feel like that shift was really brilliant, but it's really dangerous, like it was very dangerous."

Ryan recalled the incident of the Boston Marathon bomber who died, and how several individuals and organizations put out statements saying that they were going to refuse to bury him after his death. She remembers learning about this from a friend who is also Muslim. Ryan shared, "The fact that you felt like you needed to put out a statement declaring to the world that [you] won't even engage in a burial practice . . . because that would somehow signal that if you bury someone, you condone. Why, why are you even letting yourself fall into that? That's not the issue. Why are you playing into that?" Like Perla, Ryan shared an important perspective about internalized Islamophobia and how it manifests in the community.

Despite all of this, Ryan was optimistic about the shifts that at least some Muslims were making toward abolition, but she cautioned that in terms of surveillance, she hoped "there's a really solid awareness and without decentering the anti-Blackness of police. I think that's a lot of work that a lot of us need to do and understand. And I hope that we're able then to make connections to the surveillance state and not just letting Department of Homeland Security (DHS) come into our communities or not letting CVE money come into our afterschool programs or, you know, our therapists' offices and things like this, just being more conscious about it, I think."

Though Ryan was still shaping her vision of collective liberation, emphasizing that she was trying to learn from Black women, Black queer people, and the Black radical movement, what she did envision was a world without white dominance and where the idea that we're all connected is realized. Justice for Muslims in particular, to Ryan, means "not having to be particularly conscious that you're Muslim, like not having to carry or negotiate a Muslimness that's not your own but a projection of society's anti-Muslim attitudes and the state's anti-Muslim laws and policies. When this happens, insha Allah, it means that white supremacist imperialism and colonialism are no longer enacting violence on our communities. And this will only be true when the liberation of Black Muslims is achieved, because anti-Blackness and anti-Muslimness operate hand in hand. This also includes within Muslim communities."

Ryan rejected the idea that the War on Terror was over. To her, "the War on Terror is a horrific moment and we're still in [it]. And it's so deeply rooted in white supremacy and settler colonialism, anti-Blackness and capitalism and ableism and if you are worthy in terms of productivity. . . . The War on Terror is a horrific political moment that's still alive and well, and it's just another iteration of a long, ongoing chapter of just whiteness in violence."

Imrana: A Somali Lawyer and Advocate

Imrana, who identifies as Somali, was a refugee who came to the United States two months before the 9/11 attacks. Had her family tried to come two months later, she believes it would have been too late because everything, including the border, would have been closed. But the first two months of life in the United States were, as Imrana put it, "the honeymoon stage."

She was at school when the 9/11 attacks happened, and she remembers her ESL teacher wheeling in a TV and telling the class that the towers were down. Imrana didn't understand what was happening because of the language barrier, though she noticed a changed vibe in the classroom, with teachers and students crying. According to Imrana, "Every adult in the room knew the world had changed, and all of us children definitely didn't understand it." Even though Imrana couldn't immediately comprehend what had happened, she said she understood to some extent a week later because people in Somalia were calling her family and asking if they were safe.

Six months later was when she really understood the impact of the 9/11 attacks. She told me, "Islamophobia immediately hit the ground as if it was always kind of brewing and it wasn't something that had to be learned. It was sort of on the tip of the tongue . . . it's interesting, especially for children, seventh- and eighth-graders, to be able to internalize Islamophobia at that quick a rate, and then immediately regurgitate what is happening at home." Needless to say, Imrana began experiencing a constant feeling of anxiety; it lasted from seventh grade through eleventh grade in particular, because her school was a predominantly white school in Minnesota.

Imrana recalls that, during high school, there was constant talk about the 9/11 attacks, and that military recruiters were consistently telling the students to enlist. As she described it, this was part of a larger narrative around patriotism, which meant that not only could you not be anti-war, but that reciting the Pledge of Allegiance in school became mandatory, a change from pre-9/11 days.

Even though the narrative after 9/11 in the United States was focused on unity, Imrana felt that much of it was performative, based on the fact that unlike the war efforts, people were suffering domestically, whether experiencing homelessness or food insecurity. Imrana noted, "This imaginative community that they were building by force was, I think, the part that was really uncomfortable. . . . In my mind, it was specifically to drum up support for the war." The other side was that this effectively narrowed unity to mean support for war. As Imrana described, "You [couldn't] be anti-police. You [couldn't] be anti-firefighter. You [couldn't] be anti-military. You just couldn't be anti-anything."

Imrana described the War on Terror as nebulous. She told me that it was "terrorizing us, but it was also consistently there, everywhere. It wasn't just abroad, it was here, it was in the *Zeitgeist* of our conscience." As the War on Terror has become so normalized that it's often invisible, Imrana's account speaks to how Muslims like her have experienced it differently.

A lot changed post-9/11. For Imrana, one thing was the narrative that consistently pushed the idea that the US would never be really safe again. But this was by design, and by using fear in the form of colored threat levels, for example, certain things could be sanctioned:

One, it was like now more than ever we need to militarize everything. But second, we will never truly be safe because if it happened to us once, it could always happen [again]. . . . When people trusted the government, it was really like we wrote a blank check . . . and people were willing to give up anything. I remember even I had conversations with people in high school and they were just like, "So what if you are put in a room at the airport for seven, eight hours? If it makes us collectively safer, I'm okay with that." I mean, it's funny, they weren't so willing to give up *their* freedom, but they would definitely be willing to give up *mine*.

This attitude was also based on the belief that the "government knows better than us. You know, it doesn't matter if you were inconvenienced and scared and you were terrorized and you knew your rights were taken. As long as we felt a little safer because of it, it was fine. So the assumption was definitely that the government knew better and that that's predominantly one of the things that changed."

Throughout the years since 9/11, Imrana has had consistent issues when traveling. One time, she was stuck on the US-Toronto border, where she was held in a room for several hours and had her phone taken away. No one informed her about why she had been stopped, but they eventually gave her passport and phone back and told her she was free to go. Reflecting on travel issues, Imrana noted that despite her professional identity and the fact that she was an attorney, she was "just as vulnerable just sitting there." This was a powerful statement and one that casts doubt on the belief of some within the Muslim community that being a "good" Muslim will save you from being targeted.

Imrana drew attention to another aspect of identity: an experience she had when applying for a German scholarship to go to Berlin while she was in college. Despite the fact that she had the highest grades in the department, one of the evaluators for the scholarship asked her how she could represent the American identity as someone who didn't have one. For Imrana, this was indicative of the fact that it wasn't about technically being American (which she was, by citizenship) but about others' beliefs that she wasn't considered American. Of course, none of the white students had been asked the same question. She expected to be asked about her language skills, but not her identity as American.

What did being American actually mean? Imrana believed that the American identity was "constructed around war." For all the talk about Muslims being radicalized, Imrana told me, "it's funny because people talk about being radicalized but I felt like the country, the government was able to radicalize so many young folks into this idea that they needed to serve the country in this really, really violent way for themselves and for others, and so the greatest impact to me is truly, truly the militarization of young folks and the idea that your American identity and your patriotism was directly connected to your service through the military, rather than, for example, becoming a nurse."

Muslims have been denied their humanity and the assumption of innocence, Imrana told me. Because of this, many Muslims feel compelled to perform peacefulness and engage in acts of service to prove their humanity. Imrana worked at an organization whose goal was to instill the idea that everyone should be able to experience the feeling of being innocent—which is often difficult because of the stereotypes and images that have been projected onto different identities. For Imrana, innocence was something that was taken from a lot of people, particularly Black people, who are left feeling there is a burden of proof. To this end, Imrana stated, "I think that burden needs to be lifted, like you need to, without consequences, be able to walk around and say, 'My identity is innocent. I feel innocent. I feel like myself and my humanity is recognized, period, full stop.'" This is something that has not been afforded to Muslims since 9/11, particularly Black Muslims, who are doubly criminalized.

A contrasting example of people who have their innocence taken away involves people who are privileged and express shock when their idea of their innocence is threatened. For Imrana, this happened in the summer of 2020, when protestors in support of Black Lives Matter were met with a military response. Referring to the protests, Imrana told me, "At the very beginning, this white guy spoke and he said, 'And then a military officer touched my shoulder.' But you [could] see the shock that the military could be used against them. Like, that someone could violate your body and your space and you, that's innocence—like innocence to believe that your government would never use the power of the military against you and victimize you or take your civil rights away in any way, shape, or form. That guy was definitely shocked by it."

Along similar lines, Imrana expressed frustration about how Muslims are treated as collectively responsible and made to bear the burden of the acts of Muslims not connected to them at all, while white people never have to bear this burden. As she noted, "Even though white supremacy in itself is constant terror on Black bodies, yet no one feels that they have to carry that, and even now when you think about [it], white people feel a little tiny bit of that right now and they feel exhausted by it."

With everything happening in the United States and the ongoing legacy of systemic violence, Imrana said she did not believe the War on Terror was over. She told me, "I mean, can we really say that it's over when we still have so many military interventions that are rooted and hooked on the idea that there is this outside force that is coming? Our military budget wouldn't look the way that it is looking right now if it was over, and most legal justification for a lot of the action that happens under the guise of the War on Terror is still needed."

It was important for Imrana that we reflect on what the right response to the war should have been:

I think they had moments where people are like, well, we all were in it, we didn't know better, but it's like—no, we did know better. We did know better, and they could have. I think knowing that there could have been another reality in this post-911 world, [there] could have been more people to speak up and take leadership roles and say, "No, let's stop for a moment and breathe and think about how we can heal and think about what the steps should be." It's very unnatural and I think all of the impact that it has on the humans that went abroad to fight this shows that you don't come back, and so it's not a natural reaction because the psyche didn't think it was natural as humans to do harm to others, to dehumanize them and to think of them as a collective bad. It's not a human thing to do.

Ibad: A Muslim American Human Rights Lawyer

Ibad was in college when the 9/11 attacks happened. Identifying as an Algerian American, he remembers people in the dorms congregating in his room because of his identity, in order to ask him why "they" did it—*they* meaning Muslims who perpetrated the attacks. He recalls his roommate asking him, "What do they want?" Worse yet, he was still dealing with the fear he felt when he had initially not been able to reach his parents.

Ibad said he was surprised at how quickly people he considered friends otherized him and associated him with the Muslims who perpetrated the 9/11 attacks. "It was immediate—because Muslims were associated with 9/11, so was I. What was really sad was that there was absolutely no examination of the underlying reasons. . . . It was effectively a narrative that went 'Islam and savages that support Islam hit us on 9/11, and there's really no political reason—we need to get them back.'" To Ibad, the US was operating without really addressing the root causes of the attacks, while scapegoating Muslims and Islam as the problem.

For Ibad, one of the hardest aspects about the aftermath of the attacks was the way the United States responded. The declared War on Terror was a pretext to build up the military industrial complex and wage war against Muslim-majority populations. For him, the War on Terror has meant committing massive crimes in a region that had already been victimized by poor policies advanced by the United States. The shift in discourse and treatment made life as a Muslim person very challenging, and Ibad went through a tough adjustment period. It was so painful that he seriously considered moving abroad.

Even though he remembers Bush's attempt to dissociate Islam from the 9/11 attackers, he thought Bush's discourse was operating off the "good" Muslim, "bad" Muslim paradigm more than actually vindicating the religion and its followers. This dichotomy was something that took hold in the Muslim community, and Ibad told me,

Islamophobia and anti-Muslim bigotry are so central to executing the War on Terror. It is essential to sell the idea to the population that good Muslims support war while bad ones oppose [it]. . . . It's a form of white supremacy, and this deeply rooted tool is used by the elite class to divide Muslims into good Muslims or bad Muslims based on their support for war and US policy in the Middle East. That's exactly what we're seeing play out, and it works well in that we see marginalized communities pitted against each other. We have Muslims that are spying on each other at mosques across this nation, instead of organizing and unifying together to end the War on Terror. And so we have a lot of work to do as a community, and we have to really be aware that this is what anti-Muslim bigotry is actually doing.

The War on Terror is a war of destruction, and in Ibad's mind, one of the most important aspects of it was the way it pivoted away from previously established laws and policies. To him, the war meant that

our country's leaders were going to use the official and literal tools of war—for example, the use of the laws of war, instead of criminal law—because we are treating the perpetrators of the 9/11 attacks differently. Instead, we're not going to treat crimes on 9/11 as a law enforcement issue like we treat any crime. What I mean is, we could have treated [the] 9/11 attacks the same way we did the Oklahoma City bombing. After the Oklahoma City attack, we didn't say "Oh, we're going to go and declare war on crazy white men." We did say, "We're going to prosecute McVeigh in a criminal court," and he was put in jail. With the War on Terror, we took a completely different route, and our political class opted to create a new set of laws and standards for Muslims. Our country threw the rule of law and logic out the window, and politicians and elites cynically decided they were going to make a lot of money off of the atrocities on 9/11. And that's what the War on Terror is: people making money off of the 9/11 deaths by declaring war illegitimately to send defense contractors into Iraq and the Middle East to make billions at the expense of US taxpayers, our national safety, and millions of civilians.

To Ibad, the War on Terror has been about essentially giving corporations, like Haliburton and Raytheon and many others, an opportunity to make more money, because there were profits to be made. But it was also about the ways the attacks "represent misguided American adventurism in the region where they went into the Middle East using anti-Muslim big-otry, Islamophobia, and racism to make money for the military industrial complex, while bankrupting American taxpayers." There was something even worse, though—the way the War on Terror was allowing other governments globally to justify repression and abuses through the war's guise. This includes the Chinese government, which has heavily targeted Muslim Uighur populations by using the same logic as the US War on Terror.

Could Ibad say after all this that the War on Terror was over? No, he reasoned, because we have to dismantle white supremacy, and the current capitalist system fueling it, by reimagining the way we respond to violence. White supremacy and the War on Terror are inextricably linked, he believes. Thus, as long as white supremacy exists, so too will the War on Terror.

One of the more painful ways the War on Terror impacted Ibad was in the way that members of his family have been affected by the Muslim Ban. His American parent recently remarried and has been unable to bring their spouse to the United States because of the Muslim Ban. Ibad stated, "It doesn't matter that they're American and have been here for forever, or that all their kids live here . . . the visa got denied."

Internalized Islamophobia was another issue that Ibad touched on. In a climate where anti-Muslim images, movies, and narratives have run rampant, Ibad wondered how this wouldn't impact Muslims' sense of identity:

It's difficult not to absorb and internalize this sort of anti-Muslim animus and bigotry, which is everywhere. Islamophobia is . . . an openly accepted pastime in American life, and if you're a consumer of any media, or if you even live in this country, [you are] bombarded with images of Muslims doing horrific things, killing, beheading, and violating people. The mainstream narratives in pop culture from movies to mainstream TV depict one-dimensional Muslim caricatures as exceptional, extraordinary monsters who are able to do things that no one else can do while simultaneously being impotent and feeble. It's difficult to say that it hasn't affected our ability to really perceive ourselves as Muslims in an empowered, complex, and healthy way.

The road ahead, according to Ibad, requires acknowledgment of what has happened in the Middle East and "get[ting] to the truth about who we are as a nation and what we have done outside and inside the US to not only Muslims but to Black people, immigrants, and other communities." After that, Ibad said, we could move toward building a collective vision of living together in a way that accommodates everyone's needs and that doesn't reduce people to profits.

Despite all the harm and suffering created by the War on Terror, Ibad still felt hopeful, not least because of the solidarity shown to Muslims around the Muslim Ban and others standing against Guantánamo. "I hope that people remember to center the voices of Muslims who fought back against the violence of the War on Terror, not just the white allies."

Rashida: A Black American Racial Justice Advocate

When I interviewed Rashida, who identifies as Black American, her perspective of the War on Terror was shaped by the understanding of the United States as anti-Black. To Rashida, the War on Terror wasn't a new phenomenon in and of itself, but stemmed from this long, systemic history of state violence.

Rashida was in fourth grade when the 9/11 attacks happened. Though she said she always felt "weird," the attacks made her feel "a different kind of weird." She described a shift in the general way people interacted around her sometimes and the fact that the word *terrorist* became part of the vernacular.

It didn't help that Rashida faced consistent scrutiny at school. One of her memories is of a girl coming up to her and telling her that she wanted to befriend her but had been warned against it by others who said Rashida would blow her up. In her later years of school, Rashida told me there were a few times when students would just yell out, "Terrorist!" when she walked by. When her younger sister started attending the same high school with her, another student replied, "Now there are two terrorists."

As a Black American Muslim, Rashida grew up with an understanding of the United States as a violent, anti-Black country. Thus, when she heard the narrative around 9/11, because she had already been politicized about the way the United States operates, she knew it was riddled with lies. She summarized the narrative that she remembers in the following way: "I remember the narrative just being very anti-Muslim, without any understanding of who Muslims are and what Islam is. The messaging seemed to be [that] Muslims and anyone who 'looks' Muslim or Arab is bad, and that was used to somehow justify American imperialism and violence abroad."

Another piece of the post-9/11 narrative that Rashida mentioned was around Muslim women: specifically, the way that Muslim women were constructed as a threat at the same time as they were constructed as oppressed;

having to deal with being "saved" (which was condescending, racist, and not at all compassionate) and also being a target of others' outbursts and harmful actions.

In Rashida's experience, there were practical consequences to the way identity was shaped for Muslims, one of which was the fact that "as a Muslim your existence was seen as a threat, and that lie could manifest in people's actions anytime." But the post-9/11 narratives, Rashida believes, served as a way to placate the state. Rashida told me that the consequence of this was that "when we look at prisoners at Gitmo or even how folks who are incarcerated in jails and prisons are perceived and treated, I think this is connected to the state narrative that those who are condemned by the state, for whatever reason, are not worthy to be treated with dignity and respect as human beings."

The problematic narratives Rashida identified were also harmful insofar as they sanctioned abuse. For example, one of the narratives she brought up was around prisoners and how they are constructed as deserving of torture and death—tactics that have been used throughout the War on Terror. According to Rashida, "the lie that is perpetuated is that if you're in prison, you are deserving of everything that comes your way, no matter how atrocious." This is perhaps why so many of the War-on-Terror prisoners have been tortured and detained indefinitely with almost no accountability.

For Rashida, the War on Terror means a lot of things: "When I think of the War on Terror," she told me,

I think it's a system of harmful policies, practices, and narratives to take a group of people and convince the world that they are the "bad people," which is for political gain; it actually has nothing to do with safety. It is the exploitation of people's fears, loss, and desire to feel safe and secure by creating a false sense of harm against people who also have fears, loss, and a desire to be safe. Honestly, when I think of the War on Terror, I think of the violent history of this country and how it extends into today. During the racial-terror era or the lynching era in this country, there were mobs and whole towns of white people hunting Black people down and lynching them, and somehow the narrative was [that] they were deserving of it. It can be scary how history repeats itself until you remember that history includes those who are fighting for justice, and they, too, repeat and are present over time. But anyway, when I think of these different state violent tactics—the War on Terror, the War on Drugs—I remember [that] the United States is always waging a war on people and countries and often vilifies the human beings they seek to harm in order to maintain power. I'm often baffled how some folks can watch things like *Star Wars*, *Harry Potter*, and *Hunger Games* and understand resistance but completely miss it in real life. In fiction, people take for granted they would be on the side of justice, but in reality, some folks choose a false sense of ease and bliss over what is right and just.

For Rashida, one of the most critical things was to connect the legacy of tactics such as surveillance to what is happening now. "Yes, I think surveillance is deeply connected to history. When enslaved African Muslims were held hostage and brought here, they were watched, targeted, and tortured and pressured to abandon their beliefs. They had incredible fight, resilience, and faith in [the midst of] an impossible tortuous situation. Even the connection to COINTELPRO and the surveillance of freedom fighters. I think we have to see the connections and patterns in systems of oppression if we are to be in solidarity with each other and dismantle and build something better."

Further, Rashida added, "The War on Terror is a part of the terrible policies, practices, and atrocities that exist in this country and abroad. So many people and cultures have been harmed by the War on Terror. The human toll should be at the front and center of this conversation. Actual lives are devastated by these practices and policies by a government that has a pattern of engaging in imperialistic, xenophobic, anti-Black, racist, genocidal practices."

Rashida stressed identity in the interview, saying that people often think it is inconceivable to be both Black and Muslim, which amounts to erasing her identity while still condemning her for it. In addition, Islam and Arabs are often conflated so as to present a singular idea of who a Muslim is and what they look like. In high school, people confused her identity and assumed she was Arab. In fact, one time a fellow student asked if she could interview Rashida for the school paper, and one of the questions she was asked was, when she had come from Iraq and whether it was difficult to adjust to life in the United States. This wasn't necessarily surprising to Rashida because, as she told me, "I think about that initial sort of impact of 9/11, and I think about the caricature that was created."

The Muslim American response to 9/11 and the War on Terror was another issue addressed in my interview with Rashida. She felt that many non-Black Muslim Americans operated from a very defensive posture. This was in part due to the fact that they were choosing the path of Americanism, or what they considered would keep them and their families safe, which meant that Muslim Americans were forced to blatantly disavow terrorism as part of claiming their American identity and their right to be in this country.

Rashida stated powerfully,

I feel at points like giving in to the narrative of being guilty and constantly apologizing gives up human rights and shifts the lens away from the actual guilty party, actions which are often a consequence of the state's harmful actions perpetrated under the guise of security and freedom. I think about how we generally talk about protests in this country, and it's like it should be peaceful, nonviolent, and I think that sounds really good. And at the same time, Malcolm X said it is criminal to teach someone to be nonviolent when their oppressor is violent . . . or to teach them they don't have the right to defend themselves. This is a basic human right. Nonviolence seems to be the suggested method only when people of color are demanding freedom. The state knows that, which is why the messaging whenever [the state wants] to cause harm is to position itself as a bringer of peace or a defender, and somehow this idea is accepted despite the history of lying and violence [on the part] of its source. I understand some Muslims choose a defensive stance to do damage control, but it actually perpetuates the idea that we should be apologizing for just existing as Muslims. It also ignores how deeply entrenched that messaging is in racist ideology.

Rashida observed how the individual perpetrators of white supremacist violence are constructed as lone wolves, which allows for the perpetrator to be humanized and disconnected from whiteness. For example, when it is a "lone wolf" attack, the tendency has been to share details of their life, especially when it comes to demonstrating that their violent behavior was divergent from how people knew them. This idea that whiteness can't be dangerous, so when violence occurs, it's abnormal, is ridiculous because this country was founded on the violence of white supremacy. In contrast, as Rashida told me, "When it comes to Black people or people of color, there is no reason given or presented in a way that could humanize them, as if violence is inherent to them. The lack of humanization and understanding is meant to play on racist ideas that some communities are more violent than others, not due to the violence of poverty and other oppressive systems, but due to their nature or lack of 'goodness,' which is a lie."

The War on Terror and US state violence, going back to the enslavement of African Muslims, has been a hard and bitter pill to swallow, but for Rashida, the injustice of the past and of the current context makes it necessary to always work for justice. In her words, "Justice is timeless, and there is never a wrong time to be just. It's always right to be just."

I asked Rashida about collective liberation as a conversation that the social justice movement has increasingly been using as the ultimate and long-term goal. One of the powerful parts of her response was the idea of developing a relationship outside of the framing of state violence. She asked a question of her own and then offered her response:

What if you spent your time building and growing and bonding with someone without the wedge of state violence or being pushed into oppression Olympics? There are so many inter- and intra-community relationships that first have to overcome strategic efforts that pit communities against each other. I think if we can get to a place of healing and solidarity, and genuine and radical love and care for each other, we can move towards a vision and structuring of collective liberation. I think it's hard work and *heart* work that will build our communities and create space for folks to live as Allah has commanded, for us to truly know one another, with the understanding that life is sacred and we should be treating each other accordingly and spending the time we have on this earth fulfilling our purpose and being people who don't just say we believe in justice, hope, and dignity, but actually acting upon those values.

Nadia: A South-Asian Professor

When I interviewed Nadia, a professor who identifies as South-Asian Indian American, she told me that she was a college student at the time of the 9/11 attacks. Because of the fact that, as she remembers, the attacks were being framed along the lines of anti-Muslim racism, Muslim Americans worried that they would be collectively blamed.

Nadia recounted how the images of the attacks on the twin towers were played over and over, saying, "That day you kind of saw the circulation of these images being enshrined in the national memory." The national memory that was created to narrate the 9/11 attacks was almost immediately weaponized to justify the War on Terror and, more specifically, violence against Muslims.

From the beginning of the War on Terror, Nadia remembers how the attacks were framed as being black-and-white—for example, Bush's rhetoric that "you're either with us or against us." Of course, this pigeon-holed people into choosing sides, never mind the fact that the use of these basic narratives, such as "The terrorists hate our freedoms," disallowed any nuance in analysis. This, Nadia believes, was by design.

In the immediate aftermath of 9/11, Nadia recalls a particular narrative that Bush used, essentially enlisting Americans into the War on Terror by telling the public that every American was a soldier.

During tragedies, most countries call for unity, but unity was manifested in a very specific way in the United States for Muslim Americans. According to Nadia, "there was a very vocal and deliberate effort to include patriotic Muslims and patriotic others into this message. So you were allowed to be Muslim, but only if you kind of abandoned your political analysis, only if you didn't want to talk about US war-making. . . . If you could remain quiet on those things, then you were folded into this project of national unity, but if you couldn't, then you were a traitor; you were literally legally branded a traitor." Another element of the narrative around Muslim Americans was the distinct creation of "good Muslims," which Nadia defined as being "peace-loving and upwardly mobile." Ultimately, however, as Nadia told me, "the War on Terror rested on the logics of collective blame and collective responsibility, where all Muslims were expected to condemn terrorism they had nothing to do with."

Using the vague language of the War on Terror and, particularly, the idea that the US could wage a war on terrorism—a nebulous concept—was, Nadia said, "a really brilliant branding of something that would give the US state apparatus unlimited power in allaying whatever fears the American public thought they were perceiving."

Was the War on Terror over? According to Nadia, it would be taking a very narrow view to say that it was. For her, none of the wars waged by the US could really be considered over. In this vein, Nadia told me, "The Cold War is what gave birth to the War on Terror. The Cold War, literally the geopolitics that we saw shaking down in North Africa and the, quote-unquote, Middle East, really gave rise to the types of terror that would come to be extensively fought [in] the War on Terror. So I think it's helpful to think more about the continuity that exists in history, rather than beginnings and ends."

Nadia views collective liberation as a corollary to abolition. She shared her perspective beginning with the idea that collective liberation was foreign to Americans because the US is a nation of individuals who view rights individualistically: "So, to talk about collective action in the US is an act of rebellion. . . . Collective liberation is a form of rebellion against the very tenets of American liberal individualism."

That's how the framing was used to sanction abuses, among which, Nadia identified, "was the intensification of America as a carceral state—one that turns to prisons and criminalization to, quote-unquote, solve a problem." To Nadia, the 9/11 attacks completely altered the American landscape, not in the sense that the violence committed by the United States was new, but in the sense of how many people's lives have been shaped by it, whether because of family members fighting wars abroad, or students she's taught who want to work for the Department of Homeland Security, an agency that wouldn't even exist had it not been for 9/11.

Nadia told me,

One of the greatest consequences has been the immense expansion of America, American militarism. And when I say militarism, I don't just mean the technologies of warfare. I don't just mean Iraq and Afghanistan. I don't just mean the drone warfare program. I mean all of those things, but I also mean that America has sort of doubled down on its jingoism or its urgent need to defend itself against this, quote-unquote, enemy. . . . So I don't think we would have seen a Trump presidency without a September 11. . . . So I think it actually behooves us to really understand 9/11 as much broader, as actually intensifying anti-Black racism, as intensifying xenophobia, as intensifying violence against Indigenous people. I'm reminded of the 2016 protests at Standing Rock, and how they actually used counterterrorism strategies on the Indigenous people there. Well, who defined these counterterrorism strategies? I mean, these were technologies that were crafted to target Muslim terrorists, now being used against Indigenous people. So, I think it's so broad, you know, that to understand Islamophobia separate from these things, we really do ourselves a big disservice.

The War on Terror has indelibly shaped the American landscape, as well as the Muslim American experience. There were vastly different responses, according to Nadia, between elite upper-middle-class Muslim Americans and other, less-privileged Muslim Americans. Many elite Muslim Americans, for example, might be concerned and vocal about workplace discrimination but stay silent on some of the most egregious abuses directed at other Muslims, such as torture and detention. To explain this dynamic, Nadia told me, "A useful way to make sense of the fracture is along the lines of reform versus abolition." Reformist Muslim Americans might push for change through government representation or might celebrate companies seemingly catering to Muslims (for example, the Nike hijab), while anti-Islamophobia advocates address the many systems of power (including capitalism and imperialism) that are crucial to dismantling the War on Terror but that have no place in reformist politics.

When I asked Nadia what she wants remembered about resistance and challenging the state during this era, she responded,

This moment is literally people imagining systems that are not carceral and imagining systems that could liberate people; that's what this moment is about. So what I want to be remembered is that in the midst of a plague, people went out into the streets to demand an immediate demilitarization of the police, to demand an immediate moratorium on the building of new prisons or the expansion of the prison population, to demand an immediate release of prisoners in the midst of this pandemic. That's what we were doing, right? That is what we were doing in this moment. We were not asking cops to kneel with us at protests. So what I hope is remembered is just the unapologetic militancy of this moment, which has been really remarkable and remains really remarkable to witness.

Zahra: A Somali Chaplain

Zahra, another interviewee, identified as Somali and Black. On the day of the 9/11 attacks, she remembers being at school. A sliding TV was brought in front of her and her classmates, and that's where she saw images of the twin towers falling and people dying. Now working as a movement chaplain, Zahra reflected back on how traumatizing those sights were, and must have been for the children watching them.

When she and her sister got home later that day, she found her mom, who was pregnant at the time, watching the scenes of the 9/11 attacks over and over. Zahra worried about her mom, telling me, "I just think about her having to view that violence and being pregnant and how what we know about generational trauma, and this was a woman who's already had to survive two wars and migration."

One of the interesting things Zahra remembers after the 9/11 attacks is the way capitalism entered into the narrative. The message she got was that "the way that we could support, or the best way we could respond after the deaths of thousands of people, was to go consume." This was a memory that Bijan expressed as well and ties into the reality that there was much profit tied up in the War on Terror.

Though the War on Terror was being fought domestically and abroad, Zahra's perspective was that "the people who have paid the price have been outside America's borders. Really, the people who paid blood and bone, whose children have been wiped off the face of the earth, who are disappeared, or whose countries have been invaded, whose libraries have been burned in order to wipe out their history and culture—cultural genocide, you know—all these people have not been American Muslims. And the ones within American borders who have paid the price are the ones who are the most marginalized and who are not on TV."

Another important dimension of the targeting of Muslims, as Zahra explained it, was in the very real differences between Muslims and those who strove to assimilate into whiteness—for example, those who were aspiring to whiteness and "who were upset that their path to whiteness or their path to being in positions of domination in the hierarchy were disrupted." For her, it was many of these such individuals who were leading advocacy efforts and helping to shape the "good versus bad Muslim" narrative.

Acknowledging the targeting of Muslims was, for Zahra, different from performing pain. Zahra was referencing the ways in which some Muslims have talked about their struggles in a way that is meant to appeal to white liberals. "It's a performance of inferiority, pain, and domination," Zahra told me, and one that almost seems voyeuristic.

Whiteness, to Zahra, was very troubling because she said it "requires death and destruction to exist, and that pain is how they know they are still alive." This was meant to underscore the idea of whiteness as violence—something that has very much been part of the War on Terror.

Zahra's conception of the War on Terror is that it is "one of the biggest lies American empire ever told and sold. It declared war on a thing that has no ending, no beginning, no tangible embodiment except in the bodies of Muslims. It was a blank check to destroy the world, to pillage it for the profit and power of American empire."

But Islam, as Zahra told me, has always posed a threat to empire because

Islam has always been a theology and a political tool that liberates people, even when they're caged, even when they're enslaved, even when they're imprisoned. That is why you see it flourish. Among the most oppressed people, right, that even when our bodies are caged, even when we are under apartheid and in the borders of Gaza, or in the prisons in Philadelphia, or in the cages at Gitmo, Islam allows us to survive the unsurvivable. And that inherently makes you a threat to an empire whose only function since the beginning has been to dominate, oppress, pillage, and kill.

Similar to others I interviewed, Zahra contextualized the War on Terror as part of the long-standing systemic violence that has been perpetrated against Black people. Zahra told me that "to understand American empire's treatment of Muslims, you have to walk back the lineage of American surveillance and entrapment and policing, which will always lead you to Black people's homes."

Despite the narrative that the War on Terror was over, Zahra, like every other interviewee in this book, disagreed that this is actually the case. "The War on Terror is not over. It has just infiltrated the fabric of American intel and surveillance. Whether it's the government, [the] nonprofit community . . . it has just embedded itself. . . . It's become almost invisible. Like it just has been normalized, but also like the War on Terror started way before it had that name then . . . COINTELPRO. . . . For the United States to exist, it always requires, it demands, an enemy class. Right? Multiple enemy classes, and for it to be the empire, it wants, it requires, the enemy class [to be] outside of its borders."

As a movement chaplain focused on healing and collective liberation, Zahra stressed the latter as an animating principle—not just a goal. Collective liberation, according to Zahra, does not have to be fought for by everyone, but whoever fights for it has to include everyone. This was a particularly powerful point because of the many ways that the most marginalized have been left out of even the concept of who deserves freedom, much less liberation.

Zahra brought in a particular perspective about abolition and Islam. For her, it is and was important that abolition, and nothing short of it, be the goal of challenging injustice. To this end, Zahra told me that "Islam requires us as Muslims, and especially in this context, requires that we are abolitionists in the fullest forms, which to be abolitionist also means it's not about the abolishing of things, but rather the creation of societies that do not necessitate the response of violence, that don't require prisons, that do not require oppression, do not require violence and policing. . . . So as Muslims, we understand."

Asked what she hoped will be remembered about the resistance during this era, Zahra told me, "There [were] so many people who stood up, spoke out, who risked their life, their livelihood, and everything to say that this is wrong, to speak truth to power. That there was so much community, there was so much organizing, that there was solidarity internationally . . . it gave those of us who were conscious or became conscious an internationalist lens, and gave moral courage to so many people. That is what moves me."

CONCLUSION

*I consider bin Laden an evil man. And I don't think there's any reli-
gious justification for what he has in mind. Islam is a religion of love,
not hate. This is a man who hates. This is a man who's declared war
on innocent people. This is a man who doesn't mind destroying women
and children. This is a man who hates freedom. This is an evil man.*
                                                    —GEORGE W. BUSH[1]

The above quote is from a meeting between then president Bush and Muslim community leaders at the White House, on September 26, 2001. In
the same meeting, Bush was asked whether or not bin Laden had political
goals, to which he responded, "He has [got] evil goals. And it's hard to
think in conventional terms about a man so dominated by evil."[2]

What Bush was foreshadowing with his words was the rhetorical
posture that would become the core of a political strategy that capitalized
on the upheaval caused by the events of September 11, 2001, in order to
usher in a new era of executive power and impunity. In the days, months,
and ultimately years that followed the 9/11 attacks, his administration
would leverage the power of narrative to build and sustain a sprawling, self-perpetuating apparatus of state violence. By relying on familiar,
emotionally powerful archetypes to construct explanations about who
these "new" terrorists are and why they do what they do, the US was
able to sell a particular set of military interventions and policy changes
that otherwise would have been challenged at every turn. After all, the
only reasonable response to the mindlessly hateful violence of inherently evil terrorists is to annihilate them. The United States government
has been so incredibly successful at embedding this narrative into public
consciousness that not only does it define the way we think and talk
about terrorism, but the logic, goals, and tactics of counterterrorism have
permeated law and policy in an astonishing number of aspects of contemporary political life.

Twenty years after the events of September 11, 2001, the narrative
assumptions underlying the apparatus of state violence that the War

on Terror has built are so unquestioned that they have become nearly invisible. Anyone attempting to identify or address the root causes of terrorism in this environment is committing a significant political and social faux pas. Articulating this point beautifully, Dr. Lisa Stampnitzky, lecturer in politics at the University of Sheffield, writes, "It is as though the language of evil creates a 'black box' around the terrorist, which creates its own explanation: terrorists commit terrorism because they are evil. Any further attempt to pursue alternative explanations, thereby seeking to break the black box of 'evil,' is as a profanation, even a sacrilege. The root of the politics of anti-knowledge is hence that, if terrorists are evil and irrational, then one cannot—and, indeed, should not know them."[3]

The dominant narrative of the War on Terror has been able to head off serious inquiry into the nature and cause of terrorism not only because it utilizes essentializing language and themes, but because it is supported by Islamophobia that explains terrorism as a function of religious fanaticism. As in Bush's statement above, the possibility that terrorists have political motivations is completely removed from the equation.[4]

The fight against the War on Terror—the unchecked growth of which has had such devastating human consequences—is at an impasse. This is an intentionally and carefully manufactured impasse that allows the war to continue whether or not terrorism is defined, understood, or contextualized, and whether or not designations of "terrorist" are empirically supported or morally justified.

But even as the state proceeds with this ill-defined and brutal war, important and powerful narrative interventions can disrupt and subvert the dominant paradigm that provides its foundation. This is precisely what is needed—to unravel twenty years of rhetoric demonizing Muslims and Islam from the apparatus of the War on Terror, in order to challenge both. If the narrative that has long served as its legitimization and justification can be interrupted, that may be our first and best hope of making the War on Terror a relic of history.

No One Gets Off the Hook: The Normalcy of State Violence

I don't like the racism and I don't like the name-calling and I don't like the people feeling alienated.
—GEORGE W. BUSH, REFERRING TO THE TRUMP ERA[5]

They believe that no one—including the president—is above the law.
—BARACK OBAMA, REFERENCE TO JOE BIDEN AND KAMALA HARRIS
DEMOCRATIC NATIONAL CONVENTION[6]

These quotes reveal the audacity of two leaders who are perceived as very different from one another but are united in an attempt to rewrite history by setting themselves up as contrasts to Trump rather than acknowledging their role in building and perpetuating the War on Terror and justifying its excesses. In their effort to deflect "bad" behavior onto Trump—in Obama's case through highlighting a Biden-Harris presidency as a change in the current status quo—both end up highlighting precisely what they themselves are guilty of. If the War on Terror has taught us anything, it's that neither racism nor impunity can be attributed to Trump alone—temporary deflection and projection might maintain that façade, but history ultimately won't.

Their invocation of the past serves as a reminder of how sordid the history of the War on Terror is and has been, precisely because of their leadership. The War on Terror is firmly rooted in racism and Islamophobia, and it was possible for Trump to claim the breadth of executive authority that he did only because both Bush and Obama made it so. No amount of post hoc self-righteousness can undo their roles.

Looking at the War on Terror's infrastructure, which sprawls across five dimensions (militarism and warfare, immigration, federal terrorism prosecutions, surveillance, and detention and torture), the one thing that is consistently clear is that the last twenty years have been characterized, first and foremost, by violence. What has differed across administrations is not the exacting of violence but preferences for one form of violence over the others.

Any attempt at political rehabilitation should be rejected outright, whether it's regarding George W. Bush, whose administration transformed an already brutal immigration system into one even more violent through the creation of ICE, or Obama, who earned his place in history as the "deporter in chief." Trump's political rehabilitation might prove significantly more difficult, but the possibility should not be dismissed or ignored, especially if it provides a future window for the absolution of subsequent presidents' crimes. Rather, we must remain focused on dismantling the War on Terror as it *is*, not as former presidents rewrite it.

If anything needs to be rehabilitated (or completely dismantled), it is the US's legal and political system that allows war criminals not only to thrive, but to frame their crimes as benevolent and justified.

On November 7, 2020, Joe Biden and Kamala Harris celebrated their victory over Donald Trump and Mike Pence in the presidential election. For many Americans, this brought a sigh of relief and was an indication that things would soon return to "normal." Many Americans were, first and foremost, weary—weary of the constant cycle of shock and dismay that characterized politics under Trump. But for all the ways in which he laid waste to the polite norms of society and politics, for all the ways his open embrace of hatred and naked self-interest were constantly, relentlessly on display during the four years he was in power, it is dangerous to think of President Trump as an aberration. His aggressive and openly bigoted approach to wielding executive power obscures the simple fact that for the United States, state violence is the norm; the government under any leadership will inflict violence at home and abroad to the extent that it is allowed to do so. After the excesses of the Trump era, a return to more regulated and covert state violence might seem "normal," but it's not a normal to which anyone should want to return.

As Barack Obama's vice president, Joe Biden was part of the institutionalization of the Islamophobic narrative of the War on Terror and complicit in its civil and human rights abuses—abuses that inevitably result from the ongoing expansion of the power of the executive to wield state violence without accountability. Compared to the presidency of George W. Bush before him, Obama's was characterized by civility—mostly toothless efforts at reform combined with a softer rhetorical approach that paid lip service to tolerance. This polite veneer masked the fact that his administration continued many of the same policies as his predecessor while further entrenching the structures of the War on Terror and expanding its reach. Now that Biden is president, it would be a natural course of action if he repeated history and tempered only the worst and most obvious excesses of Trump-era policy while accepting and perpetuating the legacy of the War on Terror as the status quo.

This is why it's so important to challenge the narrative at its foundation. Regardless of who is in power at any given time, it will take a long time to dismantle the War on Terror and to extract its tentacles from everything we have come to perceive as normal. We have to start by de-normalizing state violence such that, among much else, the prohibition of torture returns to being unequivocal and surveillance is met with outrage—even if you "have nothing to hide."

So Now What? Paving the Road Ahead

The difficulty of meaningfully challenging the War on Terror has been exacerbated by the fact that, despite its massive footprint in domestic policy, it is pretty much out of sight, out of mind for many Americans. An op-ed by *Slate* senior editor Joshua Keating titled "The War on Terror Comes Home"[7] provides a paradigmatic example of how this blindness is reflected in the media. Keating notes, "As the threat of foreign terrorism on American soil has dwindled, these efforts have been turned on Americans." Though he addresses surveillance of Muslims by the New York Police Department as one example of how the War on Terror has been manifested domestically, this limited acknowledgment is a reminder that for many other Americans, the domestic implications of the War on Terror are just now being felt. For the Muslim American community that has resided in the United States since 9/11, the War on Terror didn't "come home"; it's always been home. They have been criminalized on the basis of their religious identity just as Muslims around the world have been demonized and targeted.

A similar lack of awareness regarding the War on Terror's true reach was evidenced in 2020 after the murder of an unarmed Black man named George Floyd by police in Minnesota sparked uprisings around the country that were met with military tactics aimed at peaceful protestors. In response, many op-eds commented that the War on Terror had "come home"—meaning to the domestic United States. In reality, this newly visible phenomenon is merely one more example of the War on Terror's pervasive, multi-pronged impacts on domestic life. It also illustrates how the now nearly unquestioned logic of counterterrorism in general facilitates the self-perpetuation of the War on Terror's underlying structure through adaptation and expansion into new contexts.

The 1033 Program, instituted as part of the National Defense Authorization Act (NDAA) of 1997, offers a powerful view into the interconnection of the War on Terror and the threat posed by the police state. This program allows the federal government to provide local police departments with "extra" tactical military equipment that has been used abroad.[8] The images of police departments armed with the leftover equipment of the War on Terror as they brutalize Black citizens were omnipresent during the summer of 2020—a chilling reminder that all state violence flows from the same source. As a bridge between policing and militarism, perhaps the 1033 Program offers a natural starting point from which we can begin talking about and dismantling the many destructive facets of the War on Terror.

At a time when calls for abolition and defunding of the police continue to grow, thanks to the leadership of Black communities, this movement and moment have forced society and the government to envision a reality outside of rampant state violence. These growing calls for abolition are as instructive as they are hopeful, and they provide one window through which to consider the possibility of not ending, but abolishing, the War on Terror.

Applying an abolitionist lens to the War on Terror has its complications because its scope is so massive, sprawling as it does across the five dimensions mentioned above and robustly supported by laws, policies, and narrative—all of which reinforce each other. Crucially, the War on Terror's intentionally created structure was meant to stymie the application of any measure designed to end it. This is where narrative becomes so important, because terrorism has been constructed as the most heinous form of violence, exceeding all other forms of violence in brutality, and therefore justifying other forms in response. Terrorism, as opposed to crime, has been elevated to an offense against the state, like treason, and removed from the purview—and protections, such as they are—of the criminal justice system. Further, there is a very different understanding of why someone deemed a terrorist commits violence versus why someone deemed a criminal commits violence. While crime is often explained by poor social conditions and the lack of having one's needs met, the narrative lens of the War on Terror allows an explanation for terrorism only in the language of essentialized characteristics.

That said, imagining abolition is the first step toward realizing it. There are many reasons to intentionally and more explicitly offer abolition as a way forward in the War on Terror. These include what Atiya Husain, assistant professor of sociology and American studies at the University of Richmond, writes in her article "Terror and Abolition": "Many domestic issues of concern to abolitionists—ranging from national inaction on climate change to the frightening political aspirations of Amazon to the state kidnapping of migrant children—have been raised in the house that counterterrorism built."[9]

Parting Words

We have been told many lies about the War on Terror—some that have been so steadfastly entrenched in the American body politic that they are nearly invisible and some that have been unraveling for years. Even the lies that come undone, however, have been quickly replaced or repurposed, while any changes made with an eye to ending the War on Terror have been piecemeal and largely superficial. Even more insidiously, attempts by former President Obama and others to change the underlying terminology of the War on Terror in order to signal a different path forward have not managed to shift the tide of this catastrophic apparatus, but rather have served to disguise it even further.

This is why we have to look through the rhetoric into the realities on the ground because they tell very different stories from the ones that the US empire has been able to broadcast so vocally from its position of power, often at literal gunpoint. These stories of empire have also been told by co-conspirators, by those who believe that this repetition will bring them in closer proximity to power, and, perhaps unconsciously, by those who seek to validate their identity by aligning themselves with the values and tropes of their oppressors. If we are truly interested in moving past the status quo of state violence, we must deconstruct, dismantle, and ultimately subvert the dominant narrative paradigm. After all, it is this paradigm that determines and justifies who gets profiled and who doesn't, who gets detained and who doesn't, who gets tortured and who doesn't, and, finally, who gets to live and who has to die.

The work of resisting and shifting the problematic narrative structures that underlie the War on Terror cannot be understated, especially since its prerogatives have become so normalized and entangled in almost every aspect of life—whether one lives in the United States or in one of the shockingly numerous countries across the globe that have felt the weight of this country's political and military interventions. Equally important—and fundamentally interrelated—is the task of recognizing the myriad and pervasive ways in which the War on Terror has facilitated the institutionalization of Islamophobia into law and policy and concretely challenging these structures systemically and in all of their manifestations. The greatest threat to the US government is that by uprooting the structures of the War on Terror from their foundations, people in this country and beyond will recalibrate how we define safety and security in a way that doesn't thrive or rely on state violence, or come at the expense of the safety and security of others.

It should be noted that none of this will be sufficient to bring justice to the many existing victims of the War on Terror—including those who have been detained, tortured, and/or murdered. These victims have not received any acknowledgment, let alone any semblance of redress, and any path forward must demand such accountability from the government for the harms it has caused. True justice, however, would have been their not being targeted in the first place.

While justice for the survivors of two decades of the War on Terror is impossible, we must move forward towards another reality that doesn't thrive on the dehumanization and demonization of Islam and Muslims. To ensure a just future we must work toward the goal of not only an end to the War on Terror but its abolition. Ending the War on Terror means uprooting the policies and laws that have targeted Muslims and other marginalized communities in its name, while abolishing it means dismantling the structures upon which it was built and which allow it to thrive. Ending the War on Terror, while important, should not be confused with abolishing it, because the former offers no assurance that an uglier, more brutal and more cruel war could not take its place because of the rampant state violence that has defined the United States since its inception. Abolition, in other words, is about the complete justice of ensuring that there are no placeholders left for further violence.

As I write these final words, I wonder if we'll ever be able to say that the War on Terror has ended and been abolished. If and hopefully when that day comes, perhaps then we'll know what justice for Muslims really looks like.

ACKNOWLEDGMENTS

When I first sat down to start writing this book, I wasn't entirely sure what to expect in the process. What, I thought, could I possibly write that would capture the War on Terror after twenty years? Though this was not an easy question, I attempted to answer it as best I could in the pages preceding this one.

To put it lightly, writing this book was a great feat. When I think about where I started and where you, the reader, will find this page, I am filled with immense gratitude for my family, friends, the communities that I belong to, and everyone who gave me the courage and strength to keep going. I owe my deepest thanks to many who supported me on this journey.

I want to start by thanking the incredible Muslim Americans who allowed me to interview them for this book and who shared the powerful stories of their lives post-9/11. Their voices shed light on the War on Terror in a way that could not have been conveyed otherwise.

I'm grateful to my friend Kris Garrity, who provided me with immeasurable support as my research assistant during the book-writing process. Kris was and has been a Godsend in my life, and without their assistance, completing this book would have been much more difficult. Kris, I'm forever grateful for your love, support, and friendship.

To my friend Katie Wylie, who spent hundreds of hours editing my book, despite the fact that I initially only asked her if she had six to eight hours of time to give. Katie was also my thought partner who patiently listened to me whenever I got stuck and reminded me that I was going to finish this book because I had to. There are friends you meet in life who you know will always be there for you no matter how much time you spend apart, and Katie is one of them. I will always be grateful for the time she invested in me and my book. I love her dearly.

To my friend Candice Camargo, who spent hours upon hours with me on Zoom as I initially struggled to fill my pages with words and who lovingly kept track of my word count to hold me accountable. I'm grateful for all the memes we shared to laugh together to raise my spirits after reading some of the most incredibly painful and violent aspects of the War on Terror. I'm eternally grateful for her love and support.

To Eugenia Podesta, who lovingly provided me with a beautiful co-working space in which I spent hours, days, and months writing and finishing my book. Her hospitality made all the difference while I was working on one of the hardest projects in my life thus far.

To my friend Helen Schietinger, who has consistently checked on me and provided me with love and support. She has been a source of encouragement as I found and took confidence in my voice.

To my friends F. Al-Rawaf and Nawal Rajeh, who sent me messages of support throughout the writing process and who always reassured me that I would finish this book. They waited for me at the finish line and for this, I'm grateful.

To my friends Michelle Munjanattu and Azza Altiraifi, who have been constant reminders of what principled fights for social justice look like.

To Dr. Shireen Lewis, who has been my support and mentor for a decade and who was there for me as I completed my dissertation and beyond. Her committed leadership has always been an inspiration to me as I've carved out my own path.

To Dr. David Fagelson, my professor and dissertation committee member during my PhD studies at American University, who has always believed in me. I owe him deep gratitude for all the time he has spent mentoring me, thinking through complex social justice issues with me, and generally offering his support however he can. It has been years since I completed my PhD, yet he is always there to get me through the toughest times in my career trajectory. He will always be one of my favorite professors.

To all my friends who have offered unflinching analysis of social justice issues that I undoubtedly learned from. And finally, to everyone who taught me that if you know the principles on which you stand, you never have to move.

NOTES

Epigraph

1. C.P. Cavafy, "Waiting for the Barbarians" quoted in Anne McClintock, "Paranoid Empire," *Small Axe* 13, No. 1 (March 2009): 54.

Introduction

1. Mobashra Tazamal and Kristin Garrity, "Islamophobia Has No Place in the Fight against COVID-19," Truthout, April 14, 2020, https://truthout.org/articles/islamophobia-has-no-place-in-the-fight-against-covid-19/.
2. Tazamal and Garrity.
3. "The Cost of the Global War on Terror," Brown University, November 13, 2019, https://www.brown.edu/news/2019-11-13/costsofwar.
4. Andrew Soergel, "War on Terror Could Be Costliest Yet," US News, September 9, 2016, https://www.usnews.com/news/articles/2016-09-09/war-on-terror-could-be-costliest-yet.
5. Andile Sicetsha, "Remembering Steve Biko: Four Quotes That Inspired Black Consciousness," South African, September 12, 2018, https://www.thesouthafrican.com/news/remembering-steve-biko-quotes/.

Part 1

1. Roberto Sirvent and Danny Haiphong, *American Exceptionalism and American Innocence: A People's History of Fake News—from the Revolutionary War to the War on Terror* (New York: Skyhorse, 2019), chap. 1, Kindle.
2. "Friedrich Nietzsche Quotable Quotes," Goodreads, accessed June 9, 2021, https://www.goodreads.com/quotes/108811-all-i-need-is-a-sheet-of-paper-and-something.
3. John Collins and Ross Glover, "Introduction," in *Collateral Language: A User's Guide to America's New War*, ed. John Collins and Ross Glover (New York: New York University Press, 2002), 1.

Chapter 1

1. "Text: President Bush Addresses the Nation," *Washington Post*, September 20, 2001, https://www.washingtonpost.com/wp-srv/nation/specials/attacked/transcripts/bushaddress_092001.html.

2. Daniel Falcone, "US Education and the Meaning of Terrorism: An Interview with Richard Falk and Lawrence Davidson," Truthout, December 30, 2015, https://truthout.org/articles/us-education-and-the-meaning-of-terrorism-an-interview-with-richard-falk-and-lawrence-davidson/.

3. Perla Thompson, Facebook message to the author, August 1, 2017.

4. Lucy Bond, *Frames of Memory after 9/11: Culture, Criticism, Politics, and Law* (London: Palgrave Macmillan, 2015), 5.

5. Susannah Radstone, "Reconceiving Binaries: The Limits of Memory," *History Workshop Journal* 59 (Spring 2005): 134–50, quoted in Bond, 5.

6. "Text of President Bush's 2002 State of the Union Address," *Washington Post*, January 29, 2002, https://www.washingtonpost.com/wp-srv/onpolitics/transcripts/sou012902.htm.

7. "Transcript: Bush Addresses Warsaw Conference," *Washington Post*, November 6, 2001, https://www.washingtonpost.com/wp-srv/nation/specials/attacked/transcripts/bush_text110601.html.

8. Natsu Taylor Saito, "Colonial Presumptions: The War on Terror and the Roots of American Exceptionalism," *Georgetown Journal of Law and Modern Critical Race Perspectives* 67 (2008): 72.

9. Samuel Huntington, *The Clash of Civilizations and the Remaking of World Order* (New York: Simon & Schuster, 1996), 258.

10. Joanne Esch, "Legitimizing the 'War on Terror': Political Myth in Official-Level Rhetoric," *Political Psychology* 31, no. 3 (June 2010): 357–91.

11. "Text of President Bush's Press Conference," *New York Times*, April 13, 2004, https://www.nytimes.com/2004/04/13/politics/text-of-president-bushs-press-conference.html.

12. Burns H. Weston and Anna Grear, *Human Rights in the World Community: Issues and Action* (Philadelphia: University of Pennsylvania Press, 2016), 407.

13. "Text: Pentagon Briefing on Military Response to Terrorist Attacks," *Washington Post*, September 18, 2001, https://www.washingtonpost.com/wp-srv/nation/specials/attacked/transcripts/rumsfeld_091801.html.

14. Esch, "Legitimizing."

15. Chiara Bottici and Benoît Challand, "Rethinking Political Myth: The Clash of Civilizations as a Self-Fulfilling Prophecy," *European Journal of Social Theory* 9, no. 3 (2009): 38, http://www.lib.csu.ru/ER/ER_Philosophy/fulltexts/BotticiC.pdf.

16. "Text of President Bush's 2002."

17. "Text of President Bush's 2003 State of the Union Address," *Washington Post*, January 28, 2003, https://www.washingtonpost.com/wp-srv/onpolitics/transcripts/bushtext_012803.html.

18. Richard Jackson, "Security, Democracy, and the Rhetoric of Counter-Terrorism," *Democracy and Security* 1, no. 2 (2005): 150, https://doi.org/10.1080/17419160 500322517.

19. Esch, "Legitimizing," 365.

20. Jackson, "Security, Democracy," 151.

21. Richard Jackson, *Writing the War on Terrorism: Language, Politics and Counter-Terrorism* (New York: Manchester University Press, 2005), 37.

22. "Bush Addresses the Nation."

23. Jenny Edkins, *Trauma and the Memory of Politics* (Cambridge: Cambridge University Press, 2003), 19, quoted in Bond, *Frames of Memory after 9/11*, 43.

24. Richard A. Clarke, "Cheney and Rice Remember 9/11. I Do, Too," *Washington Post*, May 31, 2009, https://www.washingtonpost.com/wp-dyn/content/article/2009/05/29/AR2009052901560.html, quoted in Bond, *Frames of Memory after 9/11*, 47.

25. "Text of Bush's Address," CNN, September 11, 2001, https://edition.cnn.com/2001/US/09/11/bush.speech.text/.

26. Jackson, "Security, Democracy," 153–54.

27. "Text of President Bush's 2002."

28. "Text of President Bush's 2005 State of the Union Address," *Washington Post*, February 2, 2005, https://www.washingtonpost.com/wp-srv/politics/transcripts/bushtext_020205.html.

29. Debra Merskin, "Making Enemies in George W. Bush's Post-9/11 Speeches," *Peace Review* 17, no. 4 (August 2006), https://doi.org/10.1080/10402650500374637.

30. "Bush: 'We Will Prevail,'" Associated Press, September 15, 2001, https://www.wired.com/2001/09/bush-we-will-prevail/.

31. "President Bush Honors Military in Weekly Radio Address," White House, May 17, 2003, https://georgewbush-whitehouse.archives.gov/news/releases/2003/05/20030517.html.

32. "Remarks by the President in State of the Union Address," White House, January 20, 2015, https://obamawhitehouse.archives.gov/the-press-office/2015/01/20/remarks-president-state-union-address-January-20-2015.

33. "Transcript: President Obama's Final State of the Union Address," NPR, January 12, 2016, https://www.npr.org/2016/01/12/462831088/president-obama-state-of-the-union-transcript.

34. "Donald Trump's Congress Speech (Full Text)," CNN, March 1, 2017, https://www.cnn.com/2017/02/28/politics/donald-trump-speech-transcript-full-text.

35. "Transcript of Trump's Remarks on the Death of Abu Bakr al-Baghdadi," *New York Times*, October 27, 2019, https://www.nytimes.com/2019/10/27/us/trump-transcript-isis-al-baghdadi.html.

36. "Text of President Bush's 2004 State of the Union Address," *Washington Post*, January 20, 2004, https://www.washingtonpost.com/wp-srv/politics/transcripts/bushtext_012004.html.

37. "Text of President Bush's 2005."

38. "Text of President Bush's 2004."

39. Julian Borger, "The Truth about Israel's Secret Nuclear Arsenal," *Guardian*, January 15, 2014, https://www.theguardian.com/world/2014/jan/15/truth-israels-secret-nuclear-arsenal.

40. "Text: Bush Announces Strikes against Taliban," *Washington Post*, October 7, 2001, https://www.washingtonpost.com/wp-srv/nation/specials/attacked/transcripts/bushaddress_100801.htm.

41. "Transcript: Obama's First State of the Union Speech," CNN, January 28, 2010, https://www.cnn.com/2010/POLITICS/01/27/sotu.transcript/index.html.

42. "Excerpts from Bush's Speech," *New York Times*, January 28, 2008, https://www.nytimes.com/2008/01/28/washington/28cnd-excerpts.html.

43. Michael Blain, *Power, Discourse and Victimage Ritual in the War on Terror* (New York: Routledge, 2016), 70.

44. Gabriel Rubin, *Presidential Rhetoric on Terrorism under Bush, Obama and Trump: Inflating and Calibrating the Threat after 9/11* (London: Palgrave, 2020), 52.

45. Rubin, 59.

46. Rubin, 71.

47. Trevor McCrisken, "Ten Years On: Obama's War on Terrorism in Rhetoric and Practice," *International Affairs* 87, no. 4 (July 2011): 782.

48. Rubin, *Presidential Rhetoric*, 84.

49. McCrisken, "Ten Years On," 788.

50. Rubin, *Presidential Rhetoric*, 100.

51. Rubin, 97.

52. Rubin, 52.

53. McCrisken, "Ten Years On," 787.

54. Rubin, *Presidential Rhetoric*, 60.

55. Rubin, 106.

56. Theodore Schleifer, "Donald Trump: 'I Think Islam Hates Us,'" CNN, March 10, 2016, https://www.cnn.com/2016/03/09/politics/donald-trump-islam-hates-us/index.html.

57. Jessica Taylor, "Trump Calls for 'Total and Complete Shutdown of Muslims Entering' U.S.," NPR, December 7, 2015, https://www.npr.org/2015/12/07/458836388/trump-calls-for-total-and-complete-shutdown-of-muslims-entering-u-s.

58. Allan Smith, "Trump Says Congresswomen of Color Should 'Go Back' and Fix the Places They 'Originally Came From,'" NBC News, July 14, 2019, https://www.nbcnews.com/politics/donald-trump/trump-says-progressive-congresswomen-should-go-back-where-they-came-n1029676.

59. Rubin, *Presidential Rhetoric*, 117.

60. Rubin, 117.

61. Rubin, 118.

62. Rubin, 144–45.

63. Rubin, 79.

Chapter 2

1. Friedrich Nietzsche, *Thus Spoke Zarathustra*, trans. Adrian Del Caro (New York: Cambridge University Press, 2006), 34.
2. As quoted in John Collins, "Terrorism," in Collins and Glover, *Collateral Language*, 167–68.
3. Collins, 167.
4. Collins, 169.
5. Austin T. Turk, "Sociology of Terrorism," *Annual Review of Sociology* 30 (2004): 272, https://www.jstor.org/stable/29737694.
6. Anne Schneider and Helen Ingram, "Social Construction of Target Populations: Implications for Politics and Policy," *American Political Science Review* 87, no. 2 (June 1993): 334–47, https://www.jstor.org/stable/2939044.
7. Edward W. Said, *Culture and Imperialism* (New York: Random House, 1993), 375.
8. Scott Poynting and David Whyte, "Introduction," in *Counter-Terrorism and State Political Violence: The "War on Terror" as Terror*, ed. Scott Poynting and David Whyte (New York: Routledge, 2012), 2–3.
9. Poynting and Whyte, 5.
10. "President Bush Delivers State of the Union Address," White House, January 23, 2007, https://georgewbush-whitehouse.archives.gov/news/releases/2007/01/20070 123-2.html.
11. "Bush Delivers State."
12. Alice Slater, "The US Has Military Bases in 80 Countries. All of Them Must Close," *Nation*, January 24, 2018, https://www.thenation.com/article/archive/the -us-has-military-bases-in-172-countries-all-of-them-must-close/.
13. "President Bush Signs Patriot Act," C-SPAN, June 13, 2013, 9:12, https://www.c -span.org/video/?c4455862/president-bush-signs-patriot-act.
14. Gregory Hooks and Clayton Mosher, "Outrages against Personal Dignity: Rationalizing Abuse and Torture in the War on Terror," *Social Forces* 83, no. 4 (June 2005): 1630, https://www.jstor.org/stable/3598406?seq=1.
15. "Presidential News Conference," CNN, September 15, 2006, http://transcripts.cnn .com/TRANSCRIPTS/0609/15/cnr.02.html.
16. "Remarks of President Barack Obama—State of the Union Address as Delivered," White House, January 13, 2016, https://obamawhitehouse.archives.gov/the-press -office/2016/01/12/remarks-president-barack-obama-%E2%80%93-prepared -delivery-state-union-address.
17. "Transcript: President Obama's Remarks on the Execution of Journalist James Foley by Islamic State," *Washington Post*, August 20, 2014, https://www.washington post.com/politics/transcript-president-obamas-remarks-on-the-execution-of -journalist-james-foley-by-islamic-state/2014/08/20/f5a63802-2884-11e4-8593 -da634b334390_story.html.
18. "Full Transcript: Trump's 2020 State of the Union Address," *New York Times*, February 5, 2020, https://www.nytimes.com/2020/02/05/us/politics/state-of-union -transcript.html.

19. Coleen Rowley, "Beheadings v. Drone Assassinations," *Common Dreams*, October 1, 2014, https://www.commondreams.org/views/2014/10/01/beheadings-v-drone-assassinations.

20. Collins and Glover, "Introduction," 8.

21. Susan Opotow, "Moral Exclusion and Injustice: An Introduction," *Social Issues* 46, no. 1 (Spring 1990): 1, https://doi.org/10.1111/j.1540-4560.1990.tb00268.x.

22. Opotow, 7.

23. Opotow, 10.

24. Opotow, 13.

25. Muneer I. Ahmad, "Resisting Guantánamo: Rights at the Brink of Dehumanization," *Northwestern University Law Review* 103, no. 4 (2009): 1749, https://digitalcommons.law.yale.edu/cgi/viewcontent.cgi?article=6259&context=fss_papers.

Chapter 3

1. "The Last Word Festival 2017—Poetry Slam Final—Suhaiymah Manzoor-Khan," Roundhouse, June 20, 2017, YouTube video, 2:01, https://www.youtube.com/watch?v=G9Sz2BQdMF8&feature=emb.

2. Maha Hilal, "#NeverForget: Sixteen Years into the 'War on Terror' and Institutionalized Islamophobia Lives On," Jadaliyya, September 25, 2017, https://www.jadaliyya.com/Details/34574.

3. "Researcher: It's Not Bad Apples, It's the Barrel," CNN, May 21, 2004, https://www.cnn.com/2004/US/05/21/zimbarbo.access/.

4. James Risen and Tim Golden, "3 Prisoners Commit Suicide at Guantánamo," *New York Times*, June 11, 2006, https://www.nytimes.com/2006/06/11/us/11gitmo.html.

5. Julian Brookes, "Guantanamo Has Driven Rear Admiral Harry Harris Insane," *Mother Jones*, June 11, 2006, https://www.motherjones.com/politics/2006/06/guantanamo-has-driven-rear-admiral-harry-harris-insane/#:~:text=%E2%80%9CThey%20are%20smart%2C%20they%20are,asymmetrical%20warfare%20waged%20against%20us.%E2%80%9D.

6. Risen and Golden, "3 Prisoners Commit Suicide."

7. Riazat Butts, "All the Rage—Victim of US Bloggers' Cartoon Hits Back," *Guardian*, July 23, 2007, https://www.theguardian.com/world/2007/jul/23/india.digitalmedia.

8. Bernard Lewis, "The Roots of Muslim Rage," *Atlantic*, September 1990, https://www.theatlantic.com/magazine/archive/1990/09/the-roots-of-muslim-rage/304643/.

9. Fareed Zakaria, "The Politics of Rage: Why Do They Hate Us?," *Newsweek*, October 14, 2001, https://www.newsweek.com/politics-rage-why-do-they-hate-us-154345.

10. Thomas L. Friedman, "The Core of Muslim Rage," *New York Times*, March 6, 2002, https://www.nytimes.com/2002/03/06/opinion/the-core-of-muslim-rage.html.

11. Ayaan Hirsi Ali, "Muslim Rage and the Last Gasp of Islamic Hate," *Newsweek*, September 17, 2012, https://www.belfercenter.org/publication/muslim-rage-and-last-gasp-islamic-hate.

12. Steven Kull, *Feeling Betrayed: The Roots of Muslim Anger at America* (Washington, DC: Brookings Institution Press, 2011), ix.

13. Kull, vii.
14. Kull, 3.
15. Kull, 42–43.
16. Nick Haslam and Steve Loughnan, "Dehumanization and Infrahumanization," *Annual Review of Psychology* 65 (2014): 402.
17. Nick Haslam and Steve Loughnan, "Dehumanization and Infrahumanization," *Annual Review of Psychology* 65 (2014): 402
18. Lara Winn and Randolph Cornelius, "Self-Objectification and Cognitive Performance: A Systematic Review of the Literature," *Frontiers in Psychology* 11, no. 20 (January 28, 2020), https://www.ncbi.nlm.nih.gov/pmc/articles/PMC6997128/.
19. Frederick, "Re-improved Colbert Transcript (Now with Complete Text of Colbert-Thomas Video!)," *Daily Kos* (blog), April 30, 2006, https://www.dailykos.com/stories/2006/4/30/206303/-.
20. Maha Hilal, "Abu Ghraib: The Legacy of Torture in the War on Terror," Al Jazeera, October 1, 2017, https://www.aljazeera.com/opinions/2017/10/1/abu-ghraib-the -legacy-of-torture-in-the-war-on-terror#:~:text=%E2%80%9CAmerica%20is %20the%20friend%20of,in%20the%20war%20on%20terror.
21. Antonio Taguba, *Article 15–6 Investigation of the 800th Military Police Brigade* (Tampa: United States Central Command, 2004), 16–17, https://fas.org/irp/agency/ dod/taguba.pdf.
22. George W. Bush, "Presidential Interview," interview by Al Hurra Television, C-SPAN, May 5, 2004, 12:31, https://www.c-span.org/video/?181712-1/presidential-interview.
23. Eric Bonds, "Indirect Violence and Legitimation: Torture, Surrogacy, and the U.S. War on Terror," *Societies without Borders* 7, no. 3 (2012): 296, https:// scholarlycommons.law.case.edu/swb/vol7/iss3/2.
24. Marcy Strauss, "Lessons from Abu Ghraib," *Ohio State Law Journal* 66 (2005): 1276, https://core.ac.uk/download/pdf/159609291.pdf.
25. Strauss, 1276.
26. Colin Powell, "Wake Forest University Commencement," C-SPAN, May 17, 2004, 11:34, https://www.c-span.org/video/?181990-1/wake-forest-university -commencement&showFullAbstract=1.
27. David E. Sanger, "Powell Says C.I.A. Was Misled about Weapons," *New York Times*, May 17, 2004, https://www.nytimes.com/2004/05/17/world/powell-says -cia-was-misled-about-weapons.html.
28. Charlie Savage and Elisabeth Bumiller, "An Iraqi Massacre, a Light Sentence and a Question of Military Justice," *New York Times*, January 27, 2012, https://www .nytimes.com/2012/01/28/us/an-iraqi-massacre-a-light-sentence-and-a-question -of-military-justice.html.
29. "Bush: If Marines Killed Civilians, They'll Be Punished," CNN, June 1, 2006, https://www.cnn.com/2006/WORLD/meast/05/31/haditha/index.html.
30. Marjorie Cohn, "The Haditha Massacre," *CounterPunch*, January 31, 2012, https:// www.counterpunch.org/2012/01/31/the-haditha-massacre/.
31. "Clinton Condemns 'Deplorable Behavior' in Marine Video," Reuters, January 12, 2012, YouTube video, 0:30, https://www.youtube.com/watch?v=IiNX7M3tEpE& feature=emb_err_woyt.

32. Caren Bohan and Ahmad Nadem, "Massacre Makes Obama 'More Determined' to Leave Afghanistan," Reuters, March 12, 2012, https://www.reuters.com/article/uk-afghanistan-civilians/massacre-makes-obama-more-determined-to-leave-afghanistan-idUKBRE82A02X20120313.

33. Ahmad Nadem and Ahmad Haroon, "Afghan Civilian Deaths Spark Calls for U.S. Exit," Reuters, March 11, 2012, https://www.reuters.com/article/afghanistan-civilians/afghan-civilian-deaths-spark-calls-for-u-s-exit-idINDEE82A02J20120312.

34. "Remarks of President Barack Obama," White House, May 23, 2013, https://obamawhitehouse.archives.gov/the-press-office/2013/05/23/remarks-president-barack-obama.

35. Lynn Sweet, "Obama Reacts to Torture Report: 'Documents a Troubling Program,'" Chicago Sun-Times, December 9, 2014, https://chicago.suntimes.com/2014/12/9/18467120/obama-reacts-to-torture-report-documents-a-troubling-program.

36. "Statement by the President Report of the Senate Select Committee on Intelligence," White House, December 9, 2014, https://obamawhitehouse.archives.gov/the-press-office/2014/12/09/statement-president-report-senate-select-committee-intelligence.

37. Daniel Dale (@ddale8), "Trump later boasted at length about how big a hole in the ground and how loud a noise his 'Mother of All Bombs' made in Afghanistan in 2017, then claimed," Twitter, July 22, 2019, 1:49 p.m., https://twitter.com/ddale8/status/1153361536175529996.

38. Nicholas Wu and John Fritze, "Trump Pardons Servicemembers in High Profile War Crimes Cases," USA Today, November 15, 2019, https://www.usatoday.com/story/news/politics/2019/11/15/donald-trump-pardons-clint-lorance-mathew-golsteyn-war-crime-cases/1229083001/.

39. Helene Cooper, Michael Tackett, and Taimoor Shah, "Twist in Green Beret's Extraordinary Story: Trump's Intervention after Murder Charges," New York Times, December 16, 2018, https://www.nytimes.com/2018/12/16/us/politics/major-matt-golsteyn-trump.html.

40. Wu and Fritze, "Trump Pardons Servicemembers."

41. Dave Philipps, "Trump Clears Three Service Members in War Crimes Cases," New York Times, November 22, 2019, https://www.nytimes.com/2019/11/15/us/trump-pardons.html?auth=login-email&login=email.

42. Dave Philipps, "Navy SEAL Chief Accused of War Crimes Is Found Not Guilty of Murder," New York Times, July 2, 2019, https://www.nytimes.com/2019/07/02/us/navy-seal-trial-verdict.html.

43. Philipps, "Trump Clears Three."

44. Philipps.

45. "Remarks by President Trump on the Killing of Qasem Soleimani," White House, January 3, 2020, https://trumpwhitehouse.archives.gov/briefings-statements/remarks-president-trump-killing-qasem-soleimani/.

46. "Remarks by President Trump on the Death of ISIS Leader Abu Bakr al-Baghdadi," White House, October 27, 2019, https://trumpwhitehouse.archives.gov/briefings-statements/remarks-president-trump-death-isis-leader-abu-bakr-al-baghdadi/.

47. Macon Phillips, "Osama bin Laden Dead," White House, May 2, 2011, https://obamawhitehouse.archives.gov/blog/2011/05/02/osama-bin-laden-dead.

48. "President Bush's Statement on Execution of Saddam Hussein," US Department of State, December 30, 2006, https://2001-2009.state.gov/p/nea/rls/78373.htm.

49. Phillips, "Osama bin Laden Dead."

50. Phillips.

51. "Obama Praises Killing of al-Awlaki," Associated Press, September 30, 2011, YouTube video, 0:01, https://www.youtube.com/watch?v=x43omN1yhxw&t=13s.

52. Mark Mazzetti, Charlie Savage, and Scott Shane, "How a U.S. Citizen Came to Be in America's Cross Hairs," *New York Times*, March 9, 2013, https://www.nytimes .com/2013/03/10/world/middleeast/anwar-al-awlaki-a-us-citizen-in-americas -cross-hairs.html.

53. Peter Finn and Greg Miller, "Anwar al-Awlaki's Family Speaks Out against His, Son's Deaths," *Washington Post*, October 17, 2011, https://www.washingtonpost .com/world/national-security/anwar-al-awlakis-family-speaks-out-against-his -sons-deaths/2011/10/17/gIQA8kFssL_story.html.

54. "Remarks by the President at the 'Change of Office' Chairman of the Joint Chiefs of Staff Ceremony," White House, September 30, 2011, https://obamawhitehouse .archives.gov/the-press-office/2011/09/30/remarks-president-change-office -chairman-joint-chiefs-staff-ceremony.

55. "Read the Full Text of President Obama's Address to the Nation on Terrorism," *Time*, December 6, 2015, https://time.com/4137986/obama-address-transcript -terrorism-isis-isil-oval-office/.

56. "Backgrounder: The President's Words on Islam," White House, accessed June 9, 2021, https://georgewbush-whitehouse.archives.gov/infocus/ramadan/islam.html.

Part 2

1. Ben Rhodes, "The 9/11 Era Is Over," *Atlantic*, April 6, 2020, https://www .theatlantic.com/ideas/archive/2020/04/its-not-september-12-anymore/609502/.

2. George W. Bush, "Address to the Joint Session of the 107th Congress" (September 20, 2001), in *Selected Speeches of President George W. Bush 2001–2008* (Washington, DC: George W. Bush White House Archives, n.d.), 69, https:// georgewbush-whitehouse.archives.gov/infocus/bushrecord/documents/Selected _Speeches_George_W_Bush.pdf.

3. Bush.

4. Jeremy Waldron, *Torture, Terror, and Trade-Offs: Philosophy for the White House* (Oxford: Oxford University Press, 2012), 61.

5. Gershon Shafir, Everard Meade, and William J. Aceves, ed., *Lessons and Legacies of the War on Terror: From Moral Panic to Permanent War* (London: Routledge, 2013).

6. Shafir, Meade, and Aceves, 1.

7. Stephanie Savell, "The American Empire's Long Reach," *Nation*, February 19, 2019, https://www.thenation.com/article/archive/america-empire-war-terror-counter terrorism/.

8. Poynting and Whyte, "Introduction," 2.

Chapter 4

1. "Howard Zinn on War," Zinn Education Project, accessed June 9, 2021, https:// www.zinnedproject.org/materials/howard-zinn-on-war/.
2. "Remarks of Secretary Tom Ridge to the American Enterprise Institute: 'Securing America in a Post 9/11 World,'" Office of the Press Secretary, September 2, 2003, https:// georgewbush-whitehouse.archives.gov/news/releases/2003/09/20030902-7.html.
3. Mary Ellen O'Connell, "The Legal Case against the Global War on Terror," *Case Western Reserve Journal of International Law* 36, no. 2 (2004): 349, https://core.ac .uk/download/pdf/214078602.pdf.
4. Authorization for Use of Military Force, 50 U.S.C. § 1541 (2001), https://uscode .house.gov/statutes/pl/107/40.pdf.
5. "Text of President Bush's 2002."
6. Heather Brandon-Smith, "The 2001 AUMF and Afghanistan, 18 Years Later," Friends Committee on National Legislation, September 18, 2019, https://www.fcnl .org/updates/the-2001-aumf-and-afghanistan-18-years-later-2366.
7. John C. Yoo, *The President's Constitutional Authority to Conduct Military Operations against Terrorists and Nations Supporting Them (Memorandum Opinion for the Deputy Counsel to the President)* (Washington, DC: Office of Legal Counsel, 2001), https://fas.org/irp/agency/doj/olc092501.html.
8. Savell, "American Empire's Long Reach."
9. Jeremy Scahill, "Blackwater Founder Remains Free and Rich While His Former Employees Go Down on Murder Charges," Intercept, October 22, 2014, https:// theintercept.com/2014/10/22/blackwater-guilty-verdicts/.
10. Maggie Haberman and Michael S. Schmidt, "Trump Pardons Two Russia Inquiry Figures and Blackwater Guards," *New York Times*, December 22, 2020, https:// www.nytimes.com/2020/12/22/us/politics/trump-pardons.html.
11. "Bush Announces Strikes."
12. O'Connell, "Legal Case," 350.
13. All information from this point until the next citation is drawn from this source: Craig Whitlock, Julie Vitkovskaya, and Nick Kirkpatrick, "The War in Afghanistan: A Visual Timeline of the 18-Year Conflict," *Washington Post*, December 9, 2019, https://www.washingtonpost.com/graphics/2019/investigations/amp-stories/ visual-timeline-of-the-war-in-afghanistan/.
14. Esch, "Legitimizing," 373–74.
15. Esch, 374.
16. Neta C. Crawford and Catherine Lutz, "Human Cost of Post-9/11 Wars: Direct War Deaths in Major War Zones," Watson Institute for International and Public Affairs, November 13, 2019, 1–2, https://watson.brown.edu/costsofwar/files/cow/imce/ papers/2019/Direct%20War%20Deaths%20COW%20Estimate%20November %2013%202019%20FINAL.pdf.
17. Meghan Keneally, "Why the US Got Involved in Afghanistan—and Why It's Been Difficult to Get Out," ABC News, August 21, 2017, https://abcnews.go.com/US/us -involved-afghanistan-difficult/story?id=49341264.

18. Lynsey Mitchell, "Monsters, Martyrs, Heroes, and Their Storytellers: The Enduring Attraction of Culturally Embedded Narratives in the 'War on Terror,'" *Liverpool Law Review* 35 (December 2014): 84, https://doi.org/10.1007/s10991-013-9146-8.

19. "Text of President Bush's 2002."

20. Dylan Matthews, "George W. Bush Really Did Lie about WMDs, and His Aides Are Still Lying for Him," Vox, March 20, 2019, https://www.vox.com/policy-and-politics/2019/3/20/18274228/ari-fleischer-iraq-lies-george-w-bush-wmds.

21. Jonathan Stein and Tim Dickinson, "Lie by Lie: A Timeline of How We Got into Iraq," *Mother Jones*, September/October 2006, https://www.motherjones.com/politics/2011/12/leadup-iraq-war-timeline/.

22. Wolf Blitzer, "Search for the 'Smoking Gun,'" CNN, January 10, 2003, https://www.cnn.com/2003/US/01/10/wbr.smoking.gun/.

23. Gary L. Gregg II, "George W. Bush: Foreign Affairs," Miller Center, accessed June 9, 2021, https://millercenter.org/president/gwbush/foreign-affairs.

24. Kyle Crichton, Gina Lamb, and Rogene Fisher Jacquette, "Timeline of Major Events in the Iraq War," *New York Times*, August 31, 2010, https://archive.nytimes.com/www.nytimes.com/interactive/2010/08/31/world/middleeast/20100831-Iraq-Timeline.html?src=tptw#/%23time111_3296.

25. Whitlock, Vitkovskaya, and Kirkpatrick, "War in Afghanistan."

26. "The Iraq War: 2003–2011," Council on Foreign Relations, accessed May 6, 2021, https://www.cfr.org/timeline/iraq-war.

27. Crawford and Lutz, "Cost of Post-9/11."

28. Dahr Jamail, "Iraq: War's Legacy of Cancer," Al Jazeera, March 15, 2013, https://www.aljazeera.com/indepth/features/2013/03/2013315171951838638.html.

29. John R. Bolton, "Beyond the Axis of Evil: Additional Threats from Weapons of Mass Destruction," remarks to the Heritage Foundation, US Department of State Archive, May 6, 2002, https://2001-2009.state.gov/t/us/rm/9962.htm.

30. Christopher Woody and Ryan Pickrell, "Trump Says 'ISIS Is Defeated'—the Pentagon Says Not Quite," Business Insider, October 17, 2018, https://www.businessinsider.com/trump-says-isis-is-defeated-the-pentagon-says-not-quite-2018-10.

31. Mohamad Bazzi, "America Is Likely Complicit in War Crimes in Yemen. It's Time to Hold the US to Account," *Guardian*, October 3, 2019, https://www.theguardian.com/commentisfree/2019/oct/03/yemen-airstrikes-saudi-arabia-mbs-us.

32. Tik Root, "Yemen's New Ways of Protesting Drone Strikes: Graffiti and Poetry," *Time*, November 30, 2013, https://world.time.com/2013/11/30/yemens-new-ways-of-protesting-drone-strikes-graffiti-and-poetry/.

33. Zack Beauchamp, "Why the Hell Is the US Helping Saudi Arabia Bomb Yemen? A Brief Guide," Vox, October 14, 2016, https://www.vox.com/world/2016/10/14/13269580/us-bombing-yemen-houthis.

34. Beauchamp.

35. Timothy Robbins, Hijab Shah, and Melissa Dalton, "U.S. Support for Saudi Military Operations in Yemen," Center for Strategic & International Studies, March 23, 2018, https://www.csis.org/analysis/us-support-saudi-military-operations-yemen.

36. "How the U.S. Became More Involved in the War in Yemen," *New York Times*, October 15, 2015, https://www.nytimes.com/interactive/2016/10/14/world/middle east/yemen-saudi-arabia-us-airstrikes.html.

37. Edward Wong, "U.S. Rationale for Military Aid to Saudis in Yemen War Is Fraying," *New York Times*, September 23, 2020, https://www.nytimes.com/2020/09/23/us/politics/yemen-us-weapons-saudi-arabia.html.

38. Omer Karasapan, "Yemen's Civilians: Besieged on All Sides," Brookings, March 31, 2020, https://www.brookings.edu/blog/future-development/2020/03/31/yemens-civilians-besieged-on-all-sides/.

39. Gregory Hellman, "House Declares U.S. Military Role in Yemen's Civil War Unauthorized," Politico, November 13, 2017, https://www.politico.com/story/2017/11/13/house-yemen-civil-war-authorization-244868.

40. Wong, "U.S. Rationale."

41. *Exploring the U.S. Africa Command and a New Strategic Relationship with Africa, Hearing before the Subcommittee on African Affairs of the Committee on Foreign Relations, United States Senate, One Hundred Tenth Congress, Session 1, August 1, 2007* (Washington, DC: US Government Printing Office, 2008), 9, https://fas.org/irp/congress/2007_hr/africom.pdf.

42. Nick Turse, "Pentagon's Own Map of U.S. Bases in Africa Contradicts Its Claim of 'Light' Footprint," Intercept, February 27, 2020, https://theintercept.com/2020/02/27/africa-us-military-bases-africom/.

43. Andrew Gray and Kristin Roberts, "Bush Approves New Military Command for Africa," Reuters, February 6, 2007, https://www.reuters.com/article/us-usa-pentagon-africa/bush-approves-new-military-command-for-africa-idUSWBT006 53220070206.

44. Nick Turse, *The Changing Face of Empire: Special Ops, Drones, Spies, Proxy Fighters, Secret Bases, and Cyberwarfare* (Chicago: Haymarket, 2012), 65.

45. Dan Glazebrook, "The Imperial Agenda of the US's 'African Command' Marches On," *Guardian*, June 14, 2012, https://theguardian.com/commentisfree/2012/jun/14/africom-imperial-agenda-marches-on/.

46. United Nations, "Security Council Approves 'No-Fly Zone' over Libya, Authorizing 'All Necessary Measures' to Protect Civilians, by Vote of 10 in Favour with 5 Abstentions," Department of Public Information, March 17, 2011, https://www.un.org/press/en/2011/sc10200.doc.htm.

47. Glazebrook, "Imperial Agenda."

48. Nick Turse, "Violence Has Spiked in Africa since the Military Founded AFRICOM, Pentagon Study Finds," Intercept, July 29, 2019, https://theintercept.com/2019/07/29/pentagon-study-africom-africa-violence/.

49. "U.S. out of Africa! Shut Down AFRICOM," Black Alliance for Peace, accessed June 9, 2021, https://blackallianceforpeace.com/usoutofafrica/.

50. Pew Research Center, "Muslim-Majority Countries," Future of the Global Muslim Population, January 27, 2011, https://www.pewforum.org/2011/01/27/future-of-the-global-muslim-population-muslim-majority/.

51. "U.S. out of Africa!"

52. "Summary of War Spending, in Billions of Current Dollars," Watson Institute for International and Public Affairs, November 13, 2019, https://watson.brown .edu/costsofwar/figures/2019/budgetary-costs-post-911-wars-through-fy2020-64 -trillion.

53. Jeremy Scahill, "The Drone Legacy," in *The Assassination Complex: Inside the Government's Secret Drone Warfare Program*, ed. Jeremy Scahill and the Staff of the Intercept (New York: Simon & Schuster, 2016), 2.

54. Dan Sabbagh, "Killer Drones: How Many Are There and Who Do They Target?," *Guardian*, November 18, 2019, https://www.theguardian.com/news/2019/nov/18/ killer-drones-how-many-uav-predator-reaper.

55. *The Civilian Impact of Drones: Unexamined Costs, Unanswered Questions* (Washington, DC: Center for Civilians in Conflict; New York: Human Rights Clinic at Columbia Law School, 2012), 24, https://civiliansinconflict.org/wp-content/ uploads/2017/09/The_Civilian_Impact_of_Drones_w_cover.pdf.

56. US Congress, *Joint Resolution, to Authorize the Use of United States Armed Forces against Those Responsible for the Recent Attacks Launched against the United States*, S.J. Res. 23 (H.J. Res. 64), 107th Cong., 1st sess., introduced in Senate September 14, 2001, https://www.govinfo.gov/content/pkg/PLAW-107publ40/html/ PLAW-107publ40.htm.

57. Jessica Purkiss and Jack Serle, "Obama's Covert Drone War in Numbers: Ten Times More Strikes Than Bush," Bureau of Investigative Journalism, January 17, 2017, https://www.thebureauinvestigates.com/stories/2017-01-17/obamas-covert -drone-war-in-numbers-ten-times-more-strikes-than-bush.

58. Spencer Ackerman, "Victim of Obama's First Drone Strike: 'I Am the Living Example of What Drones Are," Business Insider, January 23, 2016, https://www.businessinsider .com/there-have-been-no-reported-drone-strikes-since-joe-biden-took-office-2021-2.

59. Curtis A. Bradley and Jack Landman Goldsmith, "Obama's AUMF Legacy," *American Journal of International Law* 110 (2016): 628–45.

60. "Legality of Drone Warfare," Bureau of Investigative Journalism, accessed June 9, 2021, https://www.thebureauinvestigates.com/explainers/legality-of-drone-warfare.

61. Jennifer Williams, "From Torture to Drone Strikes: The Disturbing Legal Legacy Obama Is Leaving for Trump," Vox, January 10, 2017, https://www.vox.com/ policy-and-politics/2016/11/14/13577464/obama-farewell-speech-torture-drones -nsa-surveillance-trump.

62. "Obama's Speech on Drone Policy," *New York Times*, May 23, 2013, https:// www.nytimes.com/2013/05/24/us/politics/transcript-of-obamas-speech-on-drone -policy.html?pagewanted=all.

63. Maha Hilal, "Trump Plans to Make It Easier to Kill Civilians with Drones. We Can Thank Obama for Paving the Way," *In These Times*, October 18, 2017, https:// inthesetimes.com/article/donald-trump-drones-civilians-barack-obama.

64. Jo Becker and Scott Shane, "Secret 'Kill List' Proves a Test of Obama's Principles and Will," *New York Times*, May 29, 2012, https://www.nytimes.com/2012/05/29/ world/obamas-leadership-in-war-on-al-qaeda.html?pagewanted=9&_r=1&hp& adxnnlx=1338289213-gFazCDrgzwY2RtQCER9fGQ&pagewanted=all.

65. *Report on the Legal and Policy Frameworks Guiding the United States' Use of Military Force and Related National Security Operations* (Washington, DC: White House, 2016), 4–5, https://www.justsecurity.org/wp-content/uploads/2016/12/ framework.Report_Final.pdf.

66. *Civilian Impact of Drones*, 21.

67. Micah Zenko, "The (Not-So) Peaceful Transition of Power: Trump's Drone Strikes Outpace Obama," Council on Foreign Relations, March 2, 2017, https://www.cfr .org/blog/not-so-peaceful-transition-power-trumps-drone-strikes-outpace-obama.

68. Charles Davis, "There Have Been Zero Reported US Drone Strikes since Joe Biden Took Office," Business Insider, February 16, 2021, https://www.businessinsider.com/ there-have-been-no-reported-drone-strikes-since-joe-biden-took-office-2021-2.

69. Zenko, "(Not-So) Peaceful."

70. Tara McKelvey, "Drones Kill Rescuers in 'Double Tap,' Say Activists," BBC News, October 22, 2013, https://www.bbc.com/news/world-us-canada-24557333.

71. Kristina Benson, "Kill 'em and Sort It Out Later: Signature Drone Strikes and International Humanitarian Law," *Pacific McGeorge Global Business & Law Journal* 27, no. 1 (2014): 49, https://faculty.mcgeorge.edu/documents/Publications/02 _Benson_27_1.pdf.

72. Becker and Shane, "Secret 'Kill List.'"

73. Jeremy Scahill, *Dirty Wars* (New York: Bold Type, 2013), 351.

74. Adam Serwer, "Obama Talks Drone Strikes," *Mother Jones*, September 6, 2012, https://www.motherjones.com/politics/2012/09/obama-talks-drone-strikes/.

75. Serwer.

76. Williams, "From Torture to Drone Strikes."

77. Becker and Shane, "Secret 'Kill List.'"

78. Peter Van Buren, "Another Casualty of the War on Terror: The Fifth Amendment," *Mother Jones*, July 24, 2014, https://www.motherjones.com/politics/2014/07/death -due-process-america/.

79. *Lawfulness of a Lethal Operation Directed against a U.S. Citizen Who Is a Senior Operational Leader of Al-Qa'ida or an Associated Force* (Washington, DC: Department of Justice, 2011), 6, https://www.justice.gov/sites/default/files/oip/ legacy/2014/07/23/dept-white-paper.pdf.

80. Conor Friedersdorf, "How Team Obama Justifies the Killing of a 16-Year-Old American," *Atlantic*, October 24, 2012, https://www.theatlantic.com/politics/archive/ 2012/10/how-team-obama-justifies-the-killing-of-a-16-year-old-american/264028/.

81. Spencer Ackerman, Jason Burke, and Julian Borger, "Eight-Year-Old American Girl 'Killed in Yemen Raid Approved by Trump,'" *Guardian*, February 1, 2017, https://www.theguardian.com/world/2017/feb/01/yemen-strike-eight-year-old -american-girl-killed-al-awlaki.

82. "Current United States Counterterror War Locations," Watson Institute for International and Public Affairs, accessed June 9, 2021, https://watson.brown.edu/ costsofwar/files/cow/imce/papers/Current%20US%20Counterterror%20War %20Locations_Costs%20of%20War%20Project%20Map.pdf.

Chapter 5

1. Dawn Paley, "Violence Doesn't Spill over Borders, Militarized Borders Create Violence," Unembedded, May 22, 2012, http://dawnpaley.tumblr.com/post/23543672055/violence-doesnt-spill-over-borders-militarized, quoted in Harsha Walia, *Undoing Border Imperialism* (Chico, CA: AK, 2013), 11.
2. Paley, 25.
3. "Remarks by the President at INS Naturalization Ceremony," White House, July 10, 2001, https://georgewbush-whitehouse.archives.gov/news/releases/2001/07/20010710-1.html.
4. Michelle Mittelstadt et al., "Through the Prism of National Security: Major Immigration Policy and Program Changes in the Decade since 9/11," Migration Policy Institute, August 2011, https://www.migrationpolicy.org/research/post-9-11-immigration-policy-program-changes.
5. Mittelstadt et al., 1.
6. Alex Lubin, *Never-Ending War on Terror*, American Studies Now: Critical Histories of the Present 13 (Oakland: University of California Press, 2021), 37–38.
7. Penn State Law Immigrants' Rights Clinic and Penn State School of International Affairs, *The 9/11 Effect and Its Legacy on U.S. Immigration Laws: Essays, Remarks, and Photographs* (University Park, PA: Center for Immigrants' Rights Clinic Publication, 2011), bk. 9, https://elibrary.law.psu.edu/cgi/viewcontent.cgi?referer=https://www.google.com/&httpsredir=1&article=1007&context=irc_pubs.
8. The deputy attorney general to Immigration and Naturalization Service commissioner, Federal Bureau of Investigation director, United States Marshals Service director, United States attorneys, "Guidance for Absconder Apprehension Initiative," Office of the Deputy Attorney General, January 25, 2002, https://www.shusterman.com/pdf/absconderapprehensioninitiative.pdf.
9. Shoba S. Wadhia, "Business as Usual: Immigration and the National Security Exception," *Penn State Law Review* 114 (2010): 1499, https://elibrary.law.psu.edu/cgi/viewcontent.cgi?referer=&httpsredir=1&article=1023&context=fac_works.
10. Penn State Law Immigrants' Rights Clinic and Rights Working Group, *The NSEERS Effect: A Decade of Racial Profiling, Fear, and Secrecy* (University Park, PA: Center for Immigrants' Rights Clinic, 2012), bk. 11, p. 4, https://elibrary.law.psu.edu/irc_pubs/11.
11. Wendy Patten and Ebony Wade, "Human Rights Implications of Post-9/11 Immigration Policies," in Penn State Law Immigrants' Rights Clinic and Penn State School of International Affairs, *9/11 Effect and Its Legacy*, pp. 8–11.
12. "Removal of Regulations Relating to Special Registration Process for Certain Nonimmigrants," *Federal Register*, December 23, 2016, https://www.federalregister.gov/documents/2016/12/23/2016-30885/removal-of-regulations-relating-to-special-registration-process-for-certain-nonimmigrants.
13. "The September 11 Detainees," ACLU, accessed June 9, 2021, https://www.aclu.org/other/september-11-detainees.
14. Patten and Wade, "Human Rights Implications," 8.

15. Shubh Mathur, "Surviving the Dragnet: 'Special Interest' Detainees in the US after 9/11," *Race & Class* 47, no. 3 (2006): 35, https://doi.org/10.1177/0306396 806061085.

16. Ziglar v. Abbasi et al., 582 U.S. 1 (2017), https://supreme.justia.com/cases/federal/ us/582/15-1358/.

17. "Fact Sheet: Operation Streamline," No More Deaths / No Más Muertes, March 2012, https://nomoredeaths.org/wp-content/uploads/2014/10/nmd_fact_sheet_operation _streamline.pdf.

18. Secure Fence Act of 2006, Pub. L. No. 109-367, Stat. 120 (2006): 2638–40.

19. Sirine Shebaya, "Does the Priority Enforcement Program Solve the Constitutional Problems with ICE Detainers?," *University of St. Thomas Law Journal* 13, no. 3 (2017): 571, https://ir.stthomas.edu/cgi/viewcontent.cgi?article=1402&context=ustlj.

20. Kade Crockford, *Beyond Sanctuary: Local Strategies for Defending Civil Liberties* (New York: Century Foundation, 2018), https://production-tcf.imgix.net/app/ uploads/2018/03/03152547/beyond-sanctuary-local-strategies-for-defending-civil -liberties.pdf.

21. Crockford.

22. Crockford.

23. Priscilla Alvarez, "How Trump Is Changing Immigration Enforcement," *Atlantic*, February 3, 2017, https://www.theatlantic.com/politics/archive/2017/02/trump -executive-order-immigration/515454/.

24. Shebaya, "Constitutional Problems with ICE Detainers," 571.

25. "Enhancing Public Safety in the Interior of the United States" (Exec. Order No. 13,768), *Federal Register*, January 25, 2017, https://www.federalregister.gov/ documents/2017/01/30/2017-02102/enhancing-public-safety-in-the-interior-of-the -united-states.

26. Alvarez, "Trump Is Changing Immigration."

27. Crockford, *Beyond Sanctuary*, 5.

28. "Visa Waiver Program," US Department of State, accessed June 9, 2021, https:// travel.state.gov/content/travel/en/us-visas/tourism-visit/visa-waiver-program .html.

29. Jennie Pasquarella, *Muslims Need Not Apply: How USCIS Secretly Mandates the Discriminatory Delay and Denial of Citizenship and Immigration Benefits to Aspiring Americans* (Los Angeles: ACLU of Southern California, 2013), 2, https:// www.aclusocal.org/sites/default/files/field_documents/161849063-muslims-need -not-apply-aclu-socal-report.pdf.

30. Jonathan R. Scharfen to Field Leadership, US Citizen and Immigration Services, "Policy for Vetting and Adjudicating Cases with National Security Concerns," ACLU of Southern California, April 11, 2008, https://www.aclusocal.org/ sites/default/files/wp-content/uploads/2013/01/CARRP-Policy-for-Vetting-and -Adjudicating-Cases-w-NS-Concerns-Apr.-11-2008.pdf.

31. *U.S. Government Watchlisting: Unfair Process and Devastating Consequences* (New York: ACLU, 2014), 1, https://www.aclu.org/sites/default/files/assets/watch list_briefing_paper_v3.pdf.

32. "Terrorist Screening Center—FAQs," FBI, January 2017, 1, https://www.fbi.gov/file-repository/terrorist-screening-center-frequently-asked-questions.pdf/view.

33. Charlie Savage, "Judge Rules Terrorism Watchlist Violates Constitutional Rights," *New York Times*, September 4, 2019, https://www.nytimes.com/2019/09/04/us/politics/terrorism-watchlist-constitution.html.

34. Anas Elhady et al. v. Charles H. Kable et al., 2019 E.D. Va. (2019), 26.

35. Matthew Barakat, "Judge Orders Government to Make Changes to Terror Watchlist," Associated Press, December 27, 2019, https://abcnews.go.com/US/wireStory/judge-orders-government-make-terror-watchlist-67947844.

36. Maha Hilal, "Admitting the Terrorism Watchlist Was Unconstitutional Is Important, but Not Nearly Enough," *Newsweek*, September 17, 2019, https://www.newsweek.com/watchilist-unconstitutional-two-classes-muslims-1459463.

37. "Terrorist Screening Center—FAQs."

38. Kim Zetter, "No-Fly List Includes the Dead," *Wired*, March 10, 2010, https://www.wired.com/2010/03/no-fly-list-includes-the-dead/.

39. "Court Orders Government to Give Plaintiffs in ACLU Lawsuit a Chance to Clear Their Names," ACLU Oregon, June 24, 2014, https://aclu-or.org/en/cases/court-rules-no-fly-list-process-unconstitutional-and-must-be-reformed-0.

40. "Tanvir v. Tanzin (Formerly Tanvir v. Holder and Tanvir v. Lynch)," Center for Constitutional Rights (CCR), August 27, 2020, https://ccrjustice.org/home/what-we-do/our-cases/tanvir-v-holder.

41. "Tanzin v. Tanvir," SCOTUSblog, December 10, 2020, https://www.scotusblog.com/case-files/cases/fnu-tanzin-v-tanvir/.

42. Saba Hamedy, "Everything You Need to Know about the Travel Ban: A Timeline," CNN, June 26, 2018, https://www.cnn.com/2018/06/26/politics/timeline-travel-ban/index.html.

43. Anthony Zurcher, "Is Trump's Immigration Order Legal?," BBC, February 6, 2017, https://www.bbc.com/news/world-us-canada-38766364.

44. "Timeline of the Muslim Ban," ACLU Washington, accessed June 9, 2021, https://www.aclu-wa.org/pages/timeline-muslim-ban.

45. Nina Totenberg and Domenico Montanaro, "In Big Win for White House, Supreme Court Upholds President Trump's Travel Ban," NPR, June 26, 2018, https://www.npr.org/2018/06/26/606481548/supreme-court-upholds-trump-travel-ban.

46. "Bush Delivers State."

47. "Remarks by the President in the State of the Union Address," White House, February 12, 2013, https://obamawhitehouse.archives.gov/the-press-office/2013/02/12/remarks-president-state-union-address.

48. "Remarks by President Trump in Joint Address to Congress," White House, February 28, 2017, https://trumpwhitehouse.archives.gov/briefings-statements/remarks-president-trump-joint-address-congress/.

49. "'Home' by Warsan Shire," Facing History and Ourselves, accessed June 9, 2021, https://www.facinghistory.org/standing-up-hatred-intolerance/warsan-shire-home.

Chapter 6

1. "Informants," Al Jazeera Investigations, July 20, 2014, YouTube video, 12:38, https://www.youtube.com/watch?v=CMRns4ViuEY.
2. "Informants," 3:19.
3. Wadie Said, *Crimes of Terror: The Legal and Political Implications of Federal Terrorism Prosecutions* (Oxford: Oxford Scholarship Online, 2015), 4.
4. Providing Material Support to Terrorists, 18 U.S.C. § 2339A (1996), https://www.justice.gov/archives/jm/criminal-resource-manual-15-providing-material-support-terrorists-18-usc-2339a.
5. "Holder v. Humanitarian Law Project," Charity and Security Network, accessed April 20, 2021, https://charityandsecurity.org/litigation/hlp/#:~:text=The%20court%20ruled%20that%20training,support%20for%20nonviolence%2C%20are%20prohibited.
6. Said, *Crimes of Terror*, 6.
7. Human Rights Watch and Columbia Law School Human Rights Institute, *Illusion of Justice: Human Rights Abuses in US Terrorism Prosecutions* (New York: Human Rights Watch, 2014), https://web.law.columbia.edu/sites/default/files/microsites/human-rights-institute/files/final_report_-_illusion_of_justice.pdf.
8. Human Rights Watch and Columbia Law School Human Rights Institute, 22.
9. Human Rights Watch and Columbia Law School Human Rights Institute, 24–25.
10. Human Rights Watch and Columbia Law School Human Rights Institute, 5.
11. Human Rights Watch and Columbia Law School Human Rights Institute, 27.
12. Murtaza Hussain and Razan Ghalayini, "The Real Story behind the Fort Dix Five Terror Plot," Intercept, June 25, 2015, https://theintercept.com/2015/06/25/fort-dix-five-terror-plot-the-real-story/.
13. Ailsa Chang, "Defense Lawyers in Bronx Synagogue Terror Case Call FBI Informant a Lifelong Liar," WNYC News, September 16, 2010, https://www.wnyc.org/story/94776-defense-lawyers-bronx-synagogue-terror-case-call-fbi-informant-lifelong-liar/.
14. Paul Harris, "Newburgh Four: Poor, Black, and Jailed under FBI 'Entrapment' Tactics," *Guardian*, December 12, 2011, https://www.theguardian.com/world/2011/dec/12/newburgh-four-fbi-entrapment-terror.
15. Sara Kamali, "Informants, Provocateurs, and Entrapment: Examining the Histories of the FBI's PATCON and the NYPD's Muslim Surveillance Program," *Surveillance & Society* 15, no. 1 (2017), https://doi.org/10.24908/ss.v15i1.5254.
16. "The Holy Land Five," Al Jazeera, October 5, 2016, https://www.aljazeera.com/programmes/aljazeeraworld/2016/10/holy-land-foundation-hamas-161004083025906.html.
17. Steve Brown, "Tarek Mehanna: 'Sweet' Teacher, 'Best Son,' Terrorist?," WBUR News, October 22, 2009, https://www.wbur.org/news/2009/10/22/terrorism-suspect.
18. Sara Mulkeen and Staff, "Sudbury Man Convicted on Terrorism Charges Receives Award," *MetroWest Daily News*, January 7, 2013, https://www.metrowestdailynews.com/x1058227140/Sudbury-man-convicted-on-terrorism-charges-receives-award#ixzz2HIICJ1yN.

19. Amna Akbar, "How Tarek Mehanna Went to Prison for a Thought Crime," *Nation*, December 31, 2013, https://www.thenation.com/article/archive/how-tarek -mehanna-went-prison-thought-crime/.

20. Akbar.

21. Glenn Greenwald, "The Real Criminals in the Tarek Mehanna Case," Salon, April 13, 2012, https://www.salon.com/2012/04/13/the_real_criminals_in_the _tarek_mehanna_case/.

22. Stephen I. Vladeck, "Trying Terrorism Suspects in Article III Courts: The Lessons of *United States v. Abu Ali*," American Constitution Society for Law and Policy, August 2010, https://www.acslaw.org/wp-content/uploads/2018/04/Vladeck_Abu _Ali.pdf.

23. Vladeck, 4.

24. Murtaza Hussain and Glenn Greenwald, "Exclusive Interview: Sami Al-Arian, Professor Who Defeated Controversial Terrorism Charges, Is Deported from U.S.," Intercept, February 5, 2015, https://theintercept.com/2015/02/05/sami-al-arian -charged-terrorism-never-convicted-deported-today-u-s/.

25. Hussain and Greenwald.

26. "Live Q&A with Edward Snowden: Thursday 23rd January, 8pm GMT, 3pm EST," Courage Foundation, January 23, 2014, https://www.freesnowden.is/asksnowden/.

27. Brett Rubio and Bridget K. Baker, "Are We Targeting Our Fellow Countrymen? The Consequences of the USA PATRIOT Act," *Journal of Education Controversy* 3, no. 1 (2008): 1, https://cedar.wwu.edu/jec/vol3/iss1/4/.

28. "Are They Allowed to Do That? A Breakdown of Selected Government Surveillance Programs," Brennan Center for Justice, accessed June 9, 2021, https:// www.brennancenter.org/sites/default/files/analysis/Government%20Surveillance %20Factsheet.pdf.

29. "How the USA Patriot Act Redefines 'Domestic Terrorism,'" ACLU, accessed June 9, 2021, https://www.aclu.org/other/how-usa-patriot-act-redefines-domestic -terrorism.

30. Daniel Victor, "Ahmed Mohamed, Boy Handcuffed for Making Clock, Is Suing," *New York Times*, August 8, 2016, https://www.nytimes.com/2016/08/09/us/ahmed -mohamed-boy-handcuffed-for-making-clock-is-suing.html.

31. Barack Obama (@POTUS44), "Cool clock, Ahmed. Want to bring it to the White House? We should inspire more kids like you to like science. It's what makes America great," Twitter, September 16, 2015, 12:58 p.m., https://twitter.com/POTUS44/ status/644193755814342656.

32. Arun Kundnani and Ben Hayes, *The Globalisation of Countering Violent Extremism Policies: Undermining Human Rights, Instrumentalising Civil Society* (Amsterdam: Transnational Institute, 2018), 4, https://www.tni.org/files/publication-down loads/the_globalisation_of_countering_violent_extremism_policies.pdf.

33. Kundnani and Hayes, 8.

34. Aziz Huq, "Modeling Terrorist Radicalization the New Face of Discrimination: Muslim in America," University of Chicago Law School, 2010, https:// chicagounbound.uchicago.edu/cgi/viewcontent.cgi?article=2523&context= journal_articles.

35. "Remarks by the President in State of the Union Address," White House, January 25, 2011, https://obamawhitehouse.archives.gov/the-press-office/2011/01/25/remarks-president-state-union-address.

36. Office of President Barack Obama, *Empowering Local Partners to Prevent Violent Extremism in the United States* (Washington, DC: White House, 2011), 3, https://obamawhitehouse.archives.gov/sites/default/files/empowering_local_partners.pdf.

37. "Pilot Programs Are Key to Our Countering Violent Extremism Efforts," US Department of Justice Archives, February 18, 2015, https://www.justice.gov/archives/opa/blog/pilot-programs-are-key-our-countering-violent-extremism-efforts.

38. Faiza Patel and Meghan Koushik, *Countering Violent Extremism* (New York: Brennan Center for Justice, 2019), 8, https://www.brennancenter.org/sites/default/files/2019-08/Report_Brennan%20Center%20CVE%20Report_0.pdf.

39. Patel and Koushik, 2.

40. Office of President Barack Obama, *Empowering Local Partners*, 2.

41. Fatema Ahmad, "Why 'Countering Violent Extremism' Programs Won't Stop White Supremacists," American Friends Service Committee, August 6, 2019, https://www.afsc.org/blogs/news-and-commentary/why-countering-violent-extremism-programs-wont-stop-white-supremacists.

42. Julia Edwards Ainsley, Dustin Volz, and Kristina Cooke, "Exclusive: Trump to Focus Counter-Extremism Program Solely on Islam—Sources," Reuters, February 3, 2017, https://www.reuters.com/article/us-usa-trump-extremists-program-exclusiv/exclusive-trump-to-focus-counter-extremism-program-solely-on-islam-sources-idUSKBN15G5VO.

43. George Joseph, "Draft DHS Report Called for Long-Term Surveillance of Sunni Muslim Immigrants," *Foreign Policy*, February 5, 2018, https://foreignpolicy.com/2018/02/05/draft-dhs-report-surveillance-of-muslim-immigrants/.

44. Dina El-Rifai, "Trump Wants to Surveil Muslims in the U.S.—and Why We Should All Be Concerned," American Friends Service Committee, February 16, 2018, https://www.afsc.org/blogs/news-and-commentary/trump-wants-to-surveil-muslims.

45. "Targeted Violence and Terrorism Prevention," Department of Homeland Security, last modified April 14, 2021, https://www.dhs.gov/tvtp.

46. "Civil Rights and Community Groups Ask DHS to Halt Discriminatory Surveillance Grant Program" (press release), Muslim Advocates, June 1, 2020, https://muslimadvocates.org/2020/06/civil-rights-and-community-groups-ask-dhs-to-halt-discriminatory-surveillance-grant-program/.

47. Michel Foucault, *Discipline and Punish: The Birth of the Prison* (New York: Random House, 1995), 201.

48. "Safe Spaces Initiative: About the Paper," Muslim Public Affairs Council, accessed June 9, 2021, https://www.mpac.org/safespaces/.

49. Ahmed Shaikh, "How to Spot a Future Terrorist at Fajr: A Review of MPAC's New 'Safe Spaces,'" Muslim Matters, March 3, 2016, https://muslimmatters.org/2016/03/03/how-to-spot-a-future-terrorist-at-fajr-a-review-of-mpacs-new-safe-spaces/.

50. Ahmed Shaikh, "MPAC's Long Con: CVE and Gaslighting for the National Security State," Working towards Ehsan Newsletter, January 4, 2021, https://ehsan .substack.com/p/mpacs-long-con-cve-and-gaslighting.

51. *Safe Spaces: An Updated Toolkit for Empowering Communities and Addressing Ideological Violence* (Los Angeles: MPAC, n.d.), 8, https://www.mpac.org/ safespaces/files/MPAC-Safe-Spaces.pdf.

52. "When Engagement Brings Results: The White House CVE Summit," Muslim Public Affairs Council, February 19, 2015, https://www.mpac.org/blog/policy -analysis/when-engagement-brings-results-the-white-house-cve-summit.php.

53. "When Engagement Brings Results."

54. Masjid Muhammad Department of Homeland Security Grant Application, Department of Homeland Security, 16, accessed June 9, 2021, https://www.dhs.gov/sites/ default/files/publications/EMW-2016-CA-APP-00253%20Full%20Application .pdf.

55. "#ENOUGHISENOUGH Campaign," American Muslims Against Violence and Terrorism, accessed June 9, 2021, https://www.amateinitiative.com/enoughis enough_campaign.

56. *The National Criminal Intelligence Sharing Plan: Solutions and Approaches for a Cohesive Plan to Improve Our Nation's Ability to Develop and Share Criminal Intelligence* (Washington, DC: Department of Justice, 2003), https://it.ojp.gov/ documents/national_criminal_intelligence_sharing_plan.pdf.

57. Michael Price, *National Security and Local Police* (New York: Brennan Center for Justice, 2013), https://www.brennancenter.org/sites/default/files/publications/ NationalSecurity_LocalPolice_web.pdf.

58. *Recommendations for Fusion Centers: Preserving Privacy and Civil Liberties While Protecting against Crime and Terrorism* (Washington, DC: Constitution Project, 2012), 1, https://archive.constitutionproject.org/pdf/fusioncenterreport.pdf.

59. Dia Kayyali, "Why Fusion Centers Matter: FAQ," Electronic Frontier Foundation, April 7, 2014, https://www.eff.org/deeplinks/2014/04/why-fusion-centers-matter -faq.

60. "National Network of Fusion Centers Fact Sheet," US Department of Homeland Security, August 16, 2019, https://www.dhs.gov/national-network-fusion-centers -fact-sheet.

61. "Fusion Center Locations and Contact Information," US Department of Homeland Security, September 21, 2020, https://www.dhs.gov/fusion-center-locations-and -contact-information.

62. "Nationwide Suspicious Activity Reporting (SAR) Initiative (NSI)," Bureau of Justice Assistance, accessed June 9, 2021, https://it.ojp.gov/documents/d/NSI_PPT _GAC_fall_09.pdf.

63. *Recommendations for Fusion Centers*, 14.

64. *Recommendations for Fusion Centers*, 11.

65. Kayyali, "Why Fusion Centers Matter."

66. Price, *National Security*, 17.

67. "Targets of the Surveillance System: Muslims," Privacy SOS, accessed June 9, 2021, https://privacysos.org/targets/.

68. Spencer Ackerman, "New Evidence of Anti-Islam Bias Underscores Deep Challenges for FBI's Reform Pledge," *Wired*, September 23, 2011, https://www.wired.com/2011/09/fbi-islam-domination/.

69. Connie Hassett-Walker, "The Racist Roots of American Policing: From Slave Patrols to Traffic Stops," Conversation, June 4, 2019, https://theconversation.com/the-racist-roots-of-american-policing-from-slave-patrols-to-traffic-stops-112816.

Chapter 7

1. "Meet the Press Transcript—December 14, 2014," NBC News, December 14, 2014, https://www.nbcnews.com/meet-the-press/meet-press-transcript-december-14-2014-n268181.

2. Josh Gerstein, "Obama: 'We Tortured Some Folks,'" Politico, August 1, 2014, https://www.politico.com/story/2014/08/john-brennan-torture-cia-109654.

3. "Bush: 'We Do Not Torture' Terror Suspects," NBC News, November 7, 2005, https://www.nbcnews.com/id/wbna9956644.

4. Joseph Pugliese, *State Violence and the Execution of Law: Biopolitical Caesurae of Torture, Black Sites, Drones* (New York: Routledge, 2013), 9.

5. George Orwell, *1984: A Novel* (New York: Harcourt, 1949), 252.

6. Naomi Klein, "The True Purpose of Torture," *Guardian*, May 13, 2005, https://www.theguardian.com/world/2005/may/14/guantanamo.usa.

7. Senate Select Committee on Intelligence, *Committee Study of the Central Intelligence Agency's Detention and Interrogation Program* (Washington, DC: Government Publishing Office, 2014), 11, https://www.intelligence.senate.gov/sites/default/files/press/executive-summary_0.pdf.

8. John C. Yoo to Robert J. Delahunty, memorandum, "Treaties and Laws Applicable to the Conflict in Afghanistan and to the Treatment of Persons Captured by the U.S. Armed Forces in That Conflict," US Department of Justice, November 30, 2001, https://www.justice.gov/sites/default/files/olc/legacy/2009/12/30/aclu-ii-113001.pdf.

9. Alberto Gonzales to George W. Bush, memorandum, "Decision Re Application of the Geneva Convention on Prisoners of War to the Conflict with Al Qaeda and the Taliban," National Security Archive, January 25, 2002, https://nsarchive2.gwu.edu/torturingdemocracy/documents/20020125.pdf.

10. George W. Bush to the vice president, the secretary of state et al., memorandum, "Humane Treatment of Taliban and Al Qaeda Detainees," Project to Enforce the Geneva Conventions, February 7, 2002, section 2c, https://www.pegc.us/archive/White_House/bush_memo_20020207_ed.pdf.

11. Stephen P. Marks, "International Law and the 'War on Terrorism': Post 9/11 Responses by the United States and Asia Pacific Countries," *Asia Pacific Law Review* 14, no. 1 (2006): 61, https://cdn1.sph.harvard.edu/wp-content/uploads/sites/580/2012/09/spm_Terrorism_and_IL_APLR_2006_vol14.pdf.

12. "Remarks by Alberto R. Gonzales Counsel to the President," American Bar Association Standing Committee on Law and National Security, February 24, 2004, https://fas.org/irp/news/2004/02/gonzales.pdf.

13. Military Commissions Act of 2006, Pub. L. No. 109-366, October 17, 2006, https://www.loc.gov/rr/frd/Military_Law/pdf/PL-109-366.pdf.

14. Jay S. Bybee to John Rizzo, memorandum, "Interrogation of Al Qaeda Operative," US Department of Justice, August 1, 2002, https://www.justice.gov/sites/default/files/olc/legacy/2010/08/05/memo-bybee2002.pdf.

15. Senate Select Committee on Intelligence (SSCI), "Committee Study of the Central Intelligence Agency's Detention and Interrogation Program," S. Report 113-288, December 9, 2014, xiv, https://www.intelligence.senate.gov/sites/default/files/documents/CRPT-113srpt288.pdf.

16. Katherine Hawkins, "The Lies Hidden inside the Torture Report," *Politico Magazine*, January 28, 2015, https://www.politico.com/magazine/story/2015/01/torture-report-lies-114693.

17. "Revealed: The Boom and Bust of the CIA's Secret Torture Sites," Bureau of Investigative Journalism, October 14, 2015, https://www.thebureauinvestigates.com/stories/2015-10-14/revealed-the-boom-and-bust-of-the-cias-secret-torture-sites.

18. "Torturing Democracy: Read the Key Documents (by Chronology)," National Security Archive at George Washington University, accessed June 9, 2021, https://nsarchive2.gwu.edu/torturingdemocracy/documents/.

19. *The Report of the Constitution Project's Task Force on Detainee Treatment* (Washington, DC: Constitution Project, 2013), 152, https://docs.pogo.org/report/2013/TCP-Detainee-Task-Force-Report.pdf?_ga=2.129552655.2033079454.1615059713-1873400216.1614910032.

20. Jonathan Canfield, "The Torture Memos: The Conflict between a Shift in U.S. Policy towards a Condemnation of Human Rights and International Prohibitions against the Use of Torture," *Hofstra Law Review* 33, no. 3 (2005), https://scholarlycommons.law.hofstra.edu/cgi/viewcontent.cgi?article=2354&context=hlr.

21. Joseph Margulies, *Guantanamo and the Abuse of Presidential Power* (New York: Simon & Schuster, 2006), 108.

22. *Constitution Project's Task Force*, 154–55.

23. Jon Schwarz, "John Yoo Thinks Presidents Can Legally Torture Children. Even He Has 'Grave Concerns' about Donald Trump," Intercept, February 6, 2017, https://theintercept.com/2017/02/06/john-yoo-thinks-presidents-can-legally-torture-children-even-he-has-grave-concerns-about-donald-trump/.

24. Rachel Meeropol, ed., *America's Disappeared: Secret Imprisonment, Detainees, and the War on Terror* (New York: Seven Stories, 2005), 82.

25. *Constitution Project's Task Force*, 167.

26. Jay S. Bybee to William J. Haynes II, memorandum, "The President's Power as Commander in Chief to Transfer Captured Terrorists to the Control and Custody of Foreign Nations," US Department of Justice, March 13, 2002, 1, https://www.justice.gov/sites/default/files/olc/legacy/2009/08/24/memorandum03132002.pdf.

27. *Constitution Project's Task Force*, 140.

28. Sam Raphael, Crofton Black, and Ruth Blakeley, *CIA Torture Unredacted: An Investigation into the CIA Torture Programme* (London: Rendition Project, 2019), 18, https://www.therenditionproject.org.uk/documents/RDI/190710-TRP-TBIJ-CIA-Torture-Unredacted-Full.pdf.

29. Scahill, *Dirty Wars*, 26.

30. Jonathan Horowitz and Stacy Cammarano, "20 Extraordinary Facts about CIA Extraordinary Rendition and Secret Detention," Open Society Justice Initiative, February 5, 2013, https://www.justiceinitiative.org/voices/20-extraordinary-facts -about-cia-extraordinary-rendition-and-secret-detention.

31. *Constitution Project's Task Force*, 172.

32. Peter Jan Honigsberg, *A Place outside the Law: Forgotten Voices from Guanta-namo* (New York: Penguin Random House, 2020), 171.

33. Laura Pitter, "US: Ex-Detainees Describe Unreported CIA Torture," Human Rights Watch, October 3, 2016, https://www.hrw.org/news/2016/10/03/us-ex-detainees -describe-unreported-cia-torture#.

34. James Ross, "Black Letter Abuse: The US Legal Response to Torture Since 9/11," *International Review of the Red Cross* 89, no. 867 (September 2007): 40, https:// www.icrc.org/en/doc/assets/files/other/irrc-867-ross.pdf.

35. Pugliese, *State Violence*, 28–29.

36. Abu Zubaydah, "Abu Zubaydah," Rendition Project, accessed June 9, 2021, https://www.therenditionproject.org.uk/prisoners/zubaydah.html.

37. Charles R. Church, "What Politics and the Media Still Get Wrong about Abu Zubaydah," *Lawfare* (blog), August 1, 2018, https://www.lawfareblog.com/what -politics-and-media-still-get-wrong-about-abu-zubaydah.

38. Larry Siems, *The Torture Report* (New York: OR Books, 2011), 40.

39. Church, "What Politics."

40. Church.

41. Dexter Filkins, "How Did Abu Zubaydah Lose His Eye?," *New Yorker*, June 9, 2015, https://www.newyorker.com/news/news-desk/how-did-abu-zubaydah-lose -his-eye.

42. Mark Mazzetti, "C.I.A. Destroyed Tapes of Interrogations," *New York Times*, December 6, 2007, https://www.nytimes.com/2007/12/06/washington/06cnd-intel .html.

43. Senate Select Committee on Intelligence, "Committee Study of the Central Intelli-gence Agency's Detention and Interrogation Program," December 3, 2014, 15–16, https://fas.org/irp/congress/2014_rpt/ssci-rdi.pdf.

44. Oliver Laughland, "How the CIA Tortured Its Detainees," *Guardian*, May 20, 2015, https://www.theguardian.com/us-news/2014/dec/09/cia-torture-methods -waterboarding-sleep-deprivation.

45. Horowitz and Cammarano, "20 Extraordinary Facts."

46. Raphael, Black, and Blakeley, *CIA Torture Unredacted*, 55.

47. Raphael, Black, and Blakeley. 3.

48. Rowaida Abdelaziz, "The CIA Tortured an Afghan Suspect to Death but Refuses to Say Where His Body Is," *Huffington Post*, November 29, 2018, https://www.huffpost .com/entry/gul-rahman-cia-torture-lawsuit_n_5bff57fae4b0864f4f6a04ca.

49. "Senate Report on CIA Torture: James Mitchell and Bruce Jessen," Human Rights First, accessed June 9, 2021, https://www.humanrightsfirst.org/senate-report-cia -torture/james-mitchell-and-bruce-jessen.

50. "Report on CIA Torture."

51. Sheri Fink, "Settlement Reached in C.I.A. Torture Case," *New York Times*, August 17, 2017, https://www.nytimes.com/2017/08/17/us/cia-torture-lawsuit-settlement.html.

52. SSCI, "Committee Study," S. Report 113-288, 2.

53. Scahill, *Dirty Wars*, 28.

54. Amnesty International, *USA: Crimes and Impunity; Full Senate Committee Report on CIA Secret Detentions Must Be Released, and Accountability for Crimes under International Law Ensured* (London: Amnesty, 2015), 68, https://www.amnestyusa.org/files/cia_torture_report_amr_5114322015.pdf.

55. Scahill, *Dirty Wars*, 29.

56. Scahill, 29.

57. Andy Barr, "Bush: I'd Waterboard KSM Again," Politico, June 3, 2010, https://www.politico.com/story/2010/06/bush-id-waterboard-ksm-again-038085.

58. Khalid Sheikh Mohammed, "Khalid Sheikh Mohammed," Rendition Project, accessed June 9, 2021, https://www.therenditionproject.org.uk/prisoners/khaled-sheikh-mohammed.html.

59. Mustafa al-Hawsawi, "Mustafa al-Hawsawi," Rendition Project, accessed June 9, 2021, https://www.therenditionproject.org.uk/prisoners/hawsawi.html.

60. Ramzi bin Al-Shibh, "Ramzi bin Al-Shibh," Rendition Project, accessed June 9, 2021, https://www.therenditionproject.org.uk/prisoners/binalshibh.html.

61. Walid Mohammed bin Attash, "Walid Mohammed bin Attash," Rendition Project, accessed June 9, 2021, https://www.therenditionproject.org.uk/prisoners/walid-binattash.html.

62. Ammar Al-Baluchi, "Ammar Al-Baluchi," Rendition Project, accessed June 9, 2021, https://www.therenditionproject.org.uk/prisoners/ammar-albaluchi.html.

63. Honigsberg, *Place outside the Law*, 171–72.

64. Sacha Pfeiffer, "Trial of Sept. 11 Defendants at Guantánamo Delayed until August 2021," NPR, September 30, 2020, https://www.npr.org/2020/09/30/918454831/trial-of-sept-11-defendants-at-guant-namo-delayed-until-august-2021.

65. Michel Foucault, *Language, Counter-Memory, Practice: Selected Essays and Interviews* (Ithaca, NY: Cornell University Press, 1977), 210.

66. *Constitution Project's Task Force*, 33.

67. Honigsberg, *Place outside the Law*, 17.

68. *Constitution Project's Task Force*, 35.

69. Jane Mayer, *The Dark Side: The inside Story of How the War on Terror Turned into a War on American Ideals* (New York: Random House, 2009), 188.

70. *Constitution Project's Task Force*, 38.

71. William J. Haynes II to Donald Rumsfeld, memorandum, "Counter-Resistance Techniques," National Security Archive, November 27, 2002, 12–14, https://nsarchive2.gwu.edu//NSAEBB/NSAEBB127/02.12.02.pdf.

72. William J. Haynes II to Donald Rumsfeld, 1.

73. *Report on Torture and Cruel, Inhuman, and Degrading Treatment of Prisoners at Guantánamo Bay, Cuba* (New York: CCR, 2006), 9, https://ccrjustice.org/files/Report_ReportOnTorture.pdf.

74. Honigsberg, *Place outside the Law*, 150.

75. Pugliese, *State Violence*, 113.

76. Pugliese, 113.

77. Joseph Pugliese, "Abu Ghraib and Its Shadow Archives," *Law and Literature* 19, no. 2 (2007): 257, https://www.jstor.org/stable/10.1525/lal.2007.19.2.247 ?seq=1.

78. David Luban, "Liberalism, Torture, and the Ticking Bomb," Georgetown University Law Center, 2005, https://scholarship.law.georgetown.edu/cgi/viewcontent.cgi ?article=1163&context=facpub.

79. Michael Ratner et al., *Defendant Dossier: Geoffrey Miller* (New York: CCR, 2011), 2–3, https://ccrjustice.org/sites/default/files/assets/FINAL%20MILLER%20FOR %20FILING%20ENGLISH%202_0.pdf.

80. Scahill, *Dirty Wars*, 148.

81. Ratner et al., *Defendant Dossier*, 9.

82. Alfred W. McCoy, *A Question of Torture: CIA Interrogation, from the Cold War to the War on Terror* (New York: Henry Holt, 2006), 5–6.

83. James Sturcke, "General Approved Extreme Interrogation Methods," *Guardian*, March 30, 2005, https://www.theguardian.com/world/2005/mar/30/usa.iraq.

84. Philip Zimbardo, *The Lucifer Effect: Understanding How Good People Turn Evil* (New York: Random House, 2008), 412.

85. Sturcke, "General Approved."

86. Zimbardo, *Lucifer Effect*, 412–13.

87. *Inquiry into the Treatment of Detainees in U.S. Custody* (Washington, DC: Committee on Armed Services, 2008), xxix, https://www.armed-services.senate.gov/ imo/media/doc/Detainee-Report-Final_April-22-2009.pdf.

88. Strauss, "Lessons from Abu Ghraib," 1272.

89. "Profile: Homicide," Human Rights First Report, September 6, 2013, 1, https:// www.thetorturedatabase.org/files/foia_subsite/3._profile_homicide_manadel_al -jamadi--c05950958.pdf.

90. *Constitution Project's Task Force*, 179.

91. Jeff Stein and Adam Zagorin, "A Former CIA Interrogator on Death, Torture and the Dark Side," *Newsweek*, October 7, 2015, https://www.newsweek.com/2015/10/ 16/former-cia-interrogator-david-martines-story-380520.html.

92. Stein and Zagorin.

93. Associated Press, "U.S. Probes Death of Prisoner Seen in Photos," NBC News, May 20, 2004, https://www.nbcnews.com/id/wbna5022416.

94. Taguba, *Article 15–6 Investigation*, 16.

95. Taguba, 16–17.

96. Karen J. Greenberg and Joshua L. Dratel, *The Torture Papers: The Road to Abu Ghraib* (New York: Cambridge University Press, 2005), 524.

97. Pugliese, "Abu Ghraib," 254.

98. Pugliese, 270.

99. Pugliese, 256–57.

100. Kleanthis Kyriakidis, "Guantanamo and Abu Ghraib Revisited," Open Democracy, March 30, 2012, https://www.opendemocracy.net/en/guantanamo-and-abu -ghraib-revisited/.

101. "A System of Abuse," *Washington Post*, May 5, 2004, https://www.washingtonpost
.com/archive/opinions/2004/05/05/a-system-of-abuse/a75b435a-1109-45d1-ac9e
-888bd7f4c319/.

102. "Transcript from Bush Speech on American Strategy in Iraq," *New York Times*,
May 24, 2004, https://www.nytimes.com/2004/05/24/politics/transcript-from-bush
-speech-on-american-strategy-in-iraq.html.

103. "CMUs: The Federal Prison System's Experiment in Social Isolation," CCR,
March 31, 2010, https://ccrjustice.org/home/get-involved/tools-resources/fact
-sheets-and-faqs/cmus-federal-prison-system-s-experiment.

104. Christopher S. Stewart, "'Little Gitmo,'" *New York Magazine*, July 8, 2011, https://
nymag.com/news/features/yassin-aref-2011-7/index4.html.

105. Stewart.

106. Honigsberg, *Place outside the Law*, 213.

107. Honigsberg, 214–15.

108. William J. Aceves, "Constitutional Barriers and the Perils of Impunity," in Shafir,
Meade, and Aceves, *Lessons and Legacies*, 51.

109. Aceves, 53–54.

110. Aceves, 54–55.

111. Aceves, 59.

112. Aceves, 61.

113. Aceves, 66.

114. "Background: President Obama Signs Executive Orders on Detention and Interrogation Policy," White House, accessed June 9, 2021, https://obamawhitehouse
.archives.gov/realitycheck/the-press-office/background-president-obama-signs
-executive-orders-detention-and-interrogation-polic.

115. Adam Serwer, "Obama's Legacy of Impunity for Torture," *Atlantic*, March 14,
2018, https://www.theatlantic.com/politics/archive/2018/03/obamas-legacy-of
-impunity-for-torture/555578/.

116. David Johnston and Charlie Savage, "Obama Reluctant to Look into Bush Programs," *New York Times*, January 11, 2009, https://www.nytimes.com/2009/01/12/
us/politics/12inquire.html.

117. Serwer, "Obama's Legacy."

118. Amnesty International, *USA: Crimes and Impunity*, 57.

119. Steven Mufson, "Obama, on New Interrogations Report: 'Some of the Actions
Taken Were Contrary to Our Values,'" *Washington Post*, December 9, 2014, https://
www.washingtonpost.com/news/post-politics/wp/2014/12/09/obama-on-new
-interrogations-report-some-of-the-actions-taken-were-contrary-to-our-values/.

120. Amnesty International, *USA: Crimes and Impunity*, 10.

121. "14 Things to Know about the Use of Torture under Bush, Obama and Trump,"
TRTWorld, February 26, 2017, https://www.trtworld.com/americas/14-things-to
-know-about-american-torture-under-bush-obama-and-trump-305723.

122. Dan Mangan, "Trump Signs Executive Order to Keep Guantanamo Bay Prison
Open," CNBC, January 30, 2018, https://www.cnbc.com/2018/01/30/trump-signs-
executive-order-to-keep-guantanamo-bay-prison-open.html.

123. Khalid Qassim, "I Am in Guantánamo Bay. The US Government Is Starving Me to Death," *Guardian*, October 13, 2017, https://www.theguardian.com/commentisfree/2017/oct/13/guantanamo-bay-us-government-hunger-strike.

124. Jack Moore, "Guantanamo under Trump Is a New Hell, Says 70-Year-Old Inmate Held for 13 Years," *Newsweek*, November 18, 2017, https://www.newsweek.com/guantanamo-bays-oldest-prisoner-not-beginning-has-it-been-hell-710587.

125. Fault Lines, "The Dark Prisoners: Inside the CIA's Torture Programme," Al Jazeera, September 14, 2016, https://www.aljazeera.com/features/2016/9/14/the-dark-prisoners-inside-the-cias-torture-programme.

126. "President Bush's Speech on Terrorism," *New York Times*, September 6, 2006, https://www.nytimes.com/2006/09/06/washington/06bush_transcript.html.

127. Pugliese, *State Violence*, 181.

128. Bonds, "Indirect Violence and Legitimation," 297.

Chapter 8

1. Agence France-Presse, "Cheney Says Detainees Are Well Treated," *New York Times*, June 24, 2005, https://www.nytimes.com/2005/06/24/us/cheney-says-detainees-are-well-treated.html.

2. Mathew Sandoval, "Bodily Destruction, Bodily Empowerment: A Year of Detainee Resistance at Guantanamo Bay, Cuba" (PhD diss., University of California, 2014), 23, https://escholarship.org/content/qt9vm0d13t/qt9vm0d13t.pdf.

3. Jeffrey Mendoza, *The Significance of "Gitmo" to National Security: Whether the Prison at Guantanamo Bay, Cuba Is Necessary as a Matter of National Security* (self-pub., 2017), loc. 519, Kindle.

4. Ahmad, "Resisting Guantánamo," 1689.

5. A. Naomi Paik, "US Turned Away Thousands of Haitian Asylum-Seekers and Detained Hundreds More in the 90s," Conversation, June 28, 2018, https://theconversation.com/us-turned-away-thousands-of-haitian-asylum-seekers-and-detained-hundreds-more-in-the-90s-98611.

6. Scott Poynting, "Empire Crime, Rendition and Guantánamo Bay: The Case of David Hicks," *State Crime Journal* 4, no. 1 (Spring 2015): 25, https://www.jstor.org/stable/pdf/10.13169/statecrime.4.1.0016.pdf.

7. Tyler Pager and Paige Leskin, "Military: Gitmo Detainees Not Treated like in Early Days," Medill News Service, March 16, 2015, https://www.usatoday.com/story/news/nation/2015/03/16/gitmo-outdated-images/24874103/.

8. "Shackled Detainees Arrive in Guantanamo," CNN, January 11, 2002, https://edition.cnn.com/2002/WORLD/asiapcf/central/01/11/ret.detainee.transfer/index.html.

9. Honigsberg, *Place outside the Law*, 9.

10. Honigsberg, *Place outside the Law*, 20.

11. Andy Worthington, "The Last Prisoner to Arrive at Guantánamo, an Afghan Fascinated with US Culture, Asks Review Board to Approve His Release," *Andy Worthington* (blog), August 15, 2016, http://www.andyworthington.co.uk/2016/08/15/

the-last-prisoner-to-arrive-at-guantanamo-an-afghan-fascinated-with-us-culture
-asks-review-board-to-approve-his-release/.

12. Bridge Initiative Team, "Guantánamo Bay Military Prison: Narratives and Numbers," Bridge, November 4, 2020, https://bridge.georgetown.edu/research/guantanamo-bay -data-project/.

13. Honigsberg, *Place outside the Law*, 25.

14. "Pentagon Releases Names of Guantanamo Prisoners," NPR, April 20, 2006, https://www.npr.org/templates/story/story.php?storyId=5352799.

15. "Guantánamo by the Numbers," ACLU, November 2018, https://www.aclu.org/ issues/national-security/detention/guantanamo-numbers.

16. "Guantánamo by the Numbers," CCR, November 14, 2015, https://ccrjustice .org/home/get-involved/tools-resources/fact-sheets-and-faqs/guant-namo -numbers.

17. Mark Denbeaux, Joshua W. Denbeaux, and John Gregorek, "Report on Guantanamo Detainees: A Profile of 517 Detainees through Analysis of Department of Defense Data," Seton Hall Public Law, research paper no. 46, February 2006, 15, https://papers.ssrn.com/sol3/papers.cfm?abstract_id=885659.

18. Honigsberg, *Place outside the Law*, 15.

19. Spencer Ackerman, "Uighur Men Held for 12 Years Leave Guantánamo Bay for Slovakia," *Guardian*, December 31, 2013, https://www.theguardian.com/world/ 2013/dec/31/uighur-men-leave-guantanamo-bay-slovakia.

20. Charlie Savage, "U.S. Frees Last of the Chinese Uighur Detainees from Guantánamo Bay," *New York Times*, December 31, 2013, https://www.nytimes.com/2014/01/01/ us/us-frees-last-of-uighur-detainees-from-guantanamo.html.

21. Honigsberg, *Place outside the Law*, 35–36.

22. Neil A. Lewis, "Freedom for Chinese Detainees Hinges on Finding a New Homeland," *New York Times*, November 8, 2004, https://www.nytimes.com/2004/11/08/ us/freedom-for-chinese-detainees-hinges-on-finding-a-new-homeland.html.

23. *The Guantánamo Prisoner Hunger Strikes and Protests: February 2002–August 2005* (New York: CCR, 2005), 10, https://ccrjustice.org/files/Final%20Hunger %20Strike%20Report%20Sept%202005.pdf.

24. Shelby Sullivan-Bennis (Guantánamo attorney), in discussion with the author, January 3, 2020.

25. Richard B. Schmitt, "Detainees Told FBI of Koran Desecration," *Los Angeles Times*, May 26, 2005, https://www.latimes.com/archives/la-xpm-2005-may-26-na -gitmo26-story.html.

26. Josh White and Dan Eggen, "US Admits Koran Abuse at Cuba Base," *Guardian*, June 4, 2005, https://www.theguardian.com/world/2005/jun/05/guantanamo.usa.

27. Josh White and Dan Eggen, "Pentagon Details Mishandling of Koran," *Washington Post*, June 5, 2005, https://www.washingtonpost.com/archive/politics/2005/ 06/05/pentagon-details-mishandling-of-koran/8b172044-7dbe-489f-bf67 -5fd9d56236f7/.

28. Laurel Emile Fletcher et al., *The Guantánamo Effect: Exposing the Consequences of U.S. Detention and Interrogation Practices* (Berkeley: University of California Press, 2009), 55.

29. Honigsberg, *Place outside the Law*, 145.

30. "U.S.: Religious Humiliation of Muslim Detainees Widespread," Human Rights Watch, May 18, 2005, https://www.hrw.org/news/2005/05/18/us-religious-humiliation-muslim-detainees-widespread.

31. Carol Rosenberg, "Captives Allege Religious Abuse," *Miami Herald*, March 6, 2005, https://www.miamiherald.com/news/nation-world/world/americas/guantanamo/article1928582.html.

32. Rosenberg.

33. Sullivan-Bennis, discussion.

34. Mohamedou Ould Slahi, *The Mauritanian* (originally published as *Guantánamo Diary*), ed. Larry Siems (New York: Little, Brown, 2017), 206.

35. Michael Peppard, "The Secret Weapon," *Commonweal*, November 30, 2008, https://www.commonwealmagazine.org/secret-weapon.

36. Bob Woodward, *Bush at War* (New York: Simon & Schuster, 2002), 42, quoted in David Cole, *Justice at War: The Men and Ideas That Shaped America's War on Terror* (New York: New York Review of Books, 2008), 16.

37. Rasul v. Bush, 542 U.S. 466 (2004).

38. Hamdi v. Rumsfeld, 542 U.S. 507 (2004).

39. Hamdan v. Rumsfeld, 548 U.S. 557 (2006).

40. Boumediene v. Bush, 553 U.S. 723 (2008).

41. Rasul v. Bush, 2.

42. Hamdi v. Rumsfeld, 26.

43. Thomas R. Johnson, "Combatant Status Review Tribunals: An Ordeal through the Eyes of One 'Enemy Combatant,'" *Lewis & Clark Law Review* 11, no. 4 (2007): 948, https://law.lclark.edu/live/files/9548-lcb114art4johnsonpdf.

44. Stevie Moreno Haire, "No Way Out: The Current Military Commissions Mess at Guantanamo," *Seton Hall Law Review* 50, no. 3 (2020), https://scholarship.shu.edu/shlr/vol50/iss3/7/.

45. Detainee Treatment Act of 2005, Pub. L. No. 109-48, Stat. 119 (2005): 2739.

46. Military Commissions Act of 2006, Pub. L. No. 109-366, Stat. 120 (2006): 2600.

47. David Cole, "Military Commissions and the Paradigm of Prevention," Georgetown Law Faculty Publications and Other Works, 2013, 2, https://scholarship.law.georgetown.edu/facpub/1110.

48. Title XVIII of the National Defense Authorization Act for Fiscal Year 2010, Pub. L. No. 111-84, Stat. 123 (2009): 2190.

49. "Transcript of President Obama's National Security Address," CNN, May 21, 2009, https://www.cnn.com/2009/POLITICS/05/21/obama.transcript2/.

50. "Obama's National Security Address."

51. Cole, "Military Commissions."

52. Cole, 3.

53. Al-Hela v. Trump, No. 19-5079 (D.C. Cir. 2020), https://law.justia.com/cases/federal/appellate-courts/cadc/19-5079/19-5079-2020-08-28.html.

54. Joseph Marguiles, "Guantánamo: A Well-Studied Trunk," in *Human Rights and America's War on Terror*, ed. Satvinder S. Juss (New York: Routledge, 2019), 51.

55. A. Naomi Paik, *Rightlessness: Testimony and Redress in U.S. Prison Camps since World War II* (Chapel Hill: University of North Carolina Press, 2016), 1.

56. Paik, 1.

57. Paik, 3.

58. Paik, 13.

59. Ahmad, "Resisting Guantánamo," 1751.

60. Ahmad, 1752.

61. Ahmad, 1687.

62. Ahmad, 1755.

63. Khalid Qasim, "Hunger Striking for 'Dignity' in Guantanamo," Al Jazeera, August 24, 2016, https://www.aljazeera.com/features/2016/8/24/hunger-striking -for-dignity-in-guantanamo.

64. A. Naomi Paik, "Representing the Disappeared Body: Videos of Force-Feedings at Guantánamo," *Humanity: An International Journal of Human Rights, Humanitarianism, and Development* 9, no. 3 (2018): 437, https://doi.org/10.1353/hum.2018.0021.

65. Banu Bargu, *Starve and Immolate: The Politics of Human Weapons* (New York: Columbia University Press, 2014), 13.

66. Bargu, 14.

67. Chris Yuill, "The Body as Weapon: Bobby Sands and the Republican Hunger Strikes," *Sociological Research Online* 12, no. 2 (March 2007): 5.1, https://doi .org/10.5153/sro.1348.

68. Pugliese, *State Violence*, 4.

69. Yuill, "Body as Weapon," 5.1.

70. Ken Ballen and Peter Bergen, "The Worst of the Worst?," *Foreign Policy*, October 20, 2008, https://foreignpolicy.com/2008/10/20/the-worst-of-the-worst-4/.

71. Susan Jones, "Gen. John Kelly: Gitmo Detainees 'All Bad Boys,' but No One's Trying to Impede Their Release," CNS News, January 11, 2016, https://www .cnsnews.com/news/article/susan-jones/gen-john-kelly-gitmo-detainees-all-bad -boys-no-ones-trying-impede-their.

72. CCR, *Guantánamo Prisoner*, 7.

73. CCR, 10.

74. CCR, 10.

75. CCR, 12.

76. Corinna Howland, "To Feed or Not to Feed: Violent State Care and the Contested Medicalization of Incarcerated Hunger-Strikers in Britain, Turkey and Guantanamo Bay," *New Zealand Sociology* 28, no. 1 (2013): 106, https://www.proquest .com/docview/1429477451?fromopenview=true&pq-origsite=gscholar.

77. Samir Naji al Hasan Moqbel, "Gitmo Is Killing Me," *New York Times*, April 14, 2013, https://www.nytimes.com/2013/04/15/opinion/hunger-striking-at-guantanamo -bay.html.

78. Lakhdar Boumediene, "I Was Force-Fed at Guantanamo. What Guards Are Doing Now Is Worse," *New Republic*, October 20, 2017, https://newrepublic.com/article/ 145549/force-fed-guantanamo-guards-now-worse.

79. George J. Annas, "Hunger Strikes at Guantanamo—Medical Ethics and Human Rights in a 'Legal Black Hole,'" *New England Journal of Medicine* 355, no. 13

(September 2006): 1378, https://www.medekspert.az/en/chapter5/resources/NEJM
_The_Ethics_of_GTMO_Hunger_Strikes.pdf.

80. Joint Task Force Guantánamo Bay, Cuba, "Standard Operating Procedure: Medical
Management of Detainees on Hunger Strike," Center for the Study of Human Rights
in the Americas, March 5, 2013, 2, http://humanrights.ucdavis.edu/reports/folder
-2013-guantanamo-hunger-strike/JMG%20001%20Medical%20Management
%20of%20Detainees%20on%20Hunger%20Strike%20%285%29.pdf.

81. Howland, "To Feed or Not," 107–8.

82. James Hamblin, "Have You Ever Tried to Force-Feed a Captured Human?," *Atlantic*, May 3, 2013, https://www.theatlantic.com/health/archive/2013/05/have-you
-ever-tried-to-force-feed-a-captured-human/275507/.

83. "Guantanamo Man Tells of 'Torture,'" BBC, March 3, 2006, http://news.bbc.co
.uk/2/hi/americas/4769604.stm.

84. Brian Mishara, "Force-Feeding Is Only Part of an Ethical Intervention," *New
York Times*, May 1, 2013, https://www.nytimes.com/roomfordebate/2013/05/
01/the-ethics-of-force-feeding-inmates/force-feeding-is-only-part-of-an-ethical
-intervention.

85. Bargu, *Starve and Immolate*, 12.

86. Paik, "Representing the Disappeared Body," 431.

87. Paik, 435.

88. Bargu, *Starve and Immolate*, 85–86.

89. Sandoval, "Bodily Destruction, Bodily Empowerment," 13.

90. Yasmin Ibrahim and Anita Howarth, "Hunger Strike and the Force-Feeding
Chair: Guantanamo Bay and Corporeal Surrender," *Environment and Planning
D: Society and Space* 37, no. 2 (April 2019): 294–312, https://doi.org/10.1177/
0263775818814537.

91. Editorial Board, "The President and the Hunger Strike," *New York Times*, April 30,
2013, https://www.nytimes.com/2013/05/01/opinion/president-obama-and-the
-hunger-strike-at-guantanamo.html.

92. Ibrahim and Howarth, "Hunger Strike," 305.

93. Jason Leopold, "Guantanamo Now Calls Hunger Strikes 'Long-Term Non-
religious Fasts,'" Vice, March 11, 2014, https://www.vice.com/en/article/pa8qqz/
guantanamo-now-calls-hunger-strikes-long-term-non-religious-fasts/.

94. Associated Press, "Guantanamo Detainees' Hunger Strikes Will No Longer Be
Disclosed by U.S. Military," *Washington Post*, December 4, 2013, https://www
.washingtonpost.com/world/national-security/guantanamo-detainees-hunger
-strikes-will-no-longer-be-disclosed-by-us-military/2013/12/04/f6b1aa96-5d24
-11e3-bc56-c6ca94801fac_story.html.

95. Jason Leopold, "Gitmo Media Blackout Hopes to Undermine Hunger Strikers," Al
Jazeera America, December 11, 2013, http://america.aljazeera.com/articles/2013/
12/11/gitmo-media-blackouthopestounderminehungerstrikers.html.

96. Maha Hilal, "Will Trump Allow Gitmo Prisoners to Kill Themselves?," *Newsweek*,
November 1, 2017, https://www.newsweek.com/will-trump-allow-gitmo-prisoners
-kill-themselves-698627.

97. Hilal.

98. Paik, *Rightlessness*, 188.

99. Andy Worthington, "Another Desperate Letter from Guantánamo by Adnan Latif: 'With All My Pains, I Say Goodbye to You,'" *Andy Worthington* (blog), December 26, 2010, http://www.andyworthington.co.uk/2011/02/20/another-desper ate-letter-from-guantanamo-by-adnan-latif-with-all-my-pains-i-say-goodbye-to -you/.

100. M. Neelika Jayawardane, "The Guantanamo Art That Makes Washington Nervous," Al Jazeera, December 26, 2017, https://www.aljazeera.com/opinions/2017/ 12/26/the-guantanamo-art-that-makes-washington-nervous/.

101. "Art Therapy," *Postprint Magazine*, October 2017, 24, https://indd.adobe.com/ view/567dd3ed-81fb-43b9-83c4-869107e21d52.

102. Jayawardane, "Guantanamo Art."

103. Jacey Fortin, "Who Owns Art from Guantánamo Bay? Not Prisoners, U.S. Says," *New York Times*, November 27, 2017, https://www.nytimes.com/2017/11/27/us/ guantanamo-bay-art-exhibit.html.

104. Jayawardane, "Guantanamo Art."

105. Jayawardane.

106. Rosalyn Deutsche, "Ode to the Sea: Art from Guantánamo Bay," *ArtForum*, September 2020, https://www.artforum.com/print/202007/rosalyn-deutsche-on-ode-to -the-sea-art-from-guantanamo-bay-83687.

107. "Transcript: Out of Gitmo," *Frontline*, accessed May 27, 2021, https://www.pbs .org/wgbh/frontline/film/out-of-gitmo/transcript/.

108. Alex Potter, "Life after Guantánamo: Former Detainees Live in Limbo," *Newsweek*, September 1, 2016, https://www.newsweek.com/2016/09/09/life-after -guantanamo-former-detainees-live-limbo-494838.html.

109. Shaun Walker, "'Here I Have Nobody': Life in a Strange Country May Be Worse Than Guantánamo," *Guardian*, September 30, 2016, https://www.theguardian .com/world/2016/sep/30/worse-than-guantanamo-ex-prisoner-struggles-with-new -life-in-kazakhstan.

110. Moazzam Begg, "Just got news that Lutfi Ben Ali, Tunisian ex-Guantanamo prisoner, died last night. He had spent 13 years imprisoned by the US without charge or trial," Facebook, March 8, 2021, https://www.facebook.com/moazzam.begg/posts/ 10159388108632915.

111. Sudarsan Raghavan, "Long after His Release, an Ex-Detainee Struggles with Guantanamo's Torturous Clutches," *Washington Post*, April 25, 2018, https://www .washingtonpost.com/world/middle_east/long-after-his-release-an-ex-detainee -struggles-with-guantanamos-torturous-clutches/2018/04/25/84dfa51e-3dab-11e8 -955b-7d2e19b79966_story.html.

112. Matt Apuzzo, Sheri Fink, and James Risen, "How U.S. Torture Left a Legacy of Damaged Minds," *New York Times*, October 8, 2016, https://www.nytimes.com/ 2016/10/09/world/cia-torture-guantanamo-bay.html.

113. Alison Flood, "Guantánamo Diary Author 'Blocked from Travelling for Medical Treatment,'" *Guardian*, March 1, 2019, https://www.theguardian.com/books/2019/ mar/01/guantanamo-diary-author-blocked-from-travelling-for-medical-treatment.

114. Maha Hilal, "Freed from Guantanamo, but Imprisoned by Borders," Al Jazeera, March 13, 2019, https://www.aljazeera.com/opinions/2019/3/13/freed-from -guantanamo-but-imprisoned-by-borders/.

115. Mohamedou Slahi, WhatsApp conversation with the author, November 13, 2020.

116. Andy Worthington, "Trampling the Rights of the Child: The Treatment of Juveniles in Guantánamo," *Andy Worthington* (blog), November 24, 2008, http://www.andyworthington.co.uk/2008/11/24/trampling-the-rights-of-the-child-the -treatment-of-juveniles-in-guantanamo/.

117. Ahmad, "Resisting Guantánamo."

118. Maha Hilal, "Child Soldier in the War on Terror: The Limits of Justice for One Guantanamo Bay Survivor," *In These Times*, July 31, 2017, https://inthesetimes .com/article/omar-khadr-child-soldier-canada-institutionalized-islamophobia.

119. Morris Davis, "Today Is Guantánamo's 12th Anniversary, and There's No End in Sight," *Guardian*, November 13, 2013, https://www.theguardian.com/commentisfree/2013/nov/13/guantanamo-still-open-12-year-anniversary.

120. Marie-Danielle Smith, "'This Settlement . . . It's for Every Canadian': Highlights of Omar Khadr's Appearance on Quebec's Most Popular Talk Show," *Daily Herald Tribune*, April 22, 2019, https://www.dailyheraldtribune.com/news/politics/this-settlement-is-not-only-for-me-its-for-every-canadian-the-highlights-of-omar -khadrs-appearance-on-quebecs-most-popular-talk-show/wcm/7392a821-33a2 -4bde-b234-c6bfcc3a1e08.

121. "Key Events in the Omar Khadr Case," CBC, September 30, 2012, https://www.cbc.ca/news/canada/key-events-in-the-omar-khadr-case-1.1153759.

122. Hilal, "Child Soldier."

123. Colin Perkel, "Omar Khadr Can't Dodge US$134M Civil Judgement by Recanting Guilty Plea: U.S. Court Filing," Canadian Press, January 11, 2018, https://nationalpost.com/news/canada/u-s-plaintiffs-fire-back-at-khadr-defence-over -damages-award-enforcement-2.

124. Smith, "This Settlement."

125. Cooper Allen, "Rumsfeld Says He'll 'Clearly' Vote for Trump, Calls Him 'Known Unknown,'" *USA Today*, June 23, 2016, https://www.usatoday.com/story/news/politics/onpolitics/2016/06/23/donald-rumsfeld-donald-trump-clinton/86280248/.

126. "Summary of the Reengagement of Detainees Formerly Held at Guantanamo Bay, Cuba," Office of the Director of National Intelligence, declassified December 18, 2020, https://www.dni.gov/index.php/newsroom/reports-publications/reports-publications-2020/item/2201-summary-of-the-reengagement-of-detainees -formerly-held-at-guantanamo-bay-cuba.

127. Rebecca Lemov, "Guantánamo's Catch-22: The Uncertain Interrogation Subject," in *Modes of Uncertainty: Anthropological Cases*, ed. Limor Samimian-Darash and Paul Rabinow (Chicago: University of Chicago Press, 2015), 91.

128. Steven Lee Myers, "Bush Decides to Keep Guantánamo Open," *New York Times*, October 20, 2008, https://www.nytimes.com/2008/10/21/washington/21gitmo .html.

129. "Prepared Remarks of Attorney General Alberto R. Gonzales at the Justice Department Oversight Hearing of the Senate Judiciary Committee," Department

of Justice, July 18, 2006, https://www.justice.gov/archive/ag/speeches/2006/ag
_speech_060718.html.

130. George W. Bush, *Decision Points* (New York: Crown, 2010), 180.

131. "Obama Signs Order to Close Guantanamo Bay Facility," CNN, January 22, 2009, https://www.cnn.com/2009/POLITICS/01/22/guantanamo.order/.

132. Connie Bruck, "Why Obama Has Failed to Close Guantánamo," *New Yorker*, July 25, 2016, https://www.newyorker.com/magazine/2016/08/01/why-obama-has-failed-to-close-guantanamo.

133. "Trump Inherits Guantanamo's Remaining Detainees," NPR, January 19, 2017, https://www.npr.org/2017/01/19/510448989/trump-inherits-guantanamos-remaining-detainees.

134. "Trump Inherits."

135. "Obama's Final State."

136. David Welna, "Trump Has Vowed to Fill Guantanamo with 'Some Bad Dudes'— but Who?," NPR, November 14, 2016, https://www.npr.org/sections/parallels/2016/11/14/502007304/trump-has-vowed-to-fill-guantanamo-with-some-bad-dudes-but-who.

137. Saher Khan, "Trump Signed an Executive Order to Keep the Guantanamo Bay Prison Open. Will Anything Change?," *PBS NewsHour*, February 1, 2018, https://www.pbs.org/newshour/politics/trump-signed-an-executive-order-to-keep-the-guantanamo-bay-prison-open-will-anything-change.

138. David Welna, "First Guantanamo Inmate Released under Trump Administration," NPR, May 2, 2018, https://www.npr.org/sections/thetwo-way/2018/05/02/607878827/first-guantanamo-inmate-released-under-trump-administration.

139. Carol Rosenberg, "Guantánamo Bay as Nursing Home: Military Envisions Hospice Care as Terrorism Suspects Age," *New York Times*, April 27, 2019, https://www.nytimes.com/2019/04/27/us/politics/guantanamo-bay-aging-terrorism-suspects-medical-care.html.

Chapter 9

1. "I'm Muslim, but I'm Not . . . ," Buzzfeed Presents, September 15, 2015, YouTube video, https://www.youtube.com/watch?v=JMQjyRc7eiY.

2. Hilde Lindemann Nelson, *Damaged Identities, Narrative Repair* (Ithaca, NY: Cornell University Press, 2001), 22.

3. Karen D. Pyke, "What Is Internalized Racial Oppression and Why Don't We Study It? Acknowledging Racism's Hidden Injuries," *Sociological Perspectives* 53, no. 4 (2010): 553, https://irows.ucr.edu/cd/courses/232/pyke/intracopp.pdf.

4. G. Pheterson, "Alliances between Women," in *Bridges of Power: Women's Multicultural Alliances*, ed. L. Albrecht and R. Brewer (Philadelphia: New Society, 1990), 35.

5. Christina M. Capodilupo et al., eds., *Microaggression Theory: Influence and Implications* (Hoboken, NJ: Wiley, 2018), 126.

6. Frantz Fanon, *The Wretched of the Earth*, trans. Richard Philcox, repr. ed. (New York: Grove, 2005).

7. Albert Memmi, *The Colonizer and the Colonized* (London: Souvenir, 1974), 131.

8. Michael Schwalbe et al., "Generic Processes in the Reproduction of Inequality: An Interactionist Analysis," *Social Forces* 79, no. 2 (December 2000): 425, https://doi .org/10.2307/2675505.

9. Schwalbe et al., 426.

10. Schwalbe et al., 435.

11. Schwalbe et al., 436.

12. Abhijit Naskar, "Islam—Religion of Peace or Violence," ResearchGate, April 2017, https://www.researchgate.net/publication/316253095_Islam_-_Religion_of _Peace_or_Violence.

13. Suhaib Webb and Scott Korb, "No Room for Radicals," *New York Times*, April 24, 2013, https://www.nytimes.com/2013/04/25/opinion/no-room-for-radicals-in -mosques.html.

14. Rachel Zoll and Associated Press, "US Muslims Struggle with How They Should Condemn Extremism," *Daily Democrat*, December 6, 2015, https://www .dailydemocrat.com/2015/12/06/us-muslims-struggle-with-how-they-should -condemn-extremism/.

15. Zoll and Associated Press.

16. Maha Hilal, "It's Time for Muslim Americans to Condemn Hamza Yusuf," Al Jazeera, July 15, 2019, https://www.aljazeera.com/opinions/2019/7/15/its-time-for -muslim-americans-to-condemn-hamza-yusuf.

17. Staff, "The Muslim Moderator," *Newsweek*, August 18, 2002, https://www .newsweek.com/muslim-moderator-144091.

18. Hamza Yusuf, "The Orlando Shooter Googled My Name. I Wish He Had Reached Out to Me," *Washington Post*, June 24, 2016, https://www.washingtonpost.com/ news/in-theory/wp/2016/06/24/the-orlando-shooter-googled-my-name-i-wish-he -had-reached-out-to-me/.

19. "Witness Testimony," North Carolina Commission of Inquiry on Torture, accessed June 9, 2021, http://www.nccit.org/witnesstestimony.

20. "1I Abdullah Antepli," NC CIT, February 5, 2018, YouTube video, 10:45, https:// www.youtube.com/watch?v=xR9GnDbTvSY.

21. "1I Abdullah Antepli," 5:53.

22. "1I Abdullah Antepli," 8:43.

23. Daisy Khan, ed., *WISE Up: Knowledge Ends Extremism* (New York: Women's Islamic Initiative in Spirituality and Equality, 2017).

24. Douglas M. Stone, "Islamophobia and Domestic Security," in Khan, *WISE Up*, 50.

25. Stone, 51.

26. Stone, 52.

27. Salam Al-Marayati, "Modeling Partnership between Communities and Law Enforcement," in Khan, *WISE Up*, 53–54.

28. Al-Marayati.

29. "Full Text: Khizr Khan's Speech to the 2016 Democratic National Convention," ABC News, August 1, 2016, https://abcnews.go.com/Politics/full-text-khizr-khans -speech-2016-democratic-national/story?id=41043609.

30. Nazia Kazi, *Islamophobia, Race, and Global Politics* (Lanham: Rowman & Little-field, 2019), 82.

31. Khizr Khan, *An American Family: A Memoir of Hope and Sacrifice* (New York: Penguin Random House, 2018), 235.

32. Danielle Zoellner, "'He Will Bring the Nation Together': Gold Star Father Khizr Khan Returns to DNC Stage to Nominate Joe Biden after Impassioned Speech against Trump," *Independent*, August 19, 2020, https://www.independent.co.uk/ news/world/americas/us-election/dnc-2020-khizr-khan-gold-star-joe-biden-trump -a9677961.html.

33. Khizr Khan to "Biden for President" mailing list, "I Know Joe Biden's Heart," July 22, 2020.

34. Mansoor Shams, "I'm a Muslim U.S. Marine, but Am I American Enough?," *Newsweek*, November 22, 2018, https://www.newsweek.com/im-muslim-us-marine-am -i-american-enough-opinion-1227664.

35. "What If He Were Muslim? Colin Powell on Muslim Americans," Choowe, October 20, 2008, YouTube video, https://www.youtube.com/watch?v=dYELqbZAQ4M &feature=youtu.be.

36. Edward E. Curtis IV, *Muslim American Politics and the Future of US Democracy* (New York: New York University Press Scholarship Online, 2020), 22, https://nyu .universitypressscholarship.com/view/10.18574/nyu/9781479875009.001.0001/ upso-9781479875009-chapter-006.

37. Curtis, 24.

38. Sami H. Elmansoury, "Defining Patriotism through Legacy," in Khan, *WISE Up*, 71.

39. Elmansoury, 71.

40. Yasmina Blackburn, "Muslim American or American Muslim. Does It Matter?," *Huffington Post*, October 28, 2014, https://www.huffpost.com/entry/muslim -american-or-americ_b_6057144.

41. Blackburn.

42. Sheila Musaji, "FCNA Resolution: On Being Faithful Muslims and Loyal Americans," American Muslim, November 8, 2011, http://theamericanmuslim.org/ tam.php/features/articles/fcna-resolution-on-being-faithful-muslims-and-loyal -americans.

43. Feisal Abdul Rauf, "Five Myths about Muslims in America," *Washington Post*, April 1, 2011, https://www.washingtonpost.com/opinions/five-myths-about-muslims -in-america/2011/03/30/AFePWOIC_story.html.

44. Rauf.

45. "Muslim Voices against Extremism and Terrorism," American Muslim, June 1, 2007, http://theamericanmuslim.org/tam.php/features/articles/muslim_voices _against_extremism_and_terrorism_2/.

46. Thomas L. Friedman, "If It's a Muslim Problem, It Needs a Muslim Solution," *New York Times*, July 8, 2005, https://www.nytimes.com/2005/07/08/opinion/if-its -a-muslim-problem-it-needs-a-muslim-solution.html.

47. "Muslims Are Not Terrorists: A Factual Look at Terrorism and Islam," *Huffington Post*, December 9, 2016, https://www.huffpost.com/entry/muslims-are-not -terrorist_b_8718000.

48. Paulo Freire, "Chapter 1," in *Pedagogy of the Oppressed*, available at History Is a Weapon, accessed June 9, 2021, http://www.historyisaweapon.com/defcon2/ pedagogy/pedagogychapter1.html.

Chapter 10

1. Patsy Widakuswara, "Trump Hosts Iftar Dinner without Us Muslim Groups," Voice of America, May 14, 2019, https://www.voanews.com/usa/trump-hosts-iftar -dinner-without-us-muslim-groups.

2. "Trump Shuns American Muslims at White House Iftar," Muslim Public Affairs Council, May 13, 2019, https://www.mpac.org/blog/statements-press/trump-shuns -american-muslims-at-white-house-iftar.php.

3. Geoffrey L. Cohen and Julio Garcia, "'I Am Us': Negative Stereotypes as Collective Threats," *Journal of Personality and Social Psychology* 89, no. 4 (2005): 566.

4. Claude M. Steele and Joshua Aronson, "Stereotype Threat and the Intellectual Test Performance of African Americans," *Journal of Personality and Social Psychology* 69, no. 5 (November 1995): 797.

5. Hakeem Jerome Jefferson, "Policing Norms: Punishment and the Politics of Respectability among Black Americans" (PhD diss., University of Michigan, 2019), 19.

6. Evelyn Brooks Higginbotham, *Righteous Discontent: The Women's Movement in the Black Baptist Church, 1880–1920* (Cambridge, MA: Harvard University Press, 1993), 162.

7. Higginbotham, 162.

8. Higginbotham, 218.

9. Katharina M. Fackler, "Ambivalent Frames: Rosa Parks and the Visual Grammar of Respectability," *Souls* 18, nos. 2–4 (2016): 271–82.

10. Angela M. Banks, "Respectability and the Quest for Citizenship," *Brooklyn Law Review* 83, no. 1 (December 2017): 3, https://brooklynworks.brooklaw.edu/cgi/ viewcontent.cgi?article=2109&context=blr.

11. Allissa V. Richardson, "Dismantling Respectability: The Rise of New Womanist Communication Models in the Era of Black Lives Matter," *Journal of Communication* 69, no. 2 (April 2019): 4, https://criticalracedigitalstudies.com/wp-content/ uploads/2019/06/Dismantling-Respectability.pdf.

12. Hamza Yusuf, "We Shall Overcome," Sandala, November 15, 2016, https://sandala .org/we-shall-overcome/.

13. "More Than 300 Muslim Leaders Publish Joint Letter to Donald Trump," Democracy in Action, December 5, 2016, http://www.p2016.org/chrntran/muslim120516ltr .html.

14. "Joe Biden Speech at the Million Muslim Votes Summit Transcript July 20," Rev Transcripts, July 20, 2020, https://www.rev.com/blog/transcripts/joe-biden -speech-at-the-million-muslim-votes-summit-transcript-july-20.

15. "Joe Biden Speech."

16. "Joe Biden's Agenda for Muslim-American Communities," Joe Biden (website), accessed June 9, 2021, https://joebiden.com/muslimamerica/.

17. "Joe Biden's Agenda."

18. "Joe Biden's Agenda."

19. Azad Essa, "Joe Biden, Emgage and the Muzzling of Muslim America," Middle East Eye, October 9, 2020, https://www.middleeasteye.net/big-story/joe-biden -emgage-muslim-america-us-elections.

20. Akwalefo Bernadette Djeudo, *Concepts That Shape Politics and Government in Cameroon: A Handbook of Political Theory for Stakeholders* (Bloomington, IN: AuthorHouse UK, 2013), 54.

21. Albert O. Hirschman, *Exit, Voice, and Loyalty: Responses to Declines in Firms, Organizations, and States* (Cambridge, MA: Harvard University Press, 1970).

22. Anny Bakalian and Medhi Bozorgmehr, *Backlash 9/11: Middle Eastern and Muslim Americans Respond* (Berkeley: University of California Press, 2009).

23. "CAIR: Iraq War Dead Milestone Reinforces Need for Withdrawal," Council on American-Islamic Relations, March 24, 2008, https://www.cair.com/press _releases/cair-iraq-war-dead-milestone-reinforces-need-for-withdrawal/.

24. Patricia J. Lopez and Kathryn A. Gillespie, eds., *Economies of Death* (New York: Routledge, 2020), 19.

25. "Torture Report Quotes," National Religious Campaign against Torture, accessed May 15, 2021, http://www.nrcat.org/national-security/torture/the-torture-report/ torture-report-quotes.

26. George W. Bush, "Message to Saddam," presidentialrhetoric.com March 17, 2003, http://presidentialrhetoric.com/speeches/03.17.03.html.

27. "Statement of Fall of Saddam Hussein and Post-war Iraq," Muslim Public Affairs Council, April 10, 2003, https://www.mpac.org/issues/foreign-policy/statement-of -fall-of-saddam-hussein-post-war-iraq.php.

28. "Barack Obama's Full Statement on the Death of Osama bin Laden," *Guardian*, May 2, 2011, https://www.theguardian.com/world/2011/may/02/barack-obama -statement-bin-laden.

29. "CAIR Welcomes Elimination of Osama bin Laden," Council on American-Islamic Relations, May 2, 2011, https://www.cair.com/press_releases/cair-welcomes -elimination-of-osama-bin-laden/.

30. "CAIR Welcomes Elimination."

31. "MPAC Greets Bin Laden's Death with Sense of Relief," Muslim Public Affairs Council, accessed May 26, 2021, https://www.mpac.org/blog/updates/mpac-greets -bin-ladens-death-with-sense-of-relief.php.

32. "MPAC Greets."

33. Lopez and Gillespie, *Economies of Death*, 20.

34. "CAIR Welcomes Elimination."

35. "ICNA's Statement on Killing of Osama bin Laden," Islamic Circle of North America, May 2, 2011, https://www.icna.org/press-release/icna-statement-on-killing-of-osama-bin-laden/.

36. Sarah Galo, "How America's Politicians and Activists Reacted to Senate's CIA Torture Report," *Guardian*, December 9, 2014, https://www.theguardian.com/us-news/2014/dec/09/americas-politicians-activists-reacted-senates-cia-torture-report-twitter.

37. "CAIR Seeks 'Accountability' following Release of Senate Torture Report," Council on American-Islamic Relations, December 9, 2014, https://www.cair.com/press_releases/cair-seeks-accountability-following-release-of-senate-torture-report/.

38. "MPAC Calls on Greater CIA Oversight in Light of Torture Report," Muslim Public Affairs Council, December 10, 2014, https://www.mpac.org/blog/updates/mpac-calls-on-greater-cia-oversight-in-light-of-torture-report.php.

39. Catholic News Service, "Religious Leaders Condemn US Torture Practices as Report Is Released," December 10, 2014, https://www.ncronline.org/news/politics/religious-leaders-condemn-us-torture-practices-report-released.

40. "Targeted Killing of Terrorist Suspects Overseas," C-SPAN, April 23, 2013, https://www.c-span.org/video/?312317-1/senate-committee-examines-legality-us-drone-strikes.

41. "Drone Wars: The Constitutional and Counterterrorism Implications of Targeted Killing," Council on American-Islamic Relations, accessed June 9, 2021, https://www.cair.com/government_affairs/drone-wars-the-constitutional-and-counterterrorism-implications-of-targeted-killing/.

42. "President Obama Speaks on Attacks in Boston," Obama White House, April 16, 2013, YouTube video, 2:28, https://www.youtube.com/watch?v=Exb6ShutZ18.

43. "MPAC Commends Law Enforcement, Prays for Boston as Events Unfold," Muslim Public Affairs Council, April 19, 2013, https://www.mpac.org/issues/national-security/mpac-commends-law-enforcement-prays-for-boston-as-events-unfold.php.

44. "CAIR Urges Prayers, Blood Donations for Boston Bomb Victims" (press release), Council on American-Islamic Relations, April 16, 2013, https://www.cair.com/press_releases/cair-urges-prayers-blood-donations-for-boston-bomb-victims/.

45. "ICNA Expresses Outrage at Boston Bomb Attacks," Islamic Circle of North America, April 15, 2013, https://www.icna.org/press-release/icna-expresses-outrage-at-boston-bomb-attacks/.

Conclusion

1. "Text: Bush Welcomes Muslim Americans to White House," *Washington Post*, September 26, 2001, https://www.washingtonpost.com/wp-srv/nation/specials/attacked/transcripts/bushtext2_092601.html.

2. "Bush Welcomes Muslim Americans."

3. Lisa Stampnitzky, *Disciplining Terror: How Experts Invented "Terrorism"* (Cambridge: Cambridge University Press, 2013), 189.

4. Nisha Kappor, *Deport, Deprive, Extradite: 21st Century State Extremism* (New York: Verso, 2018), 39.

5. "George W Bush Says He 'Does Not Like the Racism' of the Donald Trump Era," *Independent*, February 28, 2017, https://www.independent.co.uk/news/world/americas/us-politics/george-w-bush-donald-trump-era-racism-does-not-press-media-a7603131.html.

6. "Read Obama's Full Speech at the Democratic National Convention," *PBS NewsHour*, August 19, 2020, https://www.pbs.org/newshour/politics/read-obamas-full-speech-at-the-democratic-national-convention.

7. Joshua Keating, "The War on Terror Comes Home," *Slate*, June 3, 2020, https://slate.com/news-and-politics/2020/06/war-on-terror-floyd-protests-military.html.

8. Brian Heater, "The 1033 Program Takes Center Stage Again, as Militarized Police Make Headlines," TechCrunch, June 8, 2020, https://techcrunch.com/2020/06/08/the-1033-program-takes-center-stage-again-as-militarized-police-make-headlines/.

9. Atiya Husain, "Terror and Abolition," *Boston Review*, June 11, 2020, http://bostonreview.net/race/atiya-husain-terror-and-abolition.